THE GROUND OF UNION

THE
GROUND
OF
UNION

⊱—◈—○—◈—⊰

Deification in Aquinas and Palamas

A. N. WILLIAMS

New York • Oxford

Oxford University Press

1999

Oxford University Press

Oxford   New York
Athens   Auckland   Bangkok   Bogotá   Buenos Aires   Calcutta
Cape Town   Chennai   Dar es Salaam   Delhi   Florence   Hong Kong   Istanbul
Karachi   Kuala Lumpur   Madrid   Melbourne   Mexico City   Mumbai
Nairobi   Paris   São Paulo   Singapore   Taipei   Tokyo   Toronto   Warsaw

and associated companies in
Berlin   Ibadan

Copyright © 1999 by A. N. Williams

Published by Oxford University Press, Inc.
198 Madison Avenue, New York, New York 10016

Oxford is a registered trademark of Oxford University Press

Library of Congress Cataloging-in-Publication Data
Williams, A. N. (Anna Ngaire)
The ground of union : deification in Aquinas
and Palamas / A. N. Williams.
p.   cm.
Includes bibliographical references and index.
ISBN 0-19-512436-7
1. Deification (Christianity)—History of doctrines—Middle Ages,
600–1500.   2. Thomas, Aquinas, Saint, 1225?–1274—Contributions in
doctrine of deification.   3. Gregory Palamas, Saint, 1296–1359—
Contributions in doctrine of deification.   I. Title.
BT767.8.W55   1999
234—dc21   98-22520

1 3 5 7 9 8 6 4 2

Printed in the United States of America
on acid-free paper

To the memory of
Francis Clive Williams
23.vii.26–19. v. 79

Ja la vostre anme nen ait sufraite!
De pareïs li seit la porte uverte!

ACKNOWLEDGMENTS

Many people supplied erudition and support during the writing of this work; my debts are too numerous to catalogue other than selectively. Chief among them are to those who commented on the manuscript in its earlier version as a dissertation: Rowan Greer, David Kelsey and Cyril O'Regan. The director of the dissertation, George Lindbeck, deserves an additional vote of thanks for his tirelessness in forming in charity a student notable for her obstinacy. I am grateful to Christopher Wells for the index; for companionship and support, my thanks go to Inger and Benjamin Brodey, Cathy Kaveny and above all my husband, Dale Gingrich, and to Merlin and Madeleine, who placed the feline seat of approval on almost all the pages.

Feast of the Holy Name, 1997   A. N. W.

CONTENTS

THE GROUND OF UNION

1

>-+-+>-+-0-+<-+-+-<

THE PROBLEM AND
ITS HISTORY

I. The Need for the Study

When Edward Gibbon pronounced Byzantine hesychasm the consummation of the "religious follies of the Greeks,"[1] he articulated no more than a commonplace judgment of the movement that has determined so much of subsequent Eastern Orthodox thought, not only in the realm of spirituality but also in dogmatic theology and theological method. Gibbon's remark is characteristic of both late medieval and modern Western appraisals of hesychasm and its chief proponent, Gregory Palamas. Ironically, it describes with equal accuracy the general tenor of Eastern estimations of the movement that revolutionized the medieval West as hesychasm galvanized the East: scholasticism. These two movements prove to be definitive moments in their respective traditions; they also occur during the period when the fracture between the two halves of Christendom hardened at last into a divide accepted by both sides as unbreachable until the midtwentieth century.

The traditional dating of the East-West schism—1054—has long been challenged.[2] Instead, the divide is viewed as the culmination of a long, slow process of mutual misunderstanding and gradual estrangement. There is, however, a modern scholarly consensus that, while exact dating may be impossible, the divide may be viewed as fixed by some point between the high Middle Ages and the early Renaissance.[3] The late Middle Ages, then, proves a decisive moment in the history of relations between the churches of East and West, the point to which any ecumenist must return if the cause of reconciliation, or even increased understanding, is to be advanced in our time. While in the views of some historians the root of the schism was political rather than religious,[4] those political factors have long since become irrelevant to the separation of the churches. What we face now are first, actual theological differences between the churches, and second, a history of bitterness. At a theological level, that bitterness is now no longer the residue of events such as the Crusaders' Sack of Constantinople; it is the consciousness of centuries of bitter polemic and mutual accusations of heresy. This problem is fortunate in the sense that while nothing can now be done to make amends for thirteenth-century barbarism, the polemic and history of theological recriminations may be reexamined with a view to establishing what legitimate problems inhere in the heap of rancorous rhetoric.

Precisely such an examination and reevaluation has been called for by several prominent students of East-West relations. John Meyendorff, for example, says:

> In order to find the mutual understanding between Easterners and Westerners once again, we should search today for the fundamental inspiration of these two modes of thought, in a patient dialogue based on the texts. It would then perhaps be possible to delineate with more precision what in the two Christian traditions belongs to the tradition of that church to which all Christians ought to refer back, in order to find once again the unity of the first centuries.[5]

Kallistos Ware's call for a reevaluation of texts is more ambiguous, oriented not toward reconciliation but vindication of the Orthodox case:

> If these charges [regarding failings of Western theological method] are to be convincing, they must be formulated with greater precision and fully supported by evidence. . . . [Orthodox critics of scholasticism] must indicate, with specific reference to the sources, how and when Anselm and Abelard, Peter Lombard and Thomas Aquinas applied logic to matters beyond logic's scope. They must indicate in detail how Aquinas relied on philosophy in a way that the Cappadocians and St John of Damascus did not.[6]

Regardless of the apparent motive, however, there is an agreement among these students of East-West relations that a return to texts is needed.

The cry for a return to the sources in turn raises the question of which among them must be examined and to what end. Ware has already furnished part of an answer: in his view, Western scholastics lie at the heart of the East's complaint, and the double mention of Aquinas in the quotation above suggests that he in particular is problematic for the Orthodox. John Meyendorff also identifies the Thomist tradition as of particular concern to the East and further indicates with whom in the Eastern tradition Thomas might be contrasted. Orthodox theologians, he maintains, would generally agree that the Greek patristic tradition finds its fulfilment in the theology of Gregory Palamas. Aquinas and Palamas, then, are immediate candidates for representatives of their respective traditions, and both date from the crucial period of final separation (Aquinas, 1225–1274; Palamas c.1296–1359). They possess a further significance in that as Aquinas is suspect in the East, so is Palamas in the West, not only on the grounds of questionable continuity with the patristic tradition but also precisely because of his relation to the Western Augustinian and Thomist tradition.[7] Even on controversies such as the filioque, which quite clearly date from well before the time of Aquinas, the opposition of East and West has been interpreted as existing directly between Aquinas and Palamas: "On this question [the filioque], it is interesting to see the conflict of the two traditions— Latin in the form of Thomism, and Orthodox in that of Palamism."[8] Contemporary Western theologians persist in claiming a fundamental clash between Palamite and scholastic theology: "The irony of Palamite theology is that . . . it is concerned with an ontology of participation by the creature in divine life through the divine energies. This allowed Gregory to affirm what scholastic theology denied: a real relation between God and the creature."[9]

Some commentators do dissent from this conventional wisdom. Meyendorff's view of the importance of Thomas is echoed on the Western side by the panel of Roman Catholic and Lutheran scholars who collaborated on the common statement in *Justification by Faith*. Nevertheless, while this group finds that Aquinas and the Eastern tradition provide useful points of comparison, it differs from Meyendorff in expecting to discover points of similarity rather than fundamental difference. Eastern theologians, the statement maintains, described human salvation in terms of a return to God of a creation that had gone forth from God, and this pattern may still be found in such strongholds of Western scholasticism as Aquinas' *Summa Theologiae*.[10] Further, while Aquinas' position as the strongman of Western scholasticism is denied only by the eccentric, Palamas' significance within his own tradition has been disputed. Nevertheless, the source of such objections to his centrality often proves to be Westerners such as Michael Fahey or the highly influential Martin Jugie, whose tendentious views of Orthodoxy in general and Palamas in particular have powerfully shaped the history of interpretation and reception. Jugie's views are debatable on many counts, but most certainly on Palamas' enduring place in the Eastern tradition. Writing in 1941, just before the great renaissance of Palamas scholarship, he predicted: "Palamism, as the dogma of the Graeco-Russian church, is truly dead, and neither its few proponents among the Greeks who have always maintained it, nor the recent sympathy for it on the part of several Russian émigrés, will be able to resuscitate it."[11] Even so cool a Western observer of Orthodoxy as Bernhard Schultze challenges this view. Remarking that not only Jugie but also Georges Florovsky noted a period of latency in attention to Palamas, he points to the resurgence of interest represented by the work of Basil Krivosheine, Cyprian Kern and Vladimir Lossky and concludes: "Moreover, in more than one recent controversy Palamism has not only been recovered, but reckoned by both parties as a badge of Orthodoxy."[12]

Although there is far from universal agreement, then, the widely accepted positions of Aquinas and Palamas within their respective traditions and the common perception of a direct opposition beteeen them are two good and obvious reasons for focusing on these two figures. The best reason for using their works as a basis for a comparison between East and West, however, is that given by Ware: when comparisons are made, the utmost care should be taken not to contrast the best on one side with the second best on the other.[13] Even if Fahey correctly regards Palamas and Aquinas as the recipients of a too exclusive focus of attention, there can be no question that both belong to the first rank of theologians in their respective traditions.

There still remains the question of why Palamas and Aquinas should be compared specifically on the issue of deification (or *theosis* or *divinization*—the three terms will be used interchangably hereafter). Many points of contention between East and West that were once debated heatedly, such as Saturday fasting and clergy beards, are no longer regarded as problematic by either side. Two questions have continued to loom very large: the filioque and papal supremacy. Are these issues not more significant for ecumenical relations than deification? Perhaps, but precisely because they recur so frequently in ecumenical discussions, they are less in need of study. Papal supremacy, in any case, is not an issue dividing East from West but an issue dividing the Roman Catholic from all other Christian churches. It does not pertain, therefore, specifically to East-West dialogue, especially since in the crucial period of separation the problem appeared in a rather different form than it does today; it was then concerned not with papal infallibility as a dogma but with the relation of the Western pope to the Eastern patriarch. Moreover, if the papacy continues to be a thorny issue in ecumenical relations, the filioque does not.

A more important reason for focusing on deification is that while it was not originally recognized as a dividing issue, it is increasingly identified as the point at which Thomistic and Palamite theology diverge. Thus the historian Steven Runciman finds in history the basis for a theological divide as fundamental as it is irrevocable:

> Gregory Palamas's doctrine of the Divine Energies not only provided the dogmatic basis to the Greek view of mysticism. It was also a restatement of the traditional interpretation of the Greek Fathers' theory of God's relation to man. It came to be accepted by a series of fourteenth-century Councils as the official doctrine of the Greek Church.[14] To Western theologians it seemed to be clear heresy. It could not be reconciled with Thomism.[15]

This stark judgment is echoed by other commentators in only slightly less dire terms. Some view the historical problem as one of correct development of doctrine. On the Orthodox side, Paul Evdokimov claims that after Augustine and Ambrose, Latin theology replaced the theology of theosis with the theology of filiation and grace,[16] an interpretation that essentially faults the West for infidelity to the true theological tradition. Fahey essentially concurs in the view that the problem is one of development, though without faulting either side.[17] We should note, however, that dispute over deification erupts not only as a point of contention between East and West but also within the Eastern church in the hesychast controversy: Palamas might well never have risen to theological prominence had he not been spurred by his dispute with Barlaam, of which we shall hear more later. As J. M. Hussey and T. A. Hart note: "It was soon apparent [in the exchange of letters between the two] that the immediate question of the validity of the hesychast prayer could not be settled without a discussion of its underlying principle, that of the deification of man."[18]

An alternate explanation of the historical cause of the divide between East and West seeks its cause in philosophical assumptions. In Catherine Mowry LaCugna's view, the difference between East and West lies in attitudes towards substance metaphysics,[19] a grounding that she believes rules out the possibility of a Western form of deification. André de Halleux more specifically links this "mystery of communion between God and humanity" to the difference between the Platonic basis of the Palamite East and the Aristotelian basis of the scholastic West.[20]

While the root causes of the differences remain debatable, there is a clear consensus that at the systematic level such a divide exists. Yves Congar, whose influential work, *After Nine Hundred Years* takes a rather pessimistic view of the possibilities of reunion, nevertheless regards theosis as a useful locus of investigation: "A study should be made of the theme of Paradise, from an ecclesiological point of view. . . . The dominant idea is of creation attaining its divine end, by the fact that in its midst there has been set a principle (the principle) of divinization."[21] While Congar recommends further study, however, he also sees the fundamental opposition between East and West of which Steven

Runciman spoke: "This same soteriology [of Oriental theology] supposes a concept of deification and of the relationship of what we call nature and grace quite different from that which animates the Latin theological construction for the same mysteries. This Latin construction depends on a distinction of nature and of grace, whose categories and vocabulary are foreign to Greek theology."[22] Indeed, Congar goes so far as to identify the conception of the ultimate end—and so the relation of nature and grace—as the *punctum saliens* of the duality of the tradition between East and West.[23] This view is echoed by Stylianos Harkianakis, who points to the same divergence that Congar does, but characterizes it as a difference in eschatology, of the connection between here and there.[24] These opinions reflect a broad consensus that holds deification, or the particular model of sanctification adopted, to be one of the decisive differences remaining between East and West, and for that reason in need of study in an ecumenical context.[25]

The final and most important reason for using the doctrine of deification as the point of comparison is its systemic significance; what at first glance might seem like a minor corner of systematic theology (sanctification per se is not even treated in many modern Western systematic theologies) actually encompasses many other doctrines. Gerry Russo points to this systemic influence: "The ecumenical question of grace is not a simple one for it presents the most comprehensive expression of the difference between Orthodox East and Latin West, touching every element of Christian life from the dogma of the Trinity down to the frequency of celebrating Eucharistic liturgy."[26] In the specifically Palamite doctrine of deification, the doctrine of God immediately rises to the fore because of the distinction Gregory makes between divine essence and energy. While the distinction seems necessary to his framework, it seems to Western eyes to tamper with the classical doctrines of God and of the Trinity. Schultze, for example, identifies as one of the particular problems of Oriental theology the problem of God and the Palamite essence-energies distinction.[27] Lossky makes the case for the connection between deification and the doctrine of God especially forcefully:

> In the West, there was no longer any place for the conception of the energies of the Trinity; nothing was admitted to exist, outside the divine essence, except created effects, acts of will analogous to the acts of creation. Western theologians must profess belief in the created character of the Glory of God and of sanctifying Grace and renounce the conception of deification or theosis; in this they are consistent with their Triadological premises.[28]

Meyendorff makes the same systematic connection between human participation in divine nature and the doctrine of God with less anti-Western sentiment, also concluding that Greek and Latin theologies of this period are "clearly incompatible."[29]

The connection between deification and the doctrine of God and the Trinity is more obvious than the link between divinization and theological method, but this latter tie is equally important. Because questions of knowledge of God and theological method become one of the most rancorous points of debate between East and West, we will not deal with them here, however, but devote a later section to this question. Suffice it to say for now that because deification entails discussion not only of sanctification and theological anthropology generally, but also the doctrines of God and the Trinity, religious knowledge and theological method, it ultimately touches on almost every major branch of Christian doctrine. Because it is so all-encompassing, then, deification provides an excellent locus for the comparison of Eastern and Western theology.

II. The Irreconcilability of Thomism and Palamism

We have already briefly noted the often expressed sensibility that there is a fundamental opposition between Aquinas and Palamas, an opposition that at least in some views renders their theologies irreconcilable. Such positions take a variety of forms. As we have seen, some claimants of incompatibility argue historically, simply noting that such assumptions were often made by parties to the hesychast controversy and its aftermath and implying that the alliance between the anti-Palamite party and advocates of Latin theology still poses problems today; others point to particular features of Thomist and Palamite theological assertion that are mutually exclusive on systematic grounds; and a large group bases its claims on a fundamental divergence over theological method. The proponents of systematic incompatibility form the largest group of commentators, although by no means all regard Palamism and Thomism as fundamentally irreconcilable.[30] We shall consider in turn these historically and systematically based claims of opposition before turning to the charges of methodological difference.

1. Interpretation of Aquinas and Palamas in the Middle Ages

Between the thirteenth and the sixteenth centuries we encounter, first, numerous attempts at a variety of levels—individual, papal and imperial—to heal the wounds of Christendom. Second, we find a controversy raging within Byzantine theological and scholarly circles over hesychasm and its theological and philosophical implications. This controversy becomes linked to the civil war shaking Byzantine society at the same time, and the fortunes of the hesychasts are linked to those of their champion in the political fray, John Cantacuzenos. While the West generally takes little note of the controversy,[31] the founding of Western religious communities near Constantinople—notably the Dominican friary at Pera, on its outskirts—means that a small group of Westerners became aware of the hesychast controversy and its implications for reunion. These Westerners are nevertheless few,[32] and thus the historical problem is largely a matter of the reception of Thomas in the East and the way in which parties in the Palamite controversy become identified as pro-Palamas and anti-Thomas or pro-Thomas and anti-Palamas. This pattern is by no means absolute, as we shall see, but we begin by examining the evidence for it.

Awareness of Thomas' work in the East coincides quite neatly with the developing furor over hesychasm. While the origins of the hesychast movement may be sought as early as the fourth century, the term *hesychasm* usually designates the ascetical practices and mystical experience that developed among monks of Mount Athos in the fourteenth century; these suggested an experiential confirmation of the Eastern churches' teaching regarding deification in this life. Palamas, himself a monk of Athos, sought to vindicate the monks by providing a theological basis for their mystical experience in his work, *Triads in Defence of the Holy Hesychasts*. His championing of the hesychasts pitted Palamas against a Calabrian monk, Barlaam, and erupted into a dispute over the foundations of theology, and especially, the rightful role of spiritual experience in theology. As this dispute has generally been interpreted, it forced Byzantine theology to choose between philosophy and spirituality as an ancillary and, following the triumph of the pro-hesychast party, sharply distinguished the East's theological method from that of the West, and especially, from that of the scholastics. Consequently, Aquinas came to be regarded as the archetypal Western theologian, whose knowledge of philosophy was as everywhere apparent as his spirituality invisible.

Before this fourteenth-century quarrel, so few Greeks knew Latin that any incursion of Aquinas into their consciousness would have been highly unlikely. Only the impact of the Latin conquest forcibly turned the attention of the Byzantines toward the West.[33] The first translations of Aquinas into Greek were completed in the fourteenth century by the Kydones brothers, Demetrios and Prochoros.[34] The manner in which Demetrios came to Aquinas is itself revealing. As secretary to the emperor, he had constantly to deal with the inept translations from the Latin of court interpreters. Although these must have been among the Greeks most competent in the language of the West, Demetrios grew frustrated by their deficiencies and undertook to learn Latin himself. The Dominican of Pera who instructed him used texts of Aquinas as teaching material. Captivated by them, Demetrios set about translating the Summa contra Gentiles into Greek and later the Summa Theologiae, eventually becoming so convinced by Thomas' arguments that he was received into the Roman church.[35] Greek texts of the two Summae thus became available in Byzantium at almost exactly the same time that the hesychast controversy was brewing.[36]

Because the clash between Palamas and Barlaam began as a dispute over the relevance of philosophy to theology, theological method and epistemology, much of the alignment of hostile parties is along these lines, and we will reserve for these issues a section of their own. We should note here, though, that while Palamas' own estimation of philosophy is complex, he evidences no attitude that would indicate a systematic rejection of Western theology.[37] His argument with Barlaam was not about Aquinas: Barlaam was in fact almost as hostile to Thomas as he was to Gregory,[38] and the latter's own view of Aquinas is not recorded.

It is therefore not in the exchange between Barlaam and Palamas that we find an alignment of pro-Thomist and anti-Palamite sentiment; this polarization occurs not around the main protagonists, but around their supporters. Some of this opposition was official, and on that count influential. Runciman notes that Paul, the Archbishop of Smyrna and a papal legate, "seems to have realized that Palamism and Thomism were mutually exclusive. . . . it was only [his] logical mind and his dislike of Palamas that drove the Palamites into the anti-Latin camp."[39] Yet the historical claim being made here can scarcely stand; given the imputation of intention to a figure long dead, it is obviously filtered through the lens of the author's assumptions. We would appear to stand on firmer ground when beginning from simple facts: the Bishop of Paris in 1241 condemned the proposition that the essence of God could never be seen, and a century later Benedict XII decreed that the saints in heaven see the divine essence.[40] However, the first of these judgements obviously cannot be taken as implying a condemnation of Palamism per se, for purely chronological reasons, and even the second is unlikely to refer to Palamas' own teachings, as his works could hardly be known in the West even at this point. By the Council of Florence, the essence-energies question had become sufficiently contentious for the emperor to forbid any attempt to raise the issue.[41] Interpretation of the Council of Florence differs widely, however. While some commentators (especially the Orthodox) have regarded the council's decrees as directly contradicting theses of Palamite theology, others have denied Florence any such relevance to the debate over the essence-energies distinction.[42]

The debate over the significance of the decrees of Florence typifies a broader problem: often official judgements pertaining to purely internal controversies of either East or West are taken as indicative of fundamental opposition between the churches, despite the fact that extrapolating from internal to external conflicts is an inherently dubious enterprise and, if undertaken at all, such comparisons must be made with great care. Thus, Runciman can take the Council of Reims' condemnation of Gilbert de la Porée as relevant to the Palamite doctrine of the energies, despite an obvious difference between the conception of relation the council condemned and that of Palamas.[43]

More significant is the Patriarch Philotheus' excommunication of Prochoros Kydones for his anti-Palamism, an attack that Joseph Gill regards as bearing as much as on his brother Demetrios as on him and one that could be interpreted as a condemnation of Thomas' teaching.[44] Most important of all, the Synod of 1368 condemned a number of theses that may be found word for word in the *Summa contra Gentiles*, for example, the identification of wisdom, truth and will with God's essence.[45] Papadopulos concludes: "Thus the scholastic theology of Aquinas is not only thrust against *individual* Byzantine theologians, but is opposed to the *whole* Orthodox church and its theology, as this was represented at the Synod through its bishops and theologians."[46] Once again, though, another commentator denies the relevance of these decrees for the interecclesial situation: "There was . . . no direct confrontation on the Palamite issue between the Latin Church and the Greek Church."[47]

Finally, however dramatic some of these pronouncements may seem, they appear to have contributed little to the worsening of relations between the churches, and history has not made much of them. What has attracted much more attention is the reception of Thomas among the small community in Constantinople that knew of his work. Stylianos Papadopulos, defining pro- and anti-Thomists not only vis-à-vis Thomas, but also equating pro-Thomistic and anti-hesychast views, determines that only a very small number of Byzantines in the period 1354 to 1435 can be termed either pro- or anti-Thomas. His count is eight pro- and twelve anti-Thomists—hardly a promising base for generalizations.[48] These Thomists begin with the brothers Kydones and include such clerics as Andreas Chrysoberges, the Bishop of Rhodes, in whose dependence on Prochoros Kydones Papadopulos finds evidence for the development of a Byzantine Thomist school,[49] and such late Byzantine thinkers as Gennadios Scholarios. Scholarios furnishes an interesting challenge to the supposition of an easy alliance between pro-Thomas and anti-Palamas sentiment, for although in most respects a convinced Thomist, he held an Eastern view on the filioque and the distinction of divine essence and energies.[50] Scholarios went so far as to maintain that had Thomas been born in the East he would have maintained the Eastern position on these issues also.[51] Scholarios was not alone in seeing the merits of both Thomas and Gregory. Thomas Tyn writes of Scholarios' contemporary, Bessarion: "A convinced Palamite in his theology, he still honoured Saint Thomas Aquinas, which assumes a truly syncretistic mind."[52] Of Tyn we shall hear much more; suffice it to note here that his view that any thinker able to see the merits of both Thomas and Gregory is guilty of syncretism is typical of the polarized mentality that still characterizes not only Tyn's work but also that of many modern commentators.[53]

Despite the very limited evidence for either pro- or anti-Thomist sentiment in Constantinople,[54] many students of the period are remarkably sanguine in their willingness to characterize Thomas' influence on Byzantine culture. R. W. Southern, for example, describes Thomas' influence as profound; although he initially limits this influence specifically to Thomas' fourteenth-century admirers, he later implies much larger consequences: "To a generation beset by uncertainty and surrounded by incalculable dangers he offered safety and certainty. To men struggling with confusion he demonstrated the possibility of systematic and clear-cut theological statements."[55] Such a portrait may well describe Aquinas' position in the West but can hardly fit the situation of the East, where so few knew of his work. Ironically, the uncertainty of life in Byzantium in the fourteenth century has also often been given as a rationale for the appeal of hesychasm. Indeed, Deno Geanakoplos finds evidence for precisely the opposite of what Southern sees: "Henceforth, with the exception of the Latinophile works produced, most theological treatises that were to be composed in the Byzantine East were apologetic or polemic in character, directed primarily against what they held to be the errors of the Latin church."[56]

Runciman differs from both Southern and Geanakoplos in finding that, with the exception of Scholarios, the translation of Aquinas' work came too late in Byzantine history to affect its scholarship.[57] Tyn, in contrast, claims that already in the Middle Ages Thomas' thought had contributed to the unification of the two churches: "In general the Greeks joyfully accepted the translations of Demetrios Kydones; even the Palamites, who later felt compelled to oppose Thomism, completely acknowledged the value of Aquinas' theology."[58] The most measured view is that of Stylianos Papadopulos who, distinguishing his own position from Chrysostomos Papadopulos' opinion that the Greek Thomas translations had no influence on Orthodox theology, notes that the effects of Aquinas' influence cannot be confined to the fourteenth and fifteenth centuries, but extend to the subsequent ages.[59] Nonetheless, he does not appear to contest the limited influence of the Thomas translations in the period of the hesychast controversy and its aftermath.

As we have noted, contemporary Western response to Palamas is even harder to determine than Aquinas' impact on the East. Runciman twice claims that the Palamite doctrine of the energies was denounced as heresy by Western theologians[60] but provides no evidence for this view. Geanakoplos, too, refers to "the West's out-of-hand rejection of Hesychasm and Palamism as doctrinally innovative and therefore heretical."[61] Like Runciman, though, Geanakoplos does not document this claim, and hence it is difficult to assess whether it is indeed historically founded or merely proceeds from the author's assumptions at the level of systematic theology.

One area of medieval Western reception of Eastern theology offers some prospect of a clear conclusion: Thomas' own anti-Greek treatise. Obviously, for chronological reasons, this cannot be taken as critical specifically of Palamas; nevertheless, because it represents Thomas' views, and not just those of the West generally, it is important in assessing the extent of historical animosity between the two sides. The most thorough study of this treatise is that of Antoine Dondaine. He establishes the important preliminary point that the Contra errores Graecorum was written at the behest of Urban IV and was therefore not a task arising out of Thomas' own spontaneous desire to dispute Eastern thought. Second, Thomas' task was to examine a florilegium of Nicholas of Cotrone, the Libellus de fide sanctae Trinitatis, and to render an evaluation of it. Dondaine concludes: "His work is less a treatise against the Greeks than an investigation of the Libellus."[62] Given that the Libellus does not accurately represent Greek thought, Thomas' treatise cannot be taken as his indictment of Eastern theology, particularly since he concludes that it is the pope's responsibility to determine what is and is not true doctrine.[63] Although Thomas was to have delivered a speech on Greek theological error at the Second Council of Lyons, another command performance, he died on the way there and the content of his paper is not known. As with Palamas, then, we have scant evidence on the basis of which to determine the opposition of Thomas and Gregory other than their own theologies.

The historical evidence for any sort of irrevocable theological divide between Aquinas and Palamas is thus very weak indeed. Commentators differ deeply on the degree and significance of data pertaining to theological differences between East and West, sometimes interpreting the same datum in radically different ways: when for example, Southern sees the uncertainty of life in fourteenth-century Byzantium as the reason for Thomas' influence, while Geanakoplos sees the same uncertainty as pushing Byzantines to an anti-Latin stance. More often, the commentators' own assumption of systematic opposition leads to claims inadequately supported by historical fact, as when Runciman sees in the Council of Reims a condemnation of Palamas or Tyn assumes syncretism in Bessarion simply because he entertained views proper to both Thomas and Gregory. Not on historical grounds, therefore, can we establish irreconcilable differences between East and West.

2. The Reception of Aquinas and Palamas in the Twentieth Century

That there is relatively little evidence with which to evaluate the reception either of Thomas or Gregory between the Renaissance and the twentieth century is not surprising in view of the Rezeptionsgeschichte of each within his own communion. One curious commonality is that although both were quickly recognized, even canonized, by their respective traditions, that recognition was followed by a long fallow period in which their work went largely unnoticed or even (in Thomas' case) maligned. The revival of interest in both begins in the nineteenth century and comes into full swing in the twentieth. If the East pays little attention to Aquinas in this period, this can be attributed at least in part to the lack of attention he receives in the West, and likewise Palamas in the East.[64]

We jump, therefore, from the late Middle Ages or early Renaissance to our own time. Once again, we are dealing with a relatively small group of people. This is especially true of Western commentators who, lacking a diaspora imposed by exile or emigration on a massive scale, have of necessity been less aware of the East than Eastern émigré theologians became of the West. Western students of Eastern Orthodoxy thus tend to be professional East-watchers, whereas one finds reference to Western theology—albeit usually its errors—quite routinely in the work of Eastern theologians. Professionalism, however, seems of little use as a predictor of acerbity: the history of reception is marked even in our time by bitterness, and often inaccuracy.

In the West, we begin the story with Adrian Fortescue. Fortescue's early twentieth-century appraisal of the Eastern Orthodox church begins with a consideration of the name by which the Orthodox are known, finding it problematic because "Orthodox in its real sense is just what we believe them not to be."[65] He concludes by declaring: "It is not, and has never been, Rome that is haughty or unconciliatory. Constantinople since Photius has always assumed a tone of arrogant defiance and insolent complacency that argues complete satisfaction with the horrible state of things produced by her schism."[66] Once again, concern for historical fact seems subordinated to the desire to proclaim one's own side as the indubitable and inevitable sole possessor of truth.

Not long after Fortescue came Martin Jugie, who contributed several articles related to Palamas to the *Dictionnaire de théologie catholique*. The assertions of the most important of these will be examined in greater detail in chapter 4. Here we focus on his historical monograph, *Le Schisme byzantin*. His title is itself, as far as the Orthodox are concerned, polemical—Philip Sherrard cannot cite it without inserting a [sic.] after *schisme*. The general tone of his work, both here and in the *Dictionnaire*, is well caught by his summary of the schism: "A constant spirit of polemic against the Roman Catholic church; an excessive conservatism, as opposed to true development of dogma with respect to the legitimate evolution of ritual and canonical forms according to the needs of time and place; doctrinal incoherence: these seem to us the general traits of the Byzantine schisme."[67] Aside from the clearly debatable contention of doctrinal incoherence and the at least mutually applicable charge of sustained polemic against the other side, there is at a strictly factual level a decided oddity in the criticism of opposition to change in ritual and canonical forms according to time and place on the part of a Roman Catholic writing in the early 1940s, of a church that had long worshiped in the vernacular and allowed for considerable local variation in liturgy and the recognition of saints, for example. Similar anomalies abound: the Orthodox defense of its doctrine against "protestant errors" was vain,[68] although by what criteria more so than Rome's own undertakings is unclear.

Jugie's animus against Palamas is particularly strong, leading him to advance claims made by no other historian: "Palamite doctrine was imposed by force on the Byzantine church by the usurper John Cantacuzenos."[69] Although Runciman also refers, on occasion, to Cantacuzenos as a usurper, the term is rather anomalous in the context of a turbulent society with no law of dynastic succession, and while the ascendancy of Palamism was undoubtedly linked to Cantacuzenos' political fortunes, it is surely cynical to suggest as Jugie does that political factors alone determined doctrinal development in any church. Of greater gravity is Jugie's attribution of views to Palamas that he does not document and which sound very unlike those Gregory usually adopts: "Palamas acknowledged he taught a new theology unknown to the ancient Fathers: 'These are,' he said, 'mysteries that have remained hidden until this day and which are indicated as enigmas in Holy Scripture,'"[70] a portrayal that differs sharply from Jugie's own charge that Palamas' theology consisted simply of "patristic florilegia."[71] Jugie even objects to the grounds for Palamas' canonization: "Our Congregation of Rites would have rejected them all as insufficient"[72]—this at a time when St. Valentine still occupied a secure place on the Roman Calendar.

Jugie's highly partisan view of Palamas might be dismissed as a period piece, dating as it does from before the rise of the ecumenical movement and the Second Vatican Council, except that his views continue to be influential. Gerhard Podskalsky, for example, who is quite critical of Meyendorff's reading of Palamas, is not at all critical of Jugie.[73] Tyn's long article, ostensibly on the Kydones brothers but largely concerned with

Palamas, draws almost entirely on Jugie and polemical works by the Kydones brothers as the basis of his information about Palamas.[74] Thus Tyn is led to some rather startling assertions. He ranges, for example, Palamism alongside existentialism and Marxism—in respect of their atheism[75]—and repeatedly refers to Palamas as a fideist, combining polemical epithets when he comments on "the Palamite fideistic-agnostic anti-Thomistic affect."[76] He continues to attribute to Palamas the claim of a superior and an inferior deity—a contention deriving from Jugie, on the basis of texts in Migne, that has long been challenged by Lossky, not on the basis of textual interpretation but on the authenticity of the texts.[77] Even in fairly recent reference works, one finds these assertions repeated: "Gregory Palamas called the divine energies 'deities' and spoke of a higher deity, that is, the being of God, and lower deities, the energies."[78] Even if one takes statements about greater and lesser divinity to be authentically those of Palamas, one is not necessarily correct in assuming, as this author does, that Palamas is simply inconsistent in also assserting the simplicity of God. Halleux, for example, notes that Palamas never speaks of the essence-energies distinction as real without adding that it does not add the least composition to divine simplicity.[79]

Although a scholar of irenic inclinations such as Halleux can acknowledge that the Palamite doctrine of divine energies, unknowable essence and uncreated grace was condemned only by non-Orthodox theologians who were too sure of themselves (and whom Halleux tactfully does not name),[80] Meyendorff's edition of the Triads seems to have been undertaken at least partly in response to Western polemic or misunderstanding.[81] Yet two decades after its publication, Western theologians continued to use far less reliable sources.

The perception of fundamental and irreconcilable differences between East and West has continued through the very end of our own century. LaCugna concludes her examination of Palamas: "On nearly every significant doctrinal point—theology of grace, theological anthropology, epistemological principles—the differences between East and West are decisive and probably irrreconcilable. Still, Palamism and Thomism remain two legitimate albeit divergent systems of thought."[82]

The situation on the Orthodox side is hardly more encouraging with respect to Aquinas. Oft-recurring objections based on contestable readings of Thomas refer to the problem of created grace (Evdokimov[83]), the supposed precedence granted to divine unity over the three hypostases[84] and beatific vision (Lossky[85]). Evdokimov and Lossky, however, are more muted in their critique of Thomas than Philip Sherrard, whose The Greek East and the Latin West fully equals Jugie for both its bitter tone and its apparent determination to misread the texts and authors it purports to analyze. However, as Sherrard's objections to Aquinas are largely concerned with method and epistemology, we shall not treat them here.

Before we turn to the purely methodological questions, we will consider some of the systematic differences between Thomas and Gregory that commentators regularly cite as obstacles to closer relations. Some of these, such as papal supremacy, lie entirely outside the scope of this study; others, such as trinitarian processions, concern us only tangentially; still others, although certainly quite problematical, pertain properly not to theology but canon law, such as clergy celibacy and divorce. Happily, a number of issues that were once deemed grave—Saturday fasting, the azymes, or use of unleavened bread in the Eucharist,[86] and clergy beardedness—have now faded in importance. The issues that remain are the ones to which we now turn: divine simplicity and its relation to the energies, created grace and the vision of God. Since these have all surfaced already in the discussion above, we will rehearse only briefly the problems they raise.

Of these three issues, the most apparently intractable is that of created grace. The reason this question looms so large is that it names the center of a much larger issue, which Meyendorff identifies as the most important element of Byzantine theology:

> The central theme, or intuition, of Byzantine theology is that man's nature is not a static, 'closed,' autonomous entity, but a dynamic reality, determined in its very existence by its relationship to God. This relationship is seen as a process of ascent and as communion— man, created in the image of God, is called to achieve a 'divine similitude'. . . . The dynamism of Byzantine anthropology can easily be contrasted with the static categories of 'nature' and 'grace' which dominated the thought of post-Augustinian Western Christianity.[87]

Viewed in this way, the issue becomes not only the nature of grace but the nature of all relations between God and humanity and necessarily implies a specific theological anthropology and a specific doctrine of God. On the anthropological side, such a theology requires a picture of the human person receptive to relation with the Utterly Other; in the Eastern Christian tradition, this receptivity is expressed in the doctrine of the *imago Dei*. As Evdokimov puts it: "The image [of God] predestines humanity to theosis."[88] On the divine side, it requires a portrait of a God who can be self-communicating without compromising transcendence, and this the Orthodox tradition came to articulate, largely because of Palamas' theology, as the distinction between divine essence and energies. How the Orthodox view this doctrine as fundamentally different from Western conceptuality is well expressed by Meyendorff: "There does not therefore exist [in Palamas' thought] any reality comparable to the 'created supernatural' of Latin thought. Such a reality would be for him a confusion of divine and human nature. . . . the hypostasis [of the one living in Christ] acquires the uncreated energies of God, which are hypostasised in it."[89]

Another way of expressing the same supposedly fundamental opposition of East and West is in terms of the relation between sanctification and consummation—that is, whether the two are considered to belong to different realms of experience or whether sanctification in this life is taken to be the initiation of consummation, so that there is an unbroken progression from this life to the next. Hussey and Hart articulate this view: "This term, χάρις, grace, is constantly used for deifying divinity, suggesting a comparison with the Thomist doctrine of beatification through supernatural grace. In contrast to St Thomas, however, they assert that this deification can and does take place in this life through a spiritualisation of the flesh which suggests the glorified body of the resurrection."[90]

A third perspective on the same problem sees it as a question of where to locate the principle of graced divine-human relation. Halleux states it thus:

> Henceforward, the mediating realities, the communal principles, could no longer constitute an intermediary ontological sphere between the uncreated and the created, but one must situate them, either in God himself, or in the creature. It is here that the theological traditions of the Orient and the Occident diverge, Palamism through the doctrine of the uncreated energies and scholasticism through that of created grace.[91]

Tyn sees the problem as quite the reverse: "What holds for some phenomena in contemporary theology applies equally to Palamas: 'Grace is for this anthropocentric theology no supernatural quality and ontological certainty [Seinsbestimmtheit]; grace is always only a certain "illumination" and heightened subjectivity.'"[92]

The two other problems we identified both relate directly to this central issue. Once the divine energies are posited as truly divine yet in some sense distinct from the essence, the problem of divine simplicity arises. The Western reservation is that Eastern doctrine seems to compromise simplicity: "The fundamental difficulty with which the Palamite distinction can be charged consists in the impossibility of assuming a real distinction in the infinite, perfect and simple God."[93] This objection is also elaborated at length in Guichardan's *Le Problème de la simplicité divine en Orient et en Occident aux XIVe et XVe siècles.* This view is not, however, shared by all Westerners, and Easterners do not generally read Palamas in this way. Both Lossky and Halleux deny that the essence-energies distinction compromises simplicity.[94] Although neither refers to precise charges, clearly there is a perception in both East and West that this issue has been a point of contention. The Eastern objection to the theology of the West concerns not the absence of a doctrine of divine energies (although this is a problem for the doctrine of grace) but the relation of the three divine hypostases to the essence, the Western portrayal of hypostatic existence being allegedly compromised by its undue emphasis on simplicity. This question—which reverts to the same issue as the filioque—does not concern us here, except insofar as it indicates that both Eastern and Western doctrines of the Trinity are challenged on the issue of simplicity and that the difference is not one of direct opposition but of charges of two quite separate forms of weakness.

Where we do encounter charges of direct opposition is on the question of the vision of God. Lossky's work demonstrates the two quite different forms this objection can take. The first concerns the encounter with divine essence: "We find ourselves confronted by two formulae neatly opposed, the first of which resolutely denies all possibility of knowing the essence of God, while the second explicitly insists on the fact that it is the actual essence of God which must be the object of beatific vision."[95] The question's second form markedly resembles one of the issues we identified as pertaining to the doctrine of grace: "No Christian theologian has ever denied *ex-professo* that the elect will have a vision of God in the state of final beatitude. . . . The question has been raised whether this vision of God is reserved exclusively for eternal life, *in patria*, or if it can in fact begin here, *in via*, in the ecstatic experience."[96] Fahey points to the perception of a direct clash between Aquinas and Palamas on this point:

> No created mind [according to Thomas] can see the essence of God unless by grace God joins Himself to that mind as something intelligible to it. Grace bestows a power of illumination called illumination of mind, the *lumen gloriae*. . . . it is not hard to see why those who follow Gregory Palamas' theory about seeing God through the divine energies will feel uneasy about the Thomistic explanation.[97]

Halleux states the conflict even more starkly. Referring to Romanides' argument, contra Meyendorff, that Barlaam's Platonism and therefore his conception of contemplation were essentially Augustinian (an argument Halleux finds persuasive), Halleux writes:

> If this thesis is to hold true, one would have to interpret the Palamite controversy not simply as a confrontation of monastic theology and humanism within the Byzantine church, but also a new encounter, and indeed a violent collision, of the Western and Eastern traditions over the vision of God. The Palamite councils constitute, as it were, the Orthodox

reply to the Latin condemnations of 1241 and 1336, and the anti-Latin character of Palamism is thus shown to be, so to speak, congenital.[98]

Against this bleak vision, Halleux offers no alternate view.

Once again, while clearly sustained and significant dispute over certain doctrinal issues continues, it is far from clear that the analysis of these issues has accurately estimated, or even identified, these problems. Accounts of which issues are significant, or what differs about Eastern and Western accounts of these doctrines, vary widely from commentator to commentator. Because so many of these commentators appear to be motivated by overt polemical intent and so many of them inadequately document the theology they describe, the modern debate, like the medieval, raises questions rather than establishes the irreconcilability of Thomist and Palamite theology.

3. The Debate over Method

The differences on individual theological loci prove to be of far-reaching significance but a significance nonetheless dwarfed by the consequence of the methodological questions underlying all these debates. Numerous ways of characterizing the methodological differences of East and West have emerged, but two sets of distinct but interrelated oppositions are frequently cited: one between East and West and one within the Eastern church, related to the hesychast controversy and coloring the East's view of the West. Thus Meyendorff describes the gap between Palamites and Latinophrones (i.e., the Latin-minded, or Greeks sympathetic to Western theology) as not over attitudes towards church union but methods and priorities.[99] The hesychast controversy itself, he points out, represents another, and highly significant, episode in the struggle over the relation of theology and philosophy in the East.[100] In so doing, he shows the way in which the intra-Byzantine controversy is inextricably connected to relations between Eastern and Western Christendom. Although the intra-Byzantine debate has long been settled, the mutual recriminations of the present are rooted in the East's struggle over hesychasm, which emerged within two centuries of those in the West over Aristotelianism and later Nominalism. The problem with assessing the various claims of methodological opposition is precisely that they become woefully intertwined.

If we start with the East's dissatisfaction with the West on the purely historical level, we see it concerns a perceived failure of development, although this time not theological but philosophical: "There is evidence to suggest that from the 15th century, if not before, some Byzantines had come to feel that the Latins were at fault, not only over particular points of doctrine, but more broadly in their entire approach to theology and their method of arguing."[101] In Orthodox perception, it is the West that is at fault because prior to the Middle Ages there was no significant difference in methodology: "As a result of intellectual developments in Western Christendom during the 11th–12th centuries, the Latins had in fact altered their interpretations of the rules of the game."[102] One problem with this diagnosis of the problem is that while no one disputes that Western theology altered dramatically as a result of the encounter with Aristotelianism, the Orthodox contention that it differs with the West primarily on this point fails to account for the many varieties of Western theology, from the medieval to the modern, that are not indebted to Aristotle, or indeed to any specific philosophical system. It especially overlooks the objections of many non–Roman Catholic theologians to the use of philosophy in theology—if attitudes towards philosophy are the main problem, why are Luther and Barth not championed by the Orthodox?

If the role of philosophy in Western theology will admit of no monolithic characterization, neither does Byzantine theology, however, for there is considerable dispute over the place of philosophy in Byzantine religious discourse. The long-seated objections of monks to "wisdom from outside" find a modern-day spokesman in the views of Alexander Kalomiros, whose views we can take as representative of one variety of Orthodox sensibility: "Protestants, humanists, atheists—the whole series of European philosophers—all graduated from the school of Catholicism. That is why they all speak the same language, the language of rationalism, and this is why, in spite of all their variances, they understand each other so famously."[103] The problem Kalomiros sees with this rationalism is exactly what monks in the fourteenth century and earlier saw: "Rationalism brings with it self-conceit; self-conceit brings estrangement; and estrangement grows with worldly power."[104] Kalomiros is not a monk, but a physician, as the prologue to his book tells us: "The author of this book is not a theologian trained in the schools where they study the unstudiable—theology. He studied medicine, something which can be studied because it is a worldly, human knowledge"[105]—an attitude that might have come directly from Mount Athos of the fourteenth century. Not surprisingly, Kalomiros' book was published in the United States by one of the leading Orthodox monasteries.

Lest Kalomiros' views be dismissed as insignificant because he is not a theologian, we note also the position of Christos Yannaras, more nuanced and sophisticated but no less hostile to what he supposes to be Western theological method:

> This "rendering manifest" [in ST I.1,8 ad 2] or explanation of revealed truth through the power of the intellect, and the vigorous use of reason within the framework of revealed truth, emphatically set a boundary between man and God, between the syllogistic capacity of the subject and the incomprehensible reality of God. In the end the boundary is set between the divine and human nature, a consequence which neglects the unity of the two natures, into one person, that is to say, the possiblity of personal participation in, and not merely logical 'clarification' of, the divine truth concerning God. The analytical scholastic methodology represents, then, a deeper stance which is essentially anthropocentric. . . . Man in the Western scholastic tradition does not participate personally in the truth of the cosmos. He does not seek to bring out the meaning, the logos of things, the disclosure of the personal activity of God in the cosmos, but seeks with his individualistic intellect to dominate the reality of the physical world.[106]

How misguided a description this is of one scholastic, Aquinas, we will see in the following two chapters. What concerns us at the moment are other claims. First, Orthodox theology requires personal participation in the truth, an attitude that could be called essentially hesychast. Second, that Western theology is (a) not the result of such personal participation, (b) analytic, scholastic and logical and (c) anthropocentric. Third, (assumed but not stated) that (a), (b) and (c) are necessarily related. If (a), (b), (c) and their relation are all eminently contestable, this invective may at least teach us that we are not here quibbling about the fine points of procedure but about the most fundamental principles of Christian theology, the source of the doctrines of God, Christology and theological anthropology.

If such attitudes are characteristic of monastic culture, however, we cannot take them to by typical of Byzantine theology in general, or of Palamas simply because he was a monk of Athos.[107] His attitudes, and those of the Byzantines, towards philosophy are nuanced and complex:

> It is clear that, for the hesychasts, the authentic 'natural' man—and therefore the whole complex of human faculties of knowledge—is the man 'in Christ', potentially transfigured, and 'deified' through participation in Christ's 'Body'. For them, secular philosophy could, at best, be still useful in the understanding of creation, but not for the knowledge of God, in which was found the ultimate meaning of human existence. This basic position of Palamas . . . did not, however, mean that the religious zealots had included in their program of action any systematic struggle against the Hellenic heritage of Byzantine civilization."[108]

Two important cautions are being offered here: first, that Byzantium, even religious Byzantium, was not hostile to the classical Greek culture that was, after all, its own ancestor; second, that the hesychasts were opposed to the use of philosophy only in theology in the narrow sense of the term—that is, to philosophy as a direct and independent informant of the doctrine of God. The attitude of the monks parallels what Meyendorff sees in Byzantine society generally: an estimation of philosophy based on a fragile equilibrium where pagan thought was not rediscovered, because it had never been forgotten, but where the memory of a gradual, painful rejection of it was still keen.[109] More recently, Stavros Yangazoglou has claimed that Palamas' attitude towards the use of philosophy in theology—and particularly towards the use of the syllogism—is considerably more nuanced than has generally been acknowledged.[110] Yangazoglou does not, however, refrain from the usual vague and unsubstantiated contrasts with Western scholasticism.

What Meyendorff deems ambivalence in Byzantine attitudes towards philosophy, however, one might be tempted to call ambiguity, given the strikingly different interpretations of other scholars. While Meyendorff is concerned to distinguish between Eastern and Western appropriations of the classical Greek philosophical tradition, Norden finds a concurrence between East and West on this very point. He sees in the Italian Renaissance the two worlds of East and West finding a commonality that all the preceding attempts at church union could not reach, "an ineradicable element of the European *Gesamtkultur* [total culture],"[111] *Gesamtkultur* being precisely what Dr. Kalomiros does not see. The more measured and scholarly Meyendorff does not see it either, however; indeed, he is adamant that the kind of secular scholarship exemplified by Palamas' predecessors such as Photius and Psellos is not appropriately termed *humanism* and is precisely not comparable to scholarship of the Italian Renaissance.[112]

Nevertheless we clearly find in Byzantium pride in its inheritance from antiquity, even a proprietary pride. When Kydones, for example, was accused of neglecting the Greek patristic heritage by following Aquinas, he is said to have replied that Aquinas was based on Aristotle, one of "our *own* Greeks."[113] Ironically, when attacking the filioque, even Photius, the namesake of the first real rift between East and West, supported his claims with reasoning based on metaphysics.[114] Damascene, too, in the philosophical chapters of his magnum opus, *The Fount of Knowledge*, laid the foundations of theology by exact definitions of being, substance, accident, species and genus, drawn from Aristotle via the Fathers.[115]

However anecdotal, these cases suggest that claims of a flat opposition between ancient philosophy and Byzantine religious culture represent a distortion. Nevertheless, there was undoubtedly in the Byzantine theological world a deep suspicion of philosophy that far overreaches any similar sensibility found in the West. In the end, the very ambivalence of Byzantine thinkers regarding philosophy renders easy classification of their views virtually impossible: "As most historians of Byzantine theology will admit, the problem of the relationship between philosophy and the facts of Christian experience remained at the center of the theological thought of Byzantium, and no safe and permanent balance between them has ever been found."[116] In this ambivalence, however, we must ask if the East is really so different from the West as a whole, if we take into account the attitudes of Justin and Tertullian, the scholastics and the reformers?

The variety of perspectives on the estimation and role of philosophy in Byzantine intellectual life generally is mirrored by the differing accounts of Palamas' own attitude towards philosophy. It is clear that Gregory received the usual foundational education of an upper-class Greek youth of his time, which certainly included training in Aristotelian logic.[117] Indeed, Palamas even expressed pride in that education; he recounted with satisfaction how the great humanist Metochites had praised his knowledge of Aristotle.[118] Nicol's claim, therefore, that although Palamas was grounded in ancient philosophy, "from the moment of his monastic vocation he turned his back on scholarly pursuits"[119] seems oddly not to regard the *Triads*, much less the quite philosophically oriented *Capita*, as scholarly pursuits; because Nicol himself notes, moreover, that Gregory's account of the cosmos in the *Capita* draws on Ptolemy and other pagan authorities,[120] it is scarcely plausible even to claim Gregory had turned his back on secular learning. Nicol's more moderate position on Palamas' attitude towards philosophy is that he thought its use should be limited or that it could become pernicious under certain circumstances: "He felt that the wisdom of the Hellenes, even of Aristotle, might be of service as an elementary preparation for higher things; but as an end in itself or worse as an alleged guide to theology it was not merely useless, it was positively dangerous."[121] The important thing for Gregory, Nicol maintains, "was to be fully aware of the limitations of philosophy and of the ways in which it had been misdirected by the Hellenes."[122] Similarly, Schultze sees Palamas as having forged a synthesis between philosophy and belief that parallels that of Western scholasticism, although it also differs.[123] Podskalsky will take no such moderate view; Palamas, he claims, wanted to banish philosophy from theology once and for all.[124] Once again, we see that the judgement of scholars differs so widely that it is hard to draw any firm conclusions from the secondary literature.

Despite the difficulty of assessing the acceptance of any philosophy in Byzantine society, some commentators have characterized the intellectual turmoil in Byzantium as a clash between Platonists and Aristotelians. Among these numbers Sherrard: "The anti-Latin elements in the Byzantine intellectual world saw in Platonism, already associated with ideas of a non-Christian Greek society, an ideological weapon with which to oppose the Christian Aristotelianism of the West."[125] A variation of this position is that of Ivánka, viewing the problem as an intra-Byzantine struggle between Palamite and Aristotelian tendencies.[126] Likewise, Halleux sees the fundamental clash as one of differing views of the "mystery of communion" between God and humanity. He claims a philosophical ground for these theologies, a difference crystallizing in the thirteenth century, with the Byzantine church opting for Platonism while the West pursued Aristotle. Halleux is even willing to use the terms *Palamism* and *scholasticism* to designate the two fundamental options, terminology that is questionable on more than one count.[127] Such is also the view of Uspensky, cited by Tatakis, which Tatakis disputes: "Despite its links to the philosophical thought of Greece, it is clear that the hesychast quarrel began and ended as a purely theological quarrel. It is the form taken in the Greek church by the debate between mysticism . . . and rationalism."[128] The reduction of scholasticism to rationalism is, of course, debatable—although we will hear this charge again and again from the Eastern side—but Tatakis' essential insight is that viewing the intra-Byzantine clash as one between two philosophies is precisely to miss the point. One might extend his insight (in terms he would doubtless reject) and question whether regarding the differences between Eastern and Western models of salvation as rooted in philosophical differences is equally to miss the point.

On this question of the appropriation of philosophy we find, as we have before, no such scholarly consensus as would render possible conclusions based on the secondary literature alone. There is slightly greater concurrence on an allied question of method—namely, the mode in which Palamas and Aquinas appropriate Denys (Pseudo-Dionysius the Areopagite[129]), or alternatively, how they position themselves in relation to the via negativa. Runciman states the purported difference thus: "Thomas indeed respects the apophatic theology of the Areopagite. He is fully conscious of the limits of human knowledge. But to him apophatic is little more than a corrective to cataphatic theology."[130] Lossky makes a very similar point but points particularly to the way in which each author works through this Dionysian inheritance. Aquinas, he claims, essentially tames the via negativa, reducing it to a via eminentiae. In Palamas, on the other hand, Lossky finds a parallel between theological method and the doctrine of God: the tension between the two ways yields an antinomy that reflects divine nature itself, with its distinction between essence and energies.[131] Kilmartin also sees the opposition as one of the apophatic and cataphatic ways, which is ultimately rooted in the doctrine of God, but claims an objection for scholasticism. Palamas, he maintains,

> speaks of a superior knowledge of God granted within the apophatic way. While the creature can never know God comprehensively, a new way of knowing God is caused by light radiating from God himself: an uncreated light, divine but distinguished from the divine essence. From the standpoint of scholastic theology this theory is untenable. It contradicts the teaching about the infinity of God. To attribute a real distinction in God other than that of the opposition of relations of Persons to one another is to predicate a superior or inferior deity in the mystery of God.[132]

Here, however, we have finally a claim of opposition, not at the methodological but the systematic level, and this tendency to slide almost imperceptibly from one level to the other we also saw in Lossky.

The problem with such analyses is that they depend on the necessary connection between method and theology to which they point, yet this connection is highly questionable. As we shall see, there is little evidence that the Palamite essence-energies distinction posits a real distinction in God, let alone an antinomy. Likewise, while Aquinas possesses no such distinction, he certainly says both that we cannot know God comprehensively and that our knowledge of God comes about from a divine light radiating from God himself. Yet where is the evidence that Aquinas finds such a theory either untenable or contradictory of divine infinity?

A less problematic suggestion is Every's, that Orthodox commitment to the *via negativa* is intimately linked to the East's contemplative inclination:

> The Greeks saw dogmas as holy images, the Christological definitions, for instance, as ikons of Christ. Like ikons they must not be broken, and they must be venerated, but they are affirmative theology, and like all positive statements, must sometimes be denied on the negative way, when the mystery is contemplated apophatically, in a wordless wonder. They are rather signposts on a way of initiation than lines on the map of heaven, and logical consequences are not naturally drawn from them.[133]

Every raises the question of the use of logic in theology, an issue as thorny for East-West dialogue as the use of philosophy, though the two are often not adequately distinguished. While his version interprets the difference as the East's non-usage of logic, an equally frequent charge is that the West misuses it. The East does not feel awed by any logical superiority of the West; on the contrary, it views the use of logic as the province of the theologically *borné*. Nicephoras Gregoras reportedly sneered that the production of proofs by syllogism is a method of argument zealously cultivated by Italians and others of mediocre intelligence, but worse than useless in the search for divine truths.[134] Again, the dispute lies not simply between East and West but also within Byzantine theological circles. Barlaam, supposedly "in love with syllogisms," maintained that Aristotelian methods of proof were applicable to all theological problems,[135] a position obviously at odds with Palamas, no matter how one construes the latter's attitude to philosophy.

The East's complaints regarding the West's excessive reliance on logic often take the form specifically of attacks on Thomas for undue rationalism. These charges reach back as far as Demetrios Kydones who, "like all antithomists," complained chiefly of Thomas' rationalism,[136] and continue in the less irenic reaches of the Greek church today:

> In its effort to Christianize the peoples of Europe who were still barbarian, the Latin Church, instead of trying to raise them to the difficult heights of Christian Faith and life, tried to present Christianity as something easy and pleasurable. . . . In this way began the spread of rationalism and the adulteration of the Christian Faith . . . which later found its best expression in the *Summa Theologica* of Thomas Aquinas.[137]

The suggestion seems to be that rationalism is somehow opposed to faith, an attitude equally evident in the late fourteenth century in the tract of Kallistos Angelikoudes, who was scandalized by Thomas' constant emphasis on the role of the intellect in the knowledge of God. Of Angelikoudes, Nicol writes: "To him it is a matter of vision, of personal experience, vouchsafed through the uncreated energies of God, through the divine light."[138] Here we see yet another problem of slippage; from the question of the legitimacy of Thomas' theological method in particular and the role of logic in general, we have moved to a false polarity of reason and spiritual experience. Thomas would have been bewildered at the suggestion that his use of either Aristotle or logical argument precluded a spiritually informed theology, because it was precisely the synthesis of the two that he sought to create. Aquinas himself, as Pelikan points out, must have been aware of arguments similar to those levelled against him after his death, for he answers them, maintaining that the warnings of the Fathers against relying on argumentation in support of the faith were meant to rule out arguments proving articles of faith from reason but that argumentation from articles of faith to their corollaries was legitimate.[139] A further problem with such Eastern criticisms of Thomas' use of reason is that they identify no trait peculiar to Thomas—they would apply equally to, say, Gregory Nazianzen.

All the aspects of the *Methodenstreit* between East and West that we have considered thus far are dwarfed by the central issue we now approach: the role of experience and mysticism in Christian theology. Runciman views this as *the* central issue obstructing the path to union of East and West:

> Every attempt at union was accompanied by a number of theological debates and supported or opposed by a number of tracts and sermons. The debates make sterile reading; for they never got down to the fundamental issue. The real bar to union was that Eastern and Western Christendom felt differently about religion; and it is difficult to debate about feelings. . . . The whole question of mysticism and mystical theory, which was of fundamental importance to the Byzantines and on which the West held other opinions, was kept out of the debates, deliberately, it seems, in the case of the Union Council of Florence, because the issue could not be resolved by the methods used in the debates.[140]

He later reduces the problems even further: "The drifting apart of the Eastern and Western branches of Christendom is clearly marked in their respective attitudes towards mysticism."[141] Another way of stating this point would be to see it as an external clash of head and heart, as does Tatakis: "The greatest interest of hesychasm is the exceptional place it gives to the heart and the sentiments. It incessantly opposes the heart and intelligence to reason."[142] Tatakis finds this trend particularly true of Palamas himself: "It is obvious that Palamas, clearly opposing the objectivism of ratiocination to Neo-Platonic ecstasy, is seeking to formulate a theory, which, being faithful to the most profound root of Christianity, wants the intelligence to be bathed in the heart and be guided by it."[143] The terms in which Tatakis describes the conflict—head versus heart, or the heart's faith-filled triumph over reason—echo, of course, Pascal, and it therefore comes as no surprise that he views Palamas as a proleptic graecophone Pascal.[144] One reason the heart-head dichotomy seems not to fit the East-West dispute very well, however, is that Gregory, at least, is not given to descriptions of affect. He does not recount visions or his personal spiritual experience or describe the experiences of others, much less state the emotional impact of such experiences. Indeed, it would be odd if he did, given that the Byzantines considered such description tasteless. Rather, he writes theology that seeks to justify the relevance of the mystical and spiritual for theology—or in other words, he champions experience as a theological informant and perhaps even a theological warrant. A second reason for rejecting the head-versus-heart perspective is that it creates an anachronistic opposition. The hesychast controversy concerned this very issue, the relevance of spiritual experience to theology, yet the eventual victory of the hesychasts esstablished a much narrower point than Angelikoudes' attitude described here would indicate. What the Orthodox church opted for was the admission of spiritual evidence in the theological realm, but in so doing, it did not reject the intellect, so central to the Fathers' conception of the spiritual life, or make any explicit pronouncement on the theological use of philosophy.

The West worries about the marginalization of scripture and tradition, about pietism, Enthusiasm and other forms of subjectivity. As Every sees it, by the seventeenth and eighteenth centuries, the Latins were prepared to denounce *any* appeal to spiritual experience as a dangerous delusion.[145] It is far from clear, however, that what the West rejected was the same as what the East affirmed. The West sought to ward off the spectre of private revelation, which the West always conceived in individualistic terms. What the East affirmed was not individual, but communal, experience, and experience, moreover, that was consonant with the prior theological tradition. It did not seek to add to the tradition novel doctrines derived solely from the experience of prayer.

The East's fear, on the other hand, is of prayer's becoming irrelevant to theology:

> In acknowledging that in the Church every Christian, and the saint in particular, possesses the privilege and opportunity of seeing and experiencing the truth, the . . . Byzantines presupposed a concept of Revelation which was substantially different from that held in the West. Because the concept *theologia* in Byzantium . . . was inseparable from *theoria* ("contemplation"), theology could not be—as it was in the West—a rational deduction from 'revealed' premises, i.e., from Scripture or from the statements of an ecclesiastical magisterium; rather, it was a vision experienced by the saints, whose authenticity was, of course, to be checked against the witness of Scripture and Tradition. . . . The true theologian was the one who saw and experienced the content of his theology; and this experience was considered to belong not to the intellect alone.[146]

Hussey and Hart echo this sentiment when they point out that Byzantines often used *theologia* to designate inwardness with God and cite Evagrius Ponticus' maxim, "If you are a theologian you pray truly, and if you pray truly you are a theologian."[147] Evagrius' work, and this thought in particular, are certainly known in the West, but neither has shaped Western theology definitively.

Nevertheless, the distinction between East and West on this point does not lie so much at the level of theory as practice. Nothing in the preceding quotations suggests attitudes or procedures condemned in the West, but increasingly since the Middle Ages the West has simply not attained the integration of theology and spiritual practice upon which the East insists so strongly as an ideal. If the East put the ideal into practice up till the fourteenth century, though, it has not often done so since then. The modern figures whom the East calls theologians are no more mystics than their Western counterparts. A more accurate point of distinction may be, therefore, not the status of spiritual experience itself but the theology inferred from it. Meyendorff writes: "For the entire patristic and Byzantine tradition, knowledge of God implies 'participation' in God—i.e., not only intellectual knowledge, but a state of the entire human being, transformed by grace, and freely cooperating with it by the efforts of both will and mind."[148] The Byzantine view of revelation and theological warrant is thus based on the assumption that human beings are radically transformed by God (theosis) and that God's nature is radically self-communicative and transcendent (the essence-energies distinction). Because of this anthropology and this theology, spiritual experience must be taken as a theological datum; conversely, to deny the validity of spiritual experience would be also to deny theosis and divine self-communication—such is the Byzantine view. Thus, the questions we are forced back upon are those of theology itself: is Western theology fundamentally in conflict with the doctrines of theosis and divine energies?

The methodological differences between East and West are real. Nevertheless, among the most vehement accounts of these also number the most prominent misreadings: Thomas Tyn's rendition of Palamas and Philip Sherrard's of Aquinas. Sherrard's, the older work, is well known among students of East-West relations, and yet he is almost always cited without any allusion to the errors of his portrayal of Aquinas. His analysis focuses on Thomas' supposed rejection of the possibility of knowledge of God from other than sensible sources: "With no innate knowledge, and unable to derive knowledge from a direct intuition of the Divine, man can in fact, according to Aquinas, only know anything by a process of abstraction from sensible objects."[149] While the latter part of this statement accurately describes an Aristotelian position regarding the physical world, it wholly misrepresents Aquinas' view of knowledge of God. Sherrard's description cannot be excused as a peripheral lapse, for he repeats essentially the same charge a few pages later: "All that man can know of [what is metaphysical and uncreated], the limit of his knowledge of the Divine, himself, and other sensible things, amounts, after he has gathered together and meditated on the abstractions he has derived from these things, to a mere collection of concepts which may be said to have an analogical likeness to the Divine, but nothing more."[150] Here, it seems the fundamental misunderstanding has broadened to include the Thomistic understanding of the nature and uses of analogy.

At first, it seems that Sherrard's problem is simply lack of familiarity with the relevant portions of the Summa Theologiae, yet he acknowledges: "That, however, Aquinas regarded the knowledge extracted by the reason from the sensible world as the only knowledge accessible to man . . . does not mean that he rejected the supra-rational truths of the Christian Revelation. On the contrary, he was most careful to acknowledge them."[151] How Sherrard's claims of Thomistic epistemology previously cited can be true in light of the latter admission is a mystery he neither acknowledges nor attempts to explain. Yet this profound misapprehension of Thomas' theology forms the basis for Sherrard's polemical comparison of Eastern and Western theological method.

On the other side stands Thomas Tyn. In his concern to distinguish Palamite from Thomistic theological method, he rightly asserts that Palamite theology does not operate on the basis of analogical thinking but then goes on to describe it as dualistic and Hegelian, with the result that "the Supernatural is only capable of representing itself as something that is either unnatural or against nature,"[152] an odd construal of a thinker celebrated for a distinction that seeks to assert precisely the authenticity of the Supernatural's engagement with creatures. Tyn raises the obvious (and legitimate) question regarding the East's appeal to experience: "However hesychasm was, as the manifestation of the energies rather than the essence of God himself, equated with an insight," but he continues with rather less justification: "To this gnosis even church tradition was supposedly subordinate."[153] Tyn's only evidence for the latter claim is Jugie's notorious article in the Dictionnaire de théologie catholique—which is not surprising, given that he would have encountered great difficulty in finding any such claim in Palamas' own work.

In the most curious turn of all, Tyn links Gregory's method to systematic emphases that are wholly out of character: "Palamism tends of its very nature more towards fideism; its basis is the same as that of rationalism: the dualism of grace and nature, so that, paradoxically, departing from fideistic premises, it can scarcely avoid rationalist (or at least anthropocentric) conclusions."[154] As we have seen, commentators from both East and West generally agree that the very categories of nature and grace are scarcely applicable to Eastern theology, and if Palamas' theology were so narrowly anthropocentric, it would surely have more to say about the effects of deification on the human person.

Both Tyn and Sherrard seem captives of their own epithets: since Thomas is rationalistic, his entire theology must be based on sense perception; since Gregory is a Hegelian, atheist, Marxist fideist,[155] he must have an inadequate sense of the supernatural—as well as a powerful intellect indeed, to synthesize these divergent philosophies. Between them, Sherrard and Tyn demonstrate in the sharpest way the need to return to the texts themselves and to attempt to interpret them on their own terms, rather than merely repeating shibboleths from the past (rationalist) or finding creative but anachronistic new ones (Marxist, Hegelian[156]).

If Sherrard and Tyn illustrate the folly of failing to return to the primary texts, a small group of scholars recognizes the necessity of doing so and of interpreting the texts in categories native to them. Lialine points to the need to study Eastern theology other than through the medium of concepts completely foreign to it,[157] a principle that applies, however, equally to appraisals of Western theology. Such interpretation might have prevented some of the polemic of the past. Philips, for example, suggests Jugie's charges of heresy against Palamas are due to his reading Eastern texts with Thomist eyes.[158] One commentator, furthermore, has not only called for a return to the texts but has made such a reexamination the basis of his study of Palamas; the difference between Jacques Lison's views of Palamas and the more usual Western readings suggests that close interpretation of the primary texts will break through many of the hoary battle lines of the past.[159]

The potential such an enterprise bears for rapprochement is noted by several commentators. For some, such as Blum, the hope of reconciliation lies at a relatively low level: East and West may be viewed as offering complementary sides of the inner unity of Christian belief.[160] Blum's vision, while making room for both Eastern and Western insights within the sphere of authentically Christian thought, nevertheless rejects the notion that the two are fundamentally similar: "Must this difference be repealed and reconciled?" he asks,[161] apparently implying that rapprochement is either undesirable or unattainable. Philips also suggests a possible coexistence of East and West but on the grounds of deficiencies in both systems rather than as a truce between fundamentally irreconcilable positions.[162] Lison likewise rejects the idea of a middle term (un moyen terme) in favor of respectful dialogue; in the end, he contends, it is impossible "not to opt for one or the other theology of grace."[163] Nevertheless, he sees Palamism as the expression of the same faith as the West's; its differences from the latter can only contribute to the catholicity of the church and the fulness of faith.[164]

Such views precisely beg the question, however: what is characteristic of Eastern and Western descriptions of God, humanity, and human sanctification, how are these different and how different are they? The possibility of acknowledging a genuine catholicity, one that includes both East and West, is possible only because the history of relations between East and West is happy in one important respect. Halleux reminds us: "If neither of the two churches has irremediably defined or condemned Palamism, the way leading from the anathemas of yesterday to the dialogue of today remains open to them."[165] If Halleux's hope rests largely on the exaggerated claims of Neopalamites to the canonicity of Palamism, we may ask whether common ground may not yet be found with Palamas. If there is reason for some optimism on that point, it is because, as Ware notes, East and West share a common past, and this past is patristic: it is false to contrast East and West as if they were mutually exclusive because such contrasts ignore the two traditions' shared past.[166] Meyendorff, indeed, finds in a return to the sources hope for bridging even the gap between Aquinas and Palamas themselves:

If, nevertheless, the doctrinal end-products of East and West seem to diverge, if the distance that separates Palamas from Thomas Aquinas seems difficult to overcome, there remains at least the fact that the two separated parts of the Christian world both go back to a common patristic tradition and, finally, to a common Biblical text. Let a common and concerted return to the sources determine our attitude towards the masters of the past: the clash between them will then perhaps become less violent.[167]

Before we embark on the direct comparison of Aquinas and Palamas, therefore, we begin with a brief excursus into their common past by reviewing the doctrine of deification as we find it in the Fathers.

III. The Patristic Concept of Deification

Our purpose here is to outline the notion of deification that had developed in Christian theology before the high Middle Ages and the end of Byzantium. In doing so, we seek merely to sketch the conventional wisdom concerning that history, to summarize its findings and illustrate them briefly from the writings of the Fathers themselves, in order to establish what kind of doctrine we are seeking in the works of Aquinas and Palamas.

Early in the Christian tradition, from the third century onwards, theosis became the dominant model of the concept of salvation.[168] The Fathers writing on deification drew on two sources: the Bible and the Platonic tradition.[169] From Plato, the tradition made use of the *Phaedo, Phaedrus, Theaetetus* and the *Republic*, in which the philosopher speaks of likening or assimilation to God, and from Plotinus, the *Enneads*, which also refers to assimilation.[170] This interweaving of Platonic and Christian elements is evident in another important source: the *Sayings of Sextus*, a pagan collection of texts dealing largely with purification, illumination and deification; although ostensible pagan, it is strongly reminiscent of Clement of Alexandria, who may have been its Christian editor.[171]

The early tradition can be viewed as too indebted to the pagan tradition, as Dalmais has, claiming, "The vocabulary of divinisation is foreign to Biblical language, which is careful to preserve the absolute of divine transcendance."[172] This view, however, vastly underestimates the importance of biblical warrants in early Christian writing on deification. Chief among the biblical sources was 2 Peter 1:4: "Thus he has given us, through these things, his precious and very great promises, so that through them you may escape from the corruption that is in the world because of passion and may become participants in divine nature." Other texts of importance include Psalm 82:6, John 10:34 (quoting Psalm 82), Romans 8:11, 1 Corinthians 15:49 and 2 Corinthians 8:9. The Fathers did not simply cite the Bible, moreover; they absorbed its essential insights, despite their proclivity for pagan texts. Lot-Borodine affirms that the Christianity of the first centuries in fact jealously guarded divine transcendence even as it proclaimed deification.[173]

The earliest Christian tradition spoke of deification using the same themes and images we will encounter in Aquinas and Palamas. The *Didache*, although not speaking of theosis directly, does consider the notions of knowledge (*gnosis*) and immortality, themes which as we shall see later, are directly linked to divinization.[174] The Apologists adapted the classic thesis of ancient Greek philosophy, both Platonic and Aristotelian, that only an unoriginate being could also be incorruptible or immortal by nature and concluded that the immortality for which the just are destined could only be a participated incorruptibility.[175] This notion of deification (a term the Apologists do not use) is clearly eschatological, although it presumes an earthly preparation, the chief notes of which are knowledge of God and a virtuous life.[176] Thus, Ignatius of Antioch speaks of a unity of the faithful paralleled by a union with God (*Letter to the Ephesians* 4). Christians are bearers of God, and the ideal term of Christian life is to be united indissolubly to him.[177] Justin Martyr, quoting Psalm 82, asserts that all are worthy of becoming gods and have the power to become sons of the Highest (*Dialogue with Trypho* 124). Tatian emphasizes recovery of the *imago Dei* and participation in the Logos (*Orations* 7) and union with the Spirit (ibid. 15) bringing knowledge and illumination (ibid. 13). Hippolytus also uses the imagery of adoption, joining it to the language of baptism and regeneration (*Discourse on the Holy Theophany* 10).

In the works of Origen, both wisdom and holiness are allied to participation in divinity (*On First Principles* 1,6,2), along with the characteristically Origenistic picture of falling away and gradual progression towards consummation, elements that did not become incorporated into the broader Christian tradition. In the *Oration on Prayer*, Origen associates humanity's being made divine with nourishment by God the Word, the exact form of this nourishment being left unspecified (27,13). Origen particularly associates deification with contemplation, in which mind (*nous*) is purified and lifted above material things to the vision of God.[178] The Origenistic scheme stresses intellect rather heavily, reducing the role of charity.[179]

The most extended early treatment of divinization occurs in the chief work of Irenaeus, *Adversus haereses*. He mentions adoption several times in connection with deification (3,6,1; 3,19, 1; 4,33, 4), and here also we find prominently, in several variants, the theme usually associated with Athanasius: God became human that humanity might become God (3,19,1; 4,33,4; 5,1,1). In *Adversus haereses*, we find also the *imago Dei* connected directly to deification, a link that will also dominate the later tradition. The image lost at the Fall is regenerated by deifying union with the incarnate Logos and the Spirit, a union attained by faith, charity and participation in the sacraments.[180] Irenaeus, perhaps foreseeing a potential difficulty that his fellow ante-Nicenes did not, speaks also of the fundamental ontological divide between created and Uncreated (4,38,3)[181] but in the same chapter associates the reception of a faculty of the Uncreated with glory and speaks of an approximation to the Uncreated. This simultaneous emphasis on the unbreachable divide between creature and Creator and on the creature's likening to the Utterly Other we will refer to as the two poles of deification. What is most characteristic of a doctrine of deification is the delicate balancing and negotiation of these two themes.[182] Also typical is the notion of a progressive assimilation to God, which finds its perfection in heavenly vision, an idea that Irenaeus borrows from Theophilus of Antioch and extends.[183]

The standard means of articulating the ground between Uncreated and creation is the Incarnation. The *locus classicus* of this form of the doctrine, as noted previously, occurs in Athanasius: "He was made human that we might be made God" (*De Inc.* 54,3). Less often cited but doctrinally much richer is the passage in *De synodis* 51. Here creation itself is depicted as a participation in the grace of God. The Son, as the Father's Word and Wisdom, is the deifying and enlightening power of the Father, through whom we partake of both Father and Son. Like Irenaeus, Athanasius also points to deification's other pole but locates the ontological distinction not in the difference between Uncreated and created but between Deifying and deified, another theme we will encounter in later theology. An important shift has taken place by the time of Athanasius, as Dalmais notes. For him, deification has become an uncontested truth, "an axiom which is possible to make into the point of departure of an argument."[184] In this respect, Athanasius anticipates later writers like Palamas.

Clement of Alexandria resumes some of the themes of earlier theology, and for the first time uses the term to deify (theopoien).[185] For Clement, the image of God resides in mind (nous) yet knowledge (gnosis) is not for the few, as it was in Greek philosophical systems, but the normal outcome of baptism, a grace that comes from God through Christ.[186] His Exhortation describes humanity as deified by heavenly teaching (chap. 11). In the same chapter, he elaborates at some length on light and illumination as freedom from ignorance, associating the mind's illumination with virtue, contemplation and salvific immortality. He also connects knowledge, contemplation and assimilation to God in the Stromata (4,23) and the connection between salvific knowledge and becoming a kindred nature to God in 7,16. Clement's bias is less exclusively intellectual than it appears, however, for he identifies knowledge not only with contemplation, knowledge and intellectual assimilation to God but also with moral assimilation via the taming of the passions (apatheia) and charity.[187] Like earlier theologians, Clement views deification as a progress through this life which is culminated only in the next.[188]

What we seldom find in the postpatristic tradition are themes deriving from the Cappadocians, for none of them treats theosis in any depth.[189] The most extended treatment occurs in Gregory of Nyssa's Catechetical Oration, where participation in the divine is linked with particular insistence to deliverance from incorruption (chap. 37), a note Palamas also sounds at times, although it is not the most important element of his doctrine of deification. In the same chapter, this corporeal element of deification joins with eucharistic theology to produce a sacramental form of deification only rarely and faintly echoed in the later tradition. Nyssa places emphasis on both knowledge and love as divine attributes on which theosis is founded: the Logos creates humanity out of the superabundance of love in order to make us participants in divine goods, but since divinity is essentially mind and word (nous kai logos), intellectual perfections must be given to humanity before all others[190]; here we find a foreshadowing of Aquinas' emphasis on intellect and will. Nazianzen also stresses both knowledge and love, since for him knowledge is wisdom illuminated by sanctifying grace and love; it is this dual engagement of mind and will which permits contemplation of God and union.[191] Perhaps Nazianzen's greatest significance for the history of deification lies in his inauguration of the term theosis.[192] Basil's Letter 234 holds great importance for the Orthodox because it outlines a rudimentary form of the essence-energies distinction. In other respects, his account of theosis is unremarkable, touching on the familiar themes of recovery of the image, the Incarnation, assimilation to God and contemplation.[193]

With Augustine, we return to an articulation of theosis that far more resembles both earlier and later theology than what we found in the Cappadocians. Drawing on the ubiquitous Psalm 82, he speaks of a deification by grace, carefully distinguishing this from the possession of divine substance. He differentiates also between the One who deifies and those who receive deification. Augustine uses the language of adoption, as Hippolytus did, but contrasts it with sonship by generation, thus pointing to the ontological divide in a slightly different way from other writers (Commentary on the Psalms 49,2 [Latin]).[194]

In Chrysostom, we find the common themes of adoption, assimilation to God, union and the need for grace. Two emphases, however, distinguish him from the earliest tradition. One is his strong stress on the sacraments: adoption is subordinated to baptismal regeneration, which is in turn accentuated by the eucharist.[195] In addition, the tradition of desert monachism, which insisted upon virtuous flight from the world, has been replaced with an emphasis on charity.[196]

Cyril of Alexandria's understanding of deification corresponds substantially with that of Athanasius; together with the latter and Gregory of Nyssa, he is the outstanding proponent of the physical concept of deification: perfection entails the remission of both fleshly corruption and fleshly passion.[197] Not surprisingly, the Incarnation is important in Cyril's theology as the means by which divine life is communicated to human nature. Nevertheless, to appropriate deification for oneself, a personal union to Christ must be effected through a sincere conversion of heart and baptism.[198] Theosis thus entails, as usual, knowledge, illumination and sacramental grace. Cyril is important, despite the conventionality of these themes by his time, for his clarity on one important issue: the relation of deification in this life and the next. Theosis indeed forms part of our earthly existence, but it is a perfectible theosis we experience now. This theosis gains in intensity, so that redemption becomes an uninterrupted process that reaches its perfection only in the parousia and resurrection.[199]

From Cyril we jump to the sixth century, to Denys. If Nazianzen is the first to use the term *theosis*, Denys is its great popularizer, and significant on that count alone.[200] In the *Celestial Hierarchy*, he identifies the hierarchy's purpose as enabling all beings to be as like as possible to God and to be at one with him (3,2). He speaks of the members of the hierarchy as images mirroring God himself. Although he uses the language of image, however, his usage leaves doubt that he has in mind the usual Christian doctrine of the *imago Dei* or its biblical sources. Denys clearly sees the beings' perfection in terms of virtue or obedience. Where he begins to sound remarkably idiosyncratic, however, is his apparent lack of concern to maintain the divide between the Giver and recipients of perfection. Some on the hierarchy purify, others are purifying. The work of purification, illumination and perfection seems not to belong exclusively to God.[201]

In the *Ecclesiastical Hierarchy*, though, he draws on a host of familiar images, echoes of which we soon hear in Aquinas and Palamas. Divinization is union with God, he maintains, using one of the most important images for deification (participation being the other). The goal of every hierarchy is a continuous love, which consists of knowledge, seeing and understanding truth, participation in the onelike perfection and "a feast upon that sacred vision which nourishes the intellect and which divinises everything rising up to it" (1,3). In the following section, he rules out the worrisome possibility left open in the *Celestial Hierarchy* 3,2: "The blessed Deity which of itself is God, is the source of all divinisation. Out of its divine generosity it grants to the divinised the fact of divinisation" (1,4). Here, the emphasis is on God as the sole bestower of theosis, and on the gratuitousness of deification.

In a move one might not expect, Denys also portrays the gift of illumination as specifically transmitted through the scriptures. He asserts in 2,1, on the basis of scriptural teaching, the attainment of likeness to and union with God through "the most loving observance of the august commandments and by the doing of sacred acts," sounding a note we will hear in different forms in both Aquinas and Palamas. He lies closer to

Aquinas, though, in stressing the intellect as the faculty through which we move towards the divine, and the love of God as that which actually moves us. Although Denys does not observe as much of a distinction between the intellect and will as Aquinas would, the emphasis on specifically these two faculties, as well as the sense of some form of connection between them, is significant.

Although one of the most important sources of the doctrine of deification for the Eastern tradition is Maximus, he does not figure in the later Western tradition, and as we will briefly treat his contribution to Palamas' thought in later chapters, we will not describe his concept of deification here. We move instead to John Damascene, whose work forms a watershed between the patristic, medieval and Byzantine periods, codifying the Fathers and providing a rich source for the later tradition in both East and West. That his codification of past thought in itself constitutes original theological thinking becomes evident in book 1 of De fide orthodoxa. We find in chapter 14, which concerns divine attributes, precisely the themes we have so often seen before: the unique role of God as the Giver, but not receiver, of goodness. Where John has surpassed the prior tradition is his location of this attribute within the doctrine of God, so that what began as a necessary caution in a certain model of sanctification comes to form part of our understanding of God. This movement, which we will observe particularly in Palamas, is also characteristic of the development of the doctrine of deification. Damascene reiterates this theme in 2,12, where he insists on the difference between participation in divine glory and change into divine being.

In one of the last chapters (4,13) of this, his greatest work, he provides a definitive summary of the entire patristic tradition on divinization. It belongs to God alone to be good in se, but he has made all things to share in that goodness. He is the source of all being, not only because he creates ex nihilo, but also because "His energy preserves and maintains all that He has made." Humanity above all has received the power of continuous union, in virtue of our possession of both reason and free will—here we see a clear foreshadowing of Aquinas. Because God bestowed on us his own image, when we fell, he took a share in our nature to purify and render us incorruptible, establishing us once more as partakers of his own divinity and making us once more children of God by adoption—and now we hear the theme of Irenaeus and Athanasius explicitly linked to the language of purification. Nyssa's sacramental proclivities emerge also, as John explores the divinizing power of baptism and the eucharist. Finally, he speaks of union with Christ (in this life) and vision (in the next), union in body and blood now being an antitype of the later mental participation through vision.

This, then, is the patristic tradition of deification. While we find few actual definitions of the term,[202] a clear enough pattern has emerged that we may make some generalizations. It asserts the imago Dei and the Incarnation as the basis of deification and construes theosis overwhelmingly in terms of knowledge, virtue, light and glory, participation and union. In some authors, the sacraments are important tradents of divinization; more often, human faculties such as the intellect and the ability to love are significant. While emphasis on the physical dimension varies, there is a broad consensus that participation in divine nature entails bodily incorruptibility. Above all, the Fathers point to the distinction between Uncreated and created, along with the Creator's desire that his creatures partake of his own life and goodness. Thus theosis, while entailing a degree of human striving towards virtuous assimilation to God and love of God remains always a divine gift, a gift of grace. The idea of uninterrupted progression towards God, a seamlessness between this life and the next, appears in the work of most of the Fathers, but hints of theosis in its fulness flowering in this life are rare.[203]

Our survey reveals considerable diversity in the ways various theologians describe deification. Some elements we have identified appear only in some texts and not in others; the sacraments, physical incorruptibility and love, for example, are not immediate markers of a doctrine of deification. Yet there is a firm core that distinguishes this doctrine from some other model of sanctification. First, we can safely say that where we find references to human participation in divine life, there we assuredly have a claim specifically of theosis. This kind of claim regarding participation in divine life is carefully to be distinguished, however, from the idea of divine indwelling in the human person. Both schemes of sanctification draw on the notion of union, but whereas the latter locates sanctification within the creature and in via, the former locates it at the level of the divine and insists upon the inseparability of life in via and in patria. A second infallible marker of the doctrine, then, is the union of God and humanity, when this union is conceived as humanity's incorporation into God, rather than God's into humanity, and when conceived as the destiny of humanity generally rather than the extraordinary experience of the few. Adoption also functions as a signal of a doctrine of deification, albeit a somewhat weaker one than participation and union. Without one of these three concepts—especially without participation and union—we are speaking of some form of sanctification that is not specifically deification. By the end of the patristic period, when the doctrine has emerged in more developed form, we can also say that the doctrine must function in close conjunction with some kind of guard around divine transcendence. Where we find the ideas of participation in divine life, union with God and humanity portrayed as human destiny, and a mode of articulating divine transcendence in this context, we can say we are dealing with a doctrine of deification. With these essential elements of the earlier tradition in mind, we turn to Aquinas and Palamas.

Our survey of the history of relations between East and West has mandated the following task: to examine one significant point of contention through a close reading of the works of two representative figures. We have already discussed reasons for examining the doctrine of theosis in Aquinas and Palamas. Our choice of texts, the *Summa Theologiae* for Aquinas and the *Triads in Defense of the Holy Hesychasts* and *Capita Physica* for Palamas, calls for some explanation, however. The advantage of these texts lies in their composition late in the careers of their authors and their relative comprehensiveness. Consideration of more texts would have yielded a broader study, but one either more shallow or more cumbersome. To compensate for the need, in the interest of close reading, to look at few texts, we need texts that are representative, hence the choice of those texts that are late, with a broad focus.

We read, then, first the *Summa* and then the *Triads* and the *Capita*, asking the nature of the doctrine of deification presented in them. In accordance with the methodological desiderata emerging from this chapter, we will try to analyze the texts in terms of their native categories, establishing these on the basis of direct references to deification (which are few in both Aquinas and Palamas) and allowing these direct references to suggest what themes and patterns we should seek elsewhere in the text. Finally, we will compare Aquinas and Palamas to determine the consonance of their doctrines of deification. We will then take the conclusions of this comparison and ask how they answer the questions and charges raised by the history of interpretation in the present chapter.

The study that follows proposes, therefore, to examine each author's work primarily from a systematic perspective and to the end of providing a detailed textual basis for dialogue between Eastern and Western theologians. While both Aquinas and Palamas have benefitted from careful, and especially in the case of the former, even revisionist readings, and while both traditions have become increasingly receptive to ecumenical rapprochement, the charges of opposition of East and West in the doctrine of deification have not been addressed in any thorough comparative study. It is to this task we now turn.

2

THE GOD TO WHOM
WE ARE LIKENED

I. Method

We begin our examination of Aquinas as we will begin with Palamas, by asking: what does it mean to be deified? To put the query thus to Aquinas is to presume more than one does in asking the same question of Palamas, however, for *The Triads* is more obviously concerned with how human persons are understood to have become holy. It is far from clear that Thomas holds a doctrine of deification in the first place. One might spend long hours searching either of his *Summae* without encountering any reference to divinization whatsoever. Nevertheless, this awkward problem recedes when we treat Aquinas as we will Gregory. We begin by looking for direct references to theosis, using them as a guide to themes elsewhere in the text and establishing the validity of the less direct passages by their affinity to the prime references.[1]

In the *Summa Theologiae* the handful of direct references are those where Thomas speaks of deiformity, principally I-II.62 but also I-II.65 and I.12.[2] The significance of these references extends in two respects beyond their value in pointing us to other parts of the *Summa*. First, I-II.62 cites the root biblical text on deification, 2 Peter 1:4 (I-II.62, 1 resp.), thus connecting Thomas' doctrine of deification to that of the Fathers before him. Second, two of the prime references to deification occur within the treatise on virtues. This location places the explicit references at the *Summa*'s heart, for the treatise on virtues is one of its mainstays, if not its very core. Thus, while Aquinas uses the technical vocabulary of theosis sparingly, when he does employ it, he does so in a context that could scarcely rank more highly in systematic importance to his work.

II. The Direct References to Deification
   in the *Summa Theologiae*

We begin by establishing the existence of a doctrine of deification in its most elementary form, with those passages where Thomas speaks directly and unambiguously of
deification, deiformity and participation in divine nature. Although few in number, these
references indicate that Thomas takes deification for granted. The best example of this
easy assumption of the doctrine occurs in the response to I-II.112,1, where he seeks to
establish that God alone is the cause of grace: "It is . . . necessary that God alone should
deify, bestowing a partaking of the divine nature." While he is here chiefly concerned
with an adjacent, but nevertheless distinct, matter, Thomas clearly indicates that he understands the creature's gracing as deification. Indeed, his description of the gift of grace in
this response indicates he views it primarily in this way: "The gift of grace surpasses
every capability of created nature, since it is nothing short of a partaking of divine Nature, which exceeds every other nature."

The prime form in which Thomas sees grace as resulting in deiformity is not through
some unspecified gift of grace but grace bestowed in the form of the theological virtues. He terms faith, hope and charity the theological virtues not because they derive
from the New Testament rather than from Aristotle but because these are the virtues
that direct us to God (I-II.62,1 s.c.). In his very definition of why a virtue might be called
theological, then, Thomas intimates his doctrine of deification. The highest of the virtues are not those which enable the right ordering of human relations but those which
order humanity to God. Sanctity is therefore defined not in human, but divine terms.
This close relation between the doctrine of sanctification and the doctrine of God is one
of the characteristics of the patristic formulation of theosis.

If we bear the salient features of the patristic doctrine in mind, we see Thomas' discussion of happiness in a new light:

> Now man's happiness is twofold. . . . One is proportionate to human nature, a happiness,
> to wit, which man can obtain by means of his natural principles. The other is a happiness
> surpassing man's nature, and which man can obtain by the power of God alone, by a kind
> of participation of the Godhead [ad quam homo sola divina virtute pervenire potest
> secundum quandam divinitatis participationem], about which it is written (2. Pet. i. 4)
> that by Christ we are made *partakers of the Divine nature*. And because such happiness surpasses
> the capacity of human nature, man's natural principles which enable him to act well
> according to his capacity, do not suffice to direct man to this same happiness. (I-II.62,
> 1 resp.)

Thomas' habit of making distinctions here serves his doctrine of deification, for he has
not only identified ultimate happiness as participation in divine nature but has also by
his distinction stressed that the higher form of happiness exceeds human powers. As we
will see in Palamas, a Christian doctrine of deification must stress the gratuitousness of
the gift of participation if it is to preserve divine transcendence and avoid pantheism.

So important is this principle of transcendence to Thomas that he gives no fewer than
three reasons for calling faith, hope and charity theological virtues: first, their object is
God; second, they are infused in us only by God; third, we know them only because
God reveals them to us in scripture (I-II.62,1 resp.). Here we see a microcosmic version
of the *Summa Theologiae* itself. The first and third reasons recall the *Prima Pars*, with its dis-

cussion both of God *in se* and as the object of human intellect, while the second summarizes Thomas' treatment of virtue and grace. Deification, then, focuses not on humanity, but on the God who invites humanity to share divine life.

While Thomas borrows the idea of theosis from the scriptures via the Fathers, he refines and clarifies it. In the first objection to I-II.62,1, Thomas establishes two principles that will be vital to our study of theosis. First, he maintains that nature may be ascribed to a subject in two ways: essentially and by participation. In this claim, Aquinas lays the foundation for the bridge that is any doctrine of divinization, a qualified spanning of the chasm between Uncreated and created. In claiming that a subject may be understood to possess nature in a manner other than by essence, Thomas provides a way of understanding theosis whereby rational creatures may be said to possess divine nature, but not as God possesses it. We are genuinely partakers of divine nature, but "after a fashion" (I-II.62,1 ad 1). The second important principle established in the reply to the first objection is one of proportionality: "These [the theological] virtues are proportionate to man in respect of the Nature of which he is made a partaker." This is the first of the analogical relationships Thomas proposes in Question 62, in which he invites the reader to see one structure in terms of another (cf. the interpretation of I-II.62,3, to follow).

Finally, Aquinas addresses the question of natural orientation towards God by analyzing the human person in terms of reason and will:

> The reason and will are naturally directed to God, inasmuch as He is the beginning and end of nature, but in proportion to nature. But the reason and will, according to their nature, are not sufficiently directed to Him in so far as He is the object of supernatural happiness. (I-II.62,1 ad 3)

The form of this analysis provides further evidence of the microcosmic structure of Question 62 for, as we shall see, the dynamic relation of intellect and will determines the structure of both his doctrine of the Trinity and his theological anthropology. If we follow the development of Thomas' argument, we see that while the root principle of the *Prima Pars* is simplicity, simplicity's correlates are intellect and will, and the culmination of the *De Deo uno* forms the foundation of the *De Trinitate* and the anthropology. It is precisely this link, the analogy between the structure of divine nature and the structure of the human person, that provides the basis for the Thomist doctrine of deification.

In asking "Whether There Are Any Theological Virtues?" then, Aquinas provides us with both a bird's-eye view of the chief structures of the *Summa* and a guide to his doctrine of theosis. In asking whether there are principles by which we attain God, Thomas affirms that we do, by means of the divine assistance working through the structures of being natural to us. From this first article of Question 62 alone, the reader is already directed to those loci elsewhere in the work where she may discover how we are made partakers of divine nature: to the discussions of human nature and grace, humanity's end, participation in the Godhead and divine being itself.

In a single article, Thomas has alluded to the main themes of the doctrine we find throughout the *Summa*. In the remaining articles of Question 62, he refines and completes this picture. In Article 2, he emphasizes the role of the theological virtues in providing the requisite supernatural assistance, again referring to the two human faculties aided by such assistance, intellect and will, and thus directing the reader's attention to two fundamental distinctions in his system. The first is the distinction between the two most important innate human faculties of reason and will, and the second, between the contexts where those faculties operate adequately on their own and those in which natural faculties require divine assistance: "The intellectual and moral virtues perfect man's intellect and appetite according to the capacity of human nature; the theological virtues, supernaturally" (I-II.62,2 ad 1). However, Article 2 also introduces a new and most important element, for it is here, in the reply to the third objection, that Aquinas introduces the unique role played by charity. The distinction he draws between love in general and charity in particular is not significant at this point; what is very important is his allusion to charity's unique position among the virtues. Since all other virtues depend on charity in some way, and since the virtues of one variety or another are the means by which we are directed to happiness in general (I-II.5,7 resp.) and to participation in God (I-II.62,1 resp.), we will obviously need to attend closely to the Summa's texts on charity if we are to grasp the Thomistic view of deification.

In the remaining two articles of Question 62, Thomas appears to add little new content. He discusses again nature and supernatural aid, and the position of charity in relation to the two other theological virtues. Yet he is not here simply repeating the claims of the first two articles, but laying down principles for understanding the relationships among the various elements of the system he has already named.

In Article 3, he takes up the questions of nature and supernatural assistance, but now he is no longer simply asserting a distinction between the two or claiming that nature alone is inadequate for certain ends. Having established the distinction, he revisits it to demonstrate that far from its two terms' standing in opposition to one another, the relation between them must be viewed analogically. This analogy is twofold in Thomas' description. First, the theological virtues direct us to supernatural happiness in the same way that natural inclinations direct us to our natural end (I-II.62,3 resp.). Second, supernatural assistance operates just as our natural capacities do, by illuminating the intellect and rightly guiding the will:

> First, as regards the intellect, man receives certain supernatural principles, which are held by means of a Divine light: these are the articles of faith, about which is faith.—Secondly, the will is directed to this end, both as to the movement of intention, which tends to that end as something attainable,—and this pertains to hope,—and as to a certain spiritual union, whereby the will is, so to speak, transformed into that end—and this belongs to charity. For the appetite of a thing is moved and tends towards its connatural end naturally; and this movement is due to a certain conformity of the thing with its end. (I-II.62,3 resp.)

The principle Aquinas works with here is paradigmatic of the method in the Summa as a whole: the realms of nature and the supernatural are portrayed as quite distinct in view of what is possible in each. Yet from the perspective of how persons attain the ends of either, the two realms overlap completely. Grace (to use a term Thomas himself does not use in these questions) does not add to the human person by creating new faculties and thus changing essentially the structure of the human being but by extending the range of possibility of those faculties the person already possesses. Grace is both foreign to us, in the sense that its effects lie beyond the attainment of our nature itself, and yet natural to us in that it does not violate or alter the composition of our nature, working instead through that nature.

The most complete account of deification emerges from the *Prima Secundae*, but a second set of direct references to deiformity is also important. This group appears in Question 12 of the *Prima Pars*. Again, the context is important, not only because Aquinas is discussing how humanity knows God but also particularly because in Article 5, with which we are concerned, he takes up the issue of the created intellect's vision of divine essence. Although we need not concern ourselves with this matter here, we should note in passing that it will prove one of the thorniest points of contention between the Eastern and Western traditions.

For the moment, however, our interest lies in the direct references to deiformity, and so we turn to the fifth and sixth articles of Question 12. Thomas begins from the same principles now familiar to us from I-II.62, nature's need for supernatural assistance if it is to attain a supernatural end: "Everything which is raised to what exceeds its nature, must be prepared by some disposition above its nature" (I.12,5 resp.). Yet in these questions on knowledge of God, Aquinas asserts something rather more than humanity's need for grace: "When any created intellect sees the essence of God, the essence of God itself becomes the intelligible form of the intellect" (ibid.). The claim that the created sees—and therefore knows—the Uncreated is a large one, and to maintain it Thomas must find extraordinary means to explain how this inconceivable could be. The form of his answer differs considerably from what any of the Fathers might have said ("becomes the intelligible form of the intellect"), but the substance does not differ: we know God because we become like to God. The knowledge of God we are said to possess is actually God's own knowledge of himself. Because Thomas goes beyond simply claiming that our intellect is strengthened, asserting instead that God inhabits it, he is perfectly consistent in using the language of divinization later in the article:

> This increase of the intellectual powers is called the illumination of the intellect, as we also call the intelligible object itself by the name of the light of illumination [lumen vel lux]. And this is the light spoken of in the Apocalypse (xxi.23). *The glory of God hath enlightened it*—viz., the society of the blessed who see God. By this light the blessed are made *deiform*—that is, like to God, according to the saying: *When He shall appear we shall be like to Him, and we shall see Him as He is* (1 John ii.2). (I.12,5 resp.)

And Thomas repeats later in the article: "By this light the rational creature is made deiform" (I.12,5 ad 3). This article confirms the conclusion drawn from study of I-II.62,1, that the intellect will occupy an important place in the Thomistic conception of divinization. In I.12, however, we see intimations we did not see in I-II.62; not only the human intellect but also the divine is central to this doctrine of theosis. More strongly than I-II.62, Question 12 of the *Prima Pars* directs us to Aquinas' doctrine of God.

Thomas gathers together many of these now familiar themes in Article 6. He begins by repeating the assertion of the previous article, that the faculty of seeing God does not belong to the created intellect naturally but is given to it by the light of glory, a gift that establishes deiformity (I.12,6 resp.), his ultimate objective being to establish degrees of participation in the light of glory. What determines the level of participation is the degree of charity one possesses:

> The intellect which has more of the light of glory will see God the more perfectly; and he will have a fuller participation of the light of glory who has more charity; because where there is the greater charity, there is the more desire, and desire in a certain degree makes

the one desiring apt and prepared to receive the object desired. Hence he who possesses the more charity, will see God the more perfectly, and will be the more beatified. (I.12, 6 resp.)

We have already seen the importance of Thomas' twin analysis of intellect and appetite, but in this question, he connects the two inextricably. Perhaps most significant for our purposes is the appearance here of charity in a question pertaining to the intellect. Aquinas is sometimes portrayed as the creator of a system that devolves purely on the intellect. Beatific vision is interpreted purely as the intellect's encounter with God and the intellect's glorification. Certainly, the Thomistic conception of salvation stresses the intellect; nevertheless, the regulative function of charity here, in the midst of the very articles dedicated to the knowledge of God, demonstrates that Aquinas' interest does not focus narrowly on the intellect. Rather, he views the intellect and the will as working together. Both are essential to the human person's functioning not only in this life but also in the next. Thomas' anthropology does not suggest one structure of human experience and existence in this life and a different structure in the next, and he definitively rules out any possibility of viewing sanctification in this life (which comes about through growth in the virtues, especially charity) as distinct and separate from salvific consummation in the next.

This handful of direct references to deiformity, to summarize, has identified the loci where we must begin our search for the Thomistic doctrine of deification: first, the doctrine of God, both the study of the one God with its consideration of God's existence and essence, God's goodness and intelligibility, God as first and final cause and the Thomistic doctrine of the Trinity, with its Augustinian exposition of the divine processions as operations of God's intellect and will; second, the theological anthropology, which describes the human person as imaging God analogically, so that the divine processions of intellect and will are mirrored in the structure of our own existence, through which grace works; third, the culmination of the anthropology and its juncture with the doctrine of God in the descriptions of participation and union with God.

III. The God to Whom We Are Likened

While it is of questionable fidelity to his spirit to follow Aquinas' editors in dividing his theology into two separate loci treating the attributes of the Godhead and the doctrine of the Trinity, for our purposes there is some value in considering these separately. The Thomistic notion of deification relies heavily on concepts established in both parts of the theology, but each part provides a distinctive means for arriving at a deifying God. In other words, Thomas provides us with two sightlines that arrive at a single vanishing point on his horizon, two distinct means of arriving at the same place. To grasp the doctrine as a whole, to see how the shapes fit together coherently, we must first grasp the distinct shape of each part.

1. The One God

We begin where Aquinas does in the Summa Theologiae, with his exposition of the one God. After what we would today call a methodological prolegomenon, he begins his

study with questions on the existence of God. Since one of these, I.2, contains the fa-
mous Five Ways, most commentators focus on the validity of the proofs presented or
more recently, on whether Thomas is actually trying to prove God's existence at all. These
issues are irrelevant for our purposes. What is highly significant in I.2, however, is that
the first proposition about God he sets out to examine is God's existence. This priority
might seem to be dictated solely by the exigency of logic: one must know a thing exists
before discussing its attributes. Question 2 of the *Prima Pars* no doubt does serve such a
role as a gesture of good faith to the requirements of logical discourse, but as we find
when we arrive at Question 3, God's existence serves a much more important role than
simply establishing the validity of the subject under examination.

If we glance ahead to Question 3, which concerns divine simplicity, we see the pains
Aquinas takes to establish the identity of existence and essence in God. Question 3 contains the full exposition of this claim. However, the beginning of his argument lies in
the Five Ways of the preceding question, in the *sed contra*'s quotation of Exodus 3:14: "It
is said in the person of God: *I am Who am.*" Because commentators tend to focus narrowly on the Five Ways qua arguments for the existence of God, their function as the
opening of Thomas' rehearsal of divine attributes is often overlooked. If, however, we
take the Five Ways as a prelude Thomas regards as necessary to the discussion of divine
simplicity, we see that the quotation from Exodus may be taken as intending to establish God not only as the proper subject of theological discourse but as the One whose
very nature it is to exist.

Just as the *sed contra* of Article 3 not only introduces the claim *that* God is, but also
indicates in some measure the nature of the one whose existence is asserted, so, too,
each of the Five Ways constitutes not only an argument for God's existence but also
entails a claim about the character of the one who exists: he is the First Mover, the first
efficient cause, necessary being (or being *a se*), the cause of being, goodness and perfection and the end of all natural bodies, or final cause. To different degrees, each of the
Five Ways provides information about Aquinas' conception of God, the bare bones of a
character sketch he will later clothe with flesh. Question 3, then, alerts the reader to what
she might otherwise have overlooked: that Thomas' description of God begins at least
in Question 2, so that this question does not merely establish the possibility of describing God, but itself begins the description.

It remains to explore, nevertheless, how this outline of a portrait of God might prove
determinative of a doctrine of theosis. It does so by establishing the two essential principles of any such doctrine. On one side, the description emphasizes God's uniqueness.
I-Am-Who-Am, after all, is the First Mover (the First Way) and therefore distinct from
all other movers; He is the first and final cause (Ways Two and Five) and thus unique
among causes; and perhaps most important, God is necessary being, unique among
beings, the uncaused causer of all being, goodness and every perfection (Ways Three
and Four). Each of the Five Ways sets God apart from creatures, so that a very deep
ontological and conceptual divide appears, which ensures that the doctrine of divinization
cannot transmute into an inadvertent form of pantheism.

On the other side, though, the Five Ways also point to a connectedness, initiated of
course on the divine side, between Uncreated and creation. One who does not move
anything cannot be a First Mover; one that does not cause anything can be neither a first
nor a final cause; if God is the source of all being, goodness and perfection, "having of

itself its own necessity, and not receiving it from another, but rather causing in others their necessity" (I.2,3 resp.), there must then be others to whom being, goodness and perfection have been imparted. The Five Ways thus establish both God's aseity and his voluntary connectedness to all that exists. The Third and Fourth Ways, moreover, indicate that what God graciously shares with creation are those features of his own life that Aquinas has told and will tell us are most characteristic of divine nature: being, goodness, perfection. In seminal form, the Five Ways argue not only God's existence, but also the existence of a Thomistic doctrine of theosis.

As Question 3 with its assertion of divine simplicity proves indispensable to the understanding of how the Five Ways contribute to the doctrine of theosis, so we must keep it firmly in mind as we read the rest of the questions of the *Prima Pars* if we are to grasp their significance. The reading that follows shows the centrality of Question 3 for the whole of the *Prima Pars* and for Thomas' doctrine of deification. The East has long criticized the West for its overemphasis on simplicity, a focus that allegedly leads to the mistaken priority of divine essence over persons. Divine simplicity has also come under attack in the West in recent years, but Thomas falls prey to neither critique if we grasp his single underlying concern in asserting it, a concern which remains valid even if the traditional doctrine of simplicity does not. The focus on Thomas' doctrine lies in securing God's uniqueness. In different ways, each of the eight articles in I.3 serves to establish the same point: God has no distinct attributes. Since God is not composed of matter and form (I.3,2), "He must be his own Godhead [deitas], His own Life, and whatever else is thus predicated of Him" (I.3,3 resp.). God is the same as his essence (I.3,3), and his existence (I.3,4), is not an individual suppositum contained in a genus (I.3,5) and has no accidents (I.3,6). Articles 3 and 4 argue, in briefer form, the principle to which Aquinas devoted an earlier opusculum, *De ente et essentia*. What has changed is the context: following the question on God's existence, the question on simplicity tells us that Aquinas considers existence not simply the precondition of all meaningful discussion of God, but the first item of our understanding of God. The focus of Thomas' doctrine lies in securing God's uniqueness.

His regard for this principle as crucial is evident in the choice he makes between it and fidelity to his philosophical guide, Aristotle. Within an Aristotelian framework, one can predicate only qualities that are general (*Categories*). Indeed, to speak of individuals at all, we must speak in terms of genus and species. This leaves Aquinas with an apparently irresoluble problem: either he must speak even of God as contained in a genus (which would severely compromise God's uniqueness) or he must step outside the Aristotelian framework (in which case he will need another account of discursive intelligibility). Not surprisingly, Thomas chooses to preserve divine uniqueness, taking Aristotle head on in I.3,5, where he bluntly denies God is contained in a genus. In doing so, he not so much rejects Aristotle as bends the Philosopher's thought to his own end: precisely because everything but God is contained in a genus, God is unique.

If we understand this purpose of the assertion of simplicity, the meaning of the rest of the *Prima Pars* becomes clearer. The questions on the knowledge of God and religious language (I.12 and 13) now appear not so much as investigations of these issues for their own sake or because of any methodological importance, but as a search for the grounds of relation between humanity and the God who is utterly Other. On the other hand, the comparatively brief treatment Thomas accords to such central divine attributes as goodness and love can be explained only with reference to the claims that God's essence is one, and all distinctions between attributes derive from the incommensurability of theological language to the object of its discussion.

We begin by investigating the consequences of asserting simplicity by turning to Question 13, the well-known discussion of analogy. In this question, Thomas treads a very fine and historically contentious line between asserting the possibility of true and faithful religious speech and acknowledging that the object of that speech utterly exceeds our descriptive capacities. He accomplishes this artful synthesis by distinguishing between the divine *signifié* and the human *signifiant*, the language which, as the product of human intellect, labors under the same constraints as the human subjects who employ it: "[God] can be named by us from creatures, yet not so that the name which signifies Him expresses the divine essence in itself" (I.13,1 resp.). The reasons underlying this position are two. The first is that names applied to God belong properly to God (I.13,3 resp.). God, after all, is in and of himself supremely intelligible (I.12,1 resp.), so he cannot be said to be unnameable because he is inherently unknowable. Indeed, because he is supremely intelligible, names applied to God belong *more* properly to him than to creatures (I.13,3 resp.).[3] The problem, then, of speaking of God lies not on the divine side but on the human side, in the *modus significandi* that is human language: "As regards [the names'] mode of signification, they do not properly and strictly apply to God; for their mode of signification applies to creatures" (I.13,3 resp.). The doctrine of analogy represents precisely a concern to hold simultaneously to the two poles of deification. In maintaining that intelligibility belongs properly to God, Aquinas once again underlines the distinction between God and all else. In showing how the human mind may nevertheless conceive of this God, he indicates a bridge over the divide.

Because human language is rooted in this creaturely world and because our intellect knows God from creatures (I.13,4 resp.), we are constrained to speak of God using a multiplicity of terms. That multiplicity indicates both the distinction between the oneness of God and the fractured diversity of all else and the fact that our language, taken as a whole, does speak accurately of God, if not entirely adequately:

> In order to understand God, [our intellect] forms conceptions proportional to the perfections flowing from God to creatures, which perfections pre-exist in God unitedly and simply, whereas in creatures they are received, divided and multiplied. . . . Therefore, although the names applied to God signify one thing, still because they signify that under many and different aspects, they are not synonymous. (I.13,4 resp.)

Aquinas' point in Article 4 indicates the basis for the celebrated *res significandum—modus significandi* distinction generally noted by his commentators. At the most fundamental level, the distinction lies between two modes of being, divine and human, between the perfect, simple, united existence of God and the composite and imperfect existence of human beings, whose very apprehension of God, more appropriate to human nature than to the divine, reflects the distinction between creature and Creator (I.13,4 ad 3).

The bridge across the ontological divide, in the sphere of language, is the doctrine of analogy. Thomas begins his discussion of analogy in Article 5 of Question 13 with the announcement that not all things said of God and creatures are either univocal or equivocal. The middle ground between these poles is analogical predication. In order to preserve both the distinctiveness of divine being and the reality of divine self-communication and human encounter with God, Aquinas avoids the Scylla of asserting univocal predication, which in making God and creation mutually intelligible would also place them on the same ontological footing, and the Charybdis of equivocal predication, whereby human access to God would be rendered a sham because our theological conceptualizing would be no more than heroic talk about ourselves. As we shall see, Thomas follows Augustine in having no use for claims to love or desire that which one does not know, nor does his understanding of knowledge limit itself to a kind of mystical apprehension that entirely bypasses rational discourse.

Hence, he rejects univocal predication as an adequate model of discourse about God on the grounds that it fails to discern the ontological divide, whose ground in the Summa is divine simplicity, the identity of essence and existence. The simple being of God is the efficient cause of all human existence and activity, but since the effects of that causality fall short of the cause itself, our language cannot represent God as God is in se but lapses into division and plurality in an inadequate gesturing towards the One (I.13,5 resp.). Thomas also rejects equivocal predication on the grounds that the inevitable fallacy entailed in equivocation would mean that nothing could be known or demonstrated about God from creatures at all (ibid.); the divide would then be so absolute that there would either be no possibility of relation or no integral connection between nature, grace and glory.

The possibility of analogical predication is based on the imperfect likeness of creatures to God (I.13,5 ad 2). The imperfection of the likeness entails two consequences. First, God remains the standard of all names applied to both God and creatures: "In names predicated of many in an analogical sense, all are predicated because they have reference to the same one thing; and this one thing must be placed in the definition of them all" (I.13,6 resp.).[4] Since God is the touchstone of all, all names designate God primarily and creatures only secondarily, because perfections flow from God to creatures and not the other way around (ibid.). The second entailment, however, pulls in a rather different direction, for although names properly designate perfections existing only in God, we apply them primarily to creatures, whom we know first (ibid.). Thus, even though the created order reflects the divine glory imperfectly and so is not the seed of analogy's truth, it remains nevertheless the realm of humanity's direct knowledge and experience, and the source, therefore, of human speech about God.

One of the major consequences of this difference between how analogical terms are applied to God and creatures leads directly back to Thomas' assertions regarding simplicity: "When any term expressing perfection is applied to a creature, it signifies that perfection distinct in idea from other perfections . . . whereas when we apply it to God, we do not mean to signify anything distinct from His essence, or power, or existence" (I.13,5 resp.). Again, while Thomas admits the validity of multiple terms for God, that multiplicity in no way should be understood as detracting from God's unicity.

The question now arises, however, whether this case for analogical naming has not led Aquinas into precisely the position that so appalled Barth: is God not now tied to the world's apron strings, dependent upon it in a manner most ill-befitting a deity? Thomas' answer is clear and unequivocal. God is outside the order of creation. It is therefore creatures who are ordered to God and not the reverse. The relation between God and the world is not bilateral: creatures are really related to God, but God is not related to creatures, properly speaking. The relation of God to the world is purely conceptual, grounded only in the fact that creatures are referred to him (I.13,7 resp.). The position Aquinas seems to be moving towards is the claim of a human participation in God that does not imply any captivity on God's part, and indeed this is the position he takes explicitly in Article 9.

Setting out to investigate whether the name God is communicable, Aquinas begins by bluntly asserting it is not (I.13,9 s.c.). Nevertheless, as usual there is a distinction to be drawn, in this instance between communication properly speaking and by similitude. Properly speaking the name God is incommunicable because the divine nature cannot be multiplied (I.13,9 resp.); by way of similitude, however, "this name God is communicable, not in its whole signification, but in some part of it by way of similitude so that those are called gods who share in divinity by likeness, according to the text I have said, You are gods (Ps lxxxi.6)" (ibid.). And in case his position remains less than fully transparent to us, he repeats in the reply to the first objection: "The divine nature is only communicable according to the participation of some similitude."[5] Thus, while surely emphasizing the qualification, he nevertheless firmly maintains, on the basis of the analysis of human discourse, a genuine participation in divine nature or divinization. By analyzing the nature of human discourse about God, Thomas has arrived at a depiction of a freely deifying God developed in close conjunction with his doctrine of divine simplicity.

Thomas' theory of theological language ultimately rests, however, on his epistemology. In the very way he frames the question of knowledge of God, he has created a foundation congenial to his doctrine, for by knowledge he means both God's knowledge of himself and our knowledge of God. The scope of the question thus encompasses divine nature, human nature, the distinction between them and the possibility of the intellectual union of the two.

He begins, as usual, by reminding the reader of the divide. Here again, we must reach back to the opening questions of the Summa's doctrine of God, where Aquinas defined God as the First Mover (I.2,3). On that basis, he reasons that God must be pure act, on the grounds that in an absolute sense, actuality is prior to potentiality. It is thus impossible that there is in God any element of potentiality whatsoever: God is defined as pure actuality (I.3,1 resp.). In Question 12, Thomas builds on this line of reasoning by claiming that since things are knowable as they are actual, God as pure act must be supremely knowable (I.12,1 resp.). If he seems to have backed himself into a corner, wilfully refusing to acknowledge the patently obvious—namely, that human beings do not have any easy or ready knowledge of God—he again rescues himself with a distinction: "But what is supremely knowable in itself, may not be knowable to a particular intellect, on account of the excess of the intelligible object above the intellect" (ibid.). The operative principle here works in exactly the same way as the one we saw governing Question 13: the obvious limitations of human conceptuality are not to be taken as indicative of God's being unknowable or unnameable. Our inability to attain to God of our own accord exposes the truth of our nature, not God's.

Having portrayed God as supremely intelligible and having acknowledged that not every intellect is capable of knowing God, Thomas obligates himself to explain how limited human intellects will, after all, attain knowledge of God. The option of simply claiming we cannot know God, while possessed of a distinguished patristic pedigree, is not available to Thomas for a variety of reasons, only one of which determines the shape of the question in hand: "The ultimate beatitude of man consists in the use of his highest function, which is the operation of the intellect; if we suppose that the created intellect could never see God, it could either never attain to beatitude, or its beatitude would consist in something else beside God; which is opposed to faith" (I.12,1 resp.). This depiction of beatitude in overwhelmingly intellectual terms is characteristically Thomistic and obliges Aquinas to find a way to show how the admittedly feeble human mind will gain its only proper end, which is felicity. Why must our beatitude consist in such intellectual fulfilment? Because Aquinas conceives the attainment of perfection as specific to the thing perfected: "The ultimate perfection of the rational creature is to be found in that which is the principle of its being; since a thing is perfect so far as it attains to its principle" (I.12,1 resp.). A rational being's fulfilment must then consist in intellectual perfection, and this perfection can take place only in the next life, as Thomas later explains, because our capacity to receive abstract intelligible things is directly proportionate to the soul's abstraction from the corporeal (I.12,11 resp.).

Thomas' ultimate answer to this conundrum scarcely surprises: the intellect will attain its end through divine aid. The specifics of his answer will nevertheless show a strong correlation with patterns we have already seen laying the foundation for a highly developed doctrine of theosis. This distinctive feature of Thomistic epistemology, the characteristic that renders it particularly suited to the development of a doctrine of theosis, is its understanding of knowledge as a form of participation.

Aquinas essentially takes for granted this principle: truly to know something is to become like it.[6] Without any great explanation or justification here, Thomas introduces this notion in the reply to Article 2,[7] where he states that both sensible and intellectual vision require two things, power of sight and the union of the thing seen with the sight. Actual vision consists in a certain kind of presence of the thing seen in the seer (I.12,2 resp.). In corporeal things, Aquinas goes on to explain, this presence of the thing seen occurs not by the presence of its essence in the one who sees but only by its likeness.

The vision of God differs from the vision of everything else in that when we see God, we are directed towards the very principle *whereby* we see. God is both end and means, final and efficient cause:

> This light is required to see the divine essence, not as a similitude in which God is seen, but as a perfection of the intellect, strengthening it to see God. Therefore it may be said that this light is to be described not as a medium in which God is seen, but as one by which He is seen [sed sub quo videtur]. (I.12,5 ad 2)

He articulates the same notion in yet stronger terms in Article 9: "According to the knowledge whereby things are known by those who see the essence of God, they are seen in God Himself not by any other similitudes but by the divine essence alone present to the intellect; by which also God Himself is seen" (I.12,9 resp.).[8] This form whereby we see God is also God. God is both the author of intellectual power and that which the intellect can see, both the means and end of the intellect's perfecting (ibid.). The paradigm Thomas articulates here bears an obvious resemblance to the root idea of deification, a similarity Thomas himself confirms when he expresses the paradigm's logical consequent: the creature's intellective power, while not the essence of God, must be some kind of participated likeness of the First Intellect (ibid.). If I.12,2 states one of deification's poles, participation in divine nature, however, Aquinas later in the same question expresses the other: "The knowledge of God's essence is by grace" (I.12,12 ad 3).[9]

We see here two principles we have already briefly noted, which Aquinas easily intertwines, but which we must keep conceptually separate. The first is that knowledge entails the likening of the knower to the known; the second is that human intellectual power being inadequate to a divine object, God must aid us if we are to attain beatitude, the vision of God. While these indeed constitute separate principles, they drive towards a common end, for together they strongly imply a doctrine of divinization.

Thomas articulates the second principle more explicitly in Article 4. Drawing on Romans 6:23, which identifies divine grace with everlasting life, he makes a further equation between eternal life and vision of divine essence, concluding that the created intellect may see the divine essence of God by grace, but only by grace and not by nature (I.12,4 s.c.). Because of the creature's need for grace to know God, that knowledge both results from and leads to a kind of triple participation in divine being:

> To know self-subsistent being is natural to the divine intellect alone; and this is beyond the natural power of any created intellect; for no creature is its own existence, forasmuch as its existence is participated [sed habet esse participatum]. Therefore the created intellect cannot see the essence of God, unless God by His grace unites Himself to the created intellect, as an object made intelligible to it [ut intelligible ab ipso]. (Ibid.)

To begin with, the creature's very existence depends upon a participation in Necessary Being; then again, God becomes intelligible because of the union of grace; finally (though not mentioned explicitly in this passage), any knowledge whatsoever results in a participation of knower in the known, as we have observed.[10]

The precise nature of this sanctifying participation becomes clearer still in the following article: "When any created intellect sees the essence of God, the essence of God itself becomes the intelligible form of the intellect" (I.12,5 resp.). In a sense, then, the union constituted by this knowledge of God consists not only of the knower and the known but also points to the unity of efficient and final causes: our consummate felicity consists in God's knowing himself in us.[11] Here, just as Aquinas broaches for the first time in the Summa the traditional imagery of theosis, he also uses its technical vocabulary for the first time, as he continues immediately on from the last passage cited:

> And this is the light spoken of in the Apocalypse (xxi.23). The glory of God hath enlightened it— viz., the society of the blessed who see God. By this light the blessed are made deiform— that is, like to God [et secundum hoc lumen efficiuntur deiformes, idest Deo similes], according to the saying: When He shall appear we shall be like to Him, and we shall see Him as He is (1 John, ii.2). (I.12,5 resp.)

In Thomas' epistemology, we thus see one distinctive element of the classic doctrine of deification, not only the idea of an eventual life with God, which any Christian eschatology affirms, but also the notion of transformation into the semblance of God. Accounts of Thomistic eschatology have tended to stress beatific vision alone; here we see that deiformity necessarily accompanies the vision of God.

The light by which we see God's essence is not something lesser that resembles God in some way but is the intellect's very perfection, which by strengthening the mind, enables it to see God (I.12,5 ad 2).[12] When the intellect attains perfection, it becomes not only most like God but also most itself, most what God created it to be. While this line of reasoning closely resembles what we have previously observed as Thomas', it immediately raises the spectre that ever haunts expositions of a doctrine of theosis: that in the elaboration, the doctrine will come to imply a breaching of the Uncreated-created distinction. Aquinas foresees such an objection and answers it forcefully: "The disposition to the form of fire can be natural only to the subject of that form. Hence the light of glory cannot be natural to a creature unless the creature has a divine nature; which is impossible. But by this light the rational creature is made deiform" (I.12,5 ad 3). While he continues to insist upon the fact of theosis, he firmly rules out the excessive claims to which the doctrine is inherently susceptible.[13]

One kind of guard against such excesses may be found in the stress on grace, a guard that, as we will see in our reading of Palamas, is the necessary accompaniment to discussions of deification. Aquinas possesses another sort of check, however, one more especially his own. Throughout the discussion of knowledge of God, Thomas has explicitly made the claim that the beatific vision consists in no less than a vision of God's essence, a claim infuriating to the Orthodox, as we have noted. While we will not examine the nature and consequences of this claim until later, we need to note here that the characteristic Thomistic distinction lies not between vision of divine essence and vision of divine something-else, but between *comprehension* of the essence and some lesser form of vision, for which Aquinas inconveniently does not supply a name. Nevertheless, he makes the substance of the distinction clear enough:

> What is comprehended is perfectly known. . . . But no created intellect can attain to that perfect mode of the knowledge of the divine intellect whereof it is intrinsically capable. . . . Since therefore the created light of glory received into any created intellect cannot be infinite, it is clearly impossible for any created intellect to know God in an infinite degree. Hence it is impossible that it should comprehend God. (I.12,7 resp.)[14]

Furthermore, seeing the essence of God does not imply that we know things other than God as God knows them; that is, seeing God's essence does not grant us a divine omniscience (I.12,8 s.c.). Because our knowledge of God is by grace and not nature, our knowledge of God is qualitatively different from God's self-knowledge, even though we participate in the latter; once again, Aquinas preserves both the distinction between Uncreated and creatures and the integrity of the creature. Still, as we have seen in other articles, Thomas wants any qualification to the claims of divinization to be taken precisely as qualifications and not as a retreat from the doctrine in its valid form, hence the distinction he draws among senses of *comprehension*:

> *Comprehension* is twofold: in one sense it is taken strictly and properly, according as something is included in the one comprehending; and thus in no way is God comprehended either by intellect, or in any other way. . . . But in another sense *comprehension* is taken more largely as opposed to *non-attainment* [insecutioni]. . . . And in this sense God is comprehended by the blessed. (I.12,7 ad 1)

"We become partakers in divine nature" may be understood in any sense that does not compromise the uniqueness of God, but conversely, any qualification made in virtue of the latter consideration may not be understood to compromise the strong and startling claim of Christian scripture, "We become partakers in divine nature."

What has seemed until this point like an exclusive focus on intellectual capacities raises the question of the relation between the deiformity resulting from knowledge of God and the deiformity resulting from formation in charity. While Question 12 by no means constitutes the definitive statement of the Thomistic conception of their relation, Article 6 does provide some preliminary guidance. We earlier noted that I.12,7 ad 1 describes the participation of vision as "the ultimate fulfilment of desire." To desire something, to be drawn towards it, is to love it, and beatific vision thus implies the active engagement of charity, as Aquinas explains in his discussion of the differences in the degree to which each of the blessed sees God:

> Hence the intellect which has more the light of glory will see God the more perfectly; and he will have a fuller participation of the light of glory who has more charity; because where there is the greater charity, there is the more desire; and desire in a certain degree makes the one desiring apt and prepared to receive the object desired. Hence he who possesses the more charity, will see God the more perfectly, and will be the more beatified. (I.12, 6 resp.)

However much he may stress the intellect as the means by which the rational creature attains the Supremely Intelligible, Aquinas seems here to suggest that formation in charity ultimately determines the limits of the intellect's attainment.

Thomas' epistemology reveals the extent to which his doctrine of deification depends on the structure of his doctrine of God. Article 6 of Question 12 brings us back to the root attribute of God in the *Prima Pars*, simplicity: "In the words, *We shall see Him as He is*, the conjunction *as* determines the mode of vision on the part of the object seen, so that the meaning is, we shall see Him to be as He is, because we shall see His existence, which is His essence" (I.12,6 ad 1). This recourse to an earlier point of doctrine illustrates Thomas' concern not simply to create a coherent and consistent structure for his work but more important, to insist always on the genuineness of divine self-communication. We are able to know God because his gift of self becomes the means by which we approach him, "In thy light we see light." What we see by means of the divine light, moreover, is not less than God, even if the limitations of our nature do not allow us such a full understanding of God as God has of himself; what we see is the one God, the only being in whom there is no division, separation or composition and in whom, therefore, essence and existence are one.

It was this claim which led Thomas also to maintain that our multiplicity of words for God, while furnishing a truthful description, does not imply that the divine nature consists of a bundle of characteristics distinguishable in any sense other than the conceptual. Nevertheless, Aquinas does provide some further insight into those attributes of God which one may predicate of the Trinity indiscriminately. This group of characteristics (some of which we have already examined) is a mixture of classical transcendentals (one, being, truth, goodness), specifically Christian and biblical attributes of God (love and mercy), and others shared by Christians and a variety of other theists, such as perfection and justice.

Even as he elaborates upon these varied traits of God, however, Thomas insists again and again that they are merely consequents of the two most important principles already established: necessary being and simplicity. The question on infinity (I.7), for example, draws so heavily on arguments presented in Questions 2 and 3 that it might justly be viewed as no more than an elucidation of them. The Thomistic argument appeals to God's immateriality as the ground of infinity, showing the relation between this immateriality and divine aseity and perfection: "Since therefore the divine being is not a being received in anything [esse divinum non sit esse receptum in aliquo], but He is His own subsistent being as was shown above, it is clear that God Himself is infinite and perfect" (I.7,1 resp.). Arguments along similar lines appear, for example, in Question 9 (on divine immutability), Question 10 (on God's eternity) and Question 11 (on the unity of God). Because these questions do little more than elaborate positions taken earlier, which we have already studied, and because they provide little new insight useful for the study of theosis, we will examine only four of these questions in detail. We need note only that, since the other questions rely heavily on the foundational principles of the identity of essence and existence, they also serve to underline the uniqueness of the Uncreated, which as we have seen, constitutes a necessary component of any doctrine of theosis. This vital element needs our attention less than four questions which provide information not regarding the God from whom we remain ever ontologically distinct but the God at whose good pleasure we become participants in divine nature. These are the questions on divine perfection, goodness, love and beatitude.

While Question 4, on God's perfection, follows immediately from the discussion of divine simplicity, our detour into the questions on religious knowledge and language will help us greatly in grasping how Thomas views the coherence of the two questions. Article 1 follows easily from notions already well established: God is perfect because, as pure actuality, he lacks nothing. Article 2, on the other hand, seems to veer dangerously (from the point of view of consistency) in the direction of a composite God. Because all created perfections are in God, he may be said to be universally perfect, not lacking any excellence that may be found in any genus (I.4,2 resp.). In the light of Questions 12 and 13 (especially the latter), we realize that Thomas doubtless intends these perfections to be taken, not as distinct qualities subsisting in God, but as an excellence that is none other than God's own being, refracted through the lens of our finite words and language into myriad separate qualities. No more will we be misled, then, when Thomas continues on to say "Since therefore God is the first effective cause of things, the perfections of all things must pre-exist in God in a more eminent way" (ibid.). Aquinas has done more here than establish God's perfection: he has connected it to all forms of excellence in humanity. While the reasoning moves from creation to Creator, he makes clear the motion of perfection itself is the reverse and thus hints that it is part of the divine character not only to create but to perfect what has been created.

Here again, we find the two essential notes of a doctrine of theosis: while the divinity's uniqueness is claimed in the strongest terms (here in the single sphere of perfection), a link between God and the created order is also asserted, a link that exists only in virtue of divine will, and the particular manner of whose existence testifies also to God's desire to share the fulness of his life with those he has created, to extend (as it were) the process of creation into a continual growth towards communion of being. While these are the essential elements of a doctrine of divinization, the doctrine they contain is no more than embryonic. The compatibility of the concept of perfection developed in Question 4 with a doctrine of theosis becomes clearest, however, in the next article, where Aquinas specifically considers whether creatures can be like God.

Again Thomas resorts to the Aristotelian framework, an analysis in terms of form and matter, genus and species. He still treads gingerly the line between similarity and distinction, maintaining the general principle of similarity between an agent and its effect but indicating the special conditions governing the case of an agent who belongs to no genus. (We observe again the great influence in later arguments of the principles laid down in Question 3 on simplicity.) Thomas continues:

> Therefore if there is an agent not contained in any *genus*, its effects will still more distantly reproduce the form of the agent, not, that is, so as to participate in the likeness of the agent's form according to the same specific or generic formality, but only according to some sort of analogy, as existence is common to all. In this way all created things, so far as they are beings, are like God as the first and universal principle of all being. (I.4,3 resp.)[15]

Two points are significant here. First, the means by which Aquinas prevents the likeness essential to theosis from becoming a matter of degrees along a continuum, where creatures slide easily into the realm of the Uncreated, is through appeal to analogy, an analogy which is precisely not any ontological similarity. Second, while the likeness Thomas is left with, the possession of existence, seems initially so weak a commonality between God and creatures as to import little for a doctrine of divinization, we must constantly bear in mind that existence is for Thomas the one essential characteristic of God. What we therefore by analogy share with God is no less than God's own essence.

Goodness consists in nothing else than that essence: "Goodness and being are really the same, and differ only in idea" (I.5,1 resp.), a claim not surprising in light of our examination of Question 13. However, in the next article, Aquinas introduces a distinction that will prove important for our purposes. While "in idea being is prior to goodness" (I.5,2 resp.), because being is the proper object of the intellect and is primarily intelligible, from the perspective of causality, the picture looks rather different:

> Goodness, since it has the aspect of the desirable, implies the idea of a final cause, the causality of which is first among causes, since an agent does not act except for some end . . . . Thus goodness, as a cause, is prior to being, as is the end to the form. Therefore among the names signifying the divine causality, goodness precedes being. (I.5,2 ad 1)

Besides positing a conceptual ordering between goodness and being, this passage is significant because once again we find desirability introduced as a prime factor in the Thomistic description of God. If we understand God as final cause primarily under the rubric of goodness, because goodness attracts agents to their proper end, then divine goodness must be taken as preeminently the label for that in divine nature in which the deified participate. Indeed, even before any sanctification takes place, the alliance of goodness and being indicates that every creature, every being, is good (I.5,3 s.c.). Article 4 reiterates this position, articulating it yet more clearly: "Since goodness is that which all things desire, and since this has the aspect of end, it is clear that goodness implies the aspect of an end" (I.5,4 resp.). Conversely, and more strongly still, Aquinas also maintains that "nothing is good except being" (I.5,2 ad 4), or in other words, there is no goodness that is not God's goodness and no possibility, therefore, of the creature's self-sanctification.

As we move from Question 5 to Question 6, we see Thomas' awareness of the precarious balance that any doctrine of theosis must maintain. No sooner has he asserted the necessity of the creature's participation in divine goodness than he takes up the theme of divine distinctiveness and pursues it vigorously. Because most of what he says here either essentially repeats what he has said earlier or draws from it correlates so obvious as to seem scarcely to require explicit statement, we can only surmise that he felt the basic point he makes to be of great importance. Thus, with logic by now entirely unremarkable, he asserts God's goodness, God as supremely good, and essential goodness as belonging to God alone. Of these claims, the argument of only one begs our attention, that of the second article. Here we find a line of reasoning very similar in structure and intent to the one in Question 13, but whose principle is applied to a slightly different end.

Although Thomas does not use the term analogy in his explanation, the underlying principle is exactly that of Question 12.[16] Thus, while good is attributed to God, the desired perfections flowing from Him "do not, however, flow from Him as from a univocal agent" (I.6,2 resp.), a position which follows naturally from I.4,2. Thomas develops this idea in the reply to the first objection: "The supreme good does not add to good any absolute thing, but only a relation. Now a relation of God to creatures, is not a reality in God, but in the creature; for it is in God in our idea only [in Deo vero secundum rationem]" (I.6,2 ad 1). The being—and therefore goodness—which God and creation both possess, does not tie them inextricably to one another; creatures indeed depend wholly on God, but the act of creating, even understood in the terms which we have seen Thomas lay out, does not irrevocably implicate God in creation nor bring about any change in divine nature. God remains the same after creation's birth as before: utterly self-sufficient and necessary Being. While this point adds no substance to the positions of Question 2, it does clarify, in the strongest possible terms, that those arguments are, as it were, still in effect. The embryonic doctrine of theosis we have been watching develop does not mitigate the sovereignty and uniqueness of the doctrine of God that Thomas began by articulating. The function of Question 6 is to show how the two are compatible, or why they are not to be understood as pulling away from one another.

If the need for such clarity arises out of a conception of divine goodness developed in a manner unfamiliar to the classical philosophical theism, the basic claim of divine goodness is not alien to that tradition. As Aquinas progresses in his exposition of the one God, however, the movement tends in an increasingly Christian direction. When we arrive at Question 20, on God's love, we have arrived on terra Christiana. The prime warrant for maintaining God is love is, not surprisingly, the text from 1 John 4:16: "God is love" (I.20,1 s.c.). Since, however, the argument in favor of this position relies heavily on preceding questions, we must glance briefly at a series of these before we turn in earnest to Question 20. In the latter, Thomas argues for the existence of love in God "because love is the first movement of the will and of every appetitive faculty" (I.20,1 resp.).

We broach here a lengthy chain of reasoning which will eventually lead us back to Question 3. God loves because he wills, Aquinas tells us (I.20). We assert will of God because will follows upon intellect, and there is intellect in God (I.19,1 resp.). While Thomas does not devote a question of the Summa to the divine intellect itself, he discusses it within Question 14, on the knowledge of God. There he provides two basic arguments in favor of a divine intellect. The more important of the two (the one to which he has more frequent recourse) is God's pure actuality:

> It must be said that the act of God's intellect is His substance. For if His act of understanding were other than His substance, then something else, as the Philosopher says, would be the act and perfection of the divine substance, to which the divine substance would be related, as potentiality is to act. (I.14, 4 resp.)[17]

The second sort of argument also reverts ultimately to Question 3, but by a more circuitous path: in I.14,1, Thomas argues for divine intellect on the basis of divine immateriality and infinity:

> Intelligent beings are distinguished from non-intelligent beings in that the latter possess only their own form; whereas the intelligent being is naturally adapted to have also the form of some other thing; for the idea of the known is in the knower. Hence it is manifest that the nature of a non-intelligent being is more contracted and limited; whereas the nature of intelligent beings has a greater amplitude and extension. . . . Now the contraction of the form comes from the matter. . . . Therefore it is clear that the immateriality of a thing is the reason why it is cognitive; and according to the mode of immateriality is the mode of knowledge. (I.14,1 resp.)

The argument for immateriality leads directly back to the claim of simplicity made in I.3,2; while the claim of infinity is made in I.7,1, it is based directly on the distinction between matter and form in that same locus (I.3,2).

The reasoning that demonstrates how 1 John 4:16 may be understood as true, then, which shows how God can be understood to be love, reverts by means either more or less circuitous, to the assertion of divine simplicity. The reason it is important to grasp this fact is not merely to admire the strong web of coherence in the Summa but to understand why Aquinas might have relatively little (four articles) to say about a tenet that lays strong claim to being the single most important Christian assertion about God. Thomas indeed finds it necessary explicitly to make the point that love is in God—he does not leave the reader to draw the logical conclusions for herself, after all. Nevertheless, given that in the context of Thomistic reasoning, God's love is a logical consequence of his simplicity, we need not marvel at the brevity of his treatment. Nor, more importantly, should we assume from that brevity that love ranks low in some Thomistic hierarchy of systematically significant divine attributes. Failure to grasp that the treatment of love is brief not because it is less important than simplicity but because it is in Thomas' view simplicity's inexorable consequent, will lead to perception of a sharp divide between, on the one hand, the Summa's exposition of the one God and his treatment of the Trinity and human sanctification on the other. In fact, all three doctrines point in the same direction, as we shall see; the differences among them lie solely in where love lies in the order of logic. In the exposition of the one God, love is an entailment rather than an axiom, but it is not on that account a less important postulate of divine being itself—though it is indeed less important in the order of our understanding of divine being, a status which may seem problematic to some.

The derivation of divine love from simplicity raises nonetheless one important problem, important both from the perspective of theological history and of the congeniality of Thomas' notion of love to a doctrine of deification. The association of love with union has always been a powerful one in Christian theology; from patristic exegesis of the sensuous imagery of the Song of Songs as God's love for the church, to the works of Bernard of Clairvaux, Christians have taken the theological meaning of charity to overlap considerably, if not entirely, with the idea of a unitive force. A doctrine of deification, moreover, implicitly claims a union of the divine and human—indeed, union and participation are often used interchangeably in treatments of theosis. The Thomistic idea of love as the correlative of simplicity therefore invites the charge of having abandoned the traditional concept of love, and one so congenial to the assertion of theosis, inasmuch as what is simple cannot be said to exist as a unitive force. While Aquinas perhaps here—uncharacteristically—replaces argument with bald assertion, he still clearly wants to remain within the traditional notion of love. Having described the act of love as a willing of good to someone, he continues:

> Love is called the unitive force, even in God [dicitur amor vis unitiva etiam in Deo], yet without implying composition; for the good that He wills for Himself, is no other than Himself, Who is good by His essence. . . . And then again the divine love is a binding force [amor divinus est vis concretiva], inasmuch as God wills good to others; yet it implies no composition in God. (I.20,1 ad 3)

The absence of a strong case for love as a unitive force may well indicate the frailty of Thomas' interest in and commitment to such a notion. The fuller exposition of how God wills good to all things in the second article provides a more typical picture of his mind's working. He begins in the response by once again making the connection between goodness and existence; since nothing can exist without God's willing it and since existence is good, God must will good to all things, which means he loves them—although Aquinas is careful in subsequent articles to show that God does not love all things equally. Nor, he tells us, does God love everything that exists as we love. The difference lies in the active agency of the love. Our love is elicited by its object; "the love of God," in contrast, "infuses and creates goodness" (I.20,2 resp.). Although Thomas has nothing further to say on the subject of infusion in these articles, the introduction of the concept here in the doctrine of God is important because of the way it foreshadows what will become a central concept of his doctrine of grace. Even here, however, the portrayal of God's love as, in part, a love for creatures that infuses goodness is significant, for it indicates that part of our understanding of the essential structure of divine being is God's active and free sharing of himself with creatures, so that his being becomes part of theirs. If love is actually the same as God's simplicity, existence, eternity, immutability and all the rest, then the love that infuses and creates goodness is not conceived as some unspecified growth in goodness but God's gift of self, the incorporation of God's being into our own, even (despite Thomas' seeming squeamishness) God's voluntary union with the human soul.

As Thomas incorporates the traditional idea of union into his doctrine of theosis, so he also accommodates the idea of contemplation. Although he himself does not use the term, the expanded description of beatitude given in Article 2 indicates a substantial similarity between the Thomistic concept of consummation and the traditional patristic understanding of theoria:

> Gregory says: He is in glory, Who whilst He rejoices in Himself, needs not further praise. To be in glory, however, is the same as to be blessed. Therefore, since we enjoy God in respect of our intellect, because vision is the whole of the reward, as Augustine says, it would seem that beatitude is said to be in God in respect of His intellect. (I.26,2 s.c.)

Despite the very strong resort to intellect, a dependence that verges on describing glory as a mental exercise, Thomas here actually overlaps substantially with standard accounts of theosis. The end of the response in Article 2, for example, depicts not a Mind conceived by other minds but a union of spiritual beings: "Beatitude must therefore be assigned to God in respect of His intellect; as also to the blessed, who are called blessed by reason of assimilation to his beatitude." While the suggestion of a sanctifying union here is strong, we must take care not to assume blithely any simple identification between *theoria* and Thomistic beatitude. The difference lies not so much on the level of assertion as in a distinction Aquinas feels necessary to make that was of less concern for the tradition before him. "Beatitude is something different from God," he states firmly (I.26,3 s.c.). The assimilation we experience in the beatific vision consists in a uniting to divine beatitude, not to divine nature. His first reason for this position is straightforward and need not detain us: "The beatitude of an intellectual nature consists in an act of the intellect" (I.26,3 resp.) and God is obviously not an act of our intellect. Thomas' second grounds introduced a distinction that will be of enormous importance, both for our grasp of the *Summa* and even more so for the analysis of East-West relations.

The distinction Aquinas makes lies essentially in the difference between the way a thing is said to exist in God and the way that same thing may exist in a creature receiving it as God's gift:

> The beatitude of an intellectual nature consists in an act of the intellect. In this we may consider two things—namely, the object of the act, which is the thing understood; and the act itself, which is to understand. If, then, beatitude be considered on the side of the object, God is the only beatitude. . . . But as regards the act of understanding, beatitude is a created thing in beatified creatures; but in God, even in this way, it is an uncreated thing. (I.26,3 resp.)

This passage reveals a pattern we will see again in the doctrine of grace: Thomas' concern to preserve the integrity of being leads him to describe a single thing in two quite different ways, according to the nature of that into which it is incorporated. The same beatitude—and it is crucial to grasp that Aquinas does not, by intention or in fact, posit two beatitudes—may be viewed as uncreated in God but created when it becomes part of the creature. Because there exist nonetheless not two beatitudes but one, the creature's beatitude is not some lesser form of what exists in God, but the creature's own experience, as creature and within the limitations of creaturely existence, of the divine. It is precisely the basic principle of deification that operates here: however we describe the creature's participation in or union with God, we do not understand that divinization as violating the ontological boundary between creature and Creator. The life in which the creature shares is genuinely God's life, but we do not live that life in precisely the way God lives it.

Properly speaking, God is the rational creature's last end; created beatitude is the end of creatures only in the sense that it is the use and fruition of their end, the creatures' own enjoyment of the end (I.26,3 ad 2). As rational creatures, our fitting and perfect end is the enjoyment of the Supremely Intelligible. While that Intelligible never alters in its uncreated status, neither do we alter, in consequence of our assimilation to it, in our status as creatures. Indeed, Aquinas reinforces the paradigm he uses here by reference, in Article 4, to an earlier procedural rule. In explaining why divine beatitude embraces all other beatitudes, he claims it is because whatever is desirable in any form of beatitude (including false beatitude) preexists in its fullest and most perfect form in the divine beatitude (I.26,4 resp.). Although Thomas himself does not allude to it, clearly the

operative principle here is that established in the response in I.13,2, analogical predication by way of the *via eminentiae*:

> These names signify the divine substance, and are predicated substantially of GOD, al-
> though they fall short of a full representation of Him. . . . Hence every creature represents
> Him, and is like Him, so far as it possesses some perfection; yet it represents Him not as
> something of the same species or genus, but as the excelling principle of whose form the
> effects fall short. (I.13,2 resp.)

While his use of phrases like *created beatitude* suggests Thomas is positing two sorts of
beatitude and therefore separating the creature from any authentic participation in precisely the Creator's own life, his own explanations of what he intends by such terminology leave no doubt as to the unicity of beatitude itself, or as we shall see, of grace itself.
Furthermore, we see how dependent is Thomas' doctrine of theosis on the reader's grasping the *Summa*'s structure. The term *created beatitude*, like its counterpart *created grace*, may
easily be misunderstood if removed from the structure into which Thomas built it. These
terms must be read in the context of his doctrine of God, which must stress divine transcendence if Thomas is also to claim theosis, and of his doctrine of language, which
specifies the way in which human speech must necessarily misrepresent divine nature
by dividing into distinct concepts what is in reality one. In that context, it is clear that
the created-Uncreated distinction refers to the ontological divide between God and humanity rather than designating fundamental divisions in grace or beatitude.

2. The Trinity

The *Summa*'s theology portrays a God intent upon drawing creatures into his own life. In
the *De Trinitate*, Thomas shows the same God as three Persons who not only desire to
engage humanity but actually do so. In the *De Deo uno*, intellect and will were the consequents of simplicity; in the *De Trinitate*, they become the leading characteristics of the
Persons of the Trinity. By the end of the treatise and the *Prima Pars*, we begin to see the
outward impetus of intellect and will in the missions of the Persons to creation. What
we will find as we explore these questions is a study of divine being that progresses
more and more towards an anthropology and a doctrine of sanctification. Thomas' exposition of the Trinity recapitulates the doctrine of the one God, rendering its systematic implications more explicit, so that by the time he begins the anthropology proper,
its outline has already been sketched out distinctly.[18]

Thomas therefore begins with the internal processions. As his doctrine of God grounds
his account of the trinitarian processions, so the internal processions ground the doctrine of mission. Initially, however, it seems his logic moves in the reverse direction,
for he opens the section on the Trinity with an argument for inward procession in God
based on the evidence of the Economy: "Since procession always supposes action, and
as there is an outward procession corresponding to the act tending to external matter,
so there must be an inward procession corresponding to the act remaining within the
agent" (I.27,1 resp.).

While these methods may appear to differ from those of the preceding section on
the one God, Aquinas soon embarks upon a line of reasoning whose chief elements will

prove very familiar to readers of his doctrine of God. The principle he uses to ground inward processions in God, the correspondence of an inward with the obvious outward procession, lends itself to the analysis of agency and intellect, of which Thomas made such great use in his doctrine of God:

> [The inward procession's corresponding to the act remaining within the agent] applies most conspicuously to the intellect, the action of which remains in the intelligent agent. For whenever we understand, by the very fact of understanding there proceeds something within us, which is a conception of the object understood, a conception issuing from our intellectual power and proceeding from our knowledge of that object. This conception is signified by the spoken word; and it is called the word of the heart signified by the word of the voice. . . . [Procession is therefore] to be understood by way of an intelligible emanation, for example, of the intelligible word which proceeds from the speaker, yet remains in him. In that sense, the Catholic Faith understands procession as existing in God. (Ibid.)[19]

This analysis simultaneously fulfils two distinct objectives: it is an explication of divine life that employs traditional biblical language (Word, Spirit) in the context of a doctrine of God already developed (God as supreme intellect and as utterly simple) in such a way that the two are shown to cohere in a single unified system.

This high degree of cohesion manifests itself yet more strongly in the following article, where Thomas undertakes to explain the procession of the Second Person as a form of generation:

> So in this manner the procession of the Word in God is generation; for He proceeds by way of intelligible action, which is a vital operation:—from a conjoined principle (as above described) [i.e., as the origin of a living being called birth]:—by way of similitude, inasmuch as the concept of the intellect is a likeness of the object conceived:—and exists in the same nature, because in God the act of understanding and His existence are the same. (I.27,2 resp.)

The lineaments of Thomas' portrayal of the one God manifest themselves strongly here, not only in the stress on divine intellect but also in the way intratrinitarian unity is explained by reference to the concept of divine simplicity that so dominated the Summa's opening chapters: it is because of that simplicity that God's existence and the exercise of his intellect—and therefore, the Father and the Son—are inseparably united and share the same nature.

Thomas' doctrine of God is, as we observed, nevertheless not monopolized by attention to intellect, for he also devoted considerable attention to the role of divine will (even if the disgruntled reader might justifiably complain that the balance tilts decidedly in the intellect's favor). This analysis in terms of two faculties is echoed by the trinitarian theology, where the spiration of the Third Person results from the operation of the divine will expressed as love. In any intellectual nature, Aquinas claims, the operation of that nature results in an intellectual act, and in God's case that act is the Word; just so:

> The operation of the will within ourselves involves also another procession, that of love, whereby the object loved is in the lover; as, by the conception of the word, the object spoken of or understood is in the intelligent agent. Hence, besides the procession of the Word in God, there exists in Him another procession called the procession of love. (I.27,3 resp.)

Furthermore, the analysis of intellectual nature as one which knows and wills not only yields a triune God; it also indicates the order of the processions and limits their number. Since one can only love what one knows, the generation of the Second Person precedes the spiration of the Third.[20] Since, moreover, in an intellectual nature those actions that remain within the agent are limited to two—namely, acts of intelligence and will—and since God is such an intellectual nature, only two divine internal processions are possible.[21]

While Thomas' account of the divine processions differs little in its essentials from the psychological model of the Trinity that had reigned in the West since Augustine, Aquinas has not simply reiterated the De Trinitate in medieval scholastic form.[22] Nor has he, by explicating first the doctrine of the one God and then the doctrine of the Trinity, divided one from the other or given priority to one over the other. Rather, he has taken Augustine's essential insight and expanded it, with a consequent image that one might call theologically Cubist: the De Deo uno and the De Trinitate are superimposed portraits of the same God viewed from different perspectives. Within the De Deo uno, the knowing and willing simple Being has one mien, within the De Trinitate, another, one in which the actions of knowing and willing take the form of Persons. Furthermore, as we will see later, this portrait will be overlaid with a third image, drawn from a differing perspective yet, in which the activities of knowing and loving take on a human form that imitates God's.

The first question raised by the manner in which Aquinas developed his own analysis of intellectual nature and aligned it with an Augustinian doctrine of the Trinity is whether the absolute divide between Uncreated and creation may now be maintained, given the essential principle that "everything that is not the divine essence is a creature" (I.28,2 s.c.). Breaching that divide would result not only in the compromising of divine simplicity, inasmuch as God would include disparate components, but would also render impossible a genuine doctrine of deification—so much is at stake here. Thomas solves this dilemma by reaching back to the principles on the knowledge of God that proved so determinative of his doctrine of the one God. Just as goodness and justice both really exist in God, but are distinguished only in our minds, so the divine relations really exist, but not in addition to the essence:

> Relation really existing in God is really the same as His essence; and only differs in its mode of intelligibility; as in relation is meant that regard to its opposite which is not expressed in the name of essence [prout in relatione importatur respectus ad suum oppositum, qui non importatur in nomine essentiae]. Thus it is clear that in God relation and essence do not differ from each other, but are one and the same. (I.28,2 resp.)

Thus a principle articulated within the doctrine of the one God provides a means for interpreting the doctrine of the Trinity so as to preserve the essential principle of the De Deo uno: "Nothing that exists in God can have any relation to that wherein it exists or of whom it is spoken, except the relation of identity;[23] and this by reason of God's extreme simplicity" (I.28,2 ad 1).

A similar pattern of recourse to a principle established within the De Deo uno to reconcile it with the developing trinitarian doctrine emerges in Aquinas' treatment of the divine Persons. The notions of Word and Spirit that Thomas developed in the first of the trinitarian questions (Question 27) need not, after all, imply that the divine processions result specifically in persons, as the tradition inherited from the Cappadocians and enshrined in the creeds would have it. What Thomas has established is that God's is an intellectual nature; that nature is said to subsist in what Anselm candidly called *nescio quids* (I don't know whats—or as an American teenager might say, whatevers), and this intellectual individual is the very definition of *person*: "Person signifies what is most perfect in all nature—that is, a subsistent individual of a rational nature [subsistens in rationali natura]" (I.29,3 resp.). Indeed, in this statement, Aquinas not only allies characteristics of God he has already established with a conventional definition of *person* but has also allied the resultant whole term and its definition with another attribute of God central to his doctrine of the one God: perfection. Furthermore, because *person* as Thomas defines it is said to signify what is most perfect in all nature, he can also tie his definition of *person* as applied to God to yet another element of his doctrine of God—namely, his miniature treatise on religious language in Question 13: not only may the name *person* be applied to God, it most properly applies to God.[24] The *via eminentiae* which Thomas described in Question 13 dictates that all terms applied to God—terms that necessarily derive from the world of creatures—will nonetheless designate God *more* truly than they do creatures. The historically problematic technical language of trinitarian theology has, in virtue of patterns set in place in the treatise on the one God, been rendered compatible with the very assertions with which it seemed headed for collision.

What Aquinas is showing us, once again, is that however varied our conceptions of God (One and Three), however numerous our designations for God (simple, perfect, intellectual, volitional), we are always led back to the same God. Each representation has its own vanishing point, but the model is always the same. To say that Aquinas' portraits of God reveal a consistent set of divine attributes does not mean that the three Persons are undifferentiated in his account. Indeed, it is in the specific character of each of the three that he lodges traits which allow us to speak of his God as unmistakably divinizing.

The Father is so called preeminently because of his relation to the divine Son: "The perfect idea of paternity and filiation is to be found in God the Father, and in God the Son, because one is the nature and glory of the Father and the Son" (I.33,3 resp.). Nevertheless, the Father's name also signifies a certain relation to creation, and in describing the nature of this relation, Aquinas uses the classic language of theosis:

> Of some, namely, the rational creature [He is the Father], by reason of the likeness of His image, according to Deut. xxxii.6: *Is He not thy Father, who possessed, and made, and created thee?* And of others He is the Father by similitude of grace, and these are also called adoptive sons, as ordained to the heritage of eternal glory by the gift of grace which they have received, according to Rom. viii.16, 17: *The Spirit Himself gives testimony to our spirit that we are the sons of God; and if sons, heirs also.* Lastly, He is the Father of others by similitude of glory, forasmuch as they have obtained possession of the heritage of glory, according to Rom. v.2: *We glory in the hope of the glory of the sons of God.* (Ibid.)

Aquinas here traces three degrees of likening to God (though he does not label them as degrees). The first is the rational creature's innate likeness, although this degree does little more than posit the creature's inalienable connectedness to God, inasmuch as God is the source of her being and her potential for further likening.[25] The second degree of likening occurs in virtue of the gift of grace; while the language of the ordaining to the heritage of eternal glory seems to postpone intimate relations with God to the afterlife, the language of adoptive sonship posits an analogical relationship between the relation of the graced creature and the Father and the relation of the divine Son to the Father. Intratrinitarian relations are mirrored in the relation of Uncreated to created, so that even though there are clear differences between the two (i.e., a shared nature in one case, the absence of such in the other), the similarity allows one to envisage the creature's gracing as a form of sharing in modes of trinitarian existence. The third degree suggests that the creature participates in the Father's glory in an even more complete way, so that now we are no longer God's adoptive children but his children pure and simple. The suggestion of an analogy between the Father's relation to the Son and to rational creatures arises again, obliquely, at the article's end, where Aquinas states that paternity designates the relation between the First and Second Persons in the first instance, and only secondarily the relation between God and creatures. While his intent here is clearly to establish the preeminence of paternity-filiation language in relation to God, this statement also assumes a proportionate likeness between the two uses of *Father*, thus suggesting a grounding of human sanctification in the intratrinitarian processions.[26]

We observe a similar pattern in the articles on the Son. Aquinas states the essential paradigm early in Question 34: "For the Father, by understanding Himself, the Son, and the Holy Ghost, and all other things comprised in this knowledge, conceives the Word; so that thus the whole Trinity is *spoken* in the Word; and likewise also all creatures" (I.34,1 ad 3). The first principle we need note here is the repetition of the now familiar notion that the Word is the Father's self-understanding. Had Aquinas stopped there, he would still have, within this question on the person of the Son, established the basis for an analogy between intratrinitarian relations and the Trinity's relation to creation; but he continues, and as he continues, he explicitly suggests the analogy. The Word represents at once the recapitulation of the Trinity and of creation; in the person of the Word, then, the Trinity in its entirety and creation in its entirety meet and converge.

Thomas does not leave this important point resting upon this single reference, however, for he devotes Article 3 wholly to the question of the Word's relation to creatures. "Word implies relation to creatures [in verbo importatur respectus ad creaturam]," he claims, "for God by knowing Himself knows every creature. . . . because God by one act understands Himself and all things, His one only Word is expressive not only of the Father, but of all creatures" (I.34,3 resp.). Here Aquinas extends a little the pattern we observed developing in Article 1. There, the Word represented the divine knowledge of self and creation; while Thomas did refer to this self-understanding as a form of speech or as resulting in speech (it is not clear which he intends), it is not until Article 3 that he so clearly claims the Word is the *expression* of world and Trinity. If understanding entails a participation of the knower in the known, so expression implies a voluntary self-giving on behalf of the other.[27]

The paradigm we have been exploring becomes at once most diffusive and most powerful in the articles on the Holy Spirit. Although there is no single passage in these articles that expresses it as concisely as passages we have examined in articles on the Father and the Son, the questions on the Holy Spirit witness profoundly to the analogy of relations among the Three and their relation to the world. We see this first in Thomas' explication of the name *Holy Spirit*:

> The name spirit in things corporeal seems to signify impulse and motion; for we call the breath and the wind by the term spirit. Now it is a property of love to move and impel the

will of the lover towards the object loved. Furthermore holiness is attributed to whatever is ordered to God. Therefore because the divine person proceeds by way of the love whereby God is loved [persona divina procedit per modum amoris quo Deus amatur], that person is most properly named The Holy Ghost. (I.36,1 resp.)

The love of God is here identified with the Spirit and is portrayed as that which moves one person towards another; while the reference is clearly to intratrinitarian relations, the applicability to the Economy is obvious, especially in light of the broad generality of "holiness is attributed to whatever is ordered to God."

The same double applicability appears in Article 37, on the significance of the Love as the Spirit's name:

For as when a thing is understood by anyone, there results in the one who understands a conception of the object understood, which conception we call word; so when anyone loves an object, a certain impression results, so to speak, of the thing loved in the affection of the lover; by reason of which the object loved is said to be in the lover. (I.37,1 resp.)

While no mention is made in this passage of what is meant by any human person's love of God, the principle's transferability is clear. The movement of the divine will that remains within God, whose name is Holy Spirit, is the bond of unity of the Father and the Son: "The Father and the Son love each other and us, by the Holy Ghost, or by love proceeding" (I.37,2 resp.).[28]

Where the implications of Thomistic pneumatology become clearest for creation, however, is in the final question treating the Spirit. Gift is said to be the Spirit's proper name, inasmuch as he proceeds from the Father and the Son (I.38,2 s.c.). Gift signifies not only the Holy Spirit's character as love but also the Spirit's procession. The gratuity that inheres in the notion of gift implies well-wishing, whose strong form is love. To give freely is an expression of love. On this basis, Aquinas concludes, love is the prime form of all gifts, that through which all gifts are given (I.38,2 resp.).[29]

The second article of Question 38 thus stipulates the sense in which gift may be taken as the proper name of the third member of the immanent Trinity. In the preceding article, however, Aquinas described the implications of the Spirit's personal name for creatures:

The word gift imports an aptitude for being given. And what is given has an aptitude or relation both to the giver and to that to which it is given. For it would not be given by anyone, unless it was his to give; and it is given to someone to be his. Now a divine person is said to belong to another, whether by origin, as the Son belongs to the Father; or as possessed by another. But we are said to possess what we can freely use or enjoy as we please: and in this way a divine person cannot be possessed, except by a rational creature united to God. . . . The rational creature does sometimes attain thereto; as when it is made partaker of of the divine Word and of the Love proceeding, so as freely to know God truly and to love God rightly. Hence the rational creature alone can possess the divine person. Nevertheless in order that it may possess Him in this manner, its own power avails nothing; hence this must be given it from above; for that is said to be given to us which we have from another source. Thus a divine person can be given and can be a gift. (I.38,1 resp.)

The first significance of the gift, then, is that it provides a common denominator between giver and recipient, and as such Aquinas may be taken as saying, with only a small interpretative stretch, that the gift links the two. A more profound parallel between giver and recipient lies in their mutual ownership of the gift, for it belongs to both, albeit in differing ways. Not only Aquinas' choice of terminology here, belonging and possessing, but also his apparent disinclination to make much of the distinction between the manner of divine and human ownership is striking. While there may be nothing surprising in maintaining that the Son belongs to the Father, Thomas certainly aligns himself with the most radical proponents of deification in claiming a divine person can be possessed by a rational creature. As he expands upon this statement, he slips into the classic language of theosis—union, participation and knowledge—to which he has added his own signature, love. The Third Person's proper names—Holy Spirit, Love and Gift—each expresses a different aspect, not only of the Spirit's particular character but also of the Spirit's connectedness to both the Trinity and the Economy: the Spirit is preeminently the bond of unity within the Trinity and also plays an important role in linking God and humanity. Because the Spirit performs both these functions, we find in the person of the Spirit a suggestive expression of humanity's entry into the divine life of the Trinity.

Question 38 also serves to specify, in a brief and preliminary way, the means by which humanity's incorporation into divine life takes place; it is, Thomas tells us, at divine instigation and only at divine instigation. This insistence grows stronger as we move towards the end of his account of the Trinity. The questions we have considered up until now have been oriented towards the Trinity's internal relations and the essential character of each of the Persons, despite the relevance for relations ad extra, which we have deliberately sought. In the final question on trinitarian doctrine, Thomas changes his focus and begins to turn his attention towards creation.

His account of missions departs from the same point as the doctrine of God with which he began the Prima Pars: God's independence of creation and creation's dependence upon God—"The notion of mission includes two things: the habitude of the one sent to the sender; and that of the one sent to the end whereto he is sent" (I.43,1 resp.).[30] The initial rubric of Aquinas' discussion of creation, then, is that creatures and the created order do not exist for their own sake but for a purpose, God's purpose. That this orientation is nevertheless grounded in the nature of the Trinity is indicated by Thomas' use of the term procession, for the mere fact of sending implies a procession from the sender (ibid.). Use of this item of trinitarian technical vocabulary invites comparison between the internal relations among the Three and their relation to the external world. The similarity between the two is further deepened when Thomas writes: "The habitude to the term to which he is sent is also shown, so that in some way he begins to be present there [ut aliquo modo ibi esse incipiat]" (ibid.). As the Three are present to one another in knowledge and love, so the Trinity's mission is present in creation's end. Thomas summarizes:

> Thus the mission of a divine person is a fitting thing, as meaning in one way the procession of origin from the sender, and as meaning a new way of existing in another [novum modum existendi in alio]; thus the Son is said to be sent by the Father into the world, inasmuch as He began to exist visibly in the world by taking our nature. (Ibid.)

Here Aquinas makes explicit what has been implicit throughout his exposition of the Trinity: the internal trinitarian processes are echoed in creation, in a way that implies creation's sanctification and participation in divine existence ("a new way of existing in another"). Reference to the Incarnation also suggests such sanctifying participation, for

Christ's person represents not only the locus of our redemption but also the personal union of divine and human nature. Aquinas thus gestures both to the anthropology of the *Secunda Pars* and the Christology of the *Tertia Pars*.

The Spirit also forms part of this sanctifying mission, and in Article 3, Aquinas begins to forge explicit links between the pneumatology of Question 38 and the doctrine of mission he has begun to elaborate. Drawing on Augustine, he characterizes mission as taking place in time, for the purpose of the creature's sanctification. Since sanctification takes place by grace, the divine missions must also be by sanctifying grace (I.43,3 s.c.). He continues in the response: "The divine person is fittingly sent in the sense that He exists newly in any one [novo modo existit in aliquo]; and He is given as possessed by anyone; and neither of these is otherwise than by sanctifying grace." Procession, God's indwelling in the human person, the Gift's belonging to its recipient, the sanctification wrought by grace: all of these elements are bound together in the Thomistic understanding of mission, the point at which trinitarian doctrine and the doctrine of sanctification meet in a form that increasingly acquires the aspect of a traditional doctrine of theosis.

The basis for grounding the notion of theosis in both the doctrine of the one God and the doctrine of the Trinity emerges clearly in the response to Article 3:

> For God is in all things by his essence, power, and presence, according to His one common mode, as the cause existing in the effects which participate in His goodness. Above and beyond this common mode, however, there is one special mode belonging to the rational nature wherein God is said to be present as the object known is in the knower, and the beloved in the lover, And since the rational creature by its operation of knowledge and love attains to God Himself, according to this special mode God is said not only to exist in the rational creature, but also to dwell therein as in His own temple. So no other effect can be put down as the reason why the divine person is in the rational creature in a new mode, except sanctifying grace. (I.43,3 resp.)

The analogy between the inner life of the Trinity and the structure of sanctification now becomes explicit, for as the internal divine processions were described in terms of knowing and loving, the motions of the intellect and the will, so the union of God and the human person comes about in virtue of the operation of knowledge and love. This union is the product of sanctifying grace, the gift of which is none other than the Spirit himself, so that one union becomes the precondition of another; God's gift of self is bestowed in order that the rational creature may know and love God, and in so doing, become divinity's proper dwelling place.

The double nature of this gift is stated more clearly in the reply to the second objection:

> Sanctifying grace disposes the soul to possess the divine person [ad habendam divinam Personam]; and this is signified when it is said that the Holy Ghost is given according to the gift of grace. Nevertheless the gift itself of grace is from the Holy Ghost; which is meant by the words, *the charity of God is poured forth in our hearts by the Holy Ghost.*

The mention of charity in this last passage should alert us, given charity's status as the chief of the deiform virtues, to the immediate applicability of these passages to a doctrine of divinzation. The reply to the first objection, moreover, states unmistakably the connection between sanctification, as Thomas conceives it, and consummation. The gift of sanctifying grace is said to perfect the rational creature in such a way that she can both use the created gift and even enjoy the divine person himself. Here Aquinas allies the gift of grace with perfection, implying precisely that kind of seamlessness between sanctification in this life and consummation in the next that is characteristic of a doctrine of theosis.[31] Even more significantly, he acknowledges that the gift of grace implies not only an effect of grace within the human person ("the created gift itself") but also an assimilation to the Uncreated ("enjoy also the divine person Himself"). That this gift is of the whole Trinity becomes apparent in the next article, where Aquinas clearly states that the Father also freely gives himself to be enjoyed by the creature (I.43,4 ad 1), this despite the fact that the Father is not sent (I.43,4 resp. and ad 2).[32]

It is perhaps because nothing less than the whole Trinity is bestowed in the gift of grace that the inner structure of the sanctified comes to resemble the inner life of God; this much Aquinas does not explicitly claim. What he does affirm outright is that through grace the human person comes to resemble God: "The soul is made like to God by grace. Hence for a divine person to be sent to anyone by grace, there must be a likening of the soul to the divine person Who is sent, by some gift of grace" (I.43,5 ad 2). Since the soul is likened to the divine person sent, sending itself must logically entail this likening. The mission of the Trinity is thus portrayed as itself an inherently deifying work.

Confirmation that this is indeed Aquinas' intention comes as he continues in the reply to the second objection:

> Because the Holy Ghost is Love, the soul is assimilated to the Holy Ghost by the gift of charity: hence the mission of the Holy Ghost is according to the mode of charity. Whereas the Son is the Word, not any sort of word, but one Who breathes forth Love. Hence Augustine says: *The Word we speak of is knowledge with love.* Thus the Son is sent not in accordance with every and any kind of intellectual perfection, but according to the intellectual illumination, which breaks forth into the affection of love.[33]

Here Aquinas has not only again asserted the significance of the infusion of charity— that it constitutes no less than the Holy Spirit's gift of self—but has also reminded the reader forcefully of the trinitarian dimension of the bestowal of charity. Not only does the language of knowing and loving recall his (and, of course, Augustine's) account of the divine processions, Thomas has now implicated the Word in the act of loving more inevitably than ever before. Until now, the relation between knowing and loving was generally portrayed as the necessity of the intellectual act's preceding that of the will— one cannot love what one does not know. Now, however, the Son's mission is associated exclusively with sanctifying knowledge. Growing in likeness to the Son is not merely a matter of extraordinary intellectual achievement but an illumination. Although Aquinas provides us with no information at this point as to how, precisely, this illumination differs from knowledge in general, the context strongly suggests that illumination pertains to God in a way that knowledge in general does not. Furthermore, this sanctification of the mind appears to lead, almost spontaneously, to the expression of love, so that this particular kind of knowledge seems inseparable from charity, just as the Son and the Spirit are united indivisibly in the Trinity.

Articles 6 and 7 merit the close attention we have given them because within their compass Thomas unites earthly sanctification and heavenly consummation. It is precisely this seamlessness that is characteristic of a doctrine of divinzation. Thus, despite the absence of the words *deification* or even *deiform* here, what one might call a theotic form of sanctification is clearly operative. The unity of experience of the wayfarers and the blessed witnesses to this theotic form, but the location of these assertions in the *Summa* also provides important evidence. The assimilation of the temporal to the eternal—and the temporal's consequent transformation—takes place within the sphere of the Trinity's activity and as a result of that activity. By expounding his notion of the unity of sanctification and consummation within his treatment of trinitarian doctrine, Aquinas suggests to his reader two ideas. First, sanctification as we commonly think of it—"grace through the sacraments," "renewal by grace," "the indwelling of grace"—is nothing other than God's self-giving to the creature. Sanctification is not the administration of some divine medicine called grace that is other or less than God. All sanctification must be understood under the rubric of the mission of the Trinity, which is the revelation of the eternal trinitarian processions in time to finite creatures consequently transformed: "The Son has been sent visibly as the author of sanctification; the Holy Ghost as the sign of sanctification" (I.43,7 resp.).

The second point follows from the first: the unity of sanctification and consummation is grounded in the unity of their cause. Aquinas does not state as much explicitly, but the structure of Question 43 suggests such as interpretation. The articles we have been considering, which essentially treat mission's effects and how they are experienced in time, all derive from the center portion of the question. They are sandwiched between articles dealing more with the immanent Trinity, mission's source and the end to which it is directed. Both the opening and closing articles affirm the unity of the Trinity, so that although the central articles necessarily distinguish the characteristic work of Son and Spirit, the opening article takes pains to indicate that the distinctive role of each of the Three implies no disunity: "The divine person sent neither begins to exist where he did not previously exist nor ceases to exist where He was. Hence such a mission takes place without a separation, having only distinction of origin" (I.43,1 ad 2). The final article stresses the unified heart of all missiological activity even more strongly.[34] Aquinas determines that a divine person is sent by one from whom he does not proceed (thus denying any absolute correspondence between the patterns of procession and mission) but takes this position in order to affirm the unity of the Trinity's operation in sending: "The whole Trinity sends the person sent" (I.43,8 resp.).[35]

Question 43 thus stresses two kinds of unity: the unity of sanctification and the unity of sanctification's cause. Nowhere in this question does Thomas explicitly link the two: nevertheless, the question's movement—from the unity of the source, to the unity of the sanctified's experience of God, back to the unity of the source—strongly suggests a connection between the two. The internal life of the Trinity is a life of unity, and our life of growing incorporation into divine existence is also a single whole which death may interrupt but not rupture.

3

᛫᛫᛫᛫᛫

THE MANNER OF
OUR LIKENING

W ith the conclusion of the doctrine of the Trinity, Aquinas turns his attention to
creation. Characteristically, the border between the doctrine of God and the doctrine of creation is indistinct. As the questions treating trinitarian doctrine drew heavily,
especially at first, on the doctrine of the one God, so the opening questions on creation
seem to flow uninterruptedly from the doctrine of the Trinity just concluded. Indeed,
so seamless is the fabric that drawing any sort of line between Questions 43 and 44 may
seem rather arbitrary. The absence of such sharp division is itself significant, for it suggests the close connection of Creator and creature that constitutes the heart of theosis.[1]

I. Nature

1. Creation

Thomas' doctrine of creation accomplishes two tasks essential to his account of creation:
it stipulates that creation results from divine desire rather than necessity, and it grounds
participation in divine Nature in the creature's very existence. The first point dictates
that while he readily uses the term *emanation*, he takes pains to distance himself from classical emanationism, the second indicates a view of participation rather more comprehensive than that of the Fathers.

As he begins to consider the emanation of things from the First Principle (Question
45), the terms in which he describes the necessary dependence of creation on God may,
especially as the question progresses, seem fundamentally Aristotelian in their reliance
on causal analysis. In the first article, however, Thomas' language sounds akin to that of

a Neoplatonist. This terminology is also, however, strongly reminiscent of the classic lexis of divinization:

> It must be said that every being in any way existing is from God. For whatever is found in anything by participation, must be caused by that to which it belongs essentially, as iron becomes ignited by fire. . . . Therefore all beings apart from God are not their own being, but are beings by participation [non sint suum esse, sed participant esse]. Therefore it must be that all things which are diversified by the diverse participation of being, so as to be more or less perfect, are caused by the one First Being, Who possesses being most perfectly. (I.44,1 resp.)

In a sense, the Thomistic understanding of participation in divine life radically exceeds classic notions of theosis in its scope, for participation in divine life occurs initially not as the sanctifying work of hypostatic union in the Son or graced renewal in the Spirit but in order for the creature to exist at all. Traditionally, divinization insists upon a continuity between sanctified existence in this life and consummate union in the next. Aquinas extends the participatory link backwards, portraying the creature as participating in divine being from the first moment of her existence, in virtue of that very existence; it is this participation which provides, logically, the base for all other varieties or degrees of participation in divine being, such as the renewal by grace and the extension of grace mentioned in I.43,6.

That this participation in being is no spontaneous eruption of divine being but God's deliberate will, Thomas makes manifest in the article on exemplary causality:

> God is the first exemplar cause of all things. In proof whereof we must consider that if for the production of any thing an exemplar is necessary, it is in order that the effect may receive a determinate form. . . . Now it is manifest that things made by nature receive determinate forms. This determination of forms must be reduced to the divine wisdom as its first principle, for divine wisdom devised the order of the universe, which order consists in the variety of things. And therefore we must say that in the divine wisdom are the types of all things, which types we have called ideas—i.e., exemplar forms existing in the divine mind. And these ideas, though multiplied by their relations to things, in reality are not apart from the divine essence, according as the likeness to that essence can be shared diversely by different things. (I.44,3 resp.)

For God to have made the world, then, he must have had a specific idea of the diverse creatures he intended to fashion, an intentionality that sits ill with a classic emanationist view, since Thomas has separated the thinking of the forms from their production.

While the argument with emanationism is not particularly significant for our purposes, the element of divine intentionality is, for this notion provides the underpinning of the Thomistic conception of God as final cause. In the following article, Thomas quotes Proverbs 16:4: "The Lord has made all things for Himself" (I.44,4 s.c.) and continues in the response: "Every agent acts for an end." God's agency differs from others in that he does not desire to acquire any end but intends only to communicate his perfection, which is his goodness. Creatures, on the other hand, intend to acquire their own perfection. Since this perfection is the likeness of divine perfection and goodness, the divine goodness must be the end of all things (I.44,4 resp.). The purpose of creation, then, is that all things become good and perfect and that all things find their consummation in divine goodness, which is none other than the divine essence (I.6,3). These two purposes are in reality the same, of course, for to become perfect, to become truly good, is to become God, and to be likened to God, at least as Thomas understands God is necessarily to become good and perfect.

The prime label for the distinction between creation and creation's Source and End is the idea of creation as *ex nihilo* (I.45,1 and 2). This constitutes no more than a restatement, in the context of the doctrine of creation, of his first and most important assertion about God, namely that God is the One whose essence is identical with his existence. God alone is necessary being; all else derives its being from God. This derivation, however, is not Being's involuntary, automatic outpouring but the result of God's act of creating from nothing. In creation, then, we have not the subdivision of the divine into lesser parcels called creatures but the consequence of a voluntary divine act: "Creation signified actively means the divine action, which is God's essence, with a relation to the creature" (I.45,3 ad 1). It is because creation is the expression of divine will, bringing something to be out of nothing, rather than the necessary outflow of Being reproducing itself according to the dictates of its nature, that Thomas can claim, as he did in I.13, a one-way ontological relationship between God and creature so that God's relation to the creature is understood as a purely conceptual relation, while the creature's relation to God is real (I.45.3 ad 1).[2]

The significance of Aquinas' repetition of this point becomes clearer when we reach Article 6, for there he begins to expound a correspondence between trinitarian procession and creation. Had this article not been preceded by the articles asserting God's utter independence of the world, Thomas would risk leaving the impression of a necessary relation between God and the world. Instead, the strong affirmation of creation *ex nihilo* clears the way for a typology with no ontological pretensions.

The intention of this doctrine is not so much to trace attractive mirror images in distinct areas of doctrine as to assert the unity of the Trinity's action *ad extra*: the act of creation belongs properly to the whole Trinity, not only one of the Persons (I.45,6 resp.).[3] Yet Aquinas clarifies, noting that although creation is the common work of the Three, it should not be taken as the work of the Three undivided; indeed, the nature of the Trinity's structure imposes a certain order in creation, because that procession imposes a certain kind of causality:

> The divine Persons, according to the nature of their procession, have a causality respecting the creation of things. . . . God the Father made the creature through His Word, which is His Son; and through His Love, which is the Holy Ghost. And so the processions of the Persons are the type [rationes] of the productions of creatures inasmuch as they include the essential attributes, knowledge, and will. (I.45,6 resp.)

Because of this typology, it is possible to say not only that the Trinity creates but also that the processions of the divine Persons are the cause of creation (I.45,6 ad 1).

As creation goes, so goes the creature. The structure of the human person mimics the divine procession, not because it is ontologically derived from the Trinity but because it is the Trinity's reflection:

> The processions of the divine Persons are referred to the acts of intellect and will. . . . For the Son proceeds as the word of the intellect ; and the Holy Ghost proceeds as the love of the will. Therefore in rational creatures, possessing intellect and will, there is found the representation of the Trinity by way of image [repraesentatio Trinitatis per modum

imaginis], inasmuch as there is found in them the word conceived, and the love proceeding. (I.45,7 resp.)

What Aquinas has chiefly sought to assert in Question 45 has been the creature's origin in the creator; however, in specifying the nature of that causality, he has established the first principle of his anthropology, as is well illustrated when he continues on from the passage just quoted: "In all creatures there is found the trace of the Trinity [repraesentatio Trinitatis per modum vestigii], inasmuch as in every creature are found some things which are necessarily reduced to the divine Persons as their cause" (ibid.). In Thomas' epistemology, then, we first heard hints of his anthropology.[4] Thomas' own priority seems to lie in establishing the fact of causality, yet the nature of the causality as he elaborates it will prove highly significant for our purposes. This is what the traces of the Trinity look like in a human being:

> For every creature subsists in its own being, and has a form, whereby it is determined to a species, and has a relation to something else. Therefore as it is a created substance, it represents the cause and principle; and so in that manner it shows the Person of the Father, Who is the *principle from no principle*. According as it has a form and species, it represents the Word as the form of the thing made by art is from the conception of the craftsman. According as it has a relation of order, it represents the Holy Ghost, inasmuch as He is love, because the order of the effect to something else is from the will of the Creator. (I.45,7 resp.)

The traces of the Trinity in the creature determined four important points in the Thomistic anthropology, therefore. First, the paternal element signifies that the human person is a creature whose origin lies in the divine principle; the creature's relation to God as effect establishes an ontological divide between the two that is eternal and inviolable, just as the Father's relation of origin in respect to the Son and Spirit is eternal and unchangeable. Second, the human species has a particular connection to the Second Person, representing the form of that Person in creation; it is therefore to Christ we look to understand what it means to be a human being as human beings were intended to be in the mind of God. Third, it is through the Holy Spirit that we are to understand the nature of our relatedness to God; it is the work of the Spirit, Thomas here implies, to preserve and strengthen that relation. Fourth, the relatedness between God and humanity, being through the Third Person, is established and strengthened particularly through love; we thus find here confirmation that love will prove especially important to Thomas' account of how the effect returns to its cause and the source of its being.

2. Imago Dei

That the divine tracery in the human person is closely related to the Thomistic view of God as final cause becomes manifest much later in the *Prima Pars*. Significantly, it is not until Question 93 that Aquinas begins his exposition of what was perhaps the single most important element of patristic anthropology, the doctrine of the *imago Dei*. Two preliminary points demand our attention before we turn to Thomas' treatment of the image of God in humanity. The first has just been suggested: for Aquinas the significance of the divine image in the human person does not lie principally in the way it describes humanity's prelapsarian state.[5] The theological import of the *imago Dei* lies not in how we are ordered to this life or what we were intended to be before we turned from God, but how we are ordered to our end. The *imago Dei* theology tells us primarily what we will be, not what we are.

The second point is that although Question 93 constitutes Thomas' initial formal broaching of the doctrine of the image in humanity, he has long before this point laid extensive groundwork for this locus. Since we have already examined much of this material, we need not review it in detail but need only trace this thread lightly so as to highlight the disparate points at which Aquinas has touched on this theme. He began in I.4,3, where he maintained that the likeness of creatures to God was by analogy and solely by analogy; we have just seen the full exposition of this position in his treatment of emanation. We saw it again in I.6, where Thomas claimed a relation between divine goodness and all other goodness, the latter participating in the exemplary and effective cause of goodness by way of an assimilation nonetheless remote and defective. In I.8, he affirmed the existence of God in all things by presence, essence and power, both as efficient cause and as the object of operation is in the operator (I.8,3 resp.). Finally, as we saw, I.45 claims an analogy of structure between the Trinity and the human person. None of these assertions in itself constitutes a doctrine of the *imago Dei*, of course. Nevertheless, all bear some resemblance to elements of that doctrine and show an affinity for its central claims. If Aquinas waits until I.93 to give the doctrine formal treatment, he has certainly hinted strongly at it from the earliest pages of the *Prima Pars*.[6]

His formal treatment begins on the same note we observed initially in Question 45, the uniqueness of God: "Equality does not belong to the essence of an image . . . . in man, there is some likeness to God, copied from God as from an exemplar; yet this likeness is not one of equality, for such an exemplar infinitely excels its copy. Therefore there is in man a likeness to God; not, indeed, a perfect likeness, but imperfect" (I.93,1 resp.). His reason is clear-cut; he wishes to preserve the uniqueness of divine nature and therefore reserves the perfect likeness to God, which could only exist in an identical nature, for Christ (I.93,1 ad 2). This affirmation echoes Question 35, on Christ as the perfect image of God. Aquinas' doctrine of the image therefore emphasizes both the unity of Persons in the Trinity (the Father and Son sharing divine essence) and humanity's simultaneous ontological distinction from and likeness to the divine Creator, a dual emphasis, both of whose distinctive impulses emerge strongly in the objections, first one pole and then the other, as if Aquinas must constantly struggle to remind the reader (and perhaps even himself) of both polarities. Thus the reply to the second objection states of the image: "It exists in man as in an alien nature," while the third proclaims: "As unity means absence of division, a species is said to be the same as far as it is one. Now a thing is said to be one not only numerically, specifically, or generically, but also according to a certain analogy or proportion. In this sense a creature is one with God, or like to Him [sic est unitas vel convenientia creaturae ad Deum]."

No more than an analogous unity can be predicated of the image because, properly speaking, a true image requires likeness of species (I.93,2 resp.). While humanity does not share species with God, human beings differ from the rest of the created world (with the exception of the angels) in possessing a higher degree of likeness to God. Likeness in virtue of existence and life is a fairly low level of likeness. What Aquinas considers far more important is the likeness in virtue of knowledge and understanding, a likeness possessed solely by intellectual creatures who alone, therefore, are properly regarded as made in the divine image (I.93,2 resp.). Indeed, this intellectual element is so important that it is what determines the angels' possessing a greater likeness to God than humanity does (I.93,3 resp.).

The significance of the intellect for the doctrine of the *imago Dei* does not lie principally in the way it distinguishes amongst degrees of likeness in creation, however, but in the way intellectual activity in the human person imitates the internal processions of the Trinity:

> Since man is said to be to the image of God by reason of his intellectual nature, he is the most perfectly like God according to that in which he can best imitate God in his intellectual nature. Now the intellectual nature imitates God chiefly in this, that God understands and loves Himself. Wherefore we see that the image of God is in man in three ways. First, inasmuch as man possesses a natural aptitude for understanding and loving God; and this aptitude consists in the very nature of the mind, which is common to all men. Secondly, inasmuch as man actually or habitually knows and loves God, though imperfectly; and this image consists in the conformity of grace. Thirdly, inasmuch as man knows and loves God perfectly; and this image consists in the likeness of glory. (I.93,4 resp.)

Aquinas here traces a three-step process of likening to God, from a likeness embedded in our nature, to a likeness that increases in this life through grace, to a likeness in the next life, when the human imitation of the Trinity's knowing and loving will be perfected. Two elements of Thomas' exposition here are striking. The first is that the three steps strongly suggest (though Aquinas himself makes little of it) an unbroken continuity. The implication is that one level of likeness depends on the other and that each succeeding level contains the preceding one within it, so that the likeness of glory encompasses also the likenesses of grace and nature. Second, although Aquinas began by stressing the intellect's significance for the likeness in this article, he has executed a subtle shift. The intellectual nature that imitates God now functions not only through the processes of understanding but also of loving, an activity that in the doctrine of the Trinity was associated exclusively with the functioning of the will. The *imago Dei*, Thomas seems to be saying, lies not solely in humanity's possession of intellectual capacities but in the possession of a rational nature broadly conceived so as to encompass the activities of both the mind and the will. (Compare Aquinas' definition of the will as a rational appetite in I.82,5 resp.) The shift of emphasis from the intellect alone to both intellect and will also recalls Thomas' doctrine of the Trinity, a suggestion confirmed by the subsequent article.

"The distinction of the Divine Persons is suitable to the Divine Nature," Aquinas reminds us in Article 5:

> and therefore to be to the image of God by imitation of the Divine Nature does not exclude being to the same image by the representation of the Divine Persons: but rather one follows from the other. We must, therefore, say that in man there exists the image of God, both as regards the Divine Nature and as regards the Trinity of Persons. (I.93,5 resp.)

Here Aquinas provides the reader with precise instructions for understanding the relation between his *De Deo uno* and his *De Trinitate* on the one hand, and his anthropology on the other. From the *De Deo uno*, he takes his definition of God as the one in whom essence and existence are identical, who is the supremely cognitive being in virtue of his immateriality and his conception of analogy; from the *De Trinitate*, he takes the processes of knowing and loving as the structure of both the entity itself (the Trinity and the human person) and its relatedness *ad extra* (the procession of the Trinity and humanity's relation to God through a progressive likening). Properly and fully to understand both humanity and humanity's link to God, therefore, we must take into account the whole of the Thomistic description of God. There is in this mode of doing theology already an intimation of a doctrine of deification, for Aquinas is claiming that we must look to God to see our truest self. In the one God as in the Trinity, we find not only divine perfection but the perfect model of humanity. To look to God is therefore to understand both what we are and what we are meant to be, both our natural condition and what we are to become.

In Article 5, this second element of the promise contained in the image is only dimly implicit, in that the divine perfection of which the human person falls short indicates what we would resemble but for that shortcoming. In later articles, however, Thomas dwells in some detail on the side of becoming, furnishing the reader with an important preview of the yet to be developed doctrine of sanctification. As Aquinas searches for the image of the Trinity in the soul, he finds it, not in the soul at rest, but in the soul in action:

> If the image of the Trinity is to be found in the soul, we must look for it where the soul approaches nearest to a representation of the species of the Divine Persons. Now the Divine Persons are distinct from each other by reason of the procession of the Word from the Speaker, and the procession of Love connecting Both. But in our soul word *cannot exist without actual thought*, as Augustine says. Therefore, first and chiefly, the image of the Trinity is to be found in the acts of the soul, that is, inasmuch as from the knowledge which we possess, by actual thought we form an internal word; and thence break forth into love. But, since the principles of acts are the habits and powers, and everything exists virtually in its principle, therefore, secondarily and consequently, the image of the Trinity may be considered as existing in the powers, and still more in the habits, forasmuch as the acts virtually exist therein. (I.93,7 resp.)

In Article 7, then, Aquinas effectively sets in motion the vast machinery of the *Secunda Pars*, with its treatment of habits and virtues. If we read the *Secunda Pars* in light of Question 93, we come to understand that the treatise on the habits and virtues is not, in the Thomistic scheme of things, a study of human endeavor—not even, in the first instance, graced human endeavor—but rather an extended meditation on the trinitarian processions. Indeed, Aquinas goes so far as to use the term *procession* of the human soul's activity, a procession of the word in the intellect, and a procession of love in the will, which in itself constitutes a created image or representation of the uncreated Trinity (I.93,6 resp.). As the mission of the Three reflects the internal processes of the Trinity, so does the internal activity of the human person reflect them, albeit imperfectly. Because the most important way in which the soul reflects the Trinity is in its activity, Thomas claims that it is in the acquisition and exercise of the habits that we most completely image God. The corollary of this claim is that the image of God is something whose fulness we grow towards. The *imago Dei* is no static endowment, a given to be taken for granted, but principally, what we become in virtue of the acquisition and exercise of habits, and secondarily, the natural precondition of the development and exercise of those habits.

If our study of the doctrine of God and the Trinity had not persuaded us that the treatise on the virtues would prove a crucial link between those doctrines and the anthropology, we have decisive proof now. The means by which we know and love God are the very means by which we mirror God in the world and the means by which we are made most like to God. Thomas states this conviction as succinctly and definitively in the response of I.93,8: "We refer the Divine image in man to the verbal concept born of the knowledge of God, and to the love derived therefrom. Thus the image of God is found in the soul according as the soul turns to God, or possesses a nature that enables it to turn to God." On the essential base of the trinitarian likeness which is the soul's capacity to know and love is fashioned an image that comes more and more to resemble God; this growing resemblance will come about through exercise of the habits, but it will be God's work, not that of the human person herself since the knowledge and love of God can exist in us only at God's good pleasure (I.93,8 ad 3). Ever so fleetingly, Aquinas alerts the reader to another theme that will prove highly determinative of his anthropology and his account of sanctification: his doctrine of grace.

Before we leave his treatment of the image for the treatise on habits and virtues, we need to note one other passing reference in Question 93 that foreshadows later developments. As we have seen, Thomas often employs some of the classic terminology of deification, such as participation and union, to describe the nature of the soul's relation to God. He does not neglect to speak of the *imago Dei* in these very terms at the end of his formal treatment of the image: "Likeness is a kind of unity, for oneness in quality causes likeness"[7] (I.93,9 resp.). Lest any reader take Thomas to be claiming in his doctrine of the image only some general affinity of the creature for the Creator, he here removes all question of such interpretation. Throughout Question 93, he has built steadily on groundwork already laid to bring us to this vantage point in the *Summa*, from which we look both backwards and forwards. The backwards glance reveals the doctrines of God and of the Trinity and tells us what we are to become: a likeness of divine nature and the Trinity. The forward glance opens up the vista of the *Secunda Pars*, whose treatment of habit, virtue and grace will tell us how this likening will be accomplished.

II. Grace

The cumulative sequence of nature-grace-glory describes humanity's growth towards God in the Thomistic vision. If nature predominated in the First Part, grace is the great theme of the Second. The link between nature and grace is, in a sense, the theory of habits, for when grace becomes ingrained, second nature as it were, the result is virtue.

1. Habits and Virtues

The progression from nature through grace to glory implies a dynamic view of humanity's relation to God, and it is in virtue of that dynamic that Thomas claims we need habits when we need to maintain a consistency in moving towards a goal. Aquinas follows Averroes in maintaining that habits are the means by which the will is able to act (I-II.49,3 s.c.).[8] We need such habits, or dispositions, when the object of desire differs in nature from the desiring subject:

> For a thing to need to be disposed to something else, three conditions are necessary. The
> first condition is that which is disposed should be distinct from that to which it is dis-

posed; and so, that it should be related to it as potentiality is to act. . . . The second condition is, that that which is in a state of potentiality in regard to something else, be capable of determination in several ways and to various things. . . . The third condition is that in disposing the subject to one of those things to which it is in potentiality several things should occur, capable of being adjusted in various ways: so as to dispose the subject well or ill to its form or to its operation. (I-II.49,4 resp.)

These three conditions clearly apply to our subject, the soul's growth towards resemblance of God, for in order to attain the end of beatitude, the soul will need to disposed towards it by habit.

At the root of the habits lie the two familiar principles of intellect and will. Intellect makes its appearance in the first instance because it is the means by which we apprehend God, and one cannot move towards an end which one cannot conceive. The mind is not only the locus of beatitude, however; it is also the seat of the will and in that capacity, determines our growth in virtue in this life. Original righteousness, in Thomas' view, requires creation in grace because original righteousness consists in the reason's subjection to God (I.95,1 resp.). The relation between intellect and will is not entirely straightforward, for each one moves the other. The will moves the intellect in respect to the carrying out of acts, but the intellect determines what acts will be carried out, and thus in one sense, may be said to move the will (I-II.9,1 ad 3). This sustenance of the mind in grace is nothing other than virtue itself: "Now the virtues are nothing but those perfections whereby reason is directed to God, and the inferior powers regulated according to the dictate of reason" (I.95,3 resp.). To grow in virtue, two things are therefore needful: reason and grace.

It is because the will operates under the aegis of reason that we can will a variety of things, indeed anything that the reason apprehends as good (I-II.13,6 resp.). Since the mind can perceive good in many things, so can the will tend toward them, or decline them, finding them lacking. Since few things are wholly good or bad, the will can freely choose amongst a great variety of things. When a thing is wholly good, however, the will cannot but incline towards it: "The perfect good alone, which is Happiness, cannot be apprehended by the reason as an evil, or as lacking in any way. Consequently man wills Happiness of necessity, nor can he will not to be happy, or to be unhappy." Yet since this willing of happiness is the willing of a means, not an end (ibid.), there is no necessary constancy in how we go about finding happiness.

Because the end we desire exceeds us, we need a principle of habit that also exceeds us:

Some habits are infused by God into man . . . because there are some habits by which man is disposed to an end which exceeds the proportion of human nature, namely, the ultimate and perfect happiness of man. . . . And since such habits need to be in proportion with that to which man is disposed by them, therefore it is necessary that those habits, which dispose to this end, exceed the proportion of human nature. Wherefore such habits can never be in man except by Divine infusion, as is the case with all gratuitous virtues. (I-II.51,4 resp.)[9]

In order to attain to God, therefore, we require infused virtue. The element of infusion, or the need for grace, we will examine later. For the moment we focus on the role of virtue in the journey to God, temporarily bracketing the no less important question of how we come by such virtue. Aquinas divides the virtues into three large groups: the intellectual, the moral and the theological. Of these, it is the particular task of only one group, the theological, to direct us towards God. For this reason, we need not consider the intellectual or moral virtues, important though they are to Thomas' system as a whole. It is the theological virtues which, by definition, direct us to God: "Faith, hope, and charity are virtues directing us to God. Therefore they are theological virtues" (I-II.62,1 s.c.).

The virtues, then, are central to deification and among the virtues, the theological take pride of place. Faith, hope and charity are, moreover, inseparable from one another in this life:

> Charity signifies not only the love of God, but also a certain friendship with Him [amicitiam quandum ad ipsum]; which implies, besides love, a certain mutual return of love, together with mutual communion [communicatione mutua]. . . . Now this fellowship of man with God, which consists in a certain familiar colloquy with Him, is begun here, in this life, by grace [inchoatur quidem hic in praesenti per gratiam], but will be perfected in the future life, by glory; each of which things we hold by faith and hope. Wherefore just as friendship with a person would be impossible, if one disbelieved in, or despaired of, the possibility of their fellowship or familiar colloquy; so too, friendship with God, which is charity, is impossible without faith, so as to believe in this fellowship and colloquy with God and hope to attain to this fellowship. Therefore charity is quite impossible without faith and hope. (I-II.65,5 resp.)

In this life, then, both the faculties of intellect and will must be graced and formed in virtue if we are to participate fully in the life of the Trinity. Similarly, charity cannot exist without the moral virtues (I-II.65,3), but Aquinas' grounds for claiming this say more about charity's priority among the virtues than its dependence on the others:

> All moral virtues are infused together with charity. . . . Charity, inasmuch as it directs man to his last end, is the principle of all the good works that are referable to his last end. Wherefore all the moral virtues must needs be infused together with charity, since it is through them that man performs each different kind of good work. (I-II.65,3 resp.)

Thus charity cannot exist without the other virtues because it is their common denominator: the infused moral virtues are connected through the cardinal virtue of prudence but also through charity (ibid.). Charity, indeed, is what gives other virtues their authentic character:

> It is possible by means of human works to acquire moral virtues. . . . But in so far as they produce good works in proportion to a supernatural last end, thus they have the character of virtue, truly and perfectly; and cannot be acquired by human acts, but are infused by God. Such like moral virtues cannot be without charity. (I-II.65,2 resp.)

Thomas' account of the relations obtaining amongst the virtues thus consistently underlines three points: the reversion of all virtue to charity, even though charity never stands alone; the need for true virtue to be infused by God rather than acquired by human effort; and the principle of the last end as determinative of the character of virtue.

2. Charity

While charity functions as the fulcrum of the treatise on habits, the latter does not contain Thomas' treatment of love in its entirety. Love in its divine aspect appears in the

Prima Pars, as we have seen, and love makes its first appearance in the anthropology in the treatise on the passions. Despite the wide range of contexts in which Thomas treats love and the several definitions he gives it, a coherent vision emerges from the Summa, a vision in which charity appears more centrally than in any other Christian theology.

Before we turn to these definitions, we will need to grasp two basic assumptions that undergird all his thought about charity. The first is the relation between love and knowledge, intellect and will. We have seen this principle operating in the De Trinitate; in the anthropology, Thomas draws even more insistently on Augustine's maxim that there can be no love without knowledge. The second is the Platonic insight that love implies a kind of likeness.

The significance of the first of these assumptions is evident in that his turn to love, and therefore the will, by no means indicates that he has ruled out a vital role for the intellect, for he gives the clearest account of the necessary relation between love and knowledge. He begins by quoting Augustine: "None can love what he does not know" (I-II.27,2 s.c.), and continues, "Good is the cause of love, as being its object. But good is not the object of the appetite, except as apprehended. And therefore love demands some apprehension of the good that is loved . . . . Accordingly knowledge is the cause of love for the same reason as good is, which can be loved only if known" (I-II.27,2 resp.). Aquinas here establishes a hierarchy: as love's precursor, knowledge is essential, but it is not unitive in the way love is. The pattern here of the relation between the intellect and will with respect to humanity's term is precisely the relation of faith, hope and charity with respect to beatitude. Charity cannot be without faith and hope, but the latter are not significant in the afterlife as is charity, for they have no place there. The intellect does not cease to function in the life of glory, but it does not attain to perfection, as love does, and this absence of perfection seems in no way to detract from the consummation of the next life:

> Something is required for the perfection of knowledge, that is not requisite for the perfection of love. For knowledge belongs to the reason, whose function it is to distinguish things that in reality are united, and to unite together, after a fashion, things that are distinct, by comparing one with another. Consequently the perfection of knowledge requires that man should know distinctly all that is in a thing, such as its parts, powers and properties. On the other hand, love is in the appetitive power, which regards a thing as it is in itself: wherefore it suffices, for the perfection of love, that a thing be loved according as it is known in itself. Hence it is, therefore, that a thing is loved more than it is known; since it can be loved perfectly, even without being perfectly known. (I-II.27,2 ad 2)

Although knowledge necessarily precedes love, then, it seems love can eventually overtake knowledge, so to speak, for if one can love that which one does not know fully, then one's love is going where no knowledge has gone before, and that love is no longer founded on knowledge.

If we place the preceding passage in the context of Thomas' doctrine of God, an even more important point emerges. Since, as we have seen, simplicity is the key element of the De Deo uno, human knowledge would appear to be particularly ill-suited to fostering fellowship with God. The intellect's modus operandi, as Aquinas describes it here, consists in dismantling, in reducing things to their component parts. While Thomistic epistemology makes clear that the assignation of distinct categories to divine being is not an illegitimate or inherently misleading enterprise, he maintains with equal steadfastness that such division reflects the structure of our minds and not God's own nature. Knowledge, as described in I-II.27,2, therefore, can never apprehend God as he truly is. Love, in contrast, can attain to perfect union.

The second fundamental assumption concerns the relation between Love and Beloved: "Likeness, properly speaking, is a cause of love," Thomas declares in the response to I-II.27,3. Although he distinguishes between two kinds of likeness, the second kind clearly does not refer to love between God and humanity inasmuch as it causes concupiscence or is based on usefulness or pleasure. The first kind of likeness causes love of friendship or well-being; this kind of likeness does not arise from one party's possessing only potentially what the other possesses actually but from "each thing having the same quality actually" (I.II.27,3 resp.). This distinction between potential and actual possession and the identification of the latter with the love of friendship reinforces the doctrine of image: friendship is not identical with likeness, but likeness forms the basis on which friendship is built.

The significance of these assumptions for Thomas' doctrine of theosis is readily apparent. In the case of the first, we see that in simultaneously deeming charity as the chief of the deiform virtues and connecting it inextricably to knowledge, Thomas has pointed to the connection between theology and anthropology. As Word and Love are inseparable in the Trinity, so knowledge and love are inseparable in humanity's ascent to God; it is through the interrelationship of intellect and will that we are bound to God, just as the Persons of the Trinity are bound to one another in knowledge and love. Second, loving presupposes likeness. Our relation to God is therefore determined, inasmuch as it is a relationship in love, by some kind of similarity between God and humanity, between the fundamentally dissimilar Uncreated and created.

We see both these foundations at work in the definition of love Thomas gives in the treatise on the passions. Here he is working at a very general level, defining love broadly enough to include eros, agape and every other form of love. He equates love with desire, a movement towards an object that culminates in joy. Love in this sense can be called a passion because it "consists in a change wrought in the appetite by the appetible object" (I.II.26,2 resp.). Thus, love is defined by its origins in the will, its transformative effects and its consummation in joy.

Such a definition necessarily leads to another, of love as union. Aquinas quotes Denys: "Every love is a unitive force [virtus unitiva]" (I-II.28, 1 s.c.) and even finds support for this view in Aristotle, who says that union is the work of love (I-II.26,2 ad 2). Union belongs to love insofar as, by reason of the complacency of the appetite, the lover stands in relation to that which he loves, as though it were himself or part of himself. Love and union are by no means identical. Aquinas' view of love does not stress rest as much as it stresses progression, as witnessed by the formulaic definition of love he gives in Article 1; namely, it is the principle of movement towards the end loved (I-II.26,1 resp.). Yet while union is the result of love rather than love itself, this result is, in Thomas' mind, definitive of its agent. This Thomistic pattern fits exactly the model of deification, emphasizing the dynamic transformation of the subject as it is drawn into fellowship with the divine.

If union belongs to the classic lexis of theosis, Thomas' second synonym for love, friendship, does not. His base definition of charity is his own and it is this conception of love that forms the centre of his doctrine of sanctification. Drawing on the saying of

Christ in the Gospel of John, "I will now not call you servants. . . but my friends," Aquinas declares: "Therefore charity is friendship" (II-II.23,1 s.c.). This definition extends well beyond Thomas' sources, for Paul in his disquisition on charity in his first letter to the Corinthians (chap. 13) does not speak of charity in such a way as to imply it is a form of friendship, and Aristotle in his treatise on friendship in the *Nicomachean Ethics* (books VIII and IX) does not consider friendship as either charity or as any relationship between God and humanity.

Thomas, on the other hand, seems to have the divine-human relationship foremost in his mind when he speaks of charity, for he defines it as humanity's friendship for God (II-II.23,1 resp.). Despite the seemingly one-way nature of the relationship implied in this dictum, Aquinas nevertheless clearly believes charity implies a mutuality:

> Neither does well-wishing suffice for friendship, for a certain mutual love is requisite, since friendship is between friend and friend: and this well-wishing is founded on some kind of communication. Accordingly, since there is a communication between man and God, inasmuch as He communicates His happiness to us, some kind of friendship must needs be based on this same communication. . . . The love which is based on this communication, is charity. (Ibid.)

Indeed, Thomas takes the implication of I-II.28,1 and makes it explicit in the subsequent article, where he refers to love as a natural indwelling, in terms that could scarcely be more intimate: "The beloved is contained in the lover, by being impressed on his heart and thus becoming the object of his complacency. On the other hand, the lover is contained in the beloved, inasmuch as the lover penetrates, so to speak, into the beloved"[10] (I-II.28,2 ad 1). What Aquinas' language here demonstrates above all else is that he does not view the friendship of lover and beloved as the joining together of entities that remain ultimately distinct. His language certainly does not suggest a melding of the two such that an amalgam results which is different from either one prior to the union. What he does claim, nevertheless, is a closeness that extends well beyond elective affinity and may aptly be termed participation in being: "Since therefore according to the same author [Denys], every love is a participated likeness of the Divine Love, it seems that every love causes ecstasy" (I.II.28,3 s.c.). Because ecstasy means being placed outside oneself (I.II.28,3 resp.), Thomas has forged a powerful connection between his doctrine of God and his anthropology: as the mission of the Trinity is loving *ek-stasis*, so humanity's love for God entails a going out, into a union that is both genuine and yet preserves distinction.

In these definitions of love, we already see the lineaments of a doctrine of deification. As Thomas explores their implications, he adds flesh to the figure. The first of these implications is the relation between sanctification and consummation, a consummation he sees evident in manifold ways. We saw intimations of this in the idea that love culminates in joy and in the definition of love as ecstasy. Most powerfully, we saw it in the claim that charity is based on communication. The ground for the claim that charity entails communication, and therefore mutuality, thus lies in the first instance at least, in God's communication of beatitude. That grounding establishes two principles: first, the initiative in divine-human relations lies entirely on the divine side, and second, beatitude is taken as the prime indicator of God's desire for friendship. One does not infer eternal communion on the basis of divine charity but charity from the fact of eternal communion. Nor does one infer humanity's love for God on the basis of human nature but rather a mutual relation between God and humanity on the basis of God's desire for it.

God's desire for fellowship reaches its fulfilment in the next life but is firmly grounded here. Aquinas expresses this conviction in two ways: first, in that fellowship is only possible in virtue of capacities granted us in creation, and second, in that charity exists in some form even now:

> Man's life is twofold. There is his outward life in respect of his sensitive and corporeal nature. . . . The other is man's spiritual life in respect of his mind, and with regard to this life there is fellowship between us and both God and the angels, imperfectly indeed in this present state of life. . . . Therefore charity is imperfect here, but will be perfected in heaven. (II-II.23,1 resp.)

While love is uniquely unitive, Thomas shows the intellect also plays a powerful role. The end of both is union, and while in this life that union is imperfect, it is not fundamentally dissimilar from the consummation of the Age to Come. In Aquinas' view, God does indeed make us for himself, creating of our nature itself the road to paradise.

Charity's connection to consummation is further demonstrated in Thomas' view of charity's relation to other virtues. What makes virtuous acts lacking in charity less than perfect, for example, is not that charity per se is the precondition of all true virtue but that only charity directs the person to her proper end.[11] Aquinas here parts company with Augustine, whom he quotes and who finds all acts of unbelievers sinful because they lack faith. The comparison with Augustine highlights the character of the Summa not only because the Bishop of Hippo deems the lack of faith the decisive factor, whereas for Aquinas it is charity, but also because Augustine's line of reasoning requires no reference to consummation. For Aquinas, in contrast, faith cannot be the argument's pivot because faith will pass away and thus says nothing of virtue's purpose, which is endless communion with God.

Similarly, charity is said to be the form of other virtues because it directs the acts of all other virtues to the last end (II-II.23,8 resp.). Charity does not direct virtues to an end that somehow differs from itself, moreover: "Charity is said to be the end of the virtues, because it directs all other virtues to its own end" (II-II.23,8 ad 3; my emphasis), nor does it urge the virtues from a point of departure alien to itself: "Charity is called the mother of the other virtues because, by commanding them, it conceives the acts of the other virtues, by the desire of the last end"[12] (ibid.). Charity is both the inception and the end of virtue—the beginning, the end and the form, therefore, of all human sanctification and the means of all human transport to beatitude.

Thomas posits a further, and even more fundamental, connection between charity and eternity and in so doing provides a further strong link between sanctification and consummation:

> In none [of the ways Thomas envisages a thing's limitations] is a limit imposed to the increase of man's charity, while he is in the state of a wayfarer. For charity itself considered as such has no limit to its increase, since it is a participation of the infinite charity which is the Holy Ghost [est enim participatio quaedam infinitae caritas, qui est Spiritus Sanctus]. In like manner the cause of the increase of charity, viz., God, is possessed of infinite power. Furthermore, on the part of its subject, no limit to this increase can be determined, because whenever charity increases, there is a corresponding increased ability to receive a further increase. It is therefore evident that it is not possible to fix any limits to the increase of charity in this life. (II-II.24,7 resp.)

The scenario Aquinas here describes closely resembles Gregory of Nyssa's notion of epectasy, although Thomas makes no mention of Nyssa in this article. The notion of perpetual growth, however, inherently suggests the seamless continuity of grace and glory, for it claims that there is a single development in the human person, which has a terminus a quo but no terminus ad quem. Each human being thus possesses one life, which is nothing other than a never-ending process of growth towards God.

As infinity characterizes eternal life, so does perfection. In answer to the question of whether charity can be perfect in this life, he gives a response that is in some ways surprising: yes. Thomas' anthropology, after all, diverged from Augustine's in that the bishop located the need for grace solely in the creature's fallen state, whereas Aquinas maintained that even without the Fall, the creature would have needed grace because without it her finite nature could never have attained to the Infinite. Article 8 of Question 24 demonstrates that the cautiousness of this anthropology by no means constitutes pessimism. Thomas' affirmation of the possibility of perfecting charity in this life is complex, resting upon a distinction, as usual. Thus, while the human person can love God perfectly with respect to her own capacities and in this way possess perfect charity, she can never love God as much as God is lovable, which is as much as God loves himself. This distinction notably allows Aquinas again to stress both of deification's poles, as well as the continuity between this life and the next. Inasmuch as God's charity remains unique, Thomas sustains the distinction between Uncreated and created; inasmuch as human creatures are deemed perfectible, and indeed perfectible during their earthly life, true deification is declared possible, for theosis is nothing other than the attainment of God's own perfect being[13]; finally, since "the perfection of the way is not perfection simply, wherefore it can always increase" (II-II.24,8 ad 3), Thomas reiterates the endlessness of human growth towards God, which is nothing other than human participation in the Inexhaustible.[14]

A further way in which he connects the charity of this life to that of the next is by insisiting that charity is a single entity binding us to God through glorification and to our neighbor and ourselves through sanctification: the act of loving God and loving our neighbor is *specifically* the same act (II-II.25,1 resp.). The appeal here to God as, in effect, the final cause of all love suggests both love's unity and also the way in which earthly love directs us immediately and essentially to God, participation in whom constitutes our glorification.

A second set of implications of Aquinas' definition of love with import for the doctrine of deification is his discussion of the ontological divide. In his treatment of charity, Thomas works from the same paradigm that informs his position on beatitude and grace. Without admitting any real division, he insists upon the creatureliness of the creature by maintaining that whatever is truly incorporated into the creature must be viewed as created. Contra Lombard, he argues that charity is something created in the soul, not the Holy Spirit *ipse* dwelling in the mind. Thomas' reason for rejecting Lombard's position springs not from any desire to diminish the reality of creaturely participation in the divine but rather to ensure the full and real agency of the human person.[15] Similarly, he will not allow that the Spirit moves the will as an instrument, for such a scenario would also compromise the will's free movement and the creature's distinctiveness and integrity. Instead, he prefers to see God's working by means of structures he himself establishes in the human person: "God, Who moves all things to their due ends, bestowed on each thing the form whereby it is inclined to the end appointed to it by Him; and in this way He *ordereth all things sweetly*" (ibid.).

Nevertheless, Aquinas does not, on the basis of the ontological distinction, claim that there is no supernatural union in the human agent:

> It is evident that the act of charity surpasses the nature of the power of the will, so that, therefore, unless some form be superadded to the natural power, inclining it to the act of love, this same act would be less perfect than the natural acts and the acts of other powers; nor would it be easy and pleasurable to perform. And this is evidently untrue, since no virtue has such a strong inclination to its act as charity has, nor does any virtue perform its act with so great pleasure. Therefore it is most necessary that, for us to perform the act of charity, there should be in us some habitual form superadded to the natural power, inclining that power to the act of charity, and causing it to act with ease and pleasure. (Ibid.)

The key factor here, for our purposes, is the notion of habitual form. This form, as supernatural, is of Uncreated provenance, yet as habitual, becomes fully incorporated into the creature.

Grasping the nature of Thomas' reasoning and the concerns which underlie it is important if we are properly to understand his quarrel with Lombard. His claim that charity is something created in the soul is not intended to deny the reality and indeed, radicality of the relationship between God and humanity. That Thomas sees no contradiction in denying the indwelling of the Spirit in the manner proposed by Lombard and maintaining a true divine-human friendship becomes evident in the replies to the objections. Because the divine essence is identical with charity the charity with which we formally love our neighbor must be a participation of the divine charity (II-II.23,2 ad 1). So strong is Aquinas' sense of charity as the medium of interaction between God and the human person that he even declares: "God is effectively the life both of the soul by charity, and of the body by the soul" (II-II.23,2 ad 2). Not only the soul's internal working, moreover, but also its union with God, results from the divine infusion of charity.[16] Aquinas thus portrays charity as the connection between the realms of time and eternity: charity permits a fellowship of two beings who differ fundamentally. While he rules out, for the sake of preserving the integrity of the person, a kind of possession of the human being by God, he by no means wishes to diminish the reality of participation, as is evident in the very next article: "Charity is superior to the soul, in as much as it is a participation of the Holy Ghost" (II-II.23,3 ad 3).[17]

Thomas' position nevertheless raises a conundrum: how a human person can truly be said to acting freely if charity's dwelling within her is the principle of her love of God and her neighbor and charity is a participation in God? His answer again parallels his reasoning on beatitude and grace. No less than faith, charity has but one object, God (II-II.23,5 s.c.), yet not God considered in himself, but God as humanity's consummation: "Since charity has for its object the last end of human life, viz., everlasting happiness, it follows that it extends to the acts of a man's whole life, by commanding them, not by eliciting immediately all acts of virtue" (II-II.23,4 ad 2). The position here is wholly consistent with Thomas' notion of the attractiveness of goodness: charity does not bring about good but brings it forth. Again, the integrity of the human person is preserved, so that she remains fully and truly human and does not become divinely controlled marionette, while at the same time God remains portrayed as the imitator and perfecter of human activity and of the divine-human friendship.

Where Lombard used the language of indwelling, Aquinas prefers the term *infusion*.[18] With his refusal of Lombard's *indwelling* and his use of a term like *caritas causata* on the one hand, and on the other, his willing employment of the language of infusion, participation and union, Thomas appears to be drawing a firm line of fine distinction, and one way of characterizing that distinction would be to say that he wishes to maintain the closest possible union between God and humanity while at the same time keeping firmly separated Uncreated and created. He does not seem to intend by *caritas causata* that what is infused into the human person differs somehow (essentially, for example) from the charity that is the Divine Essence—at least, he fails to draw the kind of distinction between the two that one might expect, given his predilection for distinctions. His intention seems rather to insist that the human person remains a creature, even though simultaneously a participant in divine nature. What Thomas took to be the significant distinction between the Spirit's infusion and the Spirit's indwelling and why he was content to accept the one designation while adamantly refusing the other remain somewhat ambiguous. One possibility, however, is that since *infusion* is a term associated almost exclusively—at least in the *Summa*—with grace, Thomas prefers it to *indwelling* because it alludes to the fundamental distinction between Creator and creature: the Creator has goodness, charity and existence of himself, whereas the creature has all only through the Creator.

Aquinas uses several different means to stress this distinction between Uncreated and created and on charity as the Creator's proper possession. One, as we have seen, is to insist that the human person's charity is created and infused. Another, obviously closely related, is to maintain that charity is always a gift of grace.[19] So strong is Thomas' conviction on this point that he is even willing to claim a certain arbitrariness in the disposal of gifts: the quantity of charity depends not on any state of the recipient but only on the Spirit's will "who divides according to his will" (ibid.), an exercise of divine inclination that determines the recipient's capacity for grace at every stage of sanctification: "The virtue in accordance with which God gives his Gifts to each one, is a disposition or previous preparation or effort of the one who receives grace. But the Holy Ghost forestalls [praevenit] even this disposition or effort, by moving man's mind either more or less, according as He will" (II-II.24,3 ad 1). Similarly, when Aquinas refers to charity as an accident (II-II.24,4 ad 3), he presumably does not mean it is so in any absolute sense; such an interpretation is ruled out by his previous identification of charity with divine essence. However, his terming charity an accident corresponds with his notion of the human person's charity as created; when charity dwells within a human subject, it remains God's possession and therefore, in some sense, remains an alien element within the human being.

Nevertheless Aquinas is always walking a fine line between the desire to draw very firm distinctions between Creator and creature and the desire, which pulls in the opposite direction, to affirm the reality of interaction between these two ontologically distinct realms. His concern to hold these two poles together in creative tension emerges distinctly in Question 24, where the emphasis in Articles 2 and 3 on the infusion, grace and accidental quality of charity is succeeded immediately by two articles on charity's increase. These articles (II-II.24,4 and 5) claim that charity increases not by addition but by gaining a deeper hold on its subject: "An essential increase of charity means nothing else but that it is yet more in its subject, which implies a greater radication in its subject [quod est magis eam radicari in subiecto]" (II-II.24,4 ad 3). Thus, although charity may be spoken of as "something created in the soul," Thomas' conception of it does not fall prey to the charge of reification. He does not portray charity as a quantifiable element superadded to human nature but as the quality of relationship between God and humanity, as he makes clear in the following article: "This is what God does when He increases charity, that is He makes it to have a greater hold on the soul, and the likeness of the Holy Ghost to be more perfectly participated by the soul"[20] (II-II.24,5 ad 3). Here we see a virtual resolution of the tension between the two poles described previously; by speaking of charity as something holding a place in the soul in virtue of divine will and power, Thomas points to the ontological divide, and by speaking of the increase of charity as deepening radication and more perfect participation in the soul, he identifies the indwelling of charity with participation of divine being. In the Thomistic depiction of the relation between charity and the human subject, therefore, both the essential elements of a doctrine of theosis find their place and are carefully treated so as to imply no incompatibility between them.

3. Grace

Although the treatise itself is of very modest proportions (five questions, I-II.109–14), the doctrine of grace informs the Summa at so many points that it must count among the most significant sections of the whole work. Certainly, it will form a vital part of our recapitulation of the Thomistic notion of theosis. Nevertheless, we come in vain to the treatise on grace seeking entirely new themes or constituents of a doctrine of divinization. What we will find, rather, is an elaboration of essential components of Aquinas' doctrine of God, his theological anthropology and the doctrine of sanctification, whose fundamental features reside in the treatment of the virtues, especially charity. While much of the treatise on grace provides vital information pertaining to Thomas' doctrine of theosis, there are many elements in it, important in themselves, which have little bearing on our question. Hence, we will not give systematic attention to the complex taxonomy of grace that Thomas provides or tarry at his doctrine of justification, crucial though it is to the Thomistic conception of salvation.

The cornerstone of that understanding of salvation is the insistence on humanity's absolute need for grace. In Aquinas' view, that need for grace extends well beyond the yawning necessity created by the Fall; humanity's need for divine assistance is fundamental. In our prelapsarian state, we could indeed avoid both mortal and venial sin without the infusion of habitual grace, acknowledges Thomas. Nevertheless, to speak of that state as one in which humanity did not need grace is absurd in his view, since without divine sustenance human persons could not exist at all—we would have fallen into nothingness (I-II.109,8 resp.). Thomas does not make a great deal of this point in the treatise on grace, but logically it is the foundation of the whole edifice. Within the doctrine of grace, this premise represents the principle in the doctrines of God and of creation ex nihilo: the sole source and cause of humanity's being is found in God.

Nevertheless, although this principle is foundational for the whole doctrine of grace, it is not Aquinas' point of departure. Just as we saw epistemological questions rise to the fore very quickly in the *Prima Pars*, so Thomas begins his account of grace with an examination of the relation between grace and knowledge. His point of departure, Aristotelian in spirit if not in detail, is the influence of the First Mover: "All movements, both corporeal and spiritual, are reduced to the simple First Mover, Who is God" (I-II.109,1 resp.). This principle, no more than an extension of the idea of God's sustaining all things in being, has far-reaching consequences for the interpretation of human behavior: "And hence no matter how perfect a corporeal or spiritual nature is supposed to be, it cannot proceed to its act unless it be moved by God" (ibid.). As if to underscore the comprehensiveness of divine causality, Thomas locates it in two distinct ways: "Not only is every motion from God as from the First Mover, but all formal perfection is from Him as from the First Act" (ibid.). The doctrine of grace that follows, therefore, constitutes not an account of how divine aid makes us perfect but a study of a divine inspiration so complete that every human action, external or internal, is seen as God's working through a divine agent.[21]

The desire to protect the integrity of human agency appears in ways other than the claim of free will, and in the epistemological sections of the treatise this strain appears as an affirmation that humanity can know truth without grace (I-II.109,1 resp.). The truth one can know, however, is only that of things intelligible through the senses. Even this kind of knowledge presupposes divine sustenance.[22] All knowing, therefore, derives in some sense from God, and all knowledge may be termed light ("the human understanding has a form, viz., intelligible light," ibid.). Thomas' language here resembles closely the traditional language of deification; he himself removes his epistemology from such a context, however: "Every truth by whomsoever spoken is from the Holy Ghost as bestowing the natural light, and moving us to understand and speak the truth, but not as dwelling in us by sanctifying grace, or as bestowing any habitual gift superadded to nature" (I-II.109,1 ad 1). Thomas' point here is not so much to deny the indwelling of the Spirit per se—for in the reply to the second objection he writes: "The intelligible Sun, Who is God, shines within us"—but to deny that superadded grace is needed for knowledge of truth deriving from sensation (cf. the first objection). He implies that such indwelling or bestowal of habitual gift is the precondition of knowing "certain truths that are known and spoken, and especially in regard to such as pertain to faith, of which the Apostle speaks" (I-II.109,1 ad 1). Thomas leaves the question of indwelling light somewhat ambiguous, however, and in the end all that can be affirmed with certainty is that he views all intellectual activity as ultimately operating with divine sustenance and views knowledge of nonsensible truth as deriving more particularly from divine aid of some variety.

The epistemology does not address at all the question of the Fall's effects. That factor is first introduced when Thomas takes up the relation of grace to good action. His point of departure remains that of Article 1, that both before and after the Fall, human nature needs the help of God as First Mover to do or wish any kind of good (I-II.109,2 resp.). Again, Thomas upholds the central principle of both his doctrine of grace and his doctrines of God and creation: that God is the sustainer of all being and the fount of all human action. Although Aquinas certainly regards the Fall as having had a devastating effect on the human capacity for good (cf. I-II.109, 3–4, 7–8), he does not view it as the principal obstacle lying in the way of humanity's ascent to God. The good originally lodged in our nature was a good sufficient unto itself but not adequate to the "surpassing good, as the good of infused virtue" (ibid.). Therefore even "in the state of perfect nature man needs a gratuitous strength superadded to natural strength for one reason, viz., in order to do and wish supernatural good." The difference between our pre-Fall and post-Fall conditions, then, lies not in the need for grace to do good but in the grounds of that need. In the case of Adam and Eve, there is a single ground, described previously, whereas after the fall, divine assistance is needed both to carry out works of supernatural virtue and in order to be healed (ibid.).

The Thomistic shift away from an Augustinian analysis, characterized by a sole emphasis on original sin, towards a scheme where grace is always requisite and the Fall only adds another dimension to an ever-present need, provides essential information about the Thomistic notion of deification. Aquinas again and again, through a variety of doctrinal devices, portrays God as the Source of all being and the End of our being; grace is an expression not only for what draws us nearer God but also quite simply, for what binds us to God in any way whatsoever. Grace is therefore not principally an entity distinct from God or an effect of God's working in us but the fact of God's indwelling, the name given to the sustenance that is God's own being, shared that we might also be divine. Although Thomas himself does not equate grace and God, he does not use the term *grace* so as to distinguish it from divine being itself, shared with creatures.

So much is the implication of Aquinas' doctrine of grace; his explicit definitions of grace fall far short of such radicality. He confines himself to discussion of grace as it affects the human soul. He says nothing that would exclude the preceding interpretation, that grace is divine being, but he discusses grace solely in terms of its effect on humanity, indicating that to the extent grace may be identified with God, it is identified as God's operation *ad extra*. "Grace implies something in the soul," he remarks in the *sed contra* of I-II.110,1, demonstrating that we can only contemplate grace in its effects on humanity. The effects, however, should not be taken as distinct from their origin: "Every love of God is followed at some time by a good caused in the creature, but not co-eternal with the eternal love"[23] (I-II.110,1 resp.). While Thomas might be taken as claiming that some fundamental difference exists between God's love as such and the good it causes in the creature, our study of the *Prima Pars* cautions against such an interpretation. Love and goodness, as attributes of God, are essentially the same, differing only in our fragmented conception (I.3 and 13). The difference Aquinas is pointing to, then, lies not in any essential distinction between love and goodness themselves but in the difference between their mode of existing in God and their mode of existing in us, which reduces once again to the distinction between creature and Creator. Thomas continues from the quotation begun previously:

> And according to this difference of good the love of God to the creature is looked at differently. For one is common, whereby He loves *all things that are*, and thereby gives things their natural being. But the second is a special love, whereby He draws the rational creature above the condition of its nature to a participation of Divine good[24]; and according to this love He is said to love anyone simply, since it is by this love that God simply wishes the eternal good, which is Himself, for the creature.[25] (I-II.110,1 resp.)

Thus while Thomas clearly prefers to view grace as divine favor bestowed upon humanity, he does, very cautiously, allow that grace may also be understood as a quality of God himself, as divine love.[26]

Thomas' hesitation in identifying grace with divine nature *tout court* is not matched by a similar reluctance to speak of grace in the human person as other than an effect. He does not, for example, equate grace and virtue. A virtue disposes one with reference to human nature:

> Whereas infused virtues dispose man in a higher manner and towards a higher end, and consequently in relation to some higher nature, i.e., in relation to a participation of the Divine Nature [which is called the light of grace [27]], according to 2 Pet. i. 4. . . . And it is in respect of receiving this nature that we are said to be born again sons of God. (I-II.110,3 resp.)

Yet more emphatically he adds a little later: "the light of grace which is a participation of the Divine Nature is something besides the infused virtues which are derived from and ordained to this light" (ibid.). Where Thomas most consistently, and apparently most comfortably, locates grace is in the center of a spectrum, at one of whose poles stands the identification of grace with divine nature, but at whose opposite pole stands the equation of grace and pure effects, such as virtue. He generally locates grace between these options, preferring to call it the creature's participation of the Uncreated. Notably, however, he rules out the equation of grace and virtue, while leaving open the possibility of equating grace and divine love, as we have seen.

The seriousness with which he takes grace as a participation in divine nature is demonstrated by the final article of this question. As he notes, the position of Article 4 merely follows from that established in Article 3. Nevertheless, the direction of Article 3 is highly instructive. Thomas asks whether grace is in the soul's essence or merely in its powers. He answers, as one would expect from his refusal to identify grace with virtue, that grace resides in the soul's essence. The intellective power participates in the divine knowledge by means of faith, the will participates in divine love through charity, and so does humanity participate in divine nature in the nature of the soul, by means of a regeneration of the likeness lost at the Fall (I-II.110,4 resp.). Grace, therefore, may be appropriately described as re-creating the human person so that her essence participates in divine knowledge and love, both of which Thomas has, in differing ways, associated with divine essence.

The theme of grace as participation continues in Question 112, where we encounter one of the strongest linkages of grace and theosis:

> The gift of grace surpasses every capability of created nature, since it is nothing short of a partaking of the Divine Nature, which exceeds every other nature. And thus it is impossible that any creature should cause grace. For it is necessary that God alone should deify, bestowing a partaking of the Divine Nature by a participated likeness, as it is impossible that anything save fire should enkindle.[28] (I-II.112,1 resp.)

Two points are significant here: the first is that deification, partaking in divine nature and possessing a participated likeness to God are unmistakably all equivalent in Aquinas' mind. The second is that viewing theosis as the gift of grace seems important to him because it stresses the inevitable distinction between creature and Creator. He makes this point in two quite different ways in this passage, first by insisting that grace lies above created nature, so that human nature is defined at the outset as finite in a way that divine nature is not, and second, by stressing that God alone can deify. The net result of both positions (and the implication of either of them alone) is that while the deified creature shares a nature with the Creator, created and Uncreated will ever differ in that only one can bestow the gift of grace, while the other is limited to receiving it. Not only the position Thomas takes here but also the mode of his argumentation is significant. He does not argue from grace's extending created nature towards deification; rather, he assumes deification and uses this theological datum to prove that grace exceeds nature. The argument's logic provides a strong indication that Thomas takes theosis for granted and assumes his readers will also.

The same logic appears later in the same question, when Aquinas considers whether one person can possess greater grace than another. His answer, as usual, entails a distinction. Sanctifying grace cannot differ in degree because its nature is to effect union with God, but grace may differ in degree when considered from the perspective of the subject, who may receive more or less of it and be more or less enlightened than another subject (I-II.112,4 resp.). Again, Thomas takes as given the union in grace to sheer Goodness, or Divine Nature, and argues from this fact to the position he is trying to establish. The connection between the Thomistic doctrine of grace and deification lies not only in the claim that grace renders us participants in divine nature but also in that God's sharing his nature with us provides valuable information about the nature of grace.

Conversely, Thomas' assumptions about grace fill out the doctrine of theosis presented in the treatise on grace. The references to theosis we have seen thus far (in Questions 109 through 113) speak of deification solely as participation in divine nature, the absent element has been the connection between sanctification of mortals and their subsequent transformation into partakers of eternity. This hitherto missing element Aquinas supplies at the very end of the treatise on grace, when he takes up the question of merit. Desiring to show why humanity cannot earn eternity, he writes: "No created nature is a sufficient principle of an act meritorious of eternal life, unless there is added a supernatural gift, which we call grace" (I-II.114,2 resp.). While his chief concern here obviously lies in eliminating what would later polemically be called works righteousness, his method of argumentation rests on two points: a supernatural end requires a supernatural means, and grace is such a supernatural means. By pointing out the common feature of grace and eternal life—their supernaturalness—and by portraying one as the means to the other, Aquinas suggests an integral connection between grace and glory. Since he has already claimed a link between grace and participation in divine nature, the reader might justifiably assume a connection between theosis and glory, even though Thomas by no means makes this connection himself in this article. He does, however, allude in somewhat stronger terms to the connection in Article 8:

> The motion of grace reaches to, falls under, condign merit. Now the motion of a mover extends not merely to the last term of the movement, but to the whole progress of the movement. But the term of the movement of grace is eternal life; and progress in this movement is by the increase of charity or grace. (I-II.114,8 resp.)

In this passage, Aquinas has clearly connected grace and glory on an uninterrupted continuum, distinguishing less sharply between means and end and instead portraying glory as grace's culmination. While he certainly makes no direct allusion to participation in divine nature, the brief mention of "increase of charity or grace" must remind the reader of theosis, first because Thomas has already spoken of grace as participation, and second because his doctrine of God has named charity as divine essence.

Perhaps the clearest statement of the relation between grace and glory, however, comes earlier, when Thomas names the effects of grace in Article 4: to heal the soul, to desire good, to carry into effect the proposed good, to persevere in good, and last, to reach glory (I-II.111,3 resp.). While this passage unmistakably connects sanctification and glory, its omission of any direct reference to theosis is striking. The overall effect of the treatise on grace, then, is that it repeatedly and clearly alludes to all the traditional components of a doctrine of theosis but in an uncodified way. It is equally clear that the Thomistic doctrine of sanctification is modeled along the lines of deification and that Aquinas feels no need to expound the latter in any remotely systematic fashion.

Despite the lack of codification, the treatise on grace leaves little doubt that Aquinas regards sanctification as an evolution toward union with God, if not union itself. Before we begin to summarize the Thomistic concepts of union and participation, a summary that will essentially entail a brief revisiting of portions of the *Summa* we have already examined, we must turn to one other portion of the text. The *Tertia Pars*, with its focus on Christology and sacramentology, will complement the account of sanctification that has been developing in the *Summa*'s first two parts, largely confirming and occasionally supplementing the doctrine we have already seen.

A Note on Created Grace.[29] One of the thorniest points of contention between East and West with respect to sanctification is the issue of created grace. For this reason alone, we would need carefully to examine the value of this term in Aquinas' thought. There is another reason yet, however, one that pertains purely to the kind of close reading of Aquinas undertaken here, and that is the questionable validity of speaking of created grace in relation to the *Summa Theologiae* in the first place.

The first indication of the oddity of applying such a category to the theology of the *Summa* is the sheer difficulty of finding uses of the term *gratia creata* at all. None appears in the treatise on grace itself, despite its elaborate taxonomy—*grace freely given, habitual, actual, operating, cooperating, prevenient grace,* to name only some of the terms Thomas uses.[30] Even the comprehensive *Lexicon of St. Thomas Aquinas* mentions created grace only in passing and furnishes no references to the *Summa*.

One might counter this line of reasoning with the objection that it suffers from the usual weakness of an argument from absence. This charge may be met with the equally formal objection that the burden of proof lies on those who make assertions. Pointing to the rarity of this term's occurrence in the *Summa* constitutes not an argument from absence but a demand that its application to Thomas' work be more carefully examined and justified than has hithero been the case. The application of the term *created grace* to the *Summa* is largely the product of an assumption of homogeneity in scholasticism—that because later scholastics (and later Thomists) used the term, it must also be appropriate for Thomas himself. Thomas' extreme hesitation in using it challenges that assumption, especially since its employment has proved so contentious in the mutual understanding of East and West.

Before we turn to the most direct reference to created grace in the *Summa*, however, we might first examine one locus classicus in the treatise on grace that is often cited as evidence of Thomas' acceptance of this concept, the first article of Question 110. The second objection argues that because nothing can come as a medium between God and the soul, grace cannot imply something created in the soul. Because the objection by definition represents a view Thomas is rejecting, one might be tempted to conclude that Thomas views grace as created. This determination is nevertheless rash, as becomes evident when one examines the reply to the objection more closely. Thomas distinguishes between the kind of causality existing between God and the soul on the one hand and between the soul and the body on the other. Because God's relation to the soul is that of agent rather than form, Thomas' metaphysics requires a form subsisting in the matter by which the agent may inform it.[31] Thomas' concern, then, is not to posit the existence of something called created grace and to array it as a form of grace alongside other different forms. His purpose, rather, is to show that grace constitutes a genuine meeting of God and humanity: the divine agent who is the source of grace does not by gracious action obliterate the human person but respects her integrity and finite status, working within her according to the form proper to her.

Significantly, in responding to an objection using the term *created grace*, Aquinas omits to use the term himself. Although we do no more than to speculate in positing a grounds for this omission, one plausible reason for Thomas' avoidance of the term does suggest itself—namely that he saw precisely the kind of problem with it that the Orthodox see. The most fundamental distinction in Christian theology, the distinction that lies at the root of both patristic and Thomistic thought, as we have seen, is the distinction betweeen Uncreated and created. Use of a term such as *created grace*, therefore, suggests the absolute and inviolable distinction of the thing designated created from the Uncreated, which is God. Such a distinction between God and his grace is clearly not the intention of the reply to the second objection and so (we may conjecture) Thomas declines to use the term, even as he insists on the working of divine grace through forms established in the human recipient of grace.

The prime reference to grace as created occurs in the Christology, in III.7,11. The context is important, for Aquinas is not here concerned with regeneration per se but with the distinctive qualities of divine and human nature. The central issue is whether the grace of Christ is infinite. The structure of Thomas' argument works always from the proper characterization of divine and human nature respectively, and reasons from that basis towards a position regarding grace. The assertion of the *sed contra* "Grace is something created in the soul" is, as always, but the reduction of a much more nuanced position. It is not a statement about grace in general, nor one side of a distinction between two varieties of grace; it is a statement about the human soul as God's creature and the authentic humanity of Christ. The doctrinal issue in question here is not the nature of grace but the spectre of Apollinarianism.

Aquinas answers the question of the grace of Christ from three perspectives. The first considers the grace of the hypostatic union, "which union has been bestowed gratis on the human nature" (III.7,11 resp.); this grace is infinite. The second kind of grace in Christ is habitual grace, which Aquinas in turn considers from two angles, as a being and in its specific nature of grace. From the latter point of view, taking the grace of Christ purely qua grace, it is infinite: "It has whatsoever can pertain to the nature of grace, and what pertains to the nature of grace is not bestowed on Him in fixed measure; seeing that *according to the purpose* of God to Whom it pertains to measure grace, it is bestowed on Christ's soul as on a universal principle for bestowing grace on human nature" (ibid.).

Considered not in its nature but as a being, however, grace conforms to the nature of its subject: "In this way it must be a finite being, since it is in the soul of Christ, as in a subject, and Christ's soul is a creature having a finite capacity; hence the being of grace cannot be infinite, since it cannot exceed its subject" (ibid.).[32] Nevertheless, grace considered as gift is not created,[33] nor is the effect of grace created.[34]

Although Aquinas does not use the terminology in this article, it seems consistent with his argumentation to say the assumption of his notion of created grace is that grace is anhypostatic. Having no hypostasis of its own, its nature assumes the limitations of its subject when enhypostasized. To acknowledge the particular character of its subject is not to claim that grace itself changes, nor that grace comes in two varieties, created and uncreated, but merely to note that grace transforms the subject, changing the subject's status from creature to Creator. In the Thomistic framework, if grace were always considered uncreated, this would imply either that grace is hypostasized, and when this hypostasis joins another, it imposes its nature on the other (which would constitute not union but annihilation of the second hypostasis) or that an anhypostatic entity, when assumed by an hypostasis, can change the nature of that hypostasis in the most fundamental way possible, so that what was once created can somehow become uncreated. Although as we shall see, in an extravagant moment, Maximus does seem to claim that deification causes such a fundamental change of status, the logical and theological problems entailed in such a claim are enormous—unless, of course, it is taken as hyperbolic doxology to the sanctifying power of the Almighty.

The fact that Thomas will consider grace created from only one of three possible perspectives—and then only to preserve the creaturely status of the human subject—leads us to a final consideration, also generally overlooked by commentators: the analogical nature of the Thomistic concept of grace.[35] Thomas states this principle himself in the treatise on the sacraments: "Grace is nothing else than a participated likeness of the Divine Nature [participata similitudo divinae naturae]" (III.62,1 resp.). What grace is, most truly and fundamentally, is *gratia increata*, the Holy Spirit, God *ipse*. The effects of grace in human persons are analogous to this essential grace, and as *inchoate* glory (II-II.24,3 ad 2) reflect, in the *viator*, the *viator*'s nature, which is finite and created.

III. Glory

Glory represents the culmination of the image of God in humanity and the culmination of the dynamic of divinization. That dynamic entails a holistic doctrine of deification in the sense that while glory surpasses nature and grace, it also includes them: "Nature is not done away, but perfected, by glory" (II-II.26,13 s.c.) and: "For grace is nothing else than a beginning of glory in us [gratia nihil est aliud quam quaedam inchoatio gloriae in nobis]" (II-II.24,3 ad 2). In this section, then, we look at nature and grace in their fulness and completion.

1. Christology and the Sacraments

We begin, as Thomas does in the *Tertia Pars*, with the Incarnation's significance. The primary reason he gives derives from the doctrine of God presented in the *Prima Pars*:

> The very nature of God is goodness. . . . Hence, what belongs to the essence of goodness befits God. But it belongs to the essence of goodness to communicate itself to others. . . . Hence it belongs to the essence of the highest good to communicate itself in the highest manner to the creature, and this is brought about chiefly by *His so joining created nature to Himself that one Person is made up of these three—the Word, a soul and flesh,* as Augustine says. (III.1,1 resp.)

The pattern here parallels that of the *Prima Pars.* As Thomas wanted to show creation as a natural but voluntary, outward expression of divine nature, so he shows the Incarnation as the fruit of divine desire for self-communication and union with humanity. To speak of Christ's significance in this way in the first instance—rather than, say, as reconciliation, redemption, atonement or sacrifice—is highly consistent with the pattern we have seen developing, for by doing so, Thomas portrays the Word's enfleshment as God's sharing of his own life with humanity.

This conviction appears again in the second article. While denying that the end of the Incarnation could have been achieved in no way other than by the Incarnation itself, Aquinas claims it was the best way of achieving that end. The first reason he gives is that humanity's furtherance in good could have been achieved by no better means. By furtherance in good, he explains, he means primarily growth in faith, hope and charity, the latter of which is "greatly enkindled [excitatur]" by the Incarnation (III.1,2 resp.). Moreover, furtherance in good may be interpreted "with regard to the full participation of the Divinity, which is the true bliss of man and end of human life; and this is bestowed upon us by Christ's humanity"[36] (ibid.). Aquinas subsequently combines both these themes at the question's end, when he contends that by the Incarnation human nature is raised to its highest perfection because the Word incarnate is the efficient cause of the perfection of human nature (III.1,6 resp.). The Incarnation thus brings about human sanctification-unto-glory in two quite distinct ways: by renovating human nature itself, a renovation effected by the hypostatic union,[37] and by some more specific form of influence, presumably over the individual human subject. Thomas has already indicated how such influence might work in the *Secunda Pars*:

> Matters concerning the Godhead are, in themselves, the strongest incentive to love and consequently to devotion, because God is supremely lovable. Yet such is the weakness of the human mind that it needs a guiding hand, not only to the knowledge, but also to the love of Divine things by means of certain sensible objects known to us. Chief among these is the humanity of Christ. (II-II.82,3 ad 2)

The Aristotelian inheritance in Thomas' epistemology is obviously decisive here. Since human beings possess bodies and therefore gather information above all through the senses, revelation becomes most readily available to us through sensible realities, and only as we know can we love. God respects the essential structures of human persons as he created them by revealing himself above all in embodied form. The Incarnation thus mediates our devotion to God by rendering the Infinite comprehensible to the finite.

Thomas follows his study of the Incarnation's benefits with an inquiry into its manner. In Question 2, we will observe again several of the themes of the treatise on grace, to which we need give no detailed scrutiny. However, a brief glance at this question will prove helpful in confirming an interpretation of a somewhat ambiguous point, given previously. The issue devolves on the person's assimilation of grace and the status of that grace henceforth as Uncreated. The principle suggested earlier was that grace, inasmuch as identified with divine being, is principally regarded as Uncreated, but once assimilated into the person becomes part of the creature and is termed created, not in virtue of its substance, but with respect to its adoptive subject.

Thomas' position on the mode of the hypostatic union confirms such a reading. To begin with, he claims the union of divine and human nature is itself created:

> The union of which we are speaking is a relation which we consider between the Divine and the human nature. . . . every relation which we consider between God and the creature is really in the creature, by whose change the relation is brought into being; whereas it is not really in God,[38] but only in our way of thinking, since it does not arise from any change in God. And hence we must say that the union of which we are speaking is not really in God, except only in our way of thinking; but in the human nature, which is a creature, it is really. Therefore we must say it is something created. (III.2,7 resp.)

Clearly, Thomas does not intend by this determination to deny the genuine divinity of one of the parties to the union, nor deny the authenticity of the union, nor claim that the hypostasis of the union, the person of Jesus Christ, is a creature pure and simple. His concern, as usual, is to distinguish clearly between Uncreated and created, and that includes presenting the essential characteristics of the divinity, one of which is impassibility. Inasmuch as the hypostatic union implies a change from one state to another, the union must be classified on the side of the created.

The mode of the hypostatic union moreover parallels that of the union between God and humanity. As grace is the medium between God and humanity in mystical union, so it is in the hypostatic union. The union of the Incarnation is said to have taken place by grace, on two grounds:

> If grace be understood as the will of God gratuitously doing something or reputing anything as well-pleasing or acceptable to Him, the union of the Incarnation took place by grace, even as the union of the saints with God by knowledge and love. But if grace be taken as the free gift of God, then the fact that the human nature is united to the Divine Person may be called a grace, inasmuch as it took place without being preceded by any merits. (III.2,10)

Here Thomas explicitly compares the union of the divine and human in Christ by grace with the human person's union with God by grace. Aquinas is not simply drawing our attention to two situations that happen to be similar; later on he makes clear that the one pattern is understood to be the form of the other: "When it is said that the *Father doth not give the Spirit by measure* . . . it may be referred to the gift which is given the human nature, to be united to the Divine Person" (III.7,11 ad 1). Not just the human nature of Christ benefits from the hypostatic union, then, but all of human nature. While this notion introduces no startling innovation into Christian thought, Aquinas pursues its implications for human sanctification in a fashion that may almost be termed dogged, and this pursuit is significant for our purposes not because of the novelty of any single claim Thomas makes but because of the comprehensiveness of the web he spins.

This communication of the hypostatic union's effects is stated with especial force in the article on Christ's priesthood. Christ is considered both priest and victim because he offers sacrifice and is himself sacrificed; sacrifice, moreover, is offered for three reasons, the third of which is in order that the human spirit may be perfectly united to God

(III.22,2 resp.). Christ merits the title *mediator* for similar reasons: it is the task of a mediator to bring about reconciliation, and Christ brings about not only reconcilation but perfect union between humanity and God (III.26,1 resp.). Christ's mediatorial role even extends to him in his humanity.[39]

An important part of the unity between God and humanity rooted in the Incarnation thus consists in its fostering of virtue in individual human subjects. Thomas alludes to this theme especially in relation to particular events in the life of Christ. The first effect Thomas names of Christ's passion, for example, is that it excites charity (III.49,1 resp.). Similarly, Christ's ascension brings about salvation by lifting up our souls to God and fostering faith, hope and charity (III.57,6 resp.). In more general terms, he writes of the Transfiguration: "It was fitting that He should show His disciples the glory of His clarity [gloriam suae claritatis] (which is to be transfigured), to which He will configure [configurabit] those who are His" (III.45,1 resp.), and: "The adoption of the sons of God is through a certain conformity of the image to the natural son of God. Now this takes place in two ways: first, by the grace of the wayfarer, which is imperfect conformity; secondly, by glory, which is perfect conformity" (III.45,4 resp.). This passage clarifies Thomas' method in elucidating the effects of the Incarnation. He wishes both to claim its sanctifying effect for humanity on earth and to indicate its ultimate salvific effects; perhaps most significant is the way he holds these two elements quite closely together, as if to insist they are not separable from one another.[40]

Perhaps the most striking example of the unity of sanctification and glory in Thomas' Christology is his analysis of the person of Christ himself. Before the passion, Christ possesses the status of both wayfarer and comprehensor—of a wayfarer chiefly with respect to the body and of a comprehensor chiefly on the part of the soul (III.11,2 resp.). Later on, Thomas specifies what each of these states means: the wayfarer tends to beatitude, while the comprehensor has already attained it (III.15,10 resp.). In Christ's person, then, we find the entire story of human sanctification: the one being perfected as she travels along the road to God and the one glorified who sees God face to face.

Because Christ contains within his person the realities of both this life and the next, he points the way to glory, standing on the road but indicating its end: "Through Him we have acquired the perfection of glory [per ipsum perfectionem gloriae adepti sumus]" (III.22,2 resp.). The end indicated by the hypostatic union is, moreover, specifically deification and not beatitude in general: "The end of grace is the union of the rational nature with God. But there can neither be nor be thought a greater union of the rational creature with God than that which is in the Person. And hence the grace of Christ reached the highest measure of grace" (III.7,12 resp.), and what grace effects is theosis: "The soul of Christ is not essentially Divine. Hence it behooves it to be Divine by participation, which is by grace"[41] (III.7,1 ad 1). Because Christ represents the pattern to which we are conformed, the participation of his soul in divine nature indicates the destiny of our souls; more important, perhaps, the fact that even Christ's soul is divine by participation indicates that our destiny is a sharing of divine life as intimate as that represented by the hypostatic union. To be divine by participation through grace constitutes no second-order, derivative union with God but a union after the manner of Christ's very own.

If Christ's own person effects salvation, it is not the only means of doing so. Aquinas' sacramental theology also indicates a way in which the grace of the hypostatic union is communicated, to the end of a wider union of humanity and God. The central principle of that theology is that the sacraments are extensions of Christ, by means of which the effects of the union may be yet more widely disseminated:

> The whole rite of the Christian religion is derived from Christ's priesthood. Consequently, it is clear that the sacramental character is specially the character of Christ, to Whose character the faithful are likened by reason of the sacramental characters,[42] which are nothing else than certain participations of Christ's Priesthood, flowing from Christ Himself. (III.63,3 resp.)

More bluntly still, he maintains that every sacrament makes the human person a participant in Christ's priesthood since every sacrament confers some effect of that priesthood (III.63,6 ad 1). Through the sacraments, then, one both participates in Christ and receives the benefits of Christ's priesthood, both of which are deifying, as we have seen. The sacraments themselves, then, are means, not just to sanctification in general, but of deification in particular.

We may note especially three ways in which Thomas speaks of the sacraments as deifying. The first is very broad: "Since, therefore, by the sacraments men are deputed to a spiritual service pertaining to the worship of God, it follows that by their means the faithful receive a certain spiritual character" (III.63,1 resp.). And he explains the nature of the character in the objections: "The faithful of Christ are destined to the reward of the glory that is to come, by the seal of Divine Predestination. But they are deputed to acts becoming the Church that is now, by a certain spiritual seal that is set on them, and is called a character" (III.63,1 ad 1), and: "From a kind of likeness, anything that assimilates [configurat] one thing to another . . . can be called a character or a seal; thus the Apostle calls Christ the figure or χαρακτήρ of the substance of the Father" (III.63,1 ad 2). More specifically still, Aquinas designates the eucharist, the preeminent sacrament of Christ's sacrifice, as deifying because its very reality is charity, with respect to both its habit and its act, which the eucharist "kindles" (III.79,4 resp.). Although Thomas does not specifically use the language of theosis here, theosis is nonetheless clearly entailed, given the views he has already expressed on charity. If charity is the substance of God and the prime means of our likening to God, the very locus of our participation in God, then the identification of the eucharist with charity implies the eucharist is also a locus of union with God. What is thus implicit in Article 4 becomes explicit in the following article. As spiritual food and spiritual medicine, Thomas tells us, the eucharist strengthens the spiritual life by uniting humanity with Christ through grace (III.79,6 resp.). Like his Christology, Thomas' sacramental theology emphasizes all the requisite elements of a doctrine of theosis, without actually using the terms *deify* or *deification*.

2. Beatitude

Human progress towards consummation begins in the very structure of our being, according to Aquinas. This is why, as we have noted, the main question in the *Summa* dealing with the image of God is entitled "The End or Term of the Production of Humanity" (I.93). Since we have already studied Thomas' doctrine of the image, here we will simply review its salient features, which are contained in Article 4. The divine image subsists in humanity in our intellectual nature, which imitates God chiefly by understanding and loving God. We possess, therefore, a natural appetite for knowing and loving God, an aptitude capable of actualization when grace brings about the development of habitual knowledge and love. Imperfection gives way to perfection when glory succeeds grace and humanity comes to know and love God perfectly. Glory, then, begins from a principle in our nature which strengthens through grace and by which humanity comes to know and love God. What we will find as we pursue other references to beatitude in the *Summa* is that all will fit into this basic scheme.

We begin, then, with the human aptitude for perfection. The most essential way in which human nature itself gestures towards glory is in the rational creature's inclination towards consummation. This inclination is expressed in the first instance in the rational creature's status as agent, since every agent, of necessity, acts for an end (I-II.1,2 resp.). Not only do human actions spring from orientation to any end whatsoever, human desiring tends toward the last end:

> Man must, of necessity, desire all, whatsoever he desires, for the last end. . . . First, because whatever man desires, he desires it under the aspect of good. And if he desire it, not as his perfect good, which is the last end, he must, of necessity, desire it as tending to the perfect good, because the beginning of anything is always ordained to its completion.[43] . . . Wherefore every beginning of perfection is ordained to complete perfection which is achieved through the last end. (I-II.1,6 resp.)

The second reason human beings necessarily desire the last end pertains more especially to humanity's rational nature: "Secondly, because the last end stands in the same relation in moving the appetite, as the first mover in other movements" (ibid.). The fact that we desire anything at all, then, derives from the beckoning, through a mass of intermediaries, of Perfection.

What is this last end? Aquinas identifies it in Article 7 simply as happiness and in Question 2 sets about determining in what happiness must consist. Since it cannot consist in wealth, fame, power and so on, Thomas concludes that no created good can constitute human happiness.[44] Although he himself does not make the connection, the implication of this line of reasoning closely resembles the logic of his *imago Dei* doctrine: human nature is naturally *capax Dei*; we tend towards that in which we participate innately. Thomas states this principle and its application to eschatology most succinctly in Article 5: "Since the end corresponds to the beginning; this argument proves that the last end is the first beginning of being, in Whom every perfection of being is" (I-II.2,5 ad 3).

Although happiness comes from God, it is not identical with God; it is not something uncreated (I-II.3,1 s.c.). The reasoning by which Thomas reaches this conclusion parallels the argument he developed regarding created and uncreated grace:

> Our end is twofold. First, there is the thing itself which we desire to attain. . . . Secondly, there is the attainment or possession, the use or enjoyment of the thing desired. . . . In the first sense, then, man's last end is the uncreated good, namely, God, Who alone by His infinite goodness can perfectly satisfy man's will. But in the second way, man's last end is something created, existing in him [creatum aliquid in ipso existens], and this is nothing else than the attainment or enjoyment of the last end. Now the last end is happiness. If, therefore, we consider man's happiness in its cause or object, then it is something uncreated; but if we consider it as to the very essence of happiness, then it is something created. (I-II.3,1 resp.)

Just as grace is essentially uncreated but when incorporated into the creature must be considered created, so happiness itself is uncreated, but any creature's happiness, inasmuch as it is truly part of the creature, is created.[45] Once again, Thomas explains his reasoning by reference to his doctrine of participation:

> God is happiness by His Essence: for He is happy not by acquisition or participation of something else, but by His Essence. On the other hand, men are happy, as Boëthius says, by participation; just as they are called *gods*, by participation. And this participation of happiness, in respect of which man is said to be happy, is something created. (I-II.3,1 ad 1)

The fundamental distinction, then, remains that between Uncreated and created. Whatever belongs essentially to God is uncreated, and in this the creature can only participate as a creature, so that the ontological divide is never considered breached. So firm is this division that Thomas prefers that his readers infer entities such as grace and happiness change their status, from uncreated to created, rather than claim that the creature becomes a composite of created and uncreated. The notion of participation functions not only to assure the authenticity of the creature's share in divine life but just as much to ensure the distinction between creature and Creator articulated through the difference in possession by essence versus participation.

An analogous way of rendering that distinction is to appeal to the cornerstone of the Thomistic doctrine of God: the identity of essence and existence in God. Aquinas contrasts divine and human happiness in Article 2. Human happiness is not only something created, since it exists in the creature, but is also aptly termed an operation (I-II.3,2 resp.). Contrast this distinction of agent and operation in the creature with their identity in God, who possesses happiness essentially, since his very being is his operation (I-II.3,2 ad 4). Since in God alone we find the identity of essence and existence, only in God is the operation of happiness identical with his being.

The lack of identity between existence and operation in the human person, on the other hand, raises the question of the nature of this operation, which Aquinas calls happiness. It turns out to consist in two activities, which are by now very familiar to us. The first is introduced in Articles 3 and 4. Since, as Thomas has tried to demonstrate in the first and second articles, human happiness consists in being united to the Uncreated Good, and the senses are not capable of attaining this union (Article 3), happiness must reside in the intellect.[46] However, despite the characteristic tidiness of the *sed contra*, Thomas very quickly introduces the second kind of operation, the motion of the will:

> Two things are needed for happiness: one, which is the essence of happiness: the other that is, as it were, its proper accident, i.e., the delight connected with it. I say, then, that as to the very essence of happiness, it is impossible for it to consist in an act of the will. For . . . happiness is the attainment of the last end. But the attainment of the end does not consist in the very act of the will. For the will is directed to the end, both absent, when it desires it; and present, when it is delighted by resting therein. Now it is evident that the desire itself of the end is not the attainment of the end, but is a movement towards the end: while delight comes to the will from the end being present. . . . Therefore, that the end be present to him who desires it, must be due to something else than an act of the will. . . . So, therefore, the essence of happiness consists in an act of the intellect; but the delight that results from happiness pertains to the will. (I-II.3,4 resp.)

While happiness essentially pertains to the intellect, the will also is immediately implicated in the enjoyment of the Last End. As we will see, these two themes become yet more entwined as his account of beatitude unfolds.

Initially, nonetheless, he focuses on what he has called the essence of happiness: the knowledge of God. Aquinas does not conceive knowledge as the passive possession of some sort of information but as the mind's active and constant engagement with its object, as contemplation of God.[47] Neither does he conceive contemplation as the culmination of development and a state of rest: "In the contemplative life man has something in common with things above him, viz., with God and the angels, to whom he is made like by happiness" (ibid.). Happiness and contemplation are therefore part of a process, the likening-to-God whose beginning lies in our nature, increases through growth in grace and virtue and culminates in the contemplation of the next life. Even though perfect happiness is reserved for the life to come, a clear continuity exists between this life and the next, inasmuch as contemplation is the context of both:

> The last and perfect happiness, which we await in the life to come, consists entirely in contemplation. But imperfect happiness, such as can be had here, consists first and principally in contemplation, but secondarily, in an operation of the practical intellect directing human actions and passions. (Ibid.)

Contemplation thus constitutes not only sanctity's fruit and perfection but also its content and perfecting. In Article 6, Thomas introduces the first hint of exactly how this perfecting-through-contemplation will come about: the intellect's perfecting is effected to the extent that it partakes of something above it, such as the intelligible light (I-II.3,6 resp.). The last phrase indicates Thomas' own awareness that he is entering the realm of indescribable experience; still, despite his proclivity for precision, he does not shy from the realm of mystical experience, even though he realizes it resists the kind of analysis he invests in most theological exposition.

The reference to light here, fleeting though it is, matters greatly because of what it gestures towards. That Aquinas claims the intellect partakes of the intelligible light in contemplation needs to be borne firmly in mind as we turn to Article 8, where he states flatly: "Final and perfect happiness can consist in nothing else than the vision of the Divine Essence" (I-II.3,8 resp.). What Thomas envisages by this vision is simply union with God, the intellect's reaching the very essence of the First Cause. Only by such union can it have perfection, for it is in God alone that our happiness consists (ibid.). For Aquinas, vision of anything less than the Divine Essence would constitute less than union with God, since what is not Divine Essence is created. His position on the vision of God is stark because of the absolute firmness of the line he draws between Uncreated and created.

Because of the creature's limitations, it cannot attain to union with God of its own accord, and the way Thomas articulates the principle of the need for divine aid in the context of beatific vision is to insist upon God's gift of light. To see how this works in practice, we must jump ahead to the account of rapture in the *Secunda Secundae*: "The Divine essence cannot be seen by a created intellect save through the light of glory, of which it is written: *In Thy light we shall see light*" (II-II.175,3 ad 2). Similarly, in addressing Christ's beatific knowledge, Thomas writes: "The vision of the Divine Essence is granted to all the blessed by a partaking of the Divine light"[48] (III.10,4 resp.). While these references occupy no great place in the *Summa*, their importance increases in virtue of their complete consistency with the Thomistic doctrine of grace. Just as we become good only by Goodness' own gift of self, so we know God only through God's own self-knowledge and see God only through the divine medium of light or glory. Strictly speaking, then, humanity does not see the divine essence, but is granted a share in God's own self-knowledge. Ultimately, the only one who really sees God is God himself, because the vision of God's essence surpasses the nature not only of the human creature but also every other creature (I-II.5,5 resp.). The reason for this lies in how human beings know. Our knowledge is according to the mode of created substance and thus necessarily falls short of the vision of the divine essence which infinitely surpasses all created substance (ibid.). The vision of God can only be had, therefore, according to the mode of uncreated substance—that is, through God's own light.

Such a position would appear to imply, however, that divine aid enables us to know God as God knows himself; in other words, the ontological divide Aquinas has so staunchly and consistently maintained would be breached by his concept of beatific vision. The question on Christ's knowledge explains how he envisages the integrity of the divine:

> The beatific vision and knowledge are to some extent above the nature of the rational soul, inasmuch as it cannot reach it of its own strength; but in another way it is in accordance with its nature, inasmuch as it is capable of it by nature, having been made to the likeness of God. . . . But the uncreated knowledge is in every way above the nature of the human soul. (III.9,2 ad 3)

Here Thomas smoothes away two potential conflicts. The easier of these is the collision course on which his doctrine of the image and his doctrine of grace are set. The assertion of a natural inclination to God would seem to undercut the need for grace. Thomas claims no more than that beatific knowledge is in *accord* with nature, but even so, shows that this perspective is only one from which the human person's knowledge of God may be viewed. From the other perspective, its actual capabilities rather than its natural aptitude, the human person is wholly inadequate to knowledge of God.

The more difficult of the two potential conflicts is specifying the difference between the graced human person and God. Like all advocates of theosis, Thomas wants to claim that human beings may truly participate in divine being—does he here not exclude humanity from such participation, inasmuch as we do not ultimately possess divine knowledge? He indeed distinguishes between the knowledge of the comprehensor and God's own self-knowledge; this distinction emerges with the greatest clarity from the reply to the second objection: "By the union this Man [Christ] is blessed with the uncreated beatitude, even as by the union He is God; yet besides the uncreated beatitude it was necessary that there should be in the human nature of Christ a created beatitude, whereby His soul was established in the last end of human nature" (III.9,2 ad 2). Despite the unmistakable message that creaturely beatitude—which is knowledge of God—differs from God's own self-knowledge, the fact that both are still called beatitude indicates that they do not constitute different species altogether. Once again, the difference between them lies in the mode in which they are appropriated. The creature possesses knowledge according to its own nature; it may be lifted beyond its own capacities, but such grace perfects nature rather than destroying it (II-II.26,13 s.c.). God also knows himself according to his own nature, and since divine and human nature are essentially distinct, the mode of this knowledge differs from the creature's mode of knowledge, even though the object of knowing, God, is the same in each case.

Even if the fundamental content of beatitude is knowledge, however, there is more to beatitude than knowing. To begin with, the effect of knowledge is joy: "Happiness is joy in truth" (I-II.4,1 s.c.), says Aquinas, quoting Augustine. The very sight of God causes delight (I-II.4,1 ad 2), he adds, and concludes the response to the same article by asserting a necessary connection between the *visio Dei* and joy: "Since happiness is nothing else but the attainment of the Sovereign Good, it cannot be without concomitant delight." This delight in turn is closely linked to charity:

> Joy is caused by love, either through the presence of the thing loved, or because the proper good of the thing loved exits and endures in it. . . . Now charity is love of God, Whose good is unchangeable, since He is His goodness, and from the very fact that He is loved, He is in those who love Him by His most excellent effect. . . . Therefore spiritual joy, which is about God, is caused by charity. (II-II.28,1 resp.)

This joy is available to us already in this life. Although we are said to be absent from God as long as we are in the body, and absent by comparison with the blessed, God may be deemed present to those who love him in this life, a presence effected by the indwelling of grace (II-II.28,1 ad 1). Indeed, it is not our own capacities in this life which are lacking and keep us from the full vision of God, but life's misery.[49] Aside from the main point of this passage, to inform us of hindrances to perfect beatitude in earthly life, it imparts another important message: that participation in the divine good, both here and later on, is a matter of both knowing and loving.

As Thomas develops this theme, the double content of glory, we will better grasp the connection he envisages between this life and the next, to which he so briefly alluded in the question on joy (II-II.28). Shortly after having defined the content of happiness as the knowledge of God (I-II.3,8), Aquinas proceeds to refine the picture:

> Since Happiness consists in gaining the last end, those things that are required for Happiness must be gathered from the way in which man is ordered to an end. Now man is ordered to an intelligible end partly through his intellect, and partly through his will:— through his intellect, in so far as a certain imperfect knowledge of the end pre-exists in the intellect:—through the will, first by love which is the will's first movement towards anything; secondly, by a real relation of the lover to the thing beloved, which relation may be threefold. For sometimes the thing beloved is present to the lover: and then it is no longer sought for. Sometimes it is not present, and it is impossible to attain it: and then, too, it is not sought for. But sometimes it is possible to attain it, yet it is raised above the capability of the attainer, so that he cannot have it forthwith: and this is the relation of one that hopes, to that which he hopes for, and this relation alone causes a search for the end. To these three, there are a corresponding three in Happiness itself. For perfect knowledge of the end corresponds to imperfect knowledge; presence of the end corresponds to the relation of hope; but delight in the end now present results from love. . . . And therefore these three must concur in Happiness; to wit, vision, which is the perfect knowledge of the intelligible end; comprehension, which implies presence of the end; and delight or enjoyment, which implies repose of the lover in the object beloved. (I-II.4,3 resp.)

The last sentence posits an equality among the three elements of happiness that chafes somewhat against its earlier exclusive identification with knowledge.

This apparent inconsistency becomes more tractable when we consider what Thomas regards as the logical ordering of the soul's movements. We have seen, in several places, Aquinas' adoption of the Augustinian maxim that one can only love what one knows. The prerequisite of all happiness, then, must be that one apprehends and possesses the object of happiness, and this is called knowledge. But one cannot know anything unless one is ordered to it.[50] Though Thomas does not claim such antecedent rectitude of will constitutes happiness directly, he does imply that the motion of the will subsists in any act of knowing. Moreover, as noted previously, the will becomes involved at a later state also:

> Concomitantly, because . . . final Happiness consists in the vision of the Divine Essence, Which is the very essence of the goodness. So that the will of him who sees the Essence of God, of necessity loves, whatever he loves, in subordination to God; just as the will of him who sees God's Essence, of necessity, loves whatever he loves, under that common notion of good which he knows. (I-II.4,4 resp.)

Although Thomas here seems curiously more interested in the ordering of loves in consequence of beatific vision, this passage nevertheless clearly assumes that the vision necessarily inspires love of its object.

The bond of love between the comprehensor and Goodness apprehended in vision forms but the most important link in a much longer chain of love. The vision of the Divine Essence is said to fill the soul with all good things, by uniting it to the source of all goodness (I-II.5,4 resp.). This union, while perfectly realized in the next life, begins imperfectly in this.[51] However imperfect the love of this life may be in comparison to that of the next, perfection in this life nevertheless consists in charity: "A thing is said to be perfect in so far as it attains its proper end, which is the ultimate perfection thereof. Now it is charity that unites us to God, Who is the last end of the human mind. . . . Therefore the perfection of the Christian life consists radically in charity"[52] (II-II.184,1 resp.). One might easily gloss over "radically" as a façon de parler, but the reply to the first objection proves Aquinas indeed sees charity as virtue's root: "The perfection of the human senses would seem to consist chiefly in their concurring together in the unity of truth. . . . Now this is effected by charity which operates consent in us men. Wherefore even the perfection of the senses consists radically in the perfection of charity." In this life, at least, even knowledge of the truth depends on charity.

If the last pronouncement might be taken as referring exclusively to knowledge obtained through the senses, Thomas suggests otherwise in the question on the contemplative life. He cites Gregory: "The contemplative life is to cling with our whole mind to the love of God and our neighbor and to desire nothing beside our Creator" (II-II.180,1 s.c.). He explains in the response that the contemplative life consists chiefly in the contemplation of the truth, whose motive cause lies in the will: "The appetitive power moves one to observe either with the senses or with the intellect, sometimes for love of the thing seen . . . sometimes for love of the very knowledge that one acquires by observation" (II-II.180,1 resp.). Here the ordering he previously took care to establish blends into a single, unified vision of sanctified life, in which the mind and the will—as well as the body, if we take into account the role accorded the senses in II-II.184, 1 ad 1—are directed to God. The unity wrought by love is, furthermore, a unity of all life, both before and after our death. The contemplative life thus consists in an anticipation of the life to come (cf. esp. II-II.180,4), in which the content of that life is to be had, only in less intense form. The difference between the two lies in degree, not kind.

To speak thus of the contemplative life suggests, perhaps, the rarified existence of the vowed monastic. Thomas' comparison of the active and contemplative lives refutes

any such notion. Although in most senses, he acknowledges, the contemplative life surpasses the active (II-II.182,1), he does not believe the active life hinders the contemplative (II-II.182,3); indeed, the active life precedes the contemplative (II-II.181,1 ad 3 and
II-II.182,1). Growth in the kind of virtue that disposes us to love of neighbor is thus not
portrayed as a lesser, temporal or temporary sanctity that is later replaced by the pure
love of God; the two are integrally connected. All charity ultimately participates in that
perfection that is God himself:

> The perfection of the Christian life consists in charity. Now perfection implies a certain
> universality. . . . Hence we may consider a threefold perfection. One is absolute and an-
> swers to a totality not only on the part of the lover, but also on the part of the object
> loved, so that God be loved as much as He is lovable. Such perfection as this is not pos-
> sible to any creature, but is competent to God alone, in Whom good is wholly and es-
> sentially. Another perfection answers to an absolute totality on the part of the lover, so
> that the affective faculty always actually tends to God as much as it possibly can; and
> such perfection as this is not possible so long as we are on the way, but we shall have it
> in heaven. The third perfection answers to a totality neither on the part of the object
> served, nor on the part of the lover as regards his always actually tending to God, but
> on the part of the lover as regards the removal of obstacles to the movement of love
> towards God. (II-II.184,2 resp.)

Here he sketches three forms of love, each of which corresponds to a state of perfection:
of the viator, the comprehensor and God. His description at this point is important, first,
because it shows each of these states to be defined by a kind of loving; second, because
it shows the three states to be interconnected; third, because while transition from the
third state to the second is possible in virtue of changes in the lover, the first state is
shown to be unique. The lover cannot be promoted to the first kind of love, and so while
all three states are intimately related, one remains unique and inviolable.

It is because of the inviolability of the divine nature that Aquinas will deny that humanity became God and will deny it at precisely the point when the logic of Christianity
might most have induced him to do so. Seeking the implications of the Incarnation, he
asks whether the statement "Humanity was made God" is true and answers: "To be made
God is the same as to be deified. Hence this is false: *Man was made God*" (III.16,7 s.c.). It
seems that he is denying either the fact or the possibility of theosis altogether. However, if we look to the authority he cites for this position, it readily becomes apparent
that such a reading is implausible: "Damascene says: *We do not say that man was deified, but
that God was humanized*" (ibid.). Clearly, Damascene, the great systematizer of the Eastern
patristic tradition and forerunner of the Byzantine, does not deviate wildly from the
Fathers before him, nor would he occupy a position of authority for those after him had
his views on such an important matter been diametrically opposed their own. The question here, as always, is what one understands by *become God*. Nowhere in the patristic or
Byzantine traditions is the notion of deification taken to mean that humanity becomes
God as God is God. The consequence of such an assertion could only be pantheism.

Given Thomas' ready resort to terminology such as *deifico, deiformis,* and *deiformitas*,
he obviously entertains no objection to every variety of theosis. The distinction he
upholds consistently is presented lucidly in III.16,5 ad 3: "What belongs to the Divine
Nature is predicated of the human nature—not, indeed, as it belongs essentially to
the Divine Nature, but as it is participated by the human nature. Hence, whatever cannot

be participated by the human nature (as to be uncreated and omnipotent), is nowise predicated of the human nature."[53] In his doctrine of consummation, therefore, he asserts the unity of sanctity and beatitude, the reality of humanity's graced growth into divine being, but refuses to do so at the cost of compromising the uniqueness of divine nature. That refusal, far from diluting his doctrine of theosis, constitutes one of its crucial components.

4

IMAGES OF
DEIFICATION

I. Method

We examine Palamas by the same means we used for Aquinas: by seeking direct references to deification and using the themes we find in these passages as a guide through the work as a whole. As with Aquinas, we seek a close reading of the primary text. This reading is needed just as much for Palamas, since so many of his commentators, both Eastern and Western, have been content to ascribe views to him with very little support from the primary text or have selected isolated statements without asking whether these are characteristic of the work as a whole.[1]

The same method applied to Aquinas and Palamas nevertheless yields results that differ in one very important way, a difference rooted in the works themselves. Whereas with Thomas the method allowed us largely to follow the structure of the *Summa*, with Gregory the structures of the *Triads* and the *Capita* will recede, becoming invisible to our study. The absence of this transparency is not as great a loss as might seem, however. The editors of two of the best modern editions of the *Triads* and the *Capita*, Meyendorff and Sinkewicz, both attempt to reduce the structure of these works to a schematic outline. In each case, the scheme corresponds only broadly to the actual work itself, inasmuch as the themes specified by the outline are at times only slightly more prominent than the many others treated in the same section. Furthermore, the outlines themselves provide little assistance in grasping the logic of Gregory's exposition, since themes constantly reappear, in different configurations, throughout the work.[2]

The irreducibility of Palamas' work to an orderly, linear outline indicates nothing whatsoever about the clarity of his thought, however. What is considered acceptable and desirable in a rhetorical structure differs from language to language, culture to culture.[3] What our study of deification will reveal in Palamas' work are highly consistent patterns of thought, developed simultaneously and diffused throughout the work. To see the coherence of Palamas' theology, however, one must look to the particular forms of his text. Those forms consist in a pattern of images, cognates for deification, that Palamas uses to convey his doctrines of God and of sanctification and by means of which he articulates the connection between these doctrines. By studying these images, a complex but coherent doctrine of deification emerges, which would be almost invisible to the reader who looked for a more linear exposition.

How, then, do we determine what these images of deification are? Our prime informant, as mentioned, will be the direct references in the text. From these direct references emerges a consistent group of images, a group that also matches the images we noted recurring in the writings of the Fathers. The direct references will tell us a little of what Palamas understands by deification and how deification funcions systematically in his theology, but only a little. They are more useful as pointers to the real tradents of his doctrine of deification, the group of images that together convey virutally all he has to say of it. We study the images because they are the doctrine and use this interpretative method because it is the imperative of the text.

The cognates have been arranged in an order that is intended to approximate the order of ascent to God. Obviously, this ordering must be taken as rough, for there are no absolute criteria for measuring the proximity of an image to theosis itself. What is clear, however, is that the first three (virtue, knowledge and vision) represent the foothills of deification, while the next four (contemplation, light, grace and glory) are nearer equivalents and three (adoption, participation and union) function virtually as synonyms for it. The borders between these groups are somewhat arbitrary, as all borders are. To an extent, this order merely represents Gregory's degree of ambivalence regarding the equation of a given cognate with theosis, the extent to which the state or entity the cognate represents may be identified with deification itself. From this perspective, for example, virtue registers lowest on the scale because while Palamas certainly regards growth in virtue as important, he portrays it more as the precondition or concomitant of deification, rather than theosis itself; union, on the other hand, is almost synonymous with deification in Palamas' thought. These differences in the correlation of the images with deification itself do not undermine the coherence of his thought, but they do add to its complexity. Gregory uses a variety of images, as do the Fathers, because of the difficulties of his subject. The doctrine of deification encompasses, as we have noted, both the doctrines of God and theological anthropology; additionally, it functions as a systematic connection between the two. The problem Gregory faces, then, is much more than the usual ones of articulating theological and mystical doctrine; it is additionally the problem of finding a systematic language, language to articulate the unity and coherence of doctrines. The quibbling we will see in the text reflects the problems inherent in that enterprise, and the quibbling is also part of the reason Gregory succeeds so well in it.

One further caveat must be issued regarding the ordering of the cognates, one which signals also the nature of the works we are about to examine. The ordering of the cognates as a ladder of ascent misrepresents the very heart of Palamas' work in one crucial respect. Gregory Palamas is not an ascetical writer. Although sometimes dismissed as such by Western historians—who, for their own reasons, have little time for what they call spirituality—Gregory is no mystic or spiritual tutor in the sense of, say, Walter Hilton,

Julian of Norwich, Teresa of Ávila or François de Sales. He is concerned neither to offer instruction in prayer or spiritual growth nor to describe mystical experiences. Although both the Triads and the Capita grew out of the historical circumstances of the hesychast controversy, Palamas does not defend his fellow monks by pointing to their experiences as evidence of divine favor. Instead, he uses the bare fact of such experience as a counter to the Barlaamite epistemology, which seemed to envisage little possibility of knowledge of God at all and considered secular philosophy as a reliable source of knowledge in general. (Thus, in any event, would run Gregory's rendition of Barlaam.) Theosis is therefore not an end which the Triads explains how to attain, but a warrant and datum in a dispute about the nature and sources of Christian claims to know God.

The Christian claim to knowledge of God is not, however, a generalized claim to know any sort of God whatsoever. The claim that God is knowable derives from a particular portrait of God, a God who makes himself known because he desires communion with those he has made. The fact of theosis thus not only grounds the possibility of making certain kinds of claims about God but also constitutes the portrait of a certain kind of God. Theosis thus implies both a particular theological method and a particular doctrine of God.

Investigation of the methodological implications of Gregory's quarrel with Barlaam lies well beyond our concerns here. The systematic implications, however, are most important. If we are correctly to understand what Palamas intends by his talk about theosis, light, union and all the rest, we must grasp the end of such talk. It is clearly not instructional, as we have said, precisely because it neither describes nor prescribes human activity. Indeed, Gregory has very little to say about humanity at all, in either the Triads or the Capita. The purpose of the voluminous discussion of theosis, we may therefore surmise, is not to furnish information about the glorification of the human being, but systematically to explore the nature of a God known to humanity by grace.

These two chapters on Palamas therefore set out, first, to establish what he understands by theosis through a close reading of the direct references to deification and texts containing cognates found in the direct references. Second, we will press the implications of the primary study, showing how Palamite discourse about deification culminates in a doctrine of God whose salient features are the desire to give to humanity no less than himself and the capacity always to transcend the creatures to whom he has granted participation in his own nature.

II. The Direct References

While Gregory frequently uses the terms divinization (usually θέωσις but occasionally compounds such as ἐκθέωσις) and divinizing or divinized (generally θεοποιός, θεουργος and θεούμενος), he does so in a way that assumes the reader understands what is meant by these terms; rarely does he define or even fully explain them.[4] The first place to look to discover what he understands by deification is this handful of definitions and near-definitions.[5]

The closest Palamas comes to a definition proper of theosis is actually a quotation from Maximus. Far from undermining the usefulness of this passage, the fact that Gregory here borrows from the Confessor is encouraging; if there is any candidate for a codifier of the patristic understanding of deification before Gregory, it is he. Here is the passage Gregory identifies as the Confessor's[6]:

Deification is an enhypostatic and direct illumination which has no beginning but appears in those worthy as something exceeding their comprehension. It is indeed a mystical union with God beyond intellect and reason, in the age when creatures will no longer know corruption [ἐν τῷ ἀφθάτῳ τῶν ὄντων αιῶνι]. Thanks to this union, the saints, observing the light of the hidden and more-than-ineffable [ὑπεραρρήτου] glory become themselves able to receive the blessed purity, in company with celestial powers. Deification is also the invocation of the great God and Father, the symbol of the authentic and real adoption, according to the gift and grace of the Holy Spirit, thanks to the bestowal of which grace the saints become and will remain the sons of God. (III.1.28)

This passage establishes a direct link between deification and many of the cognates we will consider presently: light, union, virtue, knowledge, glory, adoption and grace. However, it also points to the cognates in ways that are less direct but no less important. The characterization as enhypostatic, for example, immediately associates deification with the person. The location of deification in the realm of the personal is consistent with the testimony of the cognates, which either express that which is incorporated into the person (virtue, knowledge), or the manifestation of the personal God which the human person encounters (light, glory) or the relationship obtaining between divine and human persons (vision, adoption).

The personal nature of theosis emerges with equal clarity in a second passage, where Gregory gives what amounts to his own definition. The deifying gift of the Spirit, he writes, is:

the deifying energy of the superessential [ὑπερουσίου] divine essence, although not the totality of this energy. . . . Deification is . . . everywhere, ineffably present in the essence and inseparable from it, as its natural power [ἐνυπάρχουσα ἀφράστως ταύτῃ καὶ ἀχώριστος ἐκείνης οὖσα, ἅτε φυσικὴ δύναμις αὐτῆς]. . . . But if [the divine manifestation] seizes a suitable material, free from every veil . . . then it becomes itself visible like a spiritual light, or rather it transforms these creatures into spiritual light. (III.1.34)

Deification is both the light encountered (inasmuch as it is a visible apparition) and something that attaches to the person, becoming one with her and changing her. It is both God as other and God transforming the human person from within.

In a third passage Gregory offers a fairly detailed description of what it is to be deified, and speaks of the effects of purification by hesychasm. While he does not actually use the term *theosis*, this description may be taken as directly applicable to deification, since theosis was the culmination of hesychastic purification. He writes:

Those who have been purified by hesychasm make themselves worthy to contemplate invisible things, the essence of God remaining beyond their attainment; but those who are worthy of this contemplation can be initiated into it and make it the object of their understanding; thus they participate in the intelligible gift of the light of God in their impassible and immaterial intelligence, but they also know that the divine surpasses these contemplations and initiations, and thus they possess this superintelligible and superadded [grace] in a way that exceeds us [οὕτω τὴν ὑπὲρ νοῦν ταύτην κρεῖττον ἤ καθ' ἡμᾶς ἔχουσιν ἐπιβολήν]; they possess it not because they do not see, in the manner of those who practise negative theology, but in their very vision they know what surpasses vision, in suffering negation and not in conceptualising it [πάσχοντες οἷον τὴν ἀφαίρεσιν, ἀλλ' οὐ διανοούμενοι]. (II.3.26)

Here he identifies hesychasm's fruit as a form of contemplation that engages the intellect rather than the eye, even though what is contemplated may be described as light and the act of contemplation may be designated vision. It is a gift so fully integrated into its recipient that it may aptly be termed *participation*. Because, however, this experience remains utterly beyond all natural human capacity, it must be viewed as a form of grace.

The terms in which Palamas understands and explains deification, which we can cull from the direct references, form a group of ten images or cognates: virtue, knowledge, vision, contemplation, light, glory, grace, adoption, participation and union. He simultaneously yokes them together and denies their ultimate validity. He does so, not because he is inconsistent or his thinking muddled but because he wants to point to the way in which God both enters into human experience and exceeds it:

> Whatever name one gives it—union, vision, sensation, knowledge, intellection, illumination—does not apply to it properly, or applies properly to it alone [ἢ κυρίως ταῦτ' οὐκ ἔστιν, ἢ μόνη κυρίως ταῦτα πρόσεστιν αὐτῇ]. (II.3.33)

Although he here makes no mention of theosis, the alliance with one another of images he has frequently linked explicitly to theosis underscores the very point he is trying to make: despite the differences between them, all these terms accurately denote a quality of theosis, and all of them, even all of them collectively, fail to capture its nature definitively. The summit of our longings, to become God (Basil, quoted in the *Capita* 76), finally escapes all our knowing. Like all lovers, those who love God bewail the poverty of language to praise the beloved, and yet cannot but speak in praise. Like all lovers, Gregory both praises and quarrels with the medium of praise, his images. Paradoxically, it is only by studying the images he dismisses as inadequate that we will come to understand his doctrine of deification.

III. Deification's Cognates

1. Virtue

We begin with a cognate for theosis that is one of the most ambivalent, most problematic and most important.[7] Many of the cognates for deification, as we will see, stress divine overpowering; human effort seems either absent or is heavily discounted. In the texts on virtue and ascetical striving we will see a different emphasis. In some forms, this strain does no more than articulate the conventional wisdom of the ascetical tradition: "Perfection consists in assimilation to God and this comes about only in love by the holy practice of the divine commandments" (II.1.40; cf. also II.1.42). In such texts Gregory seems to affirm that deification comes about as the result of human striving; we become God because we try harder. Indeed, he affirms almost exactly this when he quotes Basil, writing "the prize of virtue is to become God" (III.1.34). In I.3.4, he almost seems to go out of his way to make clear that this prize is won *solely* through human effort.[8]

Passages such as these constitute but a small portion of the texts on virtue, however. More typical of his thought are affirmations of virtue as deification's threshold. Union and the divinizing end belong only to those who have purified their heart and received grace (I.3.17), he asserts, here making clear that both purification and grace are needed. Similarly, he can depict the gift of grace as a response to virtue, without specifying the precise nature of the connection between the two.[9] Is there a suggestion of a quid pro quo here? Perhaps, but what is most significant is his unconcern about the relationship between virtue and grace. That lack of concern must in part be attributable to the lack of anything like a Pelagian controversy in the East: Eastern theologians have never been as worried as Westerners about the dangers of connecting merit and grace. What Gregory's easy alliance of virtue and grace most suggests is his conviction that the saints stand constantly in need of both.

Elsewhere, he is clearer still that grace is not only a response to virtue but that purification is a necessary preparation for divinizing grace: "God will not disdain to make his dwelling in one . . . who is not only pious, but sanctified . . . by keeping the divine commandments, and is thus transformed into a vehicle appropriate to receiving the all-powerful Spirit" (III.3.5; cf. also II.3.11). He makes a similar point specifically in respect to the body in I.2.2 and with respect to the mind in II.3.11. In his view, this preparation is necessary because virtue makes the person receptive to the work of theosis: one cannot contemplate deification if there is no material ready to receive the divine apparition (III.1.34; cf. also Capita 69). In such texts, a factor of proportionality seems operative; in arguing that the divine light is not sensible, Gregory invokes such proportionality: "If [the light] were sensible, it would be visible through the air and one would therefore see it more or less directly not according to the extent of each person's virtue and the purity produced by this virtue but according to the purity of the air" (I.3.35).

At times, then, it seems the insistence on virtue claims little more than that humanity can turn from God[10]; at other times Palamas apparently intends something rather more positive, that we can through our own striving attain blessedness.[11] In the end, he is content to make no definitive determination concerning the extent to which purification really is humanity's work and the extent to which it is God's. Quoting the Gospel of John, he writes: "'For the glory which the Father gave him' he himself has given to those obedient to him" (I.3.5). Here he describes the life of virtuous striving as a preliminary step to divinizing glorification, yet the terms are not precondition followed by consequent reward but phases of growth. If anything, the implication is that obedience is not in itself the equivalent of deification and that deification can come only as gift and not as compensation. An even more striking example is this pair of texts: "It is with this power of the [passionate part of the] soul that we love and turn around" and: "Entirely seized by this love, as if they had left the body, they do not cease to commune with the divine Spirit in prayer and love." In the first, transformative love seems to originate within the human person; in the second, it seems love overshadows us. That Gregory does not see these paradigms as contradictory is clear from their proximity: both are from the same section, II.2.23.

The balance we see in II.2.23 is evident more broadly in the Triads. For every text such as those we have just seen that apparently emphasize human striving, Palamas furnishes others that portray growth in virtue as God's work. Thus he describes light as a divine and immaterial fire which reestablishes the purity of the human spirit and suppresses sin (III.1.40). In such passages, human worthiness itself is God's gift, a divinely wrought preparation for a divinely wrought gift: "The invisible vision of divine beauty deifies human persons and renders them worthy of personal relations with God" (III.3.9).

Gregory's style in the corpus on virtue must therefore often be understood as contrapuntal; the texts speaking of virtue purely in terms of human striving form a distinct and complete melodic line, but one intended to be heard in conjunction with another, which emphasizes grace, so that human striving is understood always in the context of parallel divine action. We must exercise ourselves in the observance of the commandments? Yes, but those commandments themselves sanctify, he reminds us, castigating his opponents for not considering that the evangelical commandments and the scriptures give perfect purification to the soul (II.1.36). The description, which seems to accord a quasi-sacramental power to sacred Writ, is echoed in I.2.3.[12] Here lies the difference between the kind of striving Palamas advocates and the exhortation to the virtuous life of, say, a Stoic; Christian virtue is exercised in a particular context; it is conditioned by the end to which it is ordered:

> It is not the one who kills the passionate part of the soul . . . but the one who subjugates it, so that by obedience to the Spirit . . . he will go as he should to God and tend to God through the uninterrupted memory of God. (II.2.19)

Finally, in a few texts on virtue we see Palamas approach a denial of any direct relation between human striving and deification. "This power [union] depends neither on the activity of the senses, nor on that of the intelligence," he tells us (I.3.20). Such a claim does not exclude the possibility that union might come about as a result of volition, of course, which is strictly speaking a function neither of the senses nor of the intellect, but lies somewhere between the intellect and the appetites.[13] It nevertheless seems unlikely that he here intends to exclude some human faculties as the means to union only to grant pride of place to others, especially in light of the absence of any qualification to that effect. What seems more plausible is that he here points to the transcendent element of theosis—how far beyond any purely human experience deification lies. "Every divine command and every sacred law," he tells us, "has as its term purity of heart. . . . however it is false to say that there is nothing but purity of heart beyond the accomplishment of the divine commandments. There are many other things: unspeakable vision, ecstasy in vision and hidden mysteries" (I.3.18).

Read in conjunction with the texts on other cognates for divinization, such as light and union, the passages on virtue by no means portray the divinized person as self-made. Rather, they remind us that Gregory's more customary emphasis on transcendence and divine condescension remains the theme of one steeped in Eastern synergistic theology and rigorously trained in the monastic ascetical tradition. What is surprising is not that he has so much to say regarding spiritual striving but that this element is so relatively muted.

2. Knowledge

The monastic and essentially apophatic woof of Gregory's thought is strongly counterbalanced by a kataphatic and theological warp stressing knowledge, wisdom and intellection as modes or images of deification.[14] As we will see in the texts, he manifests a marked ambivalence about identifying deification as a form of knowing, yet the sheer volume of instances in which he reaches for such images indicates that in the end he does regard deification as at least in some respects related to knowledge.

Let us begin by turning to those texts in which Palamas seems relatively content with the alliance of theosis and knowledge or intellection. The majority of these operate in accord with a common logic, a logic one might loosely call Platonic: to know something is to be at one with it. Thus he will sometimes speak as if deification obtains its purchase on the human person solely, or at least principally, via a natural faculty, the intellect[15]: "[The worthy] participate in the intelligible gift of the light of God in their impassible and immaterial intelligence" (II.3.26). In similar vein, he writes in the *Capita*: "Nothing in our nature is superior to the mind" (27).

Part of his uneasiness with the equation of deification and knowledge indeed derives from his general suspicion of secular learning and classical philosophy in particular, so it is scarcely surprising that he equivocates least when he can transmute the Platonic insight into a specifically Christian form. Thus he asserts that it is Christ who directs us toward the perfection of this saving knowledge, and Christ is Wisdom-Itself and contains in himself all true knowledge (II.1.43). Rather than viewing faith as assent to propositions entertained by the mind, Palamas reverses the pattern and shows knowledge as belief's product: "This knowledge, which is beyond all conception, is common to all who have believed in Christ" (II.3.66). Really to understand the nature of God is to become deified; those who know that God is Spirit are those who become God completely and know God in God (II.3.68).

This christological principle—that all true knowledge is in Christ—is reinforced by his articulation of its converse; in acquiring wisdom from outside, he maintains, the soul will never be conformed to truth itself (I.1.2). That this conformity to truth itself signifies divinization he later implies when he writes: "It is not study of profane science that brings salvation, purifies the faculty of knowing, and conforms it to the divine archetype" (I.1.22). It is because of the impotence of secular knowledge that Gregory exhorts his readers to prefer a wisdom that comes from God, leads towards God and conforms those who acquire it to God (I.1.2). The content of this wisdom Gregory sometimes identifies as Christ, as we have seen, but on occasion he will also identify it as the teaching of the Spirit (I.3.24), or even of the saints who have gone before.[16] Very rarely, he will even concede something like a natural theology: "One will harvest the knowledge of God from the knowledge of beings" (II.2.19).

More generally characteristic of Gregory's thought, however, is to remove deifying knowledge entirely from the natural realm. Deification signifies more than the perfection of rational nature,[17] he insists in III.1.30, and because the means by which we apprehend is supernatural, the knowledge gained can never be truly our posssession: "Those who see . . . do not know the one who enables them to see, hear and be initiated into knowlege of the future, or experience of eternal things, for the Spirit by whom they see is incomprehensible" (I.3.17). If it is correct to speak of knowlege of God at all, then, this can only mean the replacement of what we usually term knowledge with something, perhaps analogous, but entirely transcendent: in place of the intellect, the eyes and ears, the saints will acquire the incomprehensible Spirit and by him hear, see and comprehend (I.3.18). Taken in this sense, knowledge is deifying when it is the result of union with the divine mind.

Despite his assent to the traditional focus on reason as the point of similarity and contact between God and humanity, he draws the connection among knowing, doing and deification more strongly than the connection between knowledge alone and deification. In this respect, Gregory's thought remains firmly in the realm of monastic ascetical writings and tends to eschew the tradition of Christian Platonism. Hence he will describe knowledge as the fruit of a life lived in accord with the commandments. If he also insists that both fall short of deification proper, he links the three unmistakably nonetheless: "The commandments of God give knowledge, and not only knowledge, but deification" (II.3.17); more strongly still, he claims that true knowledge, union and assimilation to God come only by keeping the commandments (II.3.75).

The most persuasive evidence suggesting that knowledge and theosis are intimately connected, however, is the large group of texts in which he associates knowledge with light. Light functions as an image of theosis in two conceptually distinct ways in his thought. On the one hand, its manifestation is external, that which is encountered; on the other hand, it appears internally, as the medium through which one knows or sees. Gregory himself never makes this distinction explicitly, and in many passages the two senses of light merge, as in I.3.36. However, the distinction permits us to tease out those loci where light is associated primarily with knowledge from those where it seems more allied with vision. It is the inner, transforming light that he tends to connect to knowledge: "Knowledge . . . is called light to the extent that it is communicated by divine Light" (I.3.3). In that text, as in I.3.7 and III.1.40, knowledge is identified both as light and light's product.

While Gregory can reject the identification of light and knowledge, the apparent contradictions in his estimations of knowledge can largely be explained by looking at the fundamental distinctions he draws between varieties of it: "If this intellectual light [νοερὸν τουτὶ τὸ φῶς] does not supply knowledge, as the Fathers say, but itself constitutes knowledge . . . the life of Solomon would be more perfect and agreeable to God than those of all the saints" (I.3.50; cf. also III.1.38). Distinguishing between knowledge and wisdom does not eliminate all the textual difficulties, however, as in at least one locus, Gregory flatly denies that light and knowledge can be equated in any fashion.[18]

To a degree, the texts that deny the equation of knowledge with theosis only attest to the indisputable fact that intellectual attainment is one thing and sanctity is another, and to an extent, they simply express the apophaticism typical of both Eastern theology and monastic ascetical teaching: "Theology . . . is not a supernatural union with the super-luminous light" (I.3.15), he admonishes us, a reminder woefully unnecessary in our time, but perhaps less so in his. Even his apophaticism is tempered, however, for with surprising frequency he chides proponents of negative theology who are just as misguided as secularized students of philosophy; God, he asserts reprovingly, is not only above knowing but also above not-knowing (I.3.4).

However, Gregory at times takes an even stronger line, maintaining that deification comes only when the Martha-like intellect finally consents to rest from its self-serving labors: "The cessation of all intellectual activity [νοερᾶς ἐνργείας] . . . is an objective state and a divinising end" (I.3.17; cf. also I.3.18 and I.3.20). In part, the issue here is language and theological method; he is simply protesting the inadequacy of all language toward theology's end.[19] The problem he sees is not purely linguistic, however; it is also a matter of human finitude: "By the very fact of surpassing every cognitive activity [ἐν τῷ ὑπὲρ ὅρασιν καὶ γνῶσιν], such a person finds himself above vision and knowledge [ὁρῶν καὶ ἐνεργῶν]; that means he sees and acts in a way that exceeds us and is already God by grace" (II.3.52). It is not so much that the search for knowledge impedes the goal of deification, or leads one away from it, as that one outlives its usefulness; the intellectual faculties become superfluous when the deiform soul gives itself up, Gregory declares, citing Denys (I.3.20). Even when one may in some sense be said to have deifying knowledge, he wants to qualify severely the mode in which one may be said to have it: the very comprehension one may have, one possesses incomprehensibly (I.3.5).

It is because of this keen awareness of our limitations that he seems most content to ally knowledge and deification where knowledge is clearly not the fruit of humanity's effort to better itself.[20] On the negative side, he avers the relative uselessness of philosophical training because it is merely human; the knowledge that comes from profane education is a gift of nature and not of grace, he chides (I.1.22; cf. *Capita* 20), whereas sacred wisdom is not a natural gift but a gift of God. Not only philosophical study leads to a mistaken dependence on oneself, however, for the *via negativa* can misguide in much the same fashion: "[The negative way] lies within the powers of whoever desires it, and does not transform the soul in such a way as to bestow angelic dignity" (I.3.20).

On the positive side, Palamas is fairly sanguine about the status of knowledge bestowed as a divine gift. Knowledge of the mysteries may be conferred only on the one able to bear it (I.1.7), but it is conferred nonetheless. The knowledge of God by experience that comes from grace (as opposed, presumably, to learning) gives the human person the aspect of God (III.3.13). In a similar vein he writes: "Through this grace [of the Spirit] the mind comes to enjoy the divine effulgence [τῶν θείων μαρμαρυγῶν], and acquires an angelic and godlike form" (I.3.21). In a context that insists upon its bestowal through grace, it seems, knowledge may be viewed as deifying.

For all his reservations regarding knowledge—reservations that are entirely understandable given the rather contemptuous preference of his opponent Barlaam for philosophical over spiritual training—he will readily approach equating deification and knowledge where the intellect is seen as a point of contact at which grace and the incarnate God may do their work.[21] The consequence of this gracious activity is not solely the glorification of the mind; in the context of his very holistic anthropology, the deification of one human faculty implies its perfecting not as an end in itself but as the passage into fellowship with God: "The mind becomes supercelestial, and as it were the companion of him who passed beyond the heavens for our sake" (I.3.5).

3. Vision

Knowledge constitutes one form of apprehension; vision is another. The logic of the connection between these two cognates and theosis lies in the relation they imply between knower and known, seer and seen. Because what is known and seen is no less than God, this contact is transformative. Gregory's portrayal of vision, like his portrayal of knowledge, reflects a certain ambivalence, however. As we saw with knowledge, so we will see with vision both an affirmation and a denial that vision is deifying.

At its most optimistic, his estimation of vision often represents little more than an appreciation of the Transfiguration: "The chosen disciples . . . at Tabor saw the essential and eternal light, the invisible vision of the beauty of God" (III.3.9). The biblical description of the Transfiguration (Lk 9: 28–26 par.) came to occupy an increasingly important position in Eastern theology; by the time of Palamas it had become a locus of prime theological significance—an importance it retains in modern Orthodox theology. For him, the Transfiguration is understood not only as an historic event, but one that announces a dramatic change in the manner in which humanity will encounter God: "The Transfiguration of the Lord on Tabor is a prelude to the visible apparition of God [ὁρατῆς Θεοῦ θεοφανείας] in the glory that is yet to come" (I.3.38). As the figure of Christ is both a visible manifestation of glory and a sign pointing to what surpasses vision, so deification constitutes not only a change within, but also an apparition that may be described in physical terms: "What is this union with the illuminations if not a vision?"[22] (III.2.14).

Nevertheless, as we saw with respect to knowledge, the customary associations of his terms do not necessarily apply to his own usage: "Our holy faith is also, in a way, a vision [ὅρασιν] of our heart that surpasses all sensation and intellection, that transcends all the intellectual faculties of our soul" (II.3.40). Vision, then, both implies experiences such as Tabor that do engage the senses, and experience that is suprasensory, hence Gregory's employment of an oxymoron such as invisible vision. He does not, however, regard his usage as a façon de parler: "[Moses] knows and sees in the proper sense of these terms, since he sees only by transcendence, and does not see with any of his intellectual and sensible powers" (II.3.52). It is not his own language that is fanciful, Palamas seems to say, but our common expectations that fall short of God's intentions; beyond prayer, he tells us, there is vision unspeakable (I.3.18). The deifying gift itself is a positive and substantive encounter with God, but our description of it, utterly inadequate.[23] He stresses both the limitations of human language, or of human nature itself, and the sheer transcendence of the One encountered. While these differ for rhetorical purposes, from a theological perspective they amount to the same: God exceeds human capacities absolutely.

Gregory himself later supplies an explanation for the real experience in vision of what one cannot humanly see: "He sees God by God" (II.3.52). Vision is an appropriate way of understanding the transforming encounter with God, as long as we do not imagine this vision is a natural capacity. It is not so much the physical implications of vision that call for caution as the suggestion that deification represents a natural progression, the harvest of our own labors, for he often ranges seeing alongside knowing, impatiently deeming both as inadequate terms in which to conceive encounter with God:

> If all their intellectual activity has stopped, how could the angels and angelic persons see God except by the power of the Spirit? This is why their vision is not a sensation [αἴσθησις], since they do not receive it through the senses; nor is it an intellection [νόησις], since they do not find it through thought [λογισμῶν] or the knowledge that comes thereby. . . . It is not therefore the product of either imagination or reason. (I.3.18)

If it is not the product of natural mental faculties, no more is it the product of natural sensual ones: "Though they have indeed seen, their organ of vision was properly speaking neither the senses nor the intellect" (I.3.18), a thought he echoes in I.3.21.[24] With this proviso, that we understand our natural faculties as transformed by the encounter with God, Palamas will use the language of sense perception.[25]

Another respect in which it is clear that his demurrals do not constitute solely a flight from the material to the spiritual world, but instead emphasizes the transcending of natural human capacities, is that the content of deifying vision is not exclusively divine. Although he can say, "When we are above things we will see the eternal light directly, without any veil separating us" (II.3.24), he can also point to the implications of transformative sight for human community:

> The fire burns the beam that is in the eye and re-establishes the purity of the human spirit, so that, recovering the view that is ours by nature, one will no longer see the splinter in the eye of one's brother, but observe constantly the miracles of God. (III.1.40)

Deifying vision represents the kingdom of heaven begun among us now and continuing for all eternity; as such, it is a renovation not only of our conception of God but also of ourselves and one another.

4. Contemplation

Contemplation (θεωρία) provides a natural link between knowledge and vision because it seems to partake of the quality of both: the term *contemplation* expresses an activity that is both a form of knowing and a form of seeing. If Palamas seems at times ambivalent in his estimation of both knowledge and vision, we will see in the texts on contemplation an attitude that is almost entirely positive.

This more positive estimation may be attributable to the univocity of contemplation. Vision is susceptible of being interpreted as purely sensory, knowledge as the fruit of purely human intellectual effort; both belong to the secular realm as much as the religious. *Theoria*, on the other hand, was ever the province of monks, who did not doubt that what they experienced through it was not to be gained by human effort but could only come as a gift. Contemplation is supernatural, says Gregory flatly (II.3.23); the one who is never separated from eternal glory is the one who knows and possesses God by a true contemplation that transcends all creatures (II.3.16). Thus the light that comes from contemplation differs radically even from knowledge derived from the scriptures (II.3.18), and at times he denies that contemplation of God is any form of knowledge at all (II.3.16).

Nevertheless, with characteristic balance, he retreats from the suggestion that apophaticism pure and simple will accomplish what positive means, such as knowledge, will not: "Those worthy of this most happy contemplation recognise that this deifying action is superior to any vision, not by way of negation, but by a vision in the Spirit" (II.3.26); even as contemplation surpasses vision, it may be in a certain sense said to retain the character of this vision. On the other hand, if contemplation may not be equated with the *via negativa*, neither is it identifiable with the *via positiva*: contemplation is not simply abstraction or negation but a union and a divinization that occurs mystically and ineffably by the grace of God (I.3.17).

The balance between apophatic and kataphatic strains in Palamas' estimation of contemplation emerges clearly in a passage early in the *Triads*: "Perfect contemplation of God and divine things is not only a stripping away [ἀφαίρεσίς], but beyond this, a participation in divine things, a gift and possession more than a stripping away" (I.3.18).

The stripping away, it appears, is not an end in itself but a preparation for something positive, which must be understood entirely as a divine gift.

What is experienced in contemplation, then, is truly God, and for this reason, *theoria* must be understood not as a particular practice of prayer that can be taught but as the gift of divine grace: the saints can unite themselves to the light and see it if they have purified themselves by consecrating their mind to pure and immaterial prayer, so as to receive the supernatural power of contemplation (I.3.19). Contemplation thus functions not only as the means to theosis but as the end itself: "By unifying perfection [Denys] meant the coming and indwelling of God in us, which are accomplished in union and which nourish the spiritual eye by contemplation" (II.3.74). As an end in itself, *theoria* is rooted both in history and eternity; like theosis, it is the inauguration of the next world in this: "This contemplation has a beginning . . . but never an end, because its progress is infinite, like the ravishment of revelation" (II.3.35). Palamas connects this contemplation directly to fellowship with God.[26] Since God's fellowship is obviously only to be had at God's good pleasure, contemplation must be seen as coming at God's initiative and not as the result of assiduous ascetical practice.

5. Light

If Gregory exhibits little ambivalence with respect to contemplation, he shows even less with regard to light.[27] As we noted earlier, light stands on the border of our hierarchy of images between the lesser and the greater and reflects this status by partaking of the characteristics of both groups. He identifies light with God, as deification's source, as the agent of human sanctification, and as deification itself (αὐτοθέωσις; I.3.23). The light can be portrayed as Other and external to the human subject and as the transformative power working within. Because he portrays it in these two quite different ways, light is often linked to the other cognates, with knoweldge, glory and union, as well as with the persons of the Trinity.[28] We will therefore examine the texts on light from two perspectives: those which emphasize light as transformative and those which portray it as what we encounter.

Let us begin by noting that Gregory does not see these two facets of light as either mutually exclusive or inherently opposed, for he at times speaks of light in both ways at once, as when he quotes Denys: "This light is a supraluminous and theurgic beam, also called the deifying gift and source of Divinity"[29] (III.1.29) or when he contends in III.3.9 "the light . . . deifies those who contemplate it."[30] These texts point to his portrait of God, whom we know primarily as the one who sanctifies, and his doctrine of sanctifying grace, which is none other than God himself.

The desire to regard light in both its outer and inner aspects emerges also as he tries to describe how light engages the human person. On the one hand, he will insist it is sensible, perceptible to the senses, and on the other, insist it surpasses the senses entirely. Because the light is identified with God, Gregory is understandably ambivalent about claiming it is perceptible to the senses. Thus at times he flatly states the light is sensible, and sensible in precisely the fashion we would expect, to the eyes: "This light [that appeared on the face of Moses] was not knowledge but an illumination. . . . this light, accessible to the sensible eyes, is itself sensible" (I.3.7). This view finds support from no less than Gregory Nazianzen, who calls the light a sensible light, visible by the medium of the air (III.1.11). On other occasions, he prefers to qualify the assertion that the light is sensible, maintaining that it is so only to those whose vision has been transformed. "The light is inaccessible to senses not transformed by the Spirit" (II.3.22), he writes, implying that it is accessible to senses so transformed. More unmistakably, he says of the Transfiguration that light becomes accessible to the eyes who have spiritual power.[31] A variation of this theme is the claim that the direct vision of eternal light is reserved for a future "when we are above these things" (II.3.24).

Balancing these repeated assurances that we can indeed perceive the divine light, at least in some qualified fashion, are other passages in which he appears to claim just the opposite. The light surpasses sensations, he tells us in II.3.23, clarifying in II.3.25 that this surpassing does not imply a bypassing of sense perception: "Intelligence and sensation will receive the same and single light . . . but in a way that surpasses the senses and the intelligence."

We might justifiably take these two groups of passages as evidence of self-contradiction, if it were not for other texts in which Gregory combines both tendencies in apparent harmony. "Those who see the light consider it as invisible" (I.3.24), he writes, evidently unconcerned at the discord sounded by *see* and *invisible*. He resolves the tension by an appeal to transcendence similar to what we saw previously. He continues in I.3.24: "Those who are elevated to this degree of contemplation know that they see a light with their intellectual sense; they know this light is God." Since the light is a person, seeing the light constitutes a species of knowing or acquaintance.

Why, though, does Gregory continue to use the language of seeing at all? One possibility is that he is working within the well-established tradition of the spiritual senses, described thus by Mariette Canévet:

> The expression "spiritual sense" . . . essentially translates a simple experience: no one has ever seen God (John 1:18). But God is not thereby separated from those he has created in his own image and destined to participate in his life; God is to them, in a way, accessible. Therefore, just as the body possesses sensory organs suited to apprehending the world, so we possess one or more organs ordered to the perception of divine, spiritual, and immaterial realities: "the knowledge of God does not depend on the eye of the body, but on that of the spirit, which is in the image of the Creator and which has through God's providence received the power of knowing God" (Origen, *Contra Celsum*, VII, 33).[32]

Clearly, there are striking similarities between Gregory's ambivalent use of sensory images and this Origenistic scheme, in which the spiritual senses enable the bridging of the gap between the material and immaterial worlds. If the status of light as a perceptible phenomenon is ambiguous, the ambiguity is constructive and thoroughly consistent with his overall doctrine of theosis. The light is of genuinely divine provenance and as such, must transcend the material realm; nevertheless, light is also a point of contact between God and humanity and must therefore be somehow apprehensible by finite and material beings.

Like the Fathers before him, Gregory wants to claim that, as God creates a psychosomatic unity, so the whole person, body, mind and soul, must be divinized. Hence the simultaneous insistence on the light as both material and immaterial correlates with the insistence that the light engages the whole person. On the one hand, he claims as one of the effects of deification a regeneration of the intellect: light illuminates and deifies the intellect (I.3.23). Yet, on the other hand, illumination also engages the soul in many texts: "These sensible illuminations [αἰσθῆτοι ἐκεῖνοι φωτιμοί] produced by the ancient Law prefigured the illumination of the Spirit [φωτιμὸν τοῦ Πνεύματος] which takes place in the souls of those who believe in Christ" (I.3.12). He completes his account of the transformation wrought by light when he claims the effect of light is the power of resurrection and an energy of immortality (III.1.40). Thus, divinizing light as he portrays it engages the psychosomatic unity, the mind and the soul as well as the body:

> Since the Son of God . . . unites himself . . . to human hypostases themselves . . . since he becomes a single body with us . . . how would he not illuminate those who worthily commune with the divine ray [τῆς θεϊκῆς αὐγῆς] of his body who is in us, by lighting their souls as he illuminated the very bodies of the disciples on Tabor? For this body, the source of the light of grace, is not yet united to our bodies; it illuminates from without those who approach it worthily and sends illumination to the soul by the intermediary of the sensible eyes. (I.3.38)

These various dimensions of illumination, as inner and outer, as encountered and as transforming body, mind and soul, coalesce for Gregory in the greatest of Biblical images for both deification and light, the Transfiguration. The references to Tabor demonstrate conclusively that he conceives of theosis not as the summit of ascetical experience, the reward for spiritual striving, but as a transformation that is above all the work of God's mercy. The Transfiguration represents, above all, the christological dimension of divinization:

> Our nature has been stripped of this divine illumination and radiance as a result of the transgression. . . . [On Tabor the Word] indicated what we once were and what we shall become through him in the future age if we choose here below to live according to his ways as much as possible, as John Chrysostom says. (Capita 66)

The Transfiguration, then, represents a kind of recapitulation of the whole divine Economy; the entire story of salvation from creation, through the Fall and our redemption, to consummation, is condensed into this one moment, and thus a single moment of history stands as a comprehensive statement of Christian theology, like a creed, a symbol of the faith. The light at the Transfiguration is sacramental in Gregory's view; it not only designates the was and will be of divine action but also creates a space in which human history and destiny unite to hallow the present. The vision revealed to the apostles on Tabor was not a symbolic light that appears and then disappears; rather, it possesses the value of the second coming of Christ (I.3.26). The function of the vision at Tabor, and the evangelical witness to it, is to manifest the advent of paradise among us now, to show that the hypostatic union in Christ is both an historical event that has been accomplished and the consequent beginning of the sanctification of the entire race. The Transfiguration encompasses human history, stretching from the event at Tabor forward to the eschaton: "The light which illuminated the disciples at the most holy Transfiguration will continually and endlessly dazzle us 'with its most brilliant rays' in the Age to Come" (II.3.20; cf. also III.1.10 and III.1.16). What Tabor shows theosis to be is the transference of the principle of hypostatic union to those whose nature is solely human:

> Since the Son becomes a single body with us . . . how would he not illuminate those who worthily commune with the divine ray of his body who is in us, by lighting their souls as he illuminated the very bodies of the disciples on Tabor? (I.3.38)

In extraordinary cases, such as Paul's, the vision of light transforms the human person into a clearly superhuman being.[33]

The Transfiguration, with its dual emphasis on transformation and encounter, binds together the two chief attributes of light and so leads to the second group of texts, which portray light as hypostasized, as Other and therefore, as God:

> Those who are elevated to this degree of contemplation know they see a light with their intellectual sense; they know this light is God who by grace in union renders those who participate mysteriously luminous. (I.3.24)

Palamas also specifically identifies light with both the Second and Third Persons of the Trinity. The fact that he allies light with these two, and not with the First Person, suggests a common function of light, Christ and the Spirit: to communicate knowledge and grace within the realm of the Economy.[34] He calls Christ the true light, the radiance of glory (III.1.15) and in III.1.16 declares Jesus to be deifying light. The angels, he says, "behold the manifestation of the light of Jesus, revealed to his disciples on Tabor. . . . he himself is deifying light" (I.3.5), and he later quotes Macarius as saying the light is the glory of Christ (I.3.7). With respect to the Spirit, he writes:

> Such a divine and celestial life belongs to those who live in a manner pleasing to God participating in the life inseparable from the Spirit. . . . Such a life exists always; it exists in the very nature of the Spirit. . . . It is a light, accorded in a mysterious illumination. (III.1.9)[35]

Conclusions drawn from such texts must nevertheless be tempered by consideration of Gregory's much more cautious formulations elsewhere. For example in III.1.13 he speaks of "the grace of this light," demanding that one not believe it is a created entity, foreign to the Divinity, and implying it is also not the same as divine nature.[36] In III.1.20 he cites the evidence of hymnody as confirmation that "this light is one of the realities contemplated around God" and in III.1.12 rejects the conception of light as the created symbol of divinity, rather than the divinity itself. Similarly, he quotes Nazianzen: "One calls [the light] Divinity because it is a symbol of the Divinity" (III.1.11); the pattern here closely resembles the one just noted. Light and divinity may indeed correctly be spoken of as one and the same, but in terming light a symbol for Divinity, Nazianzen—and therefore also Gregory—to a degree undermines his own equation.

Nevertheless, Palamas perhaps does not vacillate on this point as much as might first appear. He does want to say that the light is divine, but he takes care not to make the identification absolute, hence his denial that the light is divine substance or essence: "This light is not the essence of God, because that is inaccessible and incommunicable" (II.3.9).[37] When texts such as these are ranged alongside those we examined earlier, which do seem to equate light with God, a fairly consistent pattern emerges: the light may be said to be God when we are speaking of God as self-communicating or participable. In I.3.24, for example, Gregory does not baldly assert that the light is God, but that "the light is God who by his grace renders those who participate mysteriously luminous." We need not claim that the relative clause is restrictive; it is enough that when he makes the equation, Palamas accompanies it with additional information, signalling the terms in which he is thinking of the Deity. Likewise in III.1.9, reference to the light as Spirit occurs in the context of discussion about participation in life inseparable from the Spirit. Palamas is clearly not thinking of the transcendent essence of the Spirit but the Spirit considered specifically in its communicable aspect. In this sense—and in this sense alone—light is the Spirit.

The single text that does not itself imply some such tempered interpretation is III.1.16, where light is linked directly to the Trinity and Jesus. Although we might say that speaking specifically of Jesus (rather than Christ) automatically indicates that Gregory is thinking of the Economy and the communicating, unified hypostasis rather than the transcendent Word, he remains silent regarding the Trinity. In view of the prevailing pattern already established, however, we might well assume he is associating light with what we would call the economic rather than the immanent Trinity. The conclusions one would draw from the texts regarding the divine status of light correlate with what he claims explicitly of the essence-energies distinction: the agent of divinization, that in God which we encounter and which transforms us, is the divine energy, not the divine essence.

Gregory's thought on light as deification ranges more widely and with more complexity than it does with respect to any other cognate.[38] As if realizing this, he himself supplies a capsule summary of the varied ways in which he understands light:

> This light, mysterious, inaccessible, immaterial, uncreated, deifying, eternal, this radiance of divine nature, glory of the Divinity, beauty of the celestial realm, is accessible to the senses, all the while surpassing them. (III.1.22)

6. Glory

The association of light with God is partial in Palamas' thought, as we have seen . The border between the greater and the lesser images is apparent in the much stronger association of glory with the divine. The implications of glory for the doctrine of God we will consider in the next chapter, when we examine the essence-energies distinction. Here, then, we are chiefly concerned with glory as human persons encounter it, or, to use the categories we will explore more fully in the next chapter, we will then be concerned with glory as transcendent, while we are here concerned with it as the authentic impartation of divine life to humanity. The two themes cannot entirely be separated, of course, for glory signifies the communicability of divine life: "God, while remaining entirely in himself, dwells in us by his superessential power, and communicates to us not his nature, but his proper glory and splendour" (I.3.23).

Thus, glory is that in divine nature which we contemplate, and contemplation of this glory is transformative: "We contemplate the glory of his holy nature when it pleases God to introduce us to the spiritual mysteries" (II.3.15, quoting Isaac of Nineveh), a sentiment so important to Gregory that he rewords and repeats it a little later.[39] The connection we observe here is highly significant, not only if we are to grasp what he means by glory but also in order to understand the logic of divinization in general. The vision and contemplation of glory are not simply moments in which we apprehend God but are themselves the means by which God apprehends us, rehabilitates our nature and takes us up into his own life.

Paradoxically, although glory functions as an alternate name for divine energy, Palamas does not shy from also associating it in the most intimate way with humanity: "It is not only to the human composite which is united to his hypostasis that he has given this transcendent glory, but also to his disciples,"[40] he declares in II.3.15, echoing what he said earlier: "To our human nature he has given the glory of the Godhead."[41] In such texts Gregory virtually asserts a *communicatio idiomatum* between Divinity and humanity, so that eventually what we contemplate in God is also visible in ourselves: "We possess [deification] in a perfect manner and in the Spirit, we see in ourselves the glory of God, when it pleases God to lead us to spiritual mysteries" (II.3.17). There can scarcely be any stronger affirmation of deification than this: that what we have seen in God, in virtue of God's grace alone, we will see in ourselves.

Palamas remains nonetheless clear that the glory is properly Christ's, even as he bestows it upon us. It is in the glory of the Father that Christ will come again, he asserts, and it is in the glory of their Father, Christ, that the just will shine like the sun (II.3.66). One important dimension of the christological basis for divinizing glory is his frequent insistence on the body as the recipient of glory: "We carry the Father's light in the face of Jesus Christ in earthen vessels, that is, in our bodies, in order to know the glory of the Holy Spirit" (I.2.2). As the Incarnation affirms the goodness of the human being, so it also grounds the body's divinization. At another level, however, to insist glory belongs properly to Christ is no more than to affirm glory's divine origin. He emphasizes the gratuity and divine provenance of glory in the deified most strongly in III.2.15: "[The angels] do not naturally possess the eternal vision of the eternal glory, but they receive this power and contemplation as a free gift from the Eternal Nature, just as the saints do."

While in general Palamas portrays the bestowal of glory as a gift in which the saints already participate, he appears occasionally to reserve the transformative-transfigurative experience for the second coming and the next life.[42] This eschatological dimension is however balanced by the assertion of glory as part of our unblemished nature:

> Before the transgression Adam too participated in this divine illumination and radiance, and as he was truly clothed in a garment of glory he was not naked, nor was he indecent because he was naked. (*Capita* 67)

It is this glory that is lost at the Fall:

> In shame they hid themselves, stripped of the glory which grants a more excellent life to the immortal spirits and without which the life of the spirits is believed to be and is indeed far worse than many deaths. (*Capita* 48)

The loss of glory, then, implies separation from God, and the bestowal of glory signifies both redemption and consummation, the healing and perfecting of nature by the grace of Christ:

> As to him who mysteriously possesses and sees this light, he knows and possesses God in himself . . . for he is never separated from the eternal glory. . . . Let us not, then, turn aside incredulous before the superabundance of these blessings; but let us have faith in him who has participated in our nature and granted it in return the glory of his own nature, and let us seek how to acquire this glory and see it. (II.3.16)

7. Grace

The texts surveyed thus far show that while Gregory does not abandon the monastic ascetical tradition and its emphasis on spiritual and moral striving, he nevertheless views theosis overwhelmingly as a divine gift, not as a transformation effected by the human person herself. This view of theosis demands that we raise the question of the relationship between divinization and grace. For Gregory *grace* and *gift* are often accompanied by modifiers such as *divine* or *divinizing*. Grace is for him, then, both to be identified with divine nature and not some derivative of it and with the divine engagement of humanity that results in union.

Clearly, divinization comes only as the gift of grace; so much is evident from the texts we have already seen, which do not treat grace proper. Where he allies theosis and grace, then he is only making explicit what is clearly implicit throughout his writings: "God, by his grace, renders those who participate mysteriously luminous" (I.3.24); "knowledge of God by experience comes from grace which gives man the aspect of God" (III.3.13); "through this grace [of the Spirit] the mind comes to enjoy the divine effulgence and acquires an angelic and godlike form" (I.3.20); and: "It is through grace that 'the entire Divinity comes to dwell in fullness in those deemed worthy'" (III.1.27, citing Maximus). In the clearest text of all, he speaks of Moses, who especially since Gregory of Nyssa's *Life* had been identified in the Christian spiritual tradition as the paradigm of the sanctified: "He surpasses humanity and is already God by grace" (II.3.52). Of the many ways in which Gregory allies deification and grace, this insistence upon deification as solely a divine gift is the most basic to his thought.

It is because theosis can only result from the divine act of self-giving that he reiterates over and over again that deification is not merely the perfection of nature (III.1.30; cf. also III.1.29). One cannot deify oneself, he admonishes Barlaam in III.1.25, drawing support from Maximus, and states flatly in III.1.26 that the grace of deification in perfectly free. He also cites Maximus in support of his position in the *Capita*.[43] Palamas goes beyond simply maintaining grace is supernatural, however; he also claims that regarding the grace of deification as a natural state is Messalian heresy. His utter conviction of the necessity of grace to attain a supernatural end nevertheless emerges most clearly when he asserts the need that even angels have of this grace.[44]

The characteristic insistence on grace does not prevent him from at times affirming the necessity of ascetical preparation, as we have seen, but he does so in a manner that in no way undermines the primacy of grace itself, for union and a divinzing end belong only to those who have purified their heart and received grace (I.3.17). More pointedly still, he writes in III.1.26: "Do not imagine that deification is simply the possession of the virtues; rather, it resides in the radiance and grace of God, which actually comes to us through the virtues." Grace is freely given but given freely to those worthy of it (III.1.29). Even as he seems to claim human agency, he simultaneously asserts the christological principle of divinizing grace: "The way in which the deified unite themselves to God [is] a union like that of the soul to the body, so that the entire person is deified, divinised by the grace of the God become human" (III.3.13). The stress on virtuous striving, then, is an important subtext of the main discourse, which concerns the gratuity of God's self-communication.

The degree to which grace exceeds human virtue is evident in Gregory's portrayal of it as more than a means to an end; often he appears to equate grace and theosis indistinguishably. He maintains in III.3.13: "[We become] entirely God in body and soul through grace and through the divine radiance of the blessed glory."[45] It is claims such as this that worry many Westerners, who have forgotten, or not learned, the structure of the patristic doctrine of salvation and sanctification, for such statements seem to breach the ontological divide between created and Uncreated. It is because Gregory acknowledges the inviolability of that divide that he insists that such becoming "entirely God" is by grace, not nature. The connection between divinization and grace, then, is not only to deny that human beings cannot enter into divine life of their own volition but also to affirm the ontological divide, since participation in divine nature by grace is not the same as possession of divinity by nature.

Because divinizing grace takes humanity beyond human nature, Gregory will some-times take pains to distinguish grace in this form from other varieties of grace.[46] The grace of deification surpasses nature, virtue and knowledge; it is a form of grace, it seems, that itself brings about the mysterious union (III.1.27; cf. also III.1.26 and III.1.32). One of the distinguishing marks of divinizing grace is that it not only heals or sanctifies in some general fashion but also forges a bond between donor and recipient. On one oc-casion, he expresses this sentiment in terms remarkably consonant with those favored by the Reformation traditions: "This grace is in fact a relationship, albeit not a natural one; yet it is at the same time beyond relationship"[47] (III.1.29). The terms in which he speaks of grace, in this passage as in others we have seen—as supernatural and always beyond what one may truly affirm of it—indicates that he does think of grace as divine, for these are the terms in which he habitually speaks of God.

Nevertheless, if divinizing grace differs from other varieties of grace and is at least sometimes equatable with theosis itself, it is not identifiable with God *tout court*. "The Fathers say," writes Gregory "that the divine grace of this suprasensible light is God. But God in his nature is not wholly identifiable with this grace" (I.3.23). Grace, then, is not baldly equatable with God, not because it is not authentically divine but because it does not encompass the fulness of God. On this issue, the *Capita* generally provides the most precise guide to Gregory's thought: "This very radiance and divinising energy of God . . . is a certain divine grace, but not the nature of God. This does not imply that God's nature is distant from those who receive grace" (93). If, however, Gregory exer-cises great caution in allying grace with God, refusing to equate the two fully, he never-theless does identify grace with divinity, or divine energy, on a more than occasional basis. In I.3.23, for example, he cites Denys as precedent for calling divinity the deifying gift that proceeds from God and then provides his own gloss on Denys' views of the matter:

> So the Fathers tell us that the divine grace of the suprasensible light is God. But God in his nature does not simply identify himself with this grace, because he is not only able to illuminate and deify the mind, but also to bring forth every intellectual essence from nonbeing.

If grace is not to be equated outright with divine nature, Palamas at least has no hesita-tion in claiming the closest of relations between the two short of identification. Simi-larly, he quotes Damascene, claiming that the splendor of divine grace is not something external, like the splendor possessed by Moses, but belongs to the very nature of the divine glory and splendor (III.1.22).

The desire to identify grace and theosis with God and yet not limit God to action within the sphere of the Economy—or indeed, limit divine life to action—explains, in part, why Gregory resorts to an analysis of God as being or substance on the one hand, and energy on the other. We will study this question more closely in the next chapter, but it is impossible to comment upon the relation between grace and theosis without considering grace as energy.

Part of the need for the essence-energies distinction for which he is so well known arises from the desire of the Eastern tradition, and Palamas following it, to insist upon the uncreated nature of grace. This insistence follows naturally from the fundamental premise of theosis: grace cannot render us divine if it is itself not divine, and it cannot be truly divine unless it is also uncreated. Palamas asserts the uncreated nature of grace in III.1.8; he makes the virtually equivalent assertion, that grace is without a beginning, in III.3.8. Those means of divine agency which are in themselves uncreated and fully divine are termed the energies of God, and among these energies grace is numbered. Divine and divinizing illumination and grace are the energy of God, he writes in chapter 69 of the *Capita*, reiterating in 147 that energy is none other than divine grace and illumination. That the energy is both truly that of the divine Trinity, yet nevertheless (and paradoxically) accessible to the saints he explains unmistakably: the energy and power common to the trihypostatic nature is variously and proportionately divided among its participants, and for this reason it is accessible to those who have received grace (*Capita* 109). In a deduction rather more startling, he invokes a sort of *communicatio idiomatum*, claiming that this divine energy not only deifies the saints but also dwells in them permanently: the spiritual grace that comes into the heart is a permanent energy produced by grace, tied to the soul and rooted in it (II.2.9).[48]

In the texts on grace, then, we find articulated the central principle of theosis: the bestowal of the divine gift transforms its recipient, and through this transformation is wrought a likening to God that can alone enable true fellowship. The magnitude of this fellowship—and the transformation upon which it is founded—is such that it can only come about through divine initiative, and this insistence upon the distinction between the divine source as donor and the human subject as always recipient is another hallmark of a classical doctrine of deification.

8. Adoption

As a cognate for deification, Gregory uses adoption (υἱοθεσία) far less frequently than the other images we have encountered, and those usages are largely confined to one extended section of the *Triads*, III.1.27–34. Nevertheless, these passages form the heart of his teaching on theosis, so the confined space in which the references to adoption occur provides no reliable gauge of their importance. The imagery of adoption is significant, moreover, because it underscores a key theme we have seen emerging from the texts on grace: our incorporation into divine life comes about through God's initiative and by surpassing the capacities of our nature.

At times, adoption functions as no more than a correlative to deification, as when Palamas rapidly strings together images of theosis in III.1.29: "You should not consider that God allows Himself to be seen in His superessential essence, but according to His deifying gift and energy, the grace of adoption, the uncreated deification, the enhypostatic illumination"; or when he writes in III.1.28: "Deification is also the invocation of the great God and Father, the symbol of the authentic and real adoption, according to the gift and grace of the Holy Spirit, thanks to the bestowal of which grace the saints become and will remain the sons of God" (III.1.28).

Elsewhere, however, Gregory allies adoption with more explicitly metaphysical principles: "[The Father] could be called Father and Trinity in relation to creation because there is one work of the three brought forth into creation from absolute nothingness and for the sake of adoption of sons by the grace given in common by the three" (*Capita* 132; cf. III.1.27). This passage attests to his understanding of adoption not as a juridical declaration but as God's intended culmination of creation.[49] It is this ontological regeneration that he understands by adoption, and it is because of its metaphysical implications that he asserts the adoption is hypostatic: "The saints clearly state that this adoption, actualised by faith,[50] is enhypostatic" (III.1.31).

Although less frequently employed than the other cognates, adoption is highly significant for the accuracy with which it summarizes the crucial themes of the Palamite doctrine of deification: the necessity of grace, the trancendence of natural capacities, and deification, not as the breaching of the natural order but as its consummation.

9. Participation

As we saw earlier, while Gregory generally portrays light as what the deified encounter, occasionally he speaks of it as what the saints become: "The deifying gift of the Spirit is a mysterious light and transforms into light those who receive its richness" (III.1.35). The connection between what one encounters and what one becomes is participation[51]: God by his grace renders those who participate mysteriously luminous (I.3.24; cf. also II.3.26 and *Capita* 69). One emphasis of the texts on participation is the simple fact of human participation in divine life. To affirm this participation at all, however, he must simultaneously establish a divine identity: the one who is by definition absolutely transcendent is also the one who invites and enables human participation in his being. The texts on participation thus foreshadow more strongly than those of any other cognate both the twin themes characteristic of the Palamite doctrine of deification, transcendence and authenticity, and the distinction between divine essence and energies. While study of both these areas is the task of the next chapter, we may point here to the paradox that lies at the heart of both the themes and the distinction.

On the one hand, Palamas affirms both the reality of participation in the divine and its sanctifying effect on humanity: "Those who have raised up their mind to God and have exalted their souls with divine longing . . . partake with the soul in divine communion, becoming a dwelling and possession of God" (I.2.9). Participation is not, however, the fragile spire that represents the vertex of spiritual life, but is rather its precondition. Borrowing from the Platonic intuition that only like knows like, he declares that *ta theia* (divine things) are recognized by participation only (III.1.21). Yet this recognition of *ta theia* itself constitutes the return to God; the participation on which it is based is rooted not in our nature but in God's: "A divine and celestial life belongs to those who live in a manner pleasing to God, participating in the life inseparable from the Spirit . . . . [such a life] exists in the very nature of the Spirit, whose nature it is to deify" (III.1.9). In the *Capita*, he echoes Nazianzen, describing the rationale for participation as lying immediately in human nature but ultimately, and most truly therefore, in the divine will: "For this purpose God made us, to make us partakers of his own divinity" (105; cf. also 78). The reality of participation in God is nevertheless a theme that emerges more strongly from the pages of the *Triads* than the *Capita*. The *Capita* focuses more narrowly on purely conceptual and philosophical issues, such as the logic of the energies' being uncreated. The *Triads*, in contrast, tends to argue for uncreated energy from that fact of spiritual life which Gregory takes for granted: genuine participation in God (III.2.19).

On the other hand, he recognizes the need to preserve the transcendence of divine being, a theme on the whole more typical of the *Capita* than of the *Triads*: "There will be no participation in the substance of the Creator" (*Capita* 94). Neither, he adds later, is there participation in divine hypostasis (*Capita* 109). Nevertheless, he does not neglect to make virtually the same point in the *Triads*, asking whether the divine essence transcends all that is participable (III.1.29). It seems by these statements that Gregory has impaled himself on the horns of a dilemma, and indeed he admits as much himself: "The same God is at the same time participable and imparticipable"[52] (III.2.25), he announces, and given his training in Aristotle we must presume he is fully cognizant of how close he comes to offending the most basic principle of logical argument.

His solution, of course, is the distinction for which he is above all renowned, between divine essence and energies: "All things participate in the sustaining energy but not in the substance of God" (*Capita* 104). Since the details of that distinction and its importance for Palamas' work do not concern us for the moment, suffice it to say that the texts on participation specify in what exactly we participate, in order to affirm the reality of participation in divine life. The assertion of a participable divine energy is what opens the way for the simultaneous claim of participation and transcendence, both of which he wishes to guard. The consequence of suppressing what is between the Imparticipable and its participants is, in his view, separating humanity from God. The doctrine of theosis may be described as the claim of God's gracious bridging of, without violating, the divide between ourselves and him, so that we never know the sorrow of such separation, and the essence-energies distinction, the technical grounds for those claims.

10. Union

Of all the cognates, union probably functions as the nearest equivalent to theosis.[53] Gregory's customary ambivalence is nowhere in evidence: he reveals no misgivings about describing deification as union with God.[54] He describes union in terms that are fully equatable with deification: "This union will enable persistence to the end with a pure spirit in the most narrow relations with God" (II.2.20), and he later stipulates that those most narrow relations mean direct relations with God in which no intermediary such as an angel intervenes (II.3.27 and 28). The divine indwelling implied by union entails the perfection that is theosis; he glosses Denys, equating unifying perfection with the coming and indwelling of God within us (II.3.74).

Palamas however makes clear that union in deification is not hypostatic: "Hypostatic union happens to be predicated of the Word and God-man alone . . . those deemed worthy of union with God are united to God in energy and spirit" (*Capita* 75). Once again we see him wanting to preserve both the authenticity of divine self-communication and the ultimate otherness of God. Thus while the christological hypostatic union is unique, he indicates a commonality between the union of *Deus homo* and of God with human persons: "[This] glory belongs to the divine nature, which [is] united to this adored Body in the person of one of its holy hypostases" (II.3.21). In these passages, then, Palamas sets up an is–is not tension. Union expresses the consummate quality of the relation between two natures, one divine and one human, and the fact that this term is used appropriately of both the relation of natures in Christ and the graced relation of human persons with God indicates an important parallelism between the Incarnation and deification. Nevertheless, Gregory wants to insist upon the uniqueness of the hypostatic union, so that deification cannot be taken as a potential multiplier of Christs. The Incarnation's redemptive significance establishes it as the causal principle of all reconciliation to God, and therefore all sanctification, but the Incarnation, as an event unique in human history, is not the first of a series of hypostatic unions.

Although union does not elevate human beings to the level of divine nature, it does entail the saints' transcendence of themselves.[55] Palamas associates union with transcendence in two quite distinct ways. The first lies in union's enabling us to transcend our own natural powers, particularly those of sensation and understanding: "By this union, the mind sees God in the Spirit in a manner transcending human powers" (II.3.11). The second entails our moving closer to God by understanding how God transcends all: "The mystical union with light teaches [the saints] that this light is superessentially transcendent to all things" (I.3.19). He combines both insights in II.3.36, writing: "Since [union] is brought about by the cessation of intellectual activity, how could it be accomplished if not by the Spirit?"

If in this union, we transcend ourselves, knowledge and even light, it virtually follows that union can only be with the One who himself transcends all. It is because union alone entails self-transcendence through attachment to the All-transcendent that it functions most satisfactorily as a cognate for theosis:

> What then is this union which by virtue of its transcendence is not to be identified with any being? Is it apophatic theology? . . . to practise negative theology we do not need to go out of ourselves, whereas to enter into this union, even the angels must go out from themselves. (II.3.35)

This going out, however, is not conceived solely as an exit from humanity in its natural state; it is, more positively, the acquisition of a new identity, as Gregory says of Paul, "he was that to which he was united" (II.3.37).

IV. Coda: A Note on Love in Palamite Theology

Our study of Palamas has included no treatment of love because love does not emerge as one of the prime cognates for deification in his work. Nevertheless, in order to facilitate comparison with Aquinas, it will be helpful to establish Gregory's attitude to love. In so doing, we will find that although love cannot be classed among the prime cognates, it remains an important category in the Palamite theology of theosis.[56]

The significance of Gregory's treatment of love lies perhaps in its conventionality; it is not to these passages that we should look to appreciate his insightful power to renew tradition. Rather, here he shows us how the conventional insights of the Christian theological and ascetical tradition mesh effortlessly into the Palamite synthesis.

One measure of the extent to which Palamas remains within those traditions is the evenhandedness with which he treats love as sanctification and love as union. On the one hand, he portrays love as that which inculcates holiness, and in such contexts it is often linked to the commandments: "Perfection consists in assimilation [ἀφομοίωσις] to God and . . . this comes about only in love by the holy practice of the divine commandments" (II.1.40), and: "The philosophers who believe in Christ and follow revelation hold that assimilation to Christ which is health and perfection of the soul, is only accomplished in love and observation of the commandments" (II.1.42). Palamas does not simply assert the connection between love and holiness, as he might have done, following the evangelical witness. He consistently links the two in love's tendency to be attracted towards an end: "It is with the passionate part of the soul that we love and turn around' (II.2.23) and more fully:

> It is with [the passionate part of the soul, τῇ δυνάμει τῆς ψυχῆς ἀγαπιῶμέν] that we love or else turn away, that we unite ourselves or else remain strangers. Those who love the good thus transform this power, and do not put it to death; they do not enclose it immovable in themselves [οὐκ ἀκίνητον κατακλείσαντες ἐν ἑαυτοῖς], but activate it towards love of God and and their neighbors—for, according to the Lord's words "on these two commands hang all the Law and the Prophets." (III.3.15)

The depiction of love here is highly ambivalent: because love comes from the center of passion, it has the potential to turn either towards the good or away from it.[57] This flexibility, however, does not command Gregory's interest. The focus of his concern is that to turn, to unite, one must love; for this reason one cannot simply put the passionate part of the soul to death. On this point, then, he differs from some of the more dire voices of the ascetical tradition. Passion, then, which includes love, occupies much the same place that the will might occupy in the work of another thinker. Characteristically, he gives a specifically Christian context and Christian name to a category well established in the Hellenistic philosophical tradition.

Nevertheless, he also Christianizes those categories by expanding them. In the philosophical tradition, the pursuit of knowledge is a matter of l'art pour l'art; why one seeks knowledge and why one articulates one's science, art or philosophy is self-evident. Palamas, in contrast, feels the need to explain why one communicates the matter of faith and the stuff of spiritual experience and explains this impetus in highly Christian terms: "It is because of their love of humanity that the saints speak, as far as this is possible, about ineffable things, rejecting the error of those who in their ignorance, imagine that after the abstraction from beings there remains only an absolute inaction, not an inaction surpassing all action" (I.3.19). He thus gives us a glimpse of a grounding for his theological method that lies wholly outside the exigencies of the hesychast controversy. God must be spoken of, even though speech is impossible, because humanity needs such discourse. Theology, the expression of the inexpressible, thus becomes an act of love.

Balancing this stress on love as means to an end are a group of texts in which Gregory portrays love as itself the end. In the most extended treatment of love in the Triads, he brings both emphases together but portrays the end in the most unmistakably deifying terms:

> One will harvest the knowledge of God from the knowledge of beings, since one will have seized the spiritual sense from beings, and one will practice the corresponding virtues with the aid of the passionate part of the soul which will act in conformity with the end that God proposes on creating it. With the concupiscent appetite one will embrace

charity; with the irascible appetite one will assume perseverance. It is not the one who kills the passionate part of the soul but the one who subjugates it, so that by obedience to the spirit he will go to God and tend to God through the uninterrupted memory of God; thanks to this memory he will arrive at possessing a divine disposition and make it progress towards a still better possession, which is the love of God. By this love he accomplishes the commandments given to someone who is loved, by which he learns, he puts into practice and acquires the love pure and perfect for his neighbour. It is not possible that he will not also possess impassibility. (II.2.19; cf. also II.2.23)

The movement from passion that derives from God, to God-directed loving, to the God-likeness of impassibility is a movement purely through stages of love. In another passage, Palamas goes so far as to portray love lying beyond impassibility: "Such is the way that by passing through impassibility leads to perfect love: . . . this union will create perseverance to the end with a pure spirit, in the most narrow relations with God" (II.2.20). The terms in which he describes these "most narrow relations" leave no doubt regarding the connection of love and deification: "Entirely seized by love, they leave the body and do not cease to commune with the divine spirit by prayer and love" (II.2.23).

Given this unequivocal identification of love and theosis and Gregory's ambivalence towards knowledge as a cognate for deification, the connection between love and knowledge is less predictable than it might seem in the work of another writer; he nonetheless makes it more than once: "Once reconciliation with God has been re-established by prayer and the accomplishment of the commandments, fear changes into love and the pain of prayer, transformed into joy, makes the flower of illumination appear, and like a perfume of this flower, this knowledge of the mysteries of God is conferred on the one who can bear it" (I.1.7). In this passage, as in others, Palamas is not describing the next life but deifying experience in this. Yet the exuberance of the language in such passages illustrates not the confinement of love to experience in this life but the inseparability of deifying experience in this life from that of the next, since the terms in which he portrays these mystical experiences are exactly those in which one would describe heavenly existence: "When the vision comes to him, the recipient knows well that it is that light, even though he sees but dimly; he knows this from the impassible joy akin to the vision which he experiences, from the peace which fills his mind, and the fire of love for God, which burns in him" (I.3.22; cf. also III.1.36).

While love appears in Gregory's writing with relative infrequency and assuredly possesses little systematic importance, the extravagance of his language and the strong links he forges between love and the heights of mystical experience and union concord entirely with his simple claim, echoing 1 Corinthians 13: "Love is the most perfect of all gifts" (II.2.11).

5

THEOSIS AS CONSTITUENT OF
THE DOCTRINE OF GOD

The purpose of gathering the variegated strands of Palamas' doctrine of deification and grouping them into two main themes is not simply to summarize the complex. Rather, identifying the principal themes of the Palamite doctrine of theosis will enable us better to understand how the doctrine functions in relation to Gregory's theology as a whole, and grasping this relationship is crucial to understanding the doctrine of theosis itself. Furthermore, exploring the relationship between the twin themes and the essence-energies distinction will assist in clarifying the function of the distinction in Palamas' work.

I. The Twin Themes

Throughout the analysis of the cognates, two themes surfaced with some regularity, and these now demand more deliberate scrutiny. These themes identify each of deification's poles; while conceptualizing these poles is a fairly straightforward matter, they are harder to label adequately. Two terms will therefore be used for each pole in tandem, each of which is employed in a fairly narrow sense. Transcendence, or gratuity, names the strand in Gregory's thought that emphasizes the inviolability of divine being and theosis as gift. Thus, this pole makes a statement about both the divine and human dimensions of theosis: deification is the consequence of a divine, never a human act. The same principle that proclaims humanity solely the recipient of grace also proclaims God utterly transcendent, the One never constrained by the act of self-giving. Provenance, or authenticity, expresses the notion that deification is genuine encounter with no less than the living God and not some derivative of God. What God freely gives, therefore, is none other than himself and what the deified human person receives is none other than God. This theme, too, touches both of deification's poles, specifying elements of both the theology proper and anthropology. Together these themes recapitulate all Gregory has to say regarding theosis and the Triads is largely the epic of their intertwining.

1. Transcendence-Gratuity

Gratuity labels that tendency in Gregory's thought to stress divine initiative in divinizing union and to ascribe growth in sanctity and understanding to divine action. It is also apparent (though inextricably entangled with provenance) in the emphasis on wonder, paradox, and the incomprehensibility of God's deifying embrace.

If we return to the basic definitions of theosis that Gregory borrows from Maximus (in III.1.28), we will hear unmistakable strains of this theme: "Deification . . . appears in those worthy as something exceeding their comprehension. It is indeed a mystical union with God beyond intellect and reason." Although the glory of deification is "more-than-ineffable," the saints "become themselves able to receive the blessed purity"; it is "the symbol of the hypostasised and real adoption, according to the gift and grace of the Holy Spirit, thanks to the bestowal of which grace the saints become and will remain the sons of God." Adoption, gift and grace are all cognates, as we shall see, with an especially strong link to the gratuity theme.

Similar patterns emerge from other definitions. The passage from III.1.34 speaks of the divine apparition as seizing a suitable material and then becoming visible like a spiritual light, or transforming creatures into spiritual light. Gregory here underscores God's initiative in seizing suitable material and God's action in transforming the human person through theosis. Because it provides complex but ultimately helpful evidence, the passage we considered from II.3.26 is quoted again here in its entirety:

> Those who have been purified by hesychasm make themselves worthy to contemplate invisible things, the essence of God remaining beyond their attainment; but those who are worthy of this contemplation can be initiated into it and make it the object of their understanding; thus they participate in the intelligible gift of the light of God in their impassible and immaterial intelligence, but they also know that the divine surpasses these contemplations and initiations, and thus they possess this superintelligible and superadded grace in a way that exceeds us; they possess it not because they do not see, in the manner of those who practice negative theology, but in their very vision they know what surpasses vision, in suffering negation and not in conceptualising it.

There is here an alternation between affirmation of divine and human action, an alternation entirely characteristic of the synergistic principle of Eastern theology. The Orthodox understanding of synergy is well expressed by Meyendorff in Byzantine Theology:

> It is not through his own activity or "energy" that man can be deified—this would be Pelagianism—but by divine "energy," to which his human activity is "obedient"; between the two there is a "synergy," of which the relation of the two energies in Christ is the ontological basis.[1]

This notion of synergy must be borne in mind if we are to understand how Palamas articulates the principle of transcendence within his doctrine of deification, and if our analysis intends fidelity to the author's native categories, the Westerner must leave aside the polemics of the Pelagian controversy, an exclusively Western debate. In the East's terms, the question is not whether sanctification is God's work or ours but whether our sanctification can be accomplished either against our wills or without our wills. For the East, the assertion of synergy serves not to elevate humanity to the status of cosanctifier with God but to ensure that the whole person, including the will, is regenerated; if sanctification takes place against the creature's will, so goes this logic, the will has effectively not been sanctified at all. Such an understanding helps to elucidate passages such as this one, in which it is not clear whether "those who have been purified by hesychasm" have been purified by their own spiritual discipline in practicing hesychastic prayer or whether hesychasm is simply the medium by which God grants purification. If Palamas continues on in a way more suggestive of the first possibility ("render themselves worthy of contemplating invisible things"), he later adjusts the picture. The worthy "can be initiated" into contemplation and by so doing participate in God's gift. Their possession of that gift is in a manner that "exceeds us"; their vision is of something surpassing vision and thus negation is something they "suffer." Although this passage expresses a considerable degree of support for a synergistic view—that is, that God and the saints together make theosis possible—ultimately it depicts theosis as beyond human grasp; we cannot work what we cannot begin to understand.[2] Even in this passage, so affirmative of human cooperation, Palamas clearly locates the impetus for, and accomplishment of, deification within the sphere of divine agency and desire. The transcendence theme is thus clearly present in the definitions of deification he gives, and we will find it equally present in his treatment of the cognates.

As we have seen, in the midst of his ambivalence regarding knowledge as a means to deification, Gregory nevertheless continues to use it as an image for theosis. If one interprets his intention as always to stress divine initiative, the gap between his usage and his disclaimers appears less yawning. Let us begin where we left off in the last section, with II.3.26: "The worthy participate in the intelligible gift of the light of God in their impassible and immaterial intelligence." Again, allusion to the worthy might lead a naive reader to view Gregory as holding that especially powerful intellects can attain to the vision of God by the vigorous exercise of their intelligence, yet he emphatically deems the light of God a gift. The mind is certainly the locus of its reception, but it is not the agent that brings about its bestowal.

The refusal of instrumental agency to the intellect surfaces also in claims such as that God is not only above knowing but also above not-knowing (I.3.4), that the cessation of intellectual activity is a divinizing end (I.3.17; cf. also I.13.18 and I.3.20) and that the intellectual faculties become superfluous when the deiform soul gives itself up (I.3.20). These texts do not simply repudiate knowledge or the intellect; rather, they *assume* intellectual activity in the life of the saints. What they stress is that although the intellect is clearly implicated in the divinized state (that is, we do not become mindless in virtue of becoming God), Gregory does not imply that deification means we start employing our minds more effectively than ever before and certainly not that deification is the fruit of the mind's assiduous exercise.

The converse of these disavowals is the positive emphasis on the intellect's gracing in I.1.7 and III.3.13. In the former passage Gregory writes that knowledge of God may be conferred only on the one able to bear it; although presumably it is at least in part our own preparation that enables us to bear it, knowledge remains conferred. We do not discover God, peeping at him and catching him unawares, as the elders on Susanna. More significantly still, the second of these passages tells us that knowledge of God comes from grace and it is grace that bestows the aspect of God. Taken as a whole, the texts on knowledge point strongly to the transcendence theme, for their ambivalence testifies to Gregory's conviction of the transcendence of the One who deifies. Assuming, as the Fathers before him did, that the intellect is the prime point of contact between God and humanity, he nevertheless insists that the intellect attains to God only at God's good pleasure.

The texts on contemplation point yet more clearly to theosis as God's free gift. The passage considered earlier from I.3.18 illustrates this well: "Perfect contemplation of God and divine things is not only a stripping away but beyond this, a participation in divine things, a gift and possession." If *possession* and *participation* point to the way in which contemplation becomes truly ours, *gift* firmly locates contemplation in grace's realm. Similarly, II.3.74 assumes *theoria* is the by-product of God's indwelling: "Unifying perfection . . . [means] the coming and indwelling of God in us . . . nourishing by contemplation the spiritual eye."

Finally, contemplation falls within the category of gift if for no other reason than that its object is God. It is for this reason that Gregory says that contemplation has a beginning but never an end, because its progress is infinite (II.3.35); like Nyssa, then, he seems to see sanctification a an endless process of drawing near to the One whose goodness is itself endless. Since the living God of Abraham and Sarah, Jesus and Mary, is not a jinni to be summoned at whim, contemplation will always depend on the initiative of its object, rather than the exertion of the seeker.

A similar pattern prevails in the texts on vision. What the disciples saw at Tabor, "the invisible vision of divine Beauty" (III.3.9), and what the saints will see, "the visible apparition of God in the glory that is yet to come" (I.3.38), is an encounter with the Other, with the Most High, and is therefore not manipulable or graspable by purely human means. It is for this reason that the vision "surpasses all sensation and intellection" (II.3.40). Palamas makes this theme explicit in II.3.26, when he claims the Archetype is invisible because of the fact of its transcendence; the only way to see God is by God (II.3.52).

The texts on light emphasize light or illumination as God's gift, "the deifying gift and source of Divinity" (III.1.29) and "the deifying gift of the Spirit" (III.1.7). This light is also the means "by which the beings that participate are divinized" (*Capita* 93); it is what "transforms into light those who receive its richness" (III.1.35; cf. also II.3.22). The passages speaking of the light's surpassing the power of human senses and intelligence articulate the theme of transcendence in a similar way (e.g. II.3.23 and 25).

Where the theme emerges preeminently with respect to light is in the passages treating the Transfiguration. On Tabor, Palamas tells us, the Word indicated what we once were and what we shall become through him in the future age (*Capita* 66). That future age will bring about a transcending of human capacities as we know them now, but since the vision of Tabor possesses the value of the second coming of Christ (I.3.26), the vision of radiance there is also a pledge of Christ's continuing gift:

Since the Son becomes a single body with us, how would he not illuminate those who worthily commune with the divine ray of his body who is in us, by lighting their souls as he illuminated the very bodies of the disciples on Tabor? (I.3.38)

Finally, the many passages in which Gregory refers to light as grace (I.3.26; I.3.38; II.1.12; *Capita* 69) speak persuasively of the connection between light and the theme of gratuity and transcendence in Gregory's thought. If light is both grace in itself and the occasion for the bestowal of grace, there is double cause for viewing this light imagery as a means by which Palamas claims theosis is a pure gift of God. The texts on light also draw attention to the other side of this theme, that of transcendence. When Gregory describes the divine and deifying light as inaccessible, immaterial, uncreated and eternal (III.1.22), he is reminding us that it transcends the created realm. Yet as we have seen, Palamas does more than call the light divine; he associates it directly with the Persons of the Trinity (with the Spirit in III.1.9 and with Christ and the whole Trinity in III.1.16). If Gregory's text furnishes any conclusive proof that deification lies beyond the power of human attainment, it is these texts, few though they are in number.

With the texts on participation, we return to the gratuity side of the theme we have been examining. Here Gregory's assertion that deification is granted rather than attained becomes explicit: God by his grace, renders those who participate mysteriously luminous (I.3.24; cf. II.3.26 and *Capita* 69). While our nature is in some sense susceptible to theosis, it is so by divine intention and action: God's purpose in creating us was to make us partakers of his own divinity (*Capita* 105; cf. 78). Although Gregory only hints at it, here he does suggest that even when he speaks of our own effort, as he does in the passages on virtue and striving, he is assuming this effort to be preceded and sustained by the gracious working of God within the divine Economy.

As union is the nearest functional equivalent to theosis of all the images, so it speaks directly to the theme of gratuity: unifying perfection means the coming and indwelling of God in us (II.3.74). We become perfect at God's behest and in consequence of God's gracious condescension. Union deifies because God anoints us with his presence (III.1.33). Although the human person by no means becomes passive, Palamas portrays our activity as surrender rather than seizure: "The deiform soul gives itself up to rays of inaccessible light in an unknowable union" (II.3.20); the fact that the union resulting from this surrender remains finally unknowable only underscores that it is not humanly accomplished. Even when he does ascribe agency to the saint deified by union, he does so in a way that emphasizes transcendence: "[Our spirit] possesses union that transcends the nature of the spirit and allows it to attach itself to that which surpasses it" (I.3.45); union requires that our spirit leave itself, and it does this by surpassing itself (I.3.47).

Similarly, when Palamas speaks of glory in relation to the deified, it is always a gift. We are *possessed* by glory in our innermost being, he tells us (II.3.15). He alludes to both gift and transcendence in II.3.15 when he declares: "It is not only to the human composite which is united to his hypostasis that he has given this transcendent glory, but also to his disciples." He stresses the distance that grace must wondrously overcome as he continues: "To our human nature he has given the glory of the Godhead." His use of this cognate stipulates that what we receive is simultaneously ours and yet in some sense alien: it is in the Father's glory that the just will shine like the sun, the same glory in which Christ will come again (II.3.66). Most persuasive of all in relation to the gratuity-transcendence theme is III.2.15, where he notes that not even the angels possess the vision of eternal glory by nature; like the saints, they receive it as the Eternal Nature's free gift.

Of the three remaining cognates that we have not reviewed, one (grace) so obviously presents the gratuity-transcendence theme that there is no need to reconsider it here. A second (adoption) requires no detailed review; suffice it to say that depicting theosis as adoption naturally recalls that the decisive factors in divinization are God's desire and initiative. We are left with the texts on virtue and ascetical striving, which seem to run directly counter to this theme.

To begin, let us recall that these texts most characteristically describe virtue as divinization's precondition, or conversely, that virtue merely removes obstacles to sanctification. Even if we take Palamas to be claiming that we can by our own striving make ourselves virtuous—which would be greatly to overstate his synergism—this striving would not make us *deiform*. Second, in a number of texts he denies, either virtually or explicitly, that human effort accomplishes divinization. There remain, however, a number of texts where Palamas seems directly to suggest that practice of the commandments (for example) brings about perfection (cf. II.1.40 and 42). Yet even these echo the gratuity theme, since he assumes the commandments themselves are a divine gift which bestows both knowledge and deification (II.3.17).

The texts on virtue are most accurately understood, however, in the context of the concept of synergy. We recall that the East conceives of synergy not so much as the cooperation of God and humanity considered as equals but as the process whereby human persons offer their wills to God's sanctifying action. Virtue, then, should be understood not as a human effort that results in some sort of autonomously attained state of godliness but a means by which God is able to sanctify a will rather than obliterating it. The exhortations to striving indeed emphasize the divide between Creator and creature: the difference between the two always remains, since the human person retains her own will and is not simply colonized by divine fiat.

Even in the texts on virtue, then, Gregory underlines God's freedom in bestowing participation in his life, a participation that would be impossible without the creature's holiness, and therefore, consent, but which the creature can only receive and never attain. Divine action precedes all human effort, in giving the commandments that structure virtue and the power to obey them; divine action accompanies human striving as God hallows those who do not refuse sanctification; and divine action crowns virtue by bringing it to the fulness that is participation in divine life.

The strand in Gregory's thought that we have labeled the transcendence/gratuity theme, then, stresses two aspects of what is essentially the same principle. His understanding of deification portrays God as the One who remains transcendent, even as he gives of himself to sanctify the creature and draws her into his own life. The gift must always be a free gift, one God is not constrained to bestow, but which is given at his good pleasure and which humanity can neither demand nor constrain.

2. Provenance-Authenticity

Provenance, the second of the two themes, has been creeping into this discussion because it is so often inseparable from gratuity. Gratuity, or transcendence, stresses that deification comes as a gift and indeed is such that it can only come as the gift of God. Provenance, or authenticity, stresses that this gift is genuinely a divine gift and not the product or effect of anything less than God. By pointing to divinization's source, the theme of authenticity also serves as the guarantor that theosis will be more than simple growth in goodness, something it could not be if theosis were of less than fully divine provenance.

In the explicit references to deification in the *Triads*, this theme appears only fleetingly, for in these it is virtually taken for granted. Hence in the definition borrowed from Maximus, Gregory calls theosis "a mystical union with God" (III.1.28), and in II.3.26 he speaks of "the intelligible gift of the light of God." In the explicit references, too, appear hints of the essential problem posed by the assertion of theosis, which is intimately related to the theme of authenticity. The deifying gift of the Spirit is "the deifying energy of this [superessential] divine essence" (III.1.24); here we see, in the need to allude to the essence-energies distinction, the consequences of asserting the authentically divine provenance of theosis. Although we are not now concerned with those consequences, the need for the distinction calls our attention to the provenance theme.

As we saw in the case of gratuity, provenance will emerge as a motif in the texts on all the cognates. The connection in the case of knowledge is particularly significant; for all Gregory's ambivalence about knowledge as an image for theosis, his use of the authenticity theme indicates how apt he does find the image. Knowledge points to the authentically divine provenance of theosis, not merely in that what we know is authentically God but in that the mode of our knowing is divine; hence to become God is to know God in God (II.3.68). Similarly, in II.3.43, Christ is portrayed not so much as the means by which we come to God as the one who contains all true knowledge in himself, and is indeed Wisdom-Itself. Knowledge can only be divinizing because of this divine provenance, and Gregory repeatedly draws on this connection: the goal of divinizing knowledge is to be conformed to truth itself (cf. I.1.2) and rendered like to the divine archetype (I.1.22); true knowledge is akin to assimilation to God (II.3.74) and gives the human person the aspect of God (III.3.13).

The texts on contemplation and vision, too, allude to the genuinely divine nature, not only of contemplation's object, but also its means. As in knowledge we know God by God, so in the vision of God the saint sees God by God (II.3.52). Similarly, I.3.5 asserts that we see the divine light only when we have "acquired the divinising communion of the Spirit." It is "by a vision in the Spirit" that deifying action surpasses any vision (II.3.26). Likewise, while in contemplation the mind views its object, in vision the object presents itself to the eye; in either case what one sees is not simply spiritually uplifting or magnificent but truly divine. The vision at Tabor was of no less than God, "the essential and eternal light, the invisible vision of divine Beauty" (III.3.9); it presages the glory that is to come, whose content is "the visible apparition of God" (I.3.38).

In particular, Palamas insists upon the divine provenance of light. It is the source of Divinity (III.1.29) and the "radiance of divine nature" (III.1.22). More characteristically, he presents the light as God's glory (III.1.7), a "divinising energy" (*Capita* 93), and especially "the light of grace" (I.3.3; I.3.26; I.3.38; cf. III.1.13), all allusions to the divine energy we are about to examine. What is important to grasp at this point is that although he qualifies the equation of light with God, he does identify the two. His concern in these texts is to show that the light is not a created effect, something separable from divine being or subordinate to it. If the light may be considered glory, grace and energy, such identifications do not imply that the light is less than God.

When this point is borne in mind, the outright equation of light with God becomes less startling. At times, Palamas seems to imply no more than that the light is one of God's effects, when, for example, he speaks of Christ's body as a divine ray (I.3.38) or when he calls light the life that exists in the very nature of the Spirit (III.1.9). Elsewhere, he unabashedly identifies light with God himself: "This light is God" (I.3.24), he announces, later adumbrating: "Not only the Trinity, but Jesus himself, is deifying light" (III.1.16). While he undoubtedly wants to maintain the incommunicability and inaccessibility of divine essence, as we shall shortly see, he wants just as much to portray the light as authentically divine.

That grace should be of divine origin would surprise no theologian, Eastern or Western, and the texts that do no more than assert we are divinized by grace have little to contribute to our understanding of the provenance theme. Where Gregory's claims become more remarkable, at least to Western eyes, is in the equation of grace with divine being. Twice in the *Capita* he equates grace with the radiance of God (92 and 93), and in III.1.27 he closely allies God's grace and radiance, a claim echoed by I.3.23: "The divine grace of this superessential light is God." In other texts, he speaks of grace not as the means to an end, as the agent of theosis, but as an agent whose efficacy lies precisely in that it is itself the condition of abiding in God: the divinized person "exceeds humanity and is already God by grace" (II.3.52); theosis is not simply possession of the virtues, but rather it "resides in the radiance and grace of God" (III.1.27). Most powerfully of all, he points to the divine provenance of grace by insisting it is uncreated. Since only God is uncreated, grace as he understands it cannot be less than fully and authentically divine—such is the force of the assertion in III.1.8 that grace is uncreated and the claim in III.3.8 that it has no beginning.

If discussion of grace seems a likely point at which the authenticity theme would arise, adoption might seem, of all the cognates, one of the least likely to furnish evidence for such a theme. Those who are adopted, after all, are usually thought of as less intimately related to their parent than the true daughters and sons. Yet he does not use the adoption imagery in such a way. For Gregory, the image of adoption evokes deification with especial aptness: those who are essentially separated from one another are by divinizing adoption brought into real and intimate relation. "The grace of adoption" is ranged immediately alongside "the uncreated deification" in III.1.29; the adoption by grace is "authentic and real," and because of it "the saints become and will remain the sons of God" (III.1.28), so that our rational nature is transcended (III.1.30). Because the ontological divide is bridged in adoption, God may truly be said to be our Father (*Capita* 132 and 134). This overall pattern needs to be borne in mind when we come to places in the text where Greogory seems, by Western standards, utterly conventional, as when he claims that this authentic adoption constitutes no less than a divine indwelling in believers (III.1.27). Read in light of his other statements on adoption, it would be unwise to equate this indwelling simply with graced life, as the West has usually understood it. Rather, it denotes a real union of the created with the Uncreated and a union in which the creature is drawn into the Creator's life, rather than the reverse.

Glory speaks yet more powerfully of the theme of authenticity. The same glory that is the "glory of his holy nature" is "the glory by which we are possessed at the interior of our selves" (II.3.15). This passage asserts the tight connection between God's own nature and the glory that divinizes the human race; similarly, earlier in the same section he claims that transcendent glory belongs not only to the divine hypostases but also to the disciples. More starkly still, he writes: "To our own human nature he has given the glory of the Godhead" (ibid.). That with which our nature is endowed is "a glory and splendour that is divine" (II.3.66), and our possession of God's glory is such that we will even see in ourselves the glory of God (II.3.17). This glory which we possess is not a variety of glory somehow different from God's, because although it actually becomes our vesture, it remains properly speaking Christ's: "It is in the glory of their Father, Christ, that 'the just shall shine like the sun'"[3] (II.3.66). The saints and angels alike receive the eternal vision of the eternal glory "as a free gift of Eternal Nature" (III.2.15). This last text proclaims the authentically divine provenance of glory not only in that glory is said to come from the Eternal Nature but also in that this glory is itself eternal, a point he makes also in *Capita* 39 and in II.3.66.

It lies in the nature of participation and union that they should, of all the cognates, speak most directly to the theme of provenance. Participation in divine communion is not simply some derivative experience of God for Palamas; no, to partake is to become "a domain and house of God" (I.2.9). Life in the Spirit is not simply a life in accord with the precepts of holiness (as some Westerners might take it to be), but life inseparable from the Spirit (III.1.9), a life, then, not merely holy but divine. The *Capita* sounds this theme again when Gregory asserts we were made to be partakers of his own divinity (105; cf. also 78).

As the emphasis on uncreated grace shows his desire to indicate the truly divine nature of that grace, so he points to the uncreated nature of energy, energy which must be so if it is to be the means by which we participate in God. The assertion that it is God in whom we participate leads him in these texts simultaneously to avow the imparticipability of divine essence. That he does so provides only further evidence of his commitment to the notions of authenticity and provenance, for the distinction between essence and energy, the paradoxical assertion of divine participability and imparticipability, would be entirely unnecessary if it were not for the claim of genuine participation in God in the first place.

A similar pattern is in evidence with respect to union. It is self-evident that when Christian mystics speak of union, they mean union with God, and there is no need to specify how the union texts allude to provenance in a general way. In several specific respects, however, these texts beg our attention. The first is in Gregory's insistence that in deifying union we encounter God directly, without intermediaries. He makes the point that no angel provides the means by which we are united to God twice in the *Triads*, in II.3.27 and 28. A second way in which he particularly alludes to the provenance theme is in the common usage of the term *union* for what joins Christ and humanity. Palamas is clear that the sole instance of hypostatic union between God and humanity is Christ; nevertheless, the fact that union denotes both the relation between divine and human nature in Christ and between God and human persons in deification indicates a similarity between the two and points onward to the authenticity of the contact with the divine in deification. The third, and final, way in which these texts speak of the divine provenance of deification lies in their insistence that union is achieved by the surpassing of human nature (I.3.45 and 47). If we are divinized only by departing from the limitations of human nature and we are not united to some quasi-divine being such as an angel, it follows that union can be with no less than God, the only being who transcends all.

The texts on virtue allude least of all the cognates to the theme of provenance. Nevertheless, they do address it, and the fact that even this group of texts does so indicates the theme's power and pervasiveness. The first indication of such allusion is fairly obvious: virtue consists in the practice of commandments, which are of divine provenance (cf. I.3.18; II.1.40; II.1.42; III.3.5). Gregory implies that it is only because the commandments are divine that practice of them can render holy.

A less direct way in which the virtue texts point to the authenticity theme is in their continual insistence that striving and virtue do not merely make us good but conform us to God. Nearly every one of these texts makes such an assertion in one way or another, but we will consider just a few representative examples: "Perfection consists in assimilation to God" (II.1.40; and cf. also II.3.74), "the prize of virtue is to become God" (III.1.34, after Basil), "the human person is . . . by keeping the divine commandments, transformed into a vehicle appropriate to recovering the all-powerful Spirit" (III.3.5) and "by obedience to the Spirit [one] will go to God . . . and tend to God through the uninterrupted memory of God" (II.2.19). These texts demonstrate the difference between Gregory's notions of divinization and the exhortations to virtue of, say, pagan philosophy. The beginning (the divine commandments) and the end (assimilation to God) of theosis are not conformity to one or another form of goodness but the personal God.

One important function of the provenance-authenticity theme in Gregory's thought is to counterbalance its sister theme of transcendence and gratuity. If God remains always greater than his gift, this is because it is his nature to transcend it, not because what is given is anything less than himself. On the contrary, precisely the measure of divine transcendence lies in the fact that God's self-giving can be authentic and yet not engulf God in his own creation. The provenance-authenticity theme reminds us that even though God remains above both the gift and the act of giving, he does truly give no less than himself.

II. The Essence-Energies Distinction

The twin themes highlight the way in which the Palamite doctrine of sanctification actually functions, not principally as a subsidiary of theological anthropology but as a component of the doctrine of God. The twin themes help to explain, therefore, why we must attend to a distinction pertaining to divine being in the course of our study of theosis.

The name of Gregory Palamas is historically associated above all with the theological distinction between divine essence and energies. By the Orthodox he is viewed as the consummate codifier of a long tradition, the thinker who gathers up strands stretching as far back as Irenaeus, giving them their coherent, authoritative and final expression. To Westerners he is an innovator, who as late as the fourteenth century, sought to add novel conceptualities to the depositum fidei and to add to it, moreover, in the very heart of its teaching, the doctrine of God.

We are not here concerned with either the distinction or the controversy surrounding it for its own sake. However, as we have already seen, the essence-energies distinction is inextricably bound up with Gregory's understanding of deification. The thesis we are primarily concerned to advance here is that the essence-energies distinction functions only indirectly within the doctrine of God; its primary function is as the codification of Gregory's understanding of theosis. Given that theosis itself tends to stipulate attributes of God rather than describe humanity, the distinction does operate within the doctrine of God but does so at one remove. Certainly, Gregory's purpose is not to add to the received teaching on the doctrine of God but to produce a theology with a coherent doctrine of God, one in which God *in se* and God *ad extra* and *pro nobis* are one God.

This interpretation of Palamas and his distinction runs counter to many in both East and West. While the distinction has received considerable attention from Gregory's commentators, this attention has not produced a complete consensus over whether the distinction is real or nominal in his work. Examination of this question has not been helped by the failure of many to distinguish between Gregory's own views and those of neo-Palamite theologians of the twentieth century. Among Western commentators, the confusion may be traced in part to a tendency to assume that the views of twentieth-century Orthodox writers are identical with those of Palamas himself; among Orthodox writers, the confusion results in part from the assumption that the anathemas of the Sunday of Orthodoxy are identical to assertions in Palamas' work. The anathemas, added to the Orthodox liturgy in the wake of the vindication of hesychasm, certainly celebrate Palamite theology but cannot be used instead of his own writings to establish the content of his theology. Both types of confusion are in turn related to the broader question of the distinction's dogmatic status in the Orthodox church.

In addition to the questions of the nature and function of the distinction in Gregory's work and its status in Orthodox theology, two further questions have preoccupied his commentators: the distinction's patristic pedigree and whether it compromises divine simplicity. While these latter issues have produced heated ecumenical debate, they are of minor importance for those concerned, as we are, with the interpretation of Palamas' work: in neither case is there any unclarity regarding Palamas' own view. He clearly regarded his own work as a restatement or extension of the Fathers', and there is no indication in either the *Triads* or the *Capita* that he saw himself as having lighted on some new idea. Even one of his severest critics acknowledges as much. In the same article where he accuses Palamas of having developed a system that is "incontestably a novelty in the history of Byzantine theology. Its equivalent is found nowhere in the preceding period,"[4] Jugie also charges him with composing "patristic florilegia rich in passages that are vague and without significance," upon which he drew "by exegesis that is sophistical and totally subjective,"[5] although Jugie merely asserts the flawed exegesis without offering an explanation of where its failings lie. The use of patristic source material earns Palamas the criticism that he "especially abuses the authority of the Fathers."[6] Jugie's critique merely reinforces the position taken here: whether or not sufficient patristic warrant exists for the distinction in the form it assumes in the *Triads* and the *Capita*, Gregory clearly saw it as deriving from the Fathers, or he would not have bothered to compose his "patristic florilegia."[7]

Similarly, Jugie chastises Palamas because he "platonizes without knowing it"[8] but still portrays him as erring in essentially Aristotelian terms: "The fundamental error of the system is to admit in God composition of nature and persons, of substance and accidents, of essence and physical properties proceding from the essence."[9] Because the energies do not admit of ready categorization as either substance or accident, Jugie believes Gregory is forced to term them "quasi-accidents"[10] and in so doing, compromises divine simplicity. The fact that he can term Gregory's resorting to the term συμβεβεκος πως (some form of accident or quasi-accident) and his supposed blurring of the distinction between substance and accident as "the gross philosophical error of his system"[11] does little more than demonstrate Jugie's refusal to acknowledge the validity of any base for theology other than the purely Aristotelian.[12]

In part, Jugie and his companions were simply victims of Migne, or to be more exact, the lack of any better edition of Palamas' work than Migne afforded at the time of their writing. Hence Jugie's outrage over Palamas' terming the essence as the greater divinity (ὑπερειμένη θεότης) and the energies as the lesser (ὑφειμένη θεότης) results, according to Lossky, from taking as authentically Gregory's texts which later scholarship showed unlikely to be his at all.[13] As Halleux takes pains to point out, however, whether or not one regards the distinction as finally compromising simplicity, Gregory did not view it thus, for he never speaks of the distinction as real without adding that it does not compromise divine simplicity.[14]

We leave aside, then, the questions of whether the Palamite formulation actually possesses a sufficient basis in earlier Christian theology or whether it actually compromises divine simplicity—the latter being in any case an issue of dubious importance, given the questioning by twentieth-century thinkers of the wisdom of positing divine simplicity at all.[15] Instead, we take as given that Palamas regards the distinction both as fundamentally patristic and inoffensive to the doctrine of simplicity.

The latter assumption leads us back to one of the questions we do need to examine closely: the nature of the distinction, and in particular, whether Gregory regards it as real or nominal. The weight of opinion among Gregory's commentators inclines to the view that he intends the distinction to be real: God "consists," therefore, in essence, three hypostases, and energies. This is the view of Wendebourg,[16] Ivánka,[17] Journet[18] and of course Jugie.[19] Schultze regards Halleux as also holding this view,[20] although Halleux's view may be more nuanced than Schultze allows. It is, after all, Halleux who, as we have just seen, notes that Palamas never speaks of the distinction as real without noting it does not compromise simplicity. Halleux does not explain how a real distinction would not compromise simplicity, an ambiguity that only widens when he later declares that Palamas' antinomian thought enables him to surpass the rational conception of simplicity, so that Palamism ultimately locates itself on a superior epistemological level to its objectors,[21] but this claim does little more than replace an appeal to mystery with one to antinomy and leaves unexplained how a real distinction would not compromise simplicity. Grumel's position is more subtle still: he describes the doctrine of essence and energies as a "minor real distinction."[22] A more recent proponent of a nuanced, if somewhat opaque, view is Reid, who claims that the distinction, while not nominal, is also not "sharp."[23] One of the most strenuous advocates of the reality of the distinction is Lossky, who claims it is no abstraction but designates a "strictly concrete reality."[24]

Against this large group of interpreters of Palamas stands a smaller group who are less sure Gregory intends the distinction to be real but take it rather to be conceptual or nominal. Philips unambiguously endorses this view.[25] Meyendorff's views on the matter are complex. On the one hand, he can assert: "The triple distinction—essence, hypostasis, energy—is not a division of God's being; it reflects the mysterious life of the 'One-who-is'—transcendent, tri-personal, and present to His creation."[26] Similarly, he writes: "[Byzantine theology crystallised in Palamism] affirms in God a real distinction between the Persons and the common 'essence,' just as it maintains that the same God is both transcendent (in the 'essence') and immanent (in the 'energies')."[27] Note that Meyendorff does not here claim there is a real distinction between the essence and the energies, as he does between the persons and the common essence.

Oddly, while Lossky sometimes writes unambiguously of the distinction's status as real, he can elsewhere write in terms that seem to undermine its reality: "[God's] energies . . . in no way divide His nature into two parts—knowable and unknowable—but signify two different *modes* of the divine existence, in the essence and outside of the essence" (my emphasis).[28] Later statements also undermine the idea of a real distinction; the Eastern tradition, he says, "recognizes no distinction, or rather division, save that between the created and the uncreated,"[29] and: "The energies might be described as that mode of existence of the Trinity which is outside of its inaccessible essence. God thus exists in His essence and outside of His essence."[30] While it is difficult to know precisely what to make of the the the use of *mode* in the last quotation, Lossky appears in several loci to differentiate between the relation of essence to Persons and essence to energies, the first apparently being a real distinction and the second being modal. The internal uncertainty within Lossky's writings mirrors, then, the larger dispute among the commentators as to the status of the distinction, making it difficult to draw firm conclusions from the secondary literature alone.

Because it has received far less attention, the question of how the distinction functions in Gregory's work seems less contentious than the issue of its real or nominal status. In reality, however, to the extent that his interpreters recognize the question at all, they differ rather sharply and generally along East-West lines. Western commentators, particularly pre–Vatican II Roman Catholics, have seen the distinction as an addition to the doctrine of God and as an entirely unwarranted addition at that. Those commentators who are very concerned with the distinction's ramifications for divine simplicity generally write as if Gregory were primarily concerned to contribute to the doctrine of God. Such is notably the tendency of Guichardan and Grumel, both of whom are preoccupied with the issue of how the distinction functions in relation to divine simplicity.[31] Trethowan goes so far as to identify the West's difficulty with the distinction as lying in an unintelligibility deriving especially from its incompatibility with simplicity.[32]

Wendebourg sees implications in the distinction for areas other than simplicity, but her questions have to do with the soteriological function of the doctrine of the Trinity; in her view, Palamas has rendered the latter "functionless."[33] While she is concerned with the doctrine's consequences for human persons, she is still locating the distinction entirely within the doctrine of God, leading to what she terms the defeat of trinitarian theology (a phrase and claim which LaCugna later adopts). Wendebourg writes:

> Here we have the fundamental difference between Palamas' system and the classical patristic doctrine of the Trinity, a difference that means nothing less than the complete defeat of trinitarian theology. The distinction in God, which in the eyes of the fourth century allowed men to understand his action and revelation in the world as action and revelation of his innermost, essential being, according to Palamas is raised above any connection with the world and history, closed up in itself. What we have contact with is God himself[34] but a secondary reality in his being.[35]

While in her monograph she acknowledges here and there the significance of the distinction for divinization and sanctification generally,[36] she inevitably returns to the distinction's significance for the doctrine of God: "Divinisation is . . . not only humanity's destiny, but also affects God. God must be such that humanity can be united to him, and he must also be understood in this way."[37] Wendebourg's description here resembles the central thesis of the reading that will shortly follow in these pages but differs in one important way. She sees that theosis, the essence-energies distinction and the doctrine of God are all interrelated in Palamas' thought, but she considers that Palamas uses human experience as the basis for adding to the doctrine of God. This pattern emerges most clearly in her article:

> How can we know then, that God is Father, Son, and Spirit? By means of special informa-
> tion. The Bible tells us about it, particularly the words of Christ, and several authorities of
> the Church, having received a special revelation from God. To us, ordinary Christians,
> there is nothing left but to accept that, beyond the divine reality which reveals itself to us
> in the course of our salvation, in the experience of grace, there is another level in God,
> the trinitarian one, which is God's inner, essential, primary being.[38]

As Wendebourg portrays it, human salvation is related to the distinction only as warrant; the distinction is an end in itself, the purpose of which is to add to, perhaps even
to obfuscate, the doctrine of God.

Wendebourg's sharp criticisms of Palamas' theology are related to another kind of
critique of the doctrine, one more recent than the arguments over simplicity but just as
bound up with the reader's perception of how the doctrine functions in Gregory's theology as a whole. This objection is that the effect of the distinction is to eradicate the
possibility of real contact with God, inasmuch as the energies become a substitute for
contact with the divine persons. In Gregory's theology, neither Christ nor the Holy Spirit
truly engages in the temporal realm according to Wendebourg.[39] LaCugna takes up
Wendebourg's complaint:

> God's actions or operation upon the creature are person-to-person. However, Gregory has
> set up the divine persons as a kind of intermediary level between essence and energies.
> This is the primary weakness of Palamite theology: despite its strong theology of grace,
> the creature cannot have immediate contact with a divine person, only with a person as
> expressed through an energy.[40]

The central issue that worries both LaCugna and Wendebourg hinges on the relation of
what LaCugna calls *oikonomia* and *theologia*, and Wendebourg terms the *immanent* and *economic Trinity.*[41] In either case, the concern is that the distinction serves to posit a level of
divine existence which is different or remote from that which we know: "The Biblical
notion of God's faithfulness and reliability, which precisely guarantees stability in the
midst of changing acts, does not even enter Palamas' head."[42] Thus, on both readings of
Palamas, the distinction serves to distance God from humanity or even to describe God
as one not so much transcendent as deceptive.

Ironically, Philips sees matters in completely opposite fashion, finding in Palamas
precisely the statement of twentieth-century desiderata that Wendebourg and LaCugna
regard as so imperative: "[Palamas] is struck vividly by divine transcendence and simplicity and affirms that *the energy is the essence.*"[43] Lison, similarly, reads Palamas on the
issue of divine personal communication quite differently from LaCugna and Wendebourg:
"Gregory Palamas seems to us to envisage a *personal* communication of the energy; first,
the latter is not an impersonal emanation of the essence; second, the energies are rooted

in each hypostasis and unity comes into play at the level of perichoresis. The Spirit, therefore, like the Father and the Son, has a proper and personal rapport to the energy which is common to all."[44] Lison also recognizes in Palamas an appropriation of the work of grace and energy specifically to the Spirit[45]; that is, he sees precisely the kind of personal engagement that LaCugna and Wendebourg deny.

A smaller group of commentators has not seen the distinction functioning prinicipally within the doctrine of God. Richter, for example, regards it as an ad hoc response to the hesychast controversy, not the result of philosophical deliberations over simplicity.[46] While Ivánka regards the distinction as real in Palamas' view and considers this its chief problem,[47] he sees some hope for Palamism, and for reconciliation between East and West, if it is taken as a doctrine of grace rather than as a metaphysic (Seinslehre),[48] and therefore presumably sees some justification for interpreting it in this way.

This is precisely where Orthodox commentators see the distinction's functioning. Lossky, for example, accords the distinction a fundamental place in the Orthodox doctrine of grace [49] and maintains: "The doctrine of the energies, ineffably distinct from the essence, is the dogmatic basis of the real character of all mystical experience."[50] That the distinction points not so much to an analysis of divine being per se but reflects the way in which humanity experiences divine life is also attested by both Meyendorff and Ware. Meyendorff notes: "The divine energies . . . are not 'things,' differing from one supreme 'thing' that is God's essence. Grace . . . is not something with which God rewards creatures, but a manifestation of the existence of the living God."[51] Meyendorff has often been criticized for making Palamas sound suspiciously like the midcentury French philosophers regnant during his residence in Paris, but we find a very similar reading in Ware, whom no one has accused of being a Francophilic philosopher: "Palamas' own writings make it abundantly clear that he affirmed the essence-energies distinction *not for philosophical but for experiential reasons.*"[52]

What this survey of Gregory's commentators indicates is that one's view of the essence-energies distinction will profoundly affect not only how one assesses Palamite theology as a whole but even how one describes it. Further, since the Orthodox themselves view the distinction as having direct bearing on issues often overlooked by Western commentators, we must attend to the distinction in that context if we are to arrive at any purportedly comprehensive view of Gregory's theology. The questions we are asking, then, are essentially two: what is the place of the distinction in Gregory's theological vision as a whole? and: what does the distinction tell us about his view of theosis in particular? Both of these questions obviously depend on our grasping the distinction in itself, however, and so it is to the explication of divine essence and energies in Gregory's two chief works, and especially the Capita, that we now turn.

Palamas' point of departure is the strong affirmation of transcendence he inherits from scripture and the theological tradition before him. It is because God is superessential that he is also imparticipable (III.2.25 and Capita 94), incomprehensible (Capita 81 and 94) and without manifestation (Capita 107).[53] Again and again, the Capita repeatedly provide a vivid testament to his profound sense of the ontological divide between Creator and creation:

> Every nature is utterly remote and absolutely estranged from the divine nature.[54] For if God is nature, other things are not nature, but if each of the other things is nature, he is

not nature; just as he is not a being, if others are beings; and if he is a being, the others are not beings. (*Capita* 78)

Because of this divide, there can be no participation in the substance of the Creator (*Capita* 94). This insistence on transcendence affects not only his doctrine of God but also his theological method, for he views negative theology (the ascent by negation) as amounting to no more than the apprehension of how all things are distinct from God (I.3.19).

A methodological concern for transcendence appears also in the *Triads* when Gregory complains of his opponents: "These people have arrived at a certain concept of God, but not at a conception truly worthy of him and appropriate to his blessed nature . . . . They have deprived God of his sovereignty" (I.1.18). Western theology also speaks strongly of the divide between creature and Creator but frequently does so when speaking of the consequences of the Fall. While (as we have seen earlier) the Fall is by no means theologically inconsequential for Gregory, it is not the primary reason for the divide between God and humanity. For Palamas the divide is absolute, and epistemological because ontological. "Understand the substance [of God] as inaccessible and without manifestation" (*Capita* 107), he writes, and because divine substance is unmanifested, there exists no creature capable of perceiving the nature of the Creator (*Capita* 94), a point on which there is some concurrence between Palamas and Reformed theologians.

In the *Triads* we also find a tendency to make the same point regarding transcendence both in the distinction between the essence and creation and in the distinction between the essence and energies. "God is entirely present in each of the divine energies . . . although it is clear that he transcends all of them," he writes in a characteristic note (III.2.7); more strongly, he maintains: "[The essence of God] is not only transcendent to any energy whatsoever, but . . . it transcends them 'to an infinite degree and an infinite number of times'" (III.2.8; the quoted phrase is from Maximus). However, what these texts from the *Triads* point to is not so much the desire to emphasize the transcendence of the essence in relation to the energies for its own sake as to use that comparison as a way of making the strongest possible case for the transcendence of divine essence over everything: "The essence of God, surpassing every name, also surpasses the energy" (III.2.10), "God is not only above all created things, but is even beyond Godhead"[55] (II.3.8) and more strongly still: "If God does not possess energies without beginning . . . how would he be anterior and superior to that which is without beginning?" (III.3.8). God, then, is the One who transcends all and is separated from all (I.3.18).[56]

The assertion of the imparticipability of the divine essence is not in the first instance an attempt to rescue a theology from the consequences of an unwisely asserted doctrine of sanctification wreaking systematic havoc. Palamas' concern is precisely not an ad hoc response to hesychasm; rather, reflection on hesychasm points back to central assertions about God that had been made for centuries. In the tradition of apophatic theology, Palamas insists upon divine transcendence as a key attribute of God, and one to be asserted regardless of what claims are made in the realm of theological anthropology. The distinction, then, serves as much to tell us about the distinction of God from the world as about a distinction in God, whether real or nominal. The assertion of divine transcendence in any form leaves the Christian theologian with a number of problems, not only the problem of deification itself but also any kind of sanctification, any knowledge, any revelation—in short, any contact—between God and humanity, as Palamas recognizes. The essence of God is in itself beyond all contact, he asserts (III.2.14); yet the evidence of God's engagement with humanity remains. Since the divine substance is without manifestation (Capita 107), it must be God's energy that makes him manifest, he claims in Capita 137 (cf. Triads III.2.9). The assertion of the energies serves to explain how, given the ontological divide, humanity exists and experiences God; the distinction between the divine essence and all else affirms divine transcendence as absolute and inviolable. The distinction, taken nominally, furnishes the theologian with language that accounts for the data of divine self-communication while preserving the ontological divide that any orthodox Christian must acknowledge. Taken as real, on the other hand, the distinction not only raises questions regarding the development of doctrine but also creates systematic problems, since it is unclear what the function of the energies would be prior to creation.

The datum of divine manifestation most significant for Palamas' theology is divinization. It is this that definitively identifies the energies as divine, and without divinization, he would not need to assert the divinity of the energies, but only some less radical doctrine of grace. Every union is through a contact, Gregory notes in III.2.14 (and as we recall, union is a prime cognate for theosis), and yet the divine essence is beyond all contact. "If indeed we participate in that undisclosed substance of God," he declares, "whether in all or part of it, we will be all powerful and thus each being will be all powerful. But not even all together do we possess God's substance" (Capita 108). Not only would the participation of the many in God's substance render human persons, individually or collectively, omnipotent; it would also imply a divisibility of divine substance, a contravention of the very principle of simplicity that Gregory's critics charge is violated by the distinction itself:

> One becomes a participant in God neither by substance nor by any sort of hypostasis, for neither of these can be divided in any way whatsoever. . . . the energy and power common to the trihypostatic nature is variously and proportionately divided among its participants and for this reason is accessible [χωρητή] to those who have received grace. (Capita 109)

The distinction serves a broader purpose than justifying mystical experience, however. Quite aside from the experience of divinization, there is a quantity of other evidence to suggest the distinction, in Palamas' view. To begin with, there is the fact of creation. For Palamas, divine energy is not only the reason we are divinized; it is the reason we are at all. The energies are the means by which divine intention is effected. Because of the very strong form of transcendence that dominates his theology, the existence of the world cannot be attributed to the divine essence, or the hypostases. As in the theology of the Fathers before him, however, it is difficult to separate creation from providence, and so we must speak of the role the energies play in the divine economy. The energy bestows substance, life and wisdom, he writes in Capita 87 and elaborates in Capita 78: "God is the nature of all beings and is referred to as such, since all participate in him and receive their constitution by this participation, not by participation in his nature . . . but by participation in his energy." This important link in Gregory's logic between the energies and their effect in the order of creation and providence is one which the Triads does not address as directly as the Capita. There are however hints of parallel ideas in the Triads: "We do not hold that [the demonic mind's] activity [ἐνέργειαν] comes from God, even though its possibility of acting [τὸ δύνασθαι ἐνεργεῖν] comes from him" (I.1.19). The created world would be inconceivable without the energies, not because it would not be graced and good but because it would not be at all. The precondition for deification is the existence of a world that cannot, in Gregory's view, be attributed to divine essence alone. Thus, when Palamas maintains that God's express purpose in creating us was to make us partakers of his own divinity (Capita 105), he does not mean simply that God intended to sanctify us in the most radical way possible, but that there is an intimate connection between creation and divinization, in that a God willing to divinize is a God who would also have created beings explicitly ordered to fellowship with him.

As creation is an indisputable datum for which theology must account, so is revelation. The energies allow us to explain the creatures' knowledge of the Uncreated, and the scriptural portrait of God enables us to grasp the nature of the energies. In the traditional understanding of God as Father, Son and Spirit, an understanding the church possesses only through God's self-disclosure in scripture and the church's meditation on it, Palamas finds an important tool to understand the distinction between essence and energies:

> God . . . remains absolutely immutable, and for this reason nothing could be predicated of him as an accident. Nor indeed does everything predicated of him denote the substance, for relation is predicated of him. . . . Such also is the divine energy in God, for it is neither substance nor accident.[57] (Capita 127)

He uses a similar analogy in 126 and repeats his claim that the energy is neither accidental nor nonexistent in 135. To understand the logic of the distinction, a logic which contravenes that of Aristotle, Palamas points to the divine self-disclosure the church acknowledges to have taken place. His method thus follows his epistemological claims: we know God through God.

Another respect in which the doctrine of God indicates the essence-energies distinction lies in the very distinction of God's power and effects: "If the energies of God are not in any sense distinct from the divine substance, neither will they have any distinction from one another. Therefore, God's will is not at all distinct from his foreknowledge" (Capita 100; he makes essentially the same point in 101). Since the energies are clearly distinguishable, according to Gregory, divisibility is especially predicated of them (Capita 110, following Chrysostom), and distinctions such as that between will and foreknowledge can also be maintained.

It is the simultaneous facts of divine transcendence and divine manifestation that stipulate the distinction between essence and energies, and the grounding of the doctrine in these facts also determines the doctrine's shape. The fact of transcendence stipulates a distinction of essence from both the energies and all creation; the fact of creation indicates that the energies' function is to engage that creation; the fact of divinization determines that the energies be divine; and the fact of revelation furnishes a means of understanding the relation of the essence to the energies, as well as the distinction among the energies themselves. This description of the distinction, which becomes explicit even in the discussion of its warrants, we now extend.

In order for genuine participation in a transcendent God to be possible, so goes the logic, there must be in God something other than divine substance and hypostasis, and

this Gregory calls energy. On occasion, he will term the energies the agent of divinization,[58] yet by this he does not mean to imply they are not of divine origin, and the strongest testament to Gregory's conviction on this point is his insistence on the energies'
being uncreated: "This act of creation . . . is a natural and uncreated energy of God" he
declares in *Capita* 130; it is "uncreated and coeternal with God" (*Capita* 140). The
unoriginate quality of the energies is one of the chief attributes that suggests their inseparability from the essence.[59] Uncreated, however, does not mean without a beginning, for some of the energies do indeed have a beginning and an end:

> While all the energies of God are uncreated, not all are without beginning. Indeed, be-
> ginning and end must be ascribed, if not to the creative power itself, then at least to its
> activity, that is to say, to its energy directed towards created things. (III.2.8)

Here Palamas is attempting to head off one kind of objection to divine energy as uncreated—namely, that many of the energy's effects clearly have a beginning in time.
What is significant in the way he handles that objection is that even as he allows for
effects *ad extra* to have a beginning, he continues to insist steadfastly on energy itself as
uncreated.

The second reason for insisting on the uncreated nature of the energies is to ensure
that they will not be viewed as separated from the essence. Gregory's concern in this
respect does not seem to lie so much in fear of compromising monotheism (which he
takes utterly for granted) but, again, in ensuring the energies' authentically divine nature. The divine substance and energy are inseparably present everywhere, he asserts in
the *Capita* (74), echoing what he wrote earlier in the *Triads*:

> The deifying gift of the Spirit cannot be equated with the superessential essence of God. It
> is the deifying energy of this divine essence, yet not the totality of this energy, even though
> it is indivisible in itself. . . . The essence of God is everywhere. . . . Deification is likewise
> everywhere, ineffably present in the essence and inseparable from it, as its natural power.
> (III.1.34)

Because of the inseparability of essence and energy, what the saints receive via divine
energy differs not at all from the energy of the essence (III.1.33).[60] Divine essence is
inseparable from its energy, therefore, and that energy is the very power which deifies.
This means that despite the distinction of essence from energy, deifying energy establishes a close link between the saints and the imparticipable essence itself: "This very
radiance and divinizing energy of God, by which the beings that participate are divinized,
is a certain divine grace but not the nature of God. This does not imply that God's nature is distant from those who receive grace" (*Capita* 93). Another way in which energy
establishes a link between divine essence and creation is in the equation of divine will
and energy: "What is the will of God, if not an energy of the divine nature?" Gregory
asks in III.3.7. Since God's will is preeminently associated with divine operation *ad extra*,
the characterization of energy as will inherently implies the energies are the means of
God's self-expression in the Economy.

The essential theological import of the divine energies, then, is their implication of
God's nearness to creation and the divine essence utterly beyond creation, a point that is
also clear from the connection Palamas makes between the energies and divine ubiq-
uity. He writes in the *Capita*: "The theologians maintain that these constitute an energy

of God, namely, his omnipresence" (104). Yet the converse is also true, maintains Gregory, quoting Chrysostom: "The essential energy of God consists in being nowhere; not in the sense that it does not exist, but in that it transcends place, time and nature" (III.2.9). As assertion of the essence points to God's transcendence, then, so the energies point to his immanence.

On occasion, Palamas will assert exactly the pattern we have been observing but without using the language of both essence and energy: "Even in the created realm, this glory and splendour do not pertain to essence" (II.3.66)[61] and:

> The nature of God is one thing, his glory another, even though they are inseparable from one another. However, even though this glory is different from the divine nature, it cannot be classified amongst things subject to time, for in its transcendence "it is not," because it belongs to divine nature ineffably. (II.3.15)

Another example would be III.1.29, where Palamas distinguishes between essence and relationship, associating the latter with grace and declaring the essence is beyond both.[62] He can also express the principle of transcendence without direct reference to the distinction between essence and energy and without using the term *essence*, as in III.1.33: "The principle of deification, divinity by nature, the imparticipable origin from which the deified derive their deification, beatitude itself, transcendent over all things, and supremely thearchic, is itself inaccessible to all sense perceptions and to every mind, to every incorporeal or corporeal being." This flexibility in his terminology suggests that it is the theological principles underlying the distinction that are important to him, not the codified form of the distinction itself.

The essence-energies distinction, at least as Palamas formulates and uses it, does not constitute a glib and facile answer to the problem of the manifestation of the Unmanifest, the knowledge of the Unknowable, or the apprehension of the Superessential who lies beyond all contact. His distinction is in the first instance no more than the articulation of the paradox lying at the heart of scripture itself—that the same God at once speaks and is hidden in darkness, is with us and beyond us, imparticipable and participable (III.2.25). His logical training certainly does not allow him to assert God is participable and imparticipable in the same respect, however: "[God is] imparticipable because superessential, participable because possessing a power and an energy" (ibid.). Indeed, the consequences of not asserting the energies are theologically disastrous, if one is both orthodox and logical, in his view, for suppressing what is between the Imparticipable and the participants would effectively separate us from God (III.2.24). Thus, the impossible—participation in the imparticipable—is actually necessary. Stated more positively, the assertion of energy makes sense of Christian doctrines that would otherwise be set on a collision course with divine transcendence: "God is one, the same being incomprehensible in substance but comprehensible from his creatures according to his divine energies, namely, his eternal will for us, his eternal providence for us, and his eternal wisdom concerning us" (Capita 81). Just as the supposedly antiphilosophical Palamas referred to Aristotelian categories in his explanation of the energies, so the supposedly illogical Palamas thinks through the systematic interaction of doctrines and, using language at hand in the theological tradition, develops a scheme in which contradiction is eschewed while paradox is upheld. While in substance he differs from the West, in technique he works well within the boundaries established long before his time.

We can take his doctrine as merely making explicit what is also implicit in Western theology only if the essence-energies distinction is nominal rather than real. One of the strongest objections to taking it as such are the places where it seems Palamas is proposing what would indeed constitute an addition to the traditional doctrine of God, a tripartite analysis of divine life: "There are three realities in God: substance, energy and the Trinity of divine hypostases" (*Capita* 75).[63] This is his strongest statement of this threefold analysis, and not surprisingly, it occurs in the *Capita*, which treats the essence-energies distinction much more fully than does the *Triads*. However, he does in the earlier work allude to a similar pattern of divine existence: "All the realities defined around [the essence of God] are also without a beginning: the hypostases, the relations, the distinctions and, more simply, all the manifestations of the superessential Theogony" (III.2.4). To conceive of God as essence, hypostasis (or relation) and energy (or manifestation) is to emphasize that energy is just as much divine as the undivided essence and the three Persons. These passages, however, are the only loci where Gregory seems to propose such a threefold analysis. The fact that he does at all, of course, testifies to his conviction of the energies' divine status. The fact that he does so casually, without the elaboration and justification one would expect if he imagined this analysis of divine being were intended to replace the long-accepted Cappadocian analysis in terms of essence and hypostasis, does so only once in each of his great works, and then fleetingly, suggests he attaches less significance to these statements than some of his commentators have supposed.

If Palamas does not regard the distinction as requiring the sort of justification one would expect were he intending to alter the classical doctrine of God, why would he use the terms *essence* and *energies* at all, especially in conjunction? He himself gives no explanation; he never says, "We need this distinction for such-and-such a reason." Indeed, he simply seems to assume the distinction. In that apparent assumption, we find probably the best clue to his motives. As we have seen, his talk about the energies draws often—as his writing does generally—from patristic sources. Whether or not contemporary Western scholarly opinion regards the distinction as firmly rooted in patristic thinking about God, Palamas evidently thinks it is. His discussion of essence and energies proceeds by elaboration and specification rather than according to the exigencies of justification. He argues that the essence is imparticipable, that the energies divinize and that the energies are genuinely divine and uncreated, but very rarely does he argue for the distinction itself. Perhaps the closest he comes is the bland claim in the *Triads* that essence and energies are not identical (III.2.10). Essentially, however, his argument concerns the attributes of each rather than the claim that the distinction itself is theologically necessary.[64] Thus we are brought to the difficult question of the distinction's status as dogma in the Orthodox church. While this issue concerns not so much Gregory's thought itself as its significance for ecumenical discussion, it is directly related to the assessment of how the distinction functions in Gregory's work, and so we must examine it at least briefly.

On the one hand, we have testimony of modern Orthodox writers, many of whom strenuously insist upon the distinction's indubitable status as dogma within the Orthodox tradition. Such is the view of Lossky.[65] It is also the view of Ware, although his several formulations of the assertion ultimately cast doubt upon its status. He acknowledges that the hesychast councils that affirmed the doctrine were local in character and thus do not count among the seven Ecumenical Councils whose decrees are normally taken as constituting church dogma.[66] However, because of a "gradual process of 'reception,'" the teaching of local councils has come to be accepted by the church as a whole as possessing ecumenical authority.[67] Ware thus concludes: "For Orthodox Christendom, therefore, the distinction between essence and energies is not merely a private speculation or an 'optional extra,' but an indispensable part of the faith."[68] Nevertheless, in a general discussion of sources of authority in Orthodoxy, Ware's position seems less emphatic: "While the doctrinal decisions of general councils are infallible, those of a local council or an individual bishop are always liable to error; but if such decisions are accepted by the rest of the Church, then they come to acquire Ecumenical authority (i.e., a universal authority similar to that possessed by the docrinal statements of an Ecumenical Council)."[69] Similar to certainly implies great doctrinal weight for such decrees, yet also seems to indicate that the Ecumenical Councils still stand apart and that local councils do not in the end command quite the same authority.

This ambiguity in Orthodoxy, the insistence of Lossky and Ware notwithstanding, is attested by other data. Bulgakov, for example, seems to hold that the depositum fidei is expandable only through new ecumenical councils:

> The Orthodox Church has only a small number of dogmatic definitions, forming the profession of faith obligatory for all its members. Strictly speaking, this minimum consists of the Nicene-Constantinopolitan Creed, which is read during the baptismal service and the liturgy, and the definitions of the seven ecumenical councils. This does not mean that these documents exhaust all the doctrine of the Church; but the rest has not been so formulated as to become obligatory dogma for all. . . . This is not to say that new dogmatic formulas are impossible in Orthodoxy, formulas which might be fixed by new ecumenical councils. But, strictly speaking, the minimum already existing constitutes a sufficient immovable base for the development of doctrine, without the disclosure of new dogmatic forms.[70]

Although by these criteria, the distinction would certainly not possess the status of dogma, Meyendorff offers a nuanced view which might yet permit the distinction such standing, even in Bulgakov's terms. Meyendorff regards the decision regarding the distinction rendered by the Council of 1351 as a development of the anti-Monothelite decrees of the Sixth Ecumenical Council (Constantinople III), which would seem to grant the distinction dogmatic status as defined by Bulgakov. Yet this position, while grounding Gregory's views in those of a dogmatically certain source, also acknowledges the nonidentity of source and later development, thus undermining the claim of dogmatic status.

Another variety of via media in interpreting the distinction's dogmatic status is to assert its importance for Orthodox theology without actually terming it dogma. Thus Schmemann: "[Palamas' doctrine] completes and renews in a creative way the most authentic and basic tendency in the Orthodox view of Christianity."[71] Similarly, Aghiorgoussis maintains only that the hesychast councils proclaimed Palamas' doctrine to be authentic.[72] Florovsky also sees Palamite theology to be central to the Orthodox church but apparently not exactly as dogma. He questions the restrictiveness of confining the ethos of the church to the first seven councils: "Now, in fact, St. Symeon and St. Gregory are still authoritative masters and inspirers of all those who, in the Orthodox Church, are striving after perfection, and are living the life of prayer and contemplation."[73] This statement does not mean he views Gregory purely as an ascetical writer, for he claims a little later that Palamas' teaching affects the whole body of Christian docrine[74]; nevertheless, Florovsky does not seem to view it as having dogmatic status, even though he apparently might wish it did.

A final form of evidence of the distinction's ambiguous status may be found in its absence from significant areas of Orthodox thought. No one disputes that at times between the fifteenth and twentieth centuries adherence to Palamism was spotty at best. Jugie in particular catalogues the vagaries of the doctrine's acceptance, claiming that in the seventeenth century, it was widely forgotten in the Greek church,[75] that it was absent from Russian theology from the late seventeenth century onwards,[76] and that in his day it was "just about dead."[77] The waxing and waning of the distinction's fortunes are not, unlike much of Jugie's scholarship, contested by Orthodox theologians, although the latter tend to attribute the low ebb of Palamism to the baleful influence of Western theology on their own in this period. Ware's view is typical: "After centuries of neglect, during the period when Orthodox theology was dominated by Western models, the Palamite teaching has now been rediscovered by Orthodox theologians in our own day and rightly restored to a central position."[78] Yet even this claim on behalf of the twentieth century is somewhat questionable. Stiernon, for example, cites the case of a modern Greek systematician, P. N. Trempélas, whose dogmatics (sufficiently influential to have been translated into French) seldom refers to Palamas and treats the distinction as a phenomenon purely ad extra,[79] and the distinction is mentioned neither in Karmiris' nor Pomazansky's manuals of theology, both used for training Orthodox ordinands.[80] Staniloae, author of one of the few and also most widely noticed Orthodox systematic theologies of our time, treats the distinction with great circumspection[81] and seems to regard Palamas as holding a view similar to his own.[82]

Westerners have on the whole ignored these signs that the distinction may not have quite the unambiguous place in Orthodox teaching that Lossky, for example, tends to claim for it. Wendebourg adamantly insists that the distinction's dogmatic status is beyond question.[83] LaCugna acknowledges the issue of identity between Palamism and the Orthodox position[84] but refers the issue entirely to the consistency of Gregory's views with those of the Fathers; the conciliar dimension of the question receives no treatment, and eventually she speculates: "No doubt the Orthodox will continue to defend a real distinction between essence and energies in order to make sense of their theology of deification,"[85] suggesting she does regard the distinction a nonnegotiable item of Orthodox theology. More recently, Reid asserts that the question of the distinction's dogmatic status can be dismissed; it is established, in his view, by the Palamite councils of 1341 and 1351, which gave it an official endorsement still in effect.[86]

Not all Westerners have overlooked the complexity of the evidence, however. Esser, for example, notes: "We would like . . . to question whether Palamism is the only 'legitimate' current within Eastern theology."[87] Halleux suggests that neo-Palamites exaggerate the canonicity of Palamism,[88] thus sharply contrasting Schultze's view that neo-Palamites are in fact trying to downplay it,[89] a sentiment rarely expressed elsewhere. Schultze however agrees with Ware that the significance of the distinction for ecumenical dialogue cannot be determined under present circumstances:

> The question of whether theological Palamism is the touchstone of true Orthodoxy is a significant one, not only within Orthodoxy, but also from the standpoint of ecumenism.

One would expect that the Orthodox council that has been in preparation for years . . .
would consider the extent to which Gregory Palamas' teaching is, from the Orthodox standpoint, a binding body of belief.[90]

Ware for his part acknowledges the inherent difficulty of asking those who were not
participants in a council to accept its decrees. The way he sees out of this impasse affect-
ing the essence-energies distinction is fashioned along the lines of the 1970 Geneva agreement: to distinguish between the council's intention and its terminology.[91] In particular, he sees this approach as promising with respect specifically to the reconciliation of
Palamism and Thomism.[92] It is difficult to see how such maneuvering could avail, however, if the council had intended to posit a real distinction in divine being. For the distinction not to constitute an impediment, it would have to be either nominal, or not
dogma in the fundamental sense (i.e., binding on all Christians), or both.

The difficulty becomes more acute when we try to position the distinction in relation to trinitarian theology. Is Palamas by the distinction replacing the earliest analysis
of divine being into essence and hypostases with a threefold analysis consisting of essence, hypostases, and energies? As we have seen, the Triads proposes no such doctrine,
or at most, only hints at it obliquely and inconclusively. The Capita does describe divine
life in this way, but only once and there not very fully. Had Palamas believed the distinction were, in and of itself, a necessary way of understanding God, surely he would
have attended to the tripartite distinction much more closely; certainly, had he imagined he was proposing some new and creative approach to trinitarian theology, he would
have argued more fully and more defensively, with greater consideration of opposition
(theoretical or actual) to his views, for he was nothing if not a polemicist.

Perhaps the best analogy for Gregory's position on the essence-energies distinction
is the contemporary Western distinction between the immanent and economic Trinity.
No Christian tradition regards this distinction as dogma or teaching upon which the
church stands and falls. Nevertheless, many modern theologians find it furnishes useful
categories for thinking about the Trinity in relation to creation. Indeed, the essence-
energies distinction might be taken as a prototype of the immanent-economic Trinity
distinction, for both serve to specify the ways in which God is independent of, yet will-
ingly implicated in, the created order. Such a solution would not satisfy those like Rahner,
and followers of his such as LaCugna, who find the immanent-economic Trinity distinction unacceptable, but Rahner's theology does not have the status of dogma within
the Roman Catholic church, and for other reasons (particularly its indebtedness to Kant)
affords a promising basis for ecumenical dialogue neither with the Orthodox nor with
the churches of the Reformation.

What the essence-energies distinction reduces to is a claim of divine transcendence
and immanence, together with an insistence that these must be asserted in tandem, despite the obvious inherent difficulty of doing so. Like the two natures language of
Christology, it provides a way of articulating a paradox that nevertheless does not pur-
port to resolve the tensions of the paradox. Where the essence-energies distinction more
resembles traditional christological language than the immanent-economic distinction
of modern trinitarian theology is that, for Gregory the energies do not simply represent
ways of thinking about divine activity; they are "realities in God [ὄντων τοῦ θεοῦ]"
(Capita 75) or "realities defined around the essence of God [τὰ περι αὐὴν ἀφοριζόμενα]"

(III.2.4). Once again, however, while Palamas makes this point, he does not make much of it, and his lack of attention to the real status of the energies explains what would otherwise stand as a curious, if minor, anomaly in two of his greatest commentators.

Lossky's certainty of the energies as representing real distinctions in God corresponds to Gregory's own definiteness in the last quotation (Capita 75 and III.2.4): "The doctrine concerning the energies is not a mere abstract conception, a purely intellectual distinction. We are dealing with a strictly concrete reality of the religious order."[93] Meyendorff, in contrast, uses much more muted language that suggests, or at least admits, the possibility of viewing the energies as conceptual distinctions: "The divine energies are not . . . 'things,' differing from one supreme 'thing' that is God's essence"[94] and more strongly still: "The triple distinction . . . is not a division of God's being; it reflects the mysterious life of the 'One-who-is'—transcendent, tri-personal, and present to His creation."[95] The reason two such careful readers of Gregory can regard him so differently on this point is that, while he occasionally makes the assertion of real distinctions, he appears to attach relatively little importance to it. If the distinction resembles the christological distinction between divine and human nature both in the reality of the two elements and their unity, it resembles the distinction between immanent and economic Trinity in its significance more as a theologian's tool than as an article of faith.

Nevertheless, even if Palamas did attach great dogmatic significance to the distinction for its own sake, his Western detractors would still be left with the propriety of his assertions about the essence and energies. Western theology, it is true, lacks the formal distinction; it does not, however, lack the basic concepts. No Western theologian of any stripe claims either that human beings may entirely understand God or that by grace we become wholly absorbed into divine being, or rival it, or that God is distant and without manifestation among us because transcendent. What Palamas does with the essence-energies distinction is little more than codify such commonly agreed observations and standardize the terminology for talking about them, using language that had been used loosely and informally in the theological tradition as far back as Irenaeus. Where he does extend slightly beyond pure codification of theological commonplace (e.g., in the claim that the distinctions are real), he does so only fleetingly, so that the claim can in no way be viewed as crucial to his thought.

The way in which the distinction functions in Gregory's thought, as well as the extent of its significance, is well demonstrated by considering the relation between the two elements of the distinction and the twin themes. The distinction, if taken as nominal, indicates nothing about divine nature that is not expressed by the twin themes. The themes are a better indicator of the Palamite doctrine of deification, however, for several reasons. The first is simply that the themes do not suggest a second distinction in divine being, alongside that of essence from hypostasis. Since Gregory's explicit statements do not claim a real distinction, the themes are less misleading with respect to his theological desiderata.

Not only do the themes not suggest a distinction in divine being, they do not correlate precisely with the poles of the distinction. The theme of provenance or authenticity clearly pertains to Gregory's doctrine of the energies. In asserting the existence of the energies and their relation to the essence, he wants in the first instance to ensure that the energies are regarded as divine—and not only divine but fully divine. Yet the very manner in which he goes about demonstrating the energies' authenticity indicates that the provenance theme does not concern the energies alone. As we have seen, Palamas gives two principal sorts of argument for their genuine divinity. The first of these, the energies' inseparability from the divine essence, directly engages the allusion to essence in the provenance theme. What is for Gregory definitively divine is the essence, not because it is more inherently divine than the energies but because it is incontestably so. The difference is not between the first-order authenticity of the essence and the poor-cousin authenticity of the energies, but the rhetorical necessity for asserting the energies' authenticity versus the categorical assumption of that of the essence. That the essence is divine Palamas may take for granted because his opponents, as well as the entire tradition before him, take it for granted. In the struggle to prove the energies' authenticity, the first line of attack had to be their inseparability from what no one would dispute was divine.

The second kind of argument for the energies' divine provenance is their uncreatedness. Here, too, we find inevitable connections to the essence. In claiming inoriginate status for the energies, Palamas is doing no more than taking one of the prime attributes of divine essence and transferring it to the energies. (If, as Lossky maintains, Eastern theology recognizes no division save that between created and uncreated,[96] then calling the energies uncreated essentially serves to locate them on the same side of the fundamental ontological divide as the divine essence.) Both in respect to inseparability and uncreatedness, therefore, the provenance-authenticity theme points as surely (albeit more circuitously) to essence as it does to energies.

There is significant correlation between one pole of the distinction and the theme of authenticity with respect to divinization's effects on the human person. As we have seen, while theosis is by no means the only theological reason for making the distinction between essence and energies, the distinction is extremely helpful in excluding the possibility of drawing from the doctrine of theosis certain heretical consequences. The energies perform the theological task of showing how human persons can be divinized without multiplication of the divine hypostases. To the extent that the distinction serves to specify our participation in divine life as genuinely divine because effected by the grace of the divine energies, the provenance theme corresponds neatly to the energies side of the distinction. Yet, as we have seen, Gregory's doctrine of deification is much less concerned with the human side of theosis than with the divine side. The primary theological import of the assertion of divine energies is to answer the question: what sort of God is it that Christians speak of? To this, the advocate of the energies responds: a God who creates, and desires communion with this created order. Similarly, the provenance theme answers the question by rejoining: a God whose involvement in the world is nothing less than a voluntary self-giving that is complete and yet inexhaustible. If the theme of authenticity corresponds more nearly to one pole of the distinction, then, it is in a respect—namely, that of theological anthropology—that is clearly secondary among Gregory's theological concerns.

On the side of gratuity or transcendence we observe a similar pattern. At first glance, it seems that this theme is obviously connected to the essence side of the distinction, and certainly the affirmation of imparticipable essence points unmistakably towards divine transcendence. However, when we begin to consider the gratuity side of the theme, a different pattern emerges. The assertion of gratuity (at least as it relates to theosis) concerns not only the freedom which remains God's even after the gift of deification, but also the freedom with which the gift is given. In Gregory's doctrine of God, transcendence and grace are intimately connected. We cannot become God as God is God for the fundamental reason that we are always the recipients of a divinizing grace, but never its bestowers. Since grace is always efficacious, this distinction does not make us less than divine (for Palamas insists that not only God, but also God's energy is authentically divine), but it does make us divine in a different way. To say that we become partakers of divine nature only at God's good pleasure is to stress that God does not become trapped in a web of necessity, so that he must divinize us, or that once he grants us grace, he cannot stop the tide of *Deus-homines* from storming the citadel of divine being. Such portrayals of Palamite deification are obviously wrong. It is not sufficient (and therefore not in the truest sense accurate) to say that Gregory wishes to preserve the transcendence of divine essence *and* wishes to maintain that deification is always a gift of grace. One encapsulates his thought fully only when one shows how these two elements are connected in his thought.

The nature of that connection, moreover, is not one that Palamas forges as a theological desideratum for the sake of a satisfying systematization. The connection in his thought is entirely natural: the themes of the gratuity of grace and the transcendence of the Giver of life and grace are two sides of one coin. If one accurately states Gregory's doctrine of grace, one will inevitably be drawn towards the language of transcendence. Although God's transcendence can be described without necessarily speaking of grace, and vice versa, it would be difficult to do so in the context of Gregory's doctrine of divinization.

Here, then, is one of the important differences between the twin themes and the essence-energies distinction. The provenance-authenticity theme can be made to correlate narrowly with one pole of the distinction only if one considers it exclusively in relation to anthropology; the transcendence-gratuity theme correlates neatly with the other pole only in the context of the doctrine of God. While, as we have said, Gregory's explication of theosis has far greater significance for the doctrine of God than for theological anthropology, no doctrine of God could be derived from a doctrine of theosis if there were no human person to be divinized. So we revisit the essential paradox of the distinction itself: it asserts a God who is beyond all knowing, all human describing, and yet this very assertion is the claim of those who describe God and, as Gregory constantly reminds us by his chastisement of the more extreme sides of apophatic theology, know God (albeit in a very qualified sense). It is therefore the energies that allow, indeed require, us to speak of the transcendent essence—without God's gracious self-implication in creation, there would be no need to speak of his independence of it, and certainly no possibility of our doing so.

The essence-energies distinction, then, is a powerful tool, whose function it is to ground the simultaneous assertion of several vital Christian doctrines: not only the doctrine of God and theological anthropology but also the doctrines of sanctification and grace, creation and revelation. The distinction is, as it were, the condition of the possibility of these doctrines, at least as they are articulated by Palamas. Like the doctrine of deification itself, it seems at first glance to be wholly the product of anthropological concerns: to glorify humanity, we assert divinization, then to make room for this wild form of sanctification without offending established orthodoxy, we invent the distinction. On closer examination, as we have seen, neither theosis nor the distinction proves to be chiefly concerned with theological anthropology or its systematic consequences.

Palamas begins from two chief givens: the text of 2 Peter 1:4 (and the patristic tradition following it) and the experience of the hesychast monks. These data stipulate a doctrine of deification, in his view. Like the prayer and spiritual experience of the monks, however, the doctrine leads not back towards humanity, but outward to God. The doctrine is, therefore, like the hesychasts themselves, essentially contemplative. It seeks to know the Beloved in order better to love; it seeks to love in order to be united with Love, and in the outpouring of love, it lauds the Beloved.

It is important to recognize that this necessarily contemplative tendency of a doctrine of deification is not an equally necessary tendency of any doctrine of sanctification whatsoever. A doctrine of sanctification may contain this contemplative element at its heart, inasmuch as it describes growth in holiness as growth in attributes specified as divine; however such doctrines may function adequately without significant description of the One to whom we liken. For example, one might describe sanctification as a growth in goodness because it belongs properly to God to be good. Having made that connection, though, one need say no more about God's goodness; one might simply turn towards humanity and specify what form goodness takes in human persons or how it is that we become good. Such a dwelling on the sanctified is not possible with a doctrine of theosis. Once the claim is made that humanity becomes God, only two avenues remain to be explored: how this is possible, and who it is that we become. For any orthodox doctrine of divinization, moreover, discussion of how deification is possible inevitably also focuses on God, for God must in some sense be the ground and means of its possibility.

Such an interpretation of the systematic significance of the distinction differs from both the classic Eastern and Western interpretations. The West takes the distinction as an element of the doctrine of God—one that is perhaps necessitated by a particular doctrine of sanctification but nevertheless part of the doctrine of God. Easterners tend to view it as part of the doctrine of grace. Here we are taking the distinction as an explanatory technical note to the doctrine of sanctification. Thus far, then, this reading resembles the Eastern position of the distinction's significance. This particular model of sanctification, however, is being viewed as a prime informant of the doctrine of God. The present reading thus resembles the Western view in that the essence-energies distinction ultimately does fall under the rubric of the doctrine of God. Where it differs from this view, however, is that the distinction is said to inform the doctrine of God indirectly, via the doctrine of sanctification. The significance of this indirection is that the essence-energies distinction does not serve to expand the doctrine of God, merely to clarify those elements of it susceptible to misinterpretation in the context of an asserted doctrine of theosis. The doctrine asserts the union of God and humanity even as it forges the union of theology and anthropology. This assertion is confirmed by the place of the distinction both within Gregory's own theology and in relation to Orthodox dogma. For neither Palamas nor for most Orthodox theologians in most times does the distinction furnish essential information about divine being in the sense that the essence-hypostases distinction does. Rather, it relays important information about how God relates to us and how that relatedness forms part of divine nature.

What the distinction and the doctrine of theosis tell us is that God is the divine food of believers which they nonetheless never consume, the One who enfolds believers while never engulfing them, the One who shares himself among all, yet remains one, the Giver of all who is never given away. In describing the energies, Palamas does not so much tell us *how* it is we can become God but *who* it is the divinized become: his theology in this sense is determinedly mystical rather than ascetical. We are made partakers of a life that is inherently generous, primally self-giving. The distinction's truest purpose is not to effect a logical sleight of hand, rescuing a bad theology from its worst tendencies; its truest function is to provide a small but nevertheless rich gloss and summary on theosis. In a sense too, then, Gregory's theology shapes its reader as it describes the shape of divinization, for by focusing our attention on theosis, we are brought to the contemplation of God, a contemplation that in Gregory's view is itself sanctifying.

The distinction is thus in a profound sense self-effacing, and it is important to grasp this point if we are rightly to understand its true place in Gregory's theology. If we consider the *Capita*—and even more so the *Triads*—as a whole, Palamas shows little interest in formulating a new doctrine of God or even in reworking and refurbishing an old one. He neither invents new language the better to articulate old doctrine, nor invents new doctrine the better to solve old dilemmas. With the language of divine essence and energies, he takes terminology that had long been used and refines it. In so doing, he not only provides a means for Christian theology to comprehend both the radical vision of sanctification represented most pointedly (though by no means exclusively) by 2 Peter 1:4 and the equally uncompromising insistence of monotheism in texts such as Deuteronomy 6:4, "Hear O Israel, the Lord our God is one Lord," but even more importantly, refines this language through use so that it points back to fundamental and catholic themes of Christian faith: the sovereignty of God and the grace given to humanity, the uniqueness of the Trinity and the commonality of divine life imparted through the Economy. The role of the distinction is thus entirely auxiliary. It refuses to become central and an end in itself, not only because Gregory expends far greater attention on other matters, but more significantly, because the distinction dissolves before the face of the One it describes and whom it ultimately serves.

6

CONCLUSION

I. Overview of the Thomistic and Palamite
Doctrines of Deification

We turn now from the survey of deification in Aquinas and Palamas to an assessment of their theologies in light of the charges rehearsed in chapter 1. To review, the recriminations of East and West over deification concern: the West's departure from the model of sanctification dominant in the Fathers; the particular lack of a doctrine of deification in Aquinas; Aquinas' espousal of created grace; Palamas' espousal of the essence-energies distinction; Palamas' departure from the theology of the Fathers; the uses of philosophy and logic by both figures; and the role of spiritual experience, especially in Palamas. The first two of these questions, regarding the persistence of deification in the theology of the West, and in particular, in the theology of Aquinas, has been answered by chapters 2 and 3. The question remaining is not whether Aquinas has a doctrine of deification but whether it represents a legitimate development of the patristic doctrine and whether it is compatible with that of Palamas. To begin to answer these questions, it will be helpful briely to review deification as we saw it in Aquinas and Palamas.

In the *Summa Theologiae*, the direct references of I-II.62 and 65 establish the central principles of the Thomistic doctrine of deification. These texts rely on the biblical conception of sanctification as participation in divine nature. They point to the theological virtues as means by which the human intellect and will are formed and ordered to their divine end. Finally, the explicit reference in I.12 indicates Thomas has deification firmly in mind even as he writes the doctrine of God, the foundation of the entire *Summa*.

The mainspring of Thomas' doctrine of the one God is simplicity. In simplicity, he grounds both the absolute uniqueness of God and such chief divine attributes as intellect, love and goodness. Simplicity, as it functions in the Summa, paradoxically contains in nuce the essential elements of a doctrine of deification: it articulates the absolute distinction between Uncreated and created and yet indicates the means by which these distinct entities are to be united in knowledge and love.

Later questions of the Prima Pars continue the pattern. The doctrine of analogy expounded in I.13, which at first glance seems rightly to belong in the methodological prolegomenon, may now be seen as serving to articulate the connection between simplicity and its correlate attributes. Analogical predication explains how intellect and will may be said to subsist in divine nature, simple though it is. As the Summa's first part continues, Aquinas elaborates upon attributes such as knowledge and love, finally defining the operations of knowing and loving through the category person in the De Trinitate. His description of intratrinitarian relations also implies a relation of God to humanity, a suggestion that becomes explicit in the account of the Trinity's mission to creation.

The tight structure of the Prima Pars, which connects epistemology and language to the doctrine of God, the doctrine of God to the Trinity, and the intratrinitarian relations to trinitarian missions ad extra, alerts the reader to the pattern that will become general in the Summa: Aquinas states his doctrine of deification explicitly, but also communicates it through the structure of his work, and in particular, through the interplay of intellect and will, the chief faculties of God and humanity, and the means by which God and humanity unite.

The Second and Third Parts further reveal the extent to which the Summa's doctrine of deification lodges in its structure, for we see here the principles established in the First Part applied in myriad ways in the spheres of anthropology and Christology. If we were to use Chenu's thumbnail description of the Summa (which derives, somewhat remotely, from the prologues to I.2 and the Secunda Pars), the Prima Pars describes theosis as located in the exitus, while the Secunda Pars describes the reditus. The Summa's structure is, on Chenu's account, and on that given here, theocentric, entirely defined by not-God's journey towards and union with God, of the created's participation in the Uncreated.

This theocentrism is evident throughout the Secunda Pars, but especially in the Thomistic concept of the imago Dei. Within the human person exists a trinitarian tracery consisting not only in a constitution in the faculties of knowing and loving, such as exists within the Trinity, but also in a pattern of relatedness to God similar to that within the Trinity. As the Father is the originating principle of the Trinity, so is he of all creation. As the Word knows and the Spirit loves, so is humanity bound intimately to God through knowledge and love, which is a participation in the divine Trinity's own life.

The doctrine of the imago shapes the Thomistic doctrine of deification in a second way, through the assertion of the image's threefold likening to God in nature, grace and glory. The likeness of nature demonstrates that God has made us for himself; the likeness of grace, that he draws us to himself by means of his own gift of self; of glory, that he completes nature and grace by destining us to share fully in his own nature, which sharing is beatitude. Our existence is directed to God, then, both in the sense that God's life is our destiny and in that God is where we must look in order to find our truest self. We grow towards that true self, Aquinas tells us, by growth in resemblance to God through the development of habits. The doctrine of the image thus forms a direct link between the doctrine of the Trinity and the treatises on habits and virtues.

The virtues are defined as perfections whereby the reason is directed to God, and since knowledge is a form of likeness, the virtues form the high road from grace to glory. Among the virtues, the group called theological direct us immediately to God, and of these, charity ranks first because it is the most deifying. Charity links the virtues, serving a role analogous to that of the Spirit within the Trinity, and charity constitutes the form of other virtues because it directs them to their end. Charity is one form of love; love draws humanity to God because the final cause of love is no less than God himself. It is the nature of love to bring about a change in the loving subject, and this change culminates in the union of lover and beloved. The effect of charity is infinite because it is a participation in love through union with the Holy Spirit. Nevertheless, despite the affirmation of genuine participation in the Trinity, Thomas' doctrine of divinisation stresses the inviolability of the divide between Uncreated and created, and the preservation of the creature qua creature. One form of this emphasis is his willingness to use a term such as *created beatitude*, and another is his insistence that nature is not eradicated, but perfected, by grace and glory.

The pattern of return to God which grace effects is expressed most fully in the person of Christ. The Incarnation both works sanctification on earth and bestows the ultimate salvific effect of redemption and union to God. Christ's person thus constitutes a recapitulation of the entire story and process of human sanctification. That to be divine by participation is no small and insignificant form of divinity is witnessed by the fact that Christ himself is divine in this way, as well as by hypostatic union. Christ also models our return to God in his priesthood and through the sacraments that exist in consequence of that priesthood. The sacraments set a character on their recipient, a seal that enables one thing to be assimilated to another. Since the reality of one of these (the eucharist) is charity, through the sacrament of communion the person may be said to participate in divine nature itself, which is love.

The content of participation or union is beatitude, the vision of God's essence. Seeing God must, in the Thomistic scheme, be a vision of divine essence, because all that is not created is the divine essence. Nevertheless, properly speaking, we ourselves do not see God, but God grants us a share in his own self-knowledge. Since the vision of divine essence surpasses all created substance, beatific vision can come only as God's gift of self. A single paradigm thus holds true of both Thomas' doctrine of grace and his understanding of glory. While the description of beatitude leans rather more to the side of the intellect than to the will, even in this context, Aquinas insists that participation in the divine good entails both knowing and loving, and thus beatitude itself mirrors the very structure of the Trinity.

The Thomistic doctrine of deification emphasizes resoundingly the two themes characteristic of any classic exposition of theosis. The fact of human participation in divine nature signifies God's eternal desire for communion. Much more even than creation itself, the doctrine of sanctification serves as a constituent of the doctrine of God, for it tells us not only what God would have us be but who God is, that he seeks union with those he has made. The God proclaimed by scripture and discovered in the wayfarer's experience is a God who desires communion, and contemplation of this proposition leads us to deeper knowledge and love of the One who has first sought us. Thomas is no less careful, however, to articulate deification's other pole, the ontological similarity between

Creator and creature. Because it is God who creates *ex nihilo*, and the human person whose being is therefore at every moment dependent on the act of divine will; because it is God who gives grace, and the human recipient who can never deserve it, let alone produce it; because it is God who deifies, and the creature who is graciously permitted a share of divine life, deification in Thomas' presentation never means that humanity becomes God as God is God. Union is an elective affinity brought about at God's good pleasure; it is never the amalgamation of equals into a homogeneous whole. The union between God and humanity is the fruit of divine desire alone.

Turning to Palamas, we find many of the themes and priorities we found in Aquinas. Beginning, as we did with Aquinas, with the direct references to deification, we find that Palamas provides no definition of his own, although one of his direct references employs a definition of Maximus'. Rather the direct references lead us to a clearly demarcated set of images, or cognates, for deification which we find running throughout the *Triads* and the *Capita*. Some of these cognates designate rudimentary forms of deification, or its precondition; these are virtue, knowledge and vision. A second group correlates to deification itself considerably more closely, notably contemplation, light, glory and grace. A group of three cognates, adoption, union and participation, function as virtual synonyms.

The contiguity of Palamas' doctrine of theosis with less radical forms of sanctification lies in his use of the cognates of the preparatory group. He is wary of equating deification and virtue, and yet he clearly wants to avoid the suggestion that one could be deified without also being virtuous. Likewise, while he affirms the mind's apprehension of God as encompassed within theosis, he does not want to say one becomes God by being clever, any more than one does so by being good. His ambivalence regarding vision differs slightly, for here his worry concerns the possibility of interpreting the *visio Dei* in terms too remininscent of sense perception. He uses the most suitable words he has to hand, but in the case of these cognates, he takes pains to show where they are wanting.

The cognates of the intermediate group still reveal some caution on Palamas' part, but they are intrinsically less prone to prosy misinterpretation. Contemplation expresses a notion akin to that conveyed by vision, yet because it less immediately suggests report of the senses, Gregory uses it with fewer qualifications. Now the apprehension of God can be portrayed as an encounter with a suprasensible Other, without suggesting that this encounter is procured on the human side by intelligence or diligence, or that the Ineffable becomes perceptible to human senses. Similarly, although light would seem to belong to the material world and be therefore suspect as an image for divinization, it is so often used to designate spiritual or intellectual illumination that Gregory makes use of it freely, with only a few perfunctory demurrals. Light is linked to the next two cognates inasmuch as all three denote that which is encountered, unlike virtue, knowledge, vision and contemplation, which point to elements of the saint's own experience of God. Glory, like light, designates that towards which, and grace the means by which, the saint is drawn. Glory and grace both belong properly to God and are means by which God's self-communication is actualized in humanity.

The final set of images designates neither divinized nor divinizer but the way in which the two become one. Of the three, adoption is the weakest, conveying as it does the sense of a nominal union, yet adoption also points strongly to the gracious element of deification that Gregory is always concerned to stress. That forensic element vanishes in the face of assertions of a stronger kind, such as union; perhaps for that reason, as well as its biblical grounding, Gregory privileges participation among the cognates. Conceiving of deification as participation in divine life enables him to point simultaneously to the element of gratuity (God grants us a share of his own life), the preservation of distinction (we participate in God's life rather than becoming absorbed into it) and the wondrous fact of this marriage of opposites.

Study of the direct references to deification and its cognates reveals a welter of evidence, the complexity of which seems at times to border on contradiction. Some of the ambivalence reflects the level of equation with deification that Palamas is willing to accord a particular cognate, but in many instances the lack of univocity among the texts reflects simply the author's desire not to make simple that which must eventually elude all human knowing and describing. To avoid facility, and to avoid describing deification in terms that would reduce it to a less radical model of sanctification, Gregory readily resorts to paradox. These data of his doctrine of theosis do not admit of any straightforward reduction, though they are not incoherent. Two themes appear and reappear and in these themes we find the summation of the Palamite understanding of theosis.

These two themes—transcendence or gratuity and provenance or authenticity—are expressed to some degree through each of the cognates. These serve, then, to point to the common denominators of the Palamite doctrine of theosis: God's self-communication to humanity is an authentic gift of self, and not of some lesser intermediary, yet humanity can neither force this divine gift, nor is God bound in the giving of it. These twin themes resemble the essence-energies distinction but do not correlate with it exactly: although the energies certainly correlate to provenance and authenticity, and essence corresponds to the transcendence side of the first theme, essence does not correlate to gratuity. Furthermore, the twin themes do not together point to a distinction in God, as the essence-energies distinction does. The cognates reduce to the twin themes rather than to a distinction in divine being. If the cognates are indeed where Palamas' doctrine of deification is to be found, then that doctrine is rather more concerned with the underlying principles expressed in the twin themes than with the distinction per se. The distinction itself—that is, the terms *essence* and *energies* used contrastively, rather than in isolation from one another—moreover makes the briefest of appearances in Palamas' two main works, and for this reason, it is hard to accord it the centrality to his thought given by some twentieth-century commentators, or to take it as claiming real distinction in divine being.

1. Continuity with the Patristic Tradition

The first question we face is the consonance of these doctrines of deification with the forms theosis assumes in patristic texts. If the commonality of the Thomistic and Palamite doctrines reveals itself only under close scrutiny, their fidelity to prior tradition announces itself much more readily. We can most easily describe the consonance of our various doctrines of deification via its imagery, for, with the possible exception of John Damascene, none of the Fathers presents a systematic exposition of deification, certainly not as a discrete theological locus. Here, then, we encounter the first point of similarity: the doctrine of deification is diffuse, often more implicit than explicit, and rarely communicated through a series of propositional statements. Because this diffuseness is as characteristic of the patristic and Palamite descriptions of theosis as of the Thomistic, one cannot contend that Thomas lacks a doctrine of deification simply because no single question is devoted to it in the *Summa*. Certainly, he prefers to address most issues directly, by focusing on them in a question, but to decree the individual question the *sole* means of theological assertion in the *Summa* is simply to impose one's own presuppositions upon the text. Concluding from the absence of a question "Whether deification is granted to humanity?" that Thomas has no interest in the issue would lead one to overlook his use of the explicit language of deification, his extensive use of cognate imagery, and the import of the *Summa*'s structure. It would be like squinting through a magnifying glass at the gargoyles on a cathedral while neglecting to stand back far enough to appreciate the architecture of the whole. Similarly, one can scarcely object to the diffuseness of Palamas' exposition without also condemning the Fathers—and pushing aside, moreover, the biblical data which first gave rise to the notion of theosis in the first place.

Not only the basic means of describing divinization but also the majority of specific images and concepts used to do so concur in the works of the Fathers, Aquinas and Palamas. In the corpus of any one writer, certain of these will prove more important and others less so. Those identified in these pages may well not exhaust the list actually used by any one author, but it is comprehensive enough to show the bones, and even much of the flesh, of the Christian understanding of divinization.

The key biblical proof text for these images is 2 Peter 1:4, which speaks of participation in divine nature. Participation becomes a prime image for deification in the Fathers (Origen, Athanasius, Nyssa, Denys and Damascene), as well as for Thomas and Gregory. Some of the earliest patristic literature (the *Didache*, Tatian), while not referring directly to participation, speaks of knowledge of God as sanctifying, a notion that may allude to the idea of participation, since this knowledge is of a God conceived of as *logos* and *nous*, Word and mind; given that sanctifying knowledge is of a being identified with intellect, some notion of participation may be implied. Knowledge continues as a very strong theme in the tradition, especially in the works of Origen, Clement of Alexandria, Nyssa, Nazianzen, Cyril of Alexandria and Denys. If Gregory's attitude towards knowledge is decidedly ambivalent, we cannot fault Thomas for his relentless pursuit of the theme, since he stands, on this point, far closer to the patristic consensus than does Gregory.

Union, also closely allied to participation, appears early and extensively in patristic literature (Ignatius, Tatian, Irenaeus, Chrysostom, Cyril of Alexandria, Damascene) and figures prominently in the work of both Thomas and Gregory. One important consonance among all these writers is that none is speaking of what we would properly call mystical experience—that is, an extraordinary apprehension limited to the exceptionally holy few. These authors present deifying union, as opposed to mystical rapture, as the norm of Christian growth into God.

Allied with participation, knowledge and union are the cognates light (or illumination), contemplation, vision and adoption. Of these, adoption far outranks the others in importance, appearing in Justin, Hippolytus, Augustine, Chrysostom and Damascene. As we have noted, both Aquinas and Palamas use it sparingly, but with great approval. Whatever reason underlies its apparent loss of extensive use, that diminished employment is as true of the East as of the West. Illumination appears earlier and more widely than the other optical images, but all three figure in the patristic corpus. To those who would object to the great stress on vision in the *Summa*, one can respond that while vision seems most significant to some of the more controversial Fathers, such as Origen and Denys, it is also important to Damascene, whose credentials (both orthodox and Orthodox) are impeccable.

Among the cognates focusing more on the anthropological side of deification number grace and virtue. The latter enters the literature of theosis early, for the Apologists tend to stress it heavily, but it seems less widely employed than knowledge or adoption, for example. This fact is instructive, for it indicates that the balance Gregory strikes between knowledge and virtue and the other cognates is less characteristic of patristic theology in general than that of Thomas. We note this, not to reproach Gregory, but simply to point out that the assumption that Byzantine theology clings more closely to its patristic roots than does the medieval West is not always accurate. Grace, on the other hand, seems on the whole less important to the Fathers than to either Thomas or Gregory; it not only figures less widely but appears later in connection with deification than most other cognates (we find it in Nazianzen, Augustine, Chrysostom and Cyril of Alexandria). To those who would point with great assurance to Thomas' rediscovery of the decrees of Orange as a profound influence on his doctrine of grace, we can remark only the tremendous importance of grace for Gregory also, who probably knew little or nothing of the either the Council of Orange or Pelagius. To those Westerners who believe, with considerable self-satisfaction, that down the road marked "Ignorance of Augustine" lie in wait Pelagian error and works righteousness, Gregory stands as a rebuke to parochialism.

In addition to these cognates, certain concepts provide the essential foundation upon which the doctrine is built. The *imago Dei* appears as early as Tatian and makes frequent appearances thereafter. Here again, Aquinas actually lies closer to the patristic root than Palamas, for the image is central to his exposition but does not figure prominently in that of Palamas. No difference, however, is discernible with two concepts associated particularly with Christ: the Incarnation as the paradigm of deification and the sacraments as its ecclesial mediation. Both concepts appear early (with Tatian and Hippolytus), occur frequently throughout the patristic eras, and are important to Thomas and Gregory. In this case, also, frequency of usage in and of itself places Thomas closer to the Fathers than Gregory, not only because the sacraments figure more prominently in the *Summa* than either the *Triads* or the *Capita* but also because he links the sacraments' deifying power more closely to the Incarnation. Once again, the point is not to adjudicate between Thomas and Gregory, pronouncing Thomas the champion but to illustrate how misguided is the notion that, in finding inspiration in Aristotle, the West necessarily cut itself off from the Fathers and began theology afresh. The relentless order of Thomistic theology may not resemble the usually ad hoc, discursive, pastorally and apologetically oriented, and sometimes untidy treatises of the Fathers, but the content of his theology represents no radical departure from theirs.

We are left with one of the two principles most central to the idea of deification in its Christian form: the ontological divide. While the cognates themselves convey the notion of authentic divine self-communication, none of them explicitly alludes to the divide. Yet as early as Irenaeus, the Christian tradition recognized the assertion of this divide as essential, not only for general theological purposes, but also to prevent its favored model of sanctification from becoming pantheistic, hence the repeated insistence on the point by some of divinization's strongest proponents (Athanasius, Augustine,

Denys and Damascene). Analysis of Thomas and Gregory demonstrates conclusively that both regarded this distinction as crucial, stressing it more explicitly, if anything, than their predecessors. Nevertheless, as we have seen, asserting both the divide and divine self-communication in the form of divinization places the theologian in an inherently awkward position almost inevitably resulting in an emphasis on one element over the other, just as any Christology almost inevitably ends up sounding more Antiochene or more Alexandrian. Both Thomas and Gregory appear to see the tension between these two principles even more clearly than their predecessors, and perhaps in consequence, each of them grants priority to one principle or the other when the tension between them seems too great to broker a compromise—an issue to which we will return.

What about the particular mechanism in Gregory's theology for articulating the divide, the essence-energies distinction? Is it, as the Orthodox claim, thoroughly patristic in its origins, or is it, as the West claims, a late Byzantine innovation? Orthodox writers attempting to establish the distinction's patristic pedigree appeal to two sorts of evidence: reference to divine energy and Basil's Letter 234. We did not, in the patristic survey, note usages of *energeia* because it does not emerge strongly from patristic accounts of deification, a point in favor of the Western view of the distinction. The term is not absent, however, from patristic discourse about divine activity; the Orthodox correctly point to its use early in the patristic period. The problem lies in the fact that these usages suggest little, if anything, more than that the Fathers speak of God's activity, not only as action proper but as a power that is a divine attribute. Apart from Basil's letter, there is nothing to suggest that this energy exists in some sort of symbiotic or contrastive relationship to divine essence. Use of *energeia*, therefore, does not in itself authenticate a patristic form of the essence-energies distinction. The exception, as we have noted, is Basil's Letter 234. There, however, we find a mention so brief, so fleeting, and in a context so occasional, that it seems highly questionable to propose this text as the basis of a major doctrine.

Have we then agreed with the West's claim of innovation? By no means. We assert only that the distinction does not exist in patristic literature in the form it later took in Byzantine theology. The latter, however, far from inventing new doctrine, merely drew together two elements of patristic tradition and in so doing, showed their systematic significance in a way that had hitherto gone unrecognized. It took the patristic notion of deification, along with the necessary concomitant claim of the ontological divide between creature and Creator, and paired them with the existing language of *ousia* and *energeia*. The attachment of the latter to the doctrine of deification was new, though not the doctrine or the terms themselves; new also was the pairing of the terms in a relationship of indissolubility and opposition. At the end of this process, we still end up with no more than a new and more precise means of articulating a very old idea—as long as the distinction is taken as nominal in Gregory's thought. Those who insist on an ontological distinction will encounter greater difficulty in showing its patristic pedigree. A nominal distinction, on the other hand, has quite enough patristic grounding in proportion to its actual degree of novelty, which is slight.

Finally, we find in the patristic corpus an element of the doctrine of deification to which we have until now given scant and only implicit attention. This is the idea of deification as progressive, a process that begins in this life, certainly, but finds its fulfilment only in the next. Irenaeus, Theophilus, Cyril of Alexandria and Damascene all portray deification in this way, and such a model would be consistent with Nyssa's notion of epectasy. We must note this point carefully because later Orthodox writers some-times speak of theosis as if the idea of some Taboric experience in this life were native to it. Gregory himself never makes such a claim, but neither does he espouse a solely eschatological fulfilment, despite his talk of the Age to Come. The grounding of his the-ology in the hesychasts' spirituality might, however, suggest that deification is for him inseparable from such spiritual experience. If so, he would differ significantly from Thomas, whose scheme is clearly one of graced earthly life as inchoate glory. As we have noted, though, Gregory is at most ambiguous on this point, and if he does advo-cate full divinization in this life, then on this point he would specify where the Fathers had declined to do so.

Aquinas and Palamas undoubtedly differ, then, in their appropriation of the patristic tradition, inasmuch as they emphasize different elements of it. When we measure (ad-mittedly, rather crudely) in what manner and to what extent they differ, we find the surprising result that it is Aquinas who generally lies closer to it. Nevertheless, although they sometimes represent a healthy development of the tradition (as with, for example, the vigorous insistence on grace), none of these differences represents an abandonment of the Fathers' model of deification. Rather, both theologians take patristic conceptualities and through an extended meditation on them, not so much extend, as deepen them.

2. Theological Method

A second area identified in the history as problematic was the set of issues related to theological method. Under this rubric, we include attitudes to and use of philosophy and formal logic, as well as modes of theological exposition. The disputes of the last five hundred years have centered on the first two areas, giving scant attention to the last; the contention here is that the significant differences between Eastern and Western theology pertain far more to genre and style than to logic. We will begin, however, by examining the uses of philosophy and logic in the work of Palamas and Aquinas.

The use of logic is the most straightforward issue. Accusations have come from both parties to the dispute. The East maintains that Western theology generally, and Aquinas' writings in particular, have used logic improperly; the standard complaint is against syllo-gisms. The West criticizes the East's supposed irrationality, particularly in relation to the use of, and appeals to, antinomy. Neither charge holds up very well under scrutiny.

To begin with, a justification for the polemic against syllogism is needed. Eastern critics of Aquinas, and of Western theological method generally, have assumed that the problem is self-evident. It is not. The critique is unclear on two counts. The first con-cerns what one acknowledges as an instance of syllogistic reasoning and the second, the reason that the syllogism is objectionable. With respect to the first, Eastern critics need to acknowledge that explicit use of the syllogism is quite rare in Western theology; cer-tainly, in the *Summa Theologiae*, Aquinas does not overtly use the form. It is true that in some places his reasoning might be expressed in a syllogism, but so could the argu-ments of the Fathers at times. While it could be argued that his thought itself was syllo-gistic, such a claim would need extended documentation; as Ware points out, the time is long overdue for some specificity to charges of this kind on the part of Eastern critics. While Ware's call for a substantiated critique is certainly commendable, his point is so obvious one wonders that it need have been made at all.

Even if his theology were unambiguously syllogistic, however, we would still be left with the question of why this would be objectionable. Ware's remark concerning the use of logic beyond logic's scope suggests that what worries the East is that logic would be used to arrive at conclusions that are unbiblical or unpatristic—that theologians will believe they can arrive at theological truth that is not grounded in God's self-disclosure in scripture or to the church through the workings of the Spirit. The syllogism, understood in this way, would function as a speculative tool. If syllogisms may be used in this way at all, Aquinas has not done so. His thought is not remarkable for the originality of his conclusions but for the rigor with which he attempts to expound Christian doctrine systematically. If he can be said to use syllogistic reasoning in any sense, it is as an aid in clarification, and this usage the East has never deemed objectionable.

Nor does the more vague charge of rationalism hold. Thomas does not develop his theological positions deductively, by writing from supposedly self-evident premises towards Christian doctrine, so as to establish a particular theological position without reference to scripture or tradition. His doctrine of the Trinity, for instance, starts from the assumption of a triune God and of trinitarian processions, both givens of either scripture or prior tradition, and from there attempts to describe the nature of the relations among the Three, not according to the conventions of formal logic, nor in an effort to render the supernatural transparent to human minds, but so as to draw as coherent as possible a portrait of God. To be intelligible to human beings, Thomas must use human language, rooted though it is in conceptualities pertaining solely to human experience. His description of divine Persons in terms of intellect and will nevertheless reflects not an attempt to establish theological truth on the basis of logical deduction, but to describe the God of scripture and tradition in what is, after all, the only language we have. To deny the validity of such language or the use of conceptualities derived from human experience altogether would also invalidate the theological method of the Fathers and Palamas.

If Thomas is not hyperrational, is Gregory irrational? While Western critics of the East tend to be somewhat specific in their complaints, we are often still faced, as we were with Eastern complaints about the West, with charges so general they are difficult to rebut. Let us first address the more general sort of complaint, that of simple irrationality. Opposition to Palamas' work often assumes that because its logical development is less than transparent to an outsider's eyes, it lacks any logical structure whatsoever. Few commentators (Lison is an exception) have recognized the need to interpret the texts as far as possible, at least initially, on their own terms. The overall assertion of the analysis of Palamas presented here is that when his work itself furnishes the categories for analysis, a logical structure and consistency emerge that are much clearer than would seem if one looked, for instance, to schematic outlines of the text that attempt to render it as a linear progression of loci. When we explored Gregory's thought using its native categories, we found a high degree of internal consistency, a quality only more striking given the inherent difficulties of his subject matter. Although neither the *Triads* nor the *Capita* is given over to descriptions of visionary experience per se, Gregory's extensive treatments of Taboric light and glory approach the realm of mystical experience more closely than Thomas' do in the *Summa*, yet his work maintains both coherence and, for the most part, a degree of intelligibility despite the difficulties of his subject. Not even his commitment to apophaticism deters him from mounting a reasoned, theological defense of the hesychasts. It is as inaccurate to see Gregory's work as a flight from reason as it is to view Thomas' as derived chiefly from logical explanation.

Not different attitudes towards logic, therefore, distinguish Aquinas and Palamas. Perhaps the use of philosophy, then? Certainly, no one will deny that despite the fact that both knew Aristotle well, there are clear and large differences in the ways that acquaintance influences their work. It is much too simplistic, however, to assert that Thomas merely shoehorns Christian doctrine into an unquestioned Aristotelian framework or that Gregory dispenses with logical discourse altogether.

The essential similarity in the Thomist and Palamite philosophical usages lies in their common purpose. Both Thomas and Gregory seek to write theology. This apparently banal point is important because it has so often been overlooked, or even obscured, in the secondary literature. Even today, Thomas is frequently treated essentially as a philosopher, not only on the basis of the works that are clearly philosophical, such as the *De ente et essentia*, but also on the basis of the *Summa Theologiae* itself, which sounds in some discussions to be solely concerned with such issues as substance metaphysics, epistemology, ethics, and proofs of the existence of God. The Eastern perception of Thomas, an undercover philosopher masquerading as a Christian theologian in a show of extremely bad faith, is justified to the extent that those who should have known Thomas best presented a picture of his thought that was conducive to such an interpretation. Nevertheless, Orthodox commentators who choose to pronounce on Thomas on the basis of secondary sources alone are still culpable for failing to inform themselves properly whereof they wrote and what they criticized.

The perception of Gregory as a mystic opposed to philosophy because he cannot understand it is harder to account for, given that his own works do not relate his own or anyone else's experiences and that Orthodox secondary literature treats him as a theologian rather than as a mystical writer, and given the well-known facts of his education. The West's tendency to ignore the specifically theological content of his work perhaps stems from the association of his major work with the hesychast controversy: if the forms and experience of prayer furnish the occasion for his thought, Gregory must be a mystic. Such a misconception overlooks not only his marked disinclination to discuss the specifics of mystical experience (as well as the East's general disapproval of such talk) but, more oddly still, the fact that his concern in the *Triads* and the *Capita* lies entirely on the side of showing the theological presuppositions and entailments of humanity's experience of God.

Once we renounce the notion that we are comparing a philosopher and a mystic, we are nevertheless left with the question of what kinds of theologians we have in Thomas and Gregory. Thomas no doubt bears a keen resemblance to what we in the twentieth century would call a systematician, while the structure of Gregory's prose seems to preclude viewing him thus. The method of examination used in this study, however, challenges the easy judgement that in the *Summa* we have a system for the sake of a system, while in Gregory we have a collection of incoherent polemic and antirational spiritual miscellany. The very orderly structure of the *Summa* points to a larger than systematic purpose. The import of that structure is the thesis of a mystical theology. If in its particulars the *Summa* undoubtedly belongs largely to the genres of philosophical and systematic theology, its design identifies it as a mystical theology concerned with humanity's union with God and with contemplation of God.[1] Here, indeed, comparison with Gre-

gory proves instructive: the absence of references to mystical experience proves no reliable guide to a work's status as mystical theology. As we do not doubt the *Triads* is in
this sense a mystical work, wrought of the conviction that the contemplation of the divine sanctifies, so we ought not doubt that the *Summa* is also a mystical theology, whose
meditation is intended not only to instruct the reader, but to increase in her the virtues
of faith and love. Comparison with Palamas thus allows us to see the possibility of intra-
Western similarities that are often denied, such as that between Aquinas and Bonaventure.

If we grant this important similarity—that both Thomas and Gregory are in some
sense mystical theologians—we are still left with the question of their respective relations to philosophy. We are not dealing with opposite ends of a spectrum, with Thomas
as the embracer of Aristotelianism and Gregory as the categorical rejector of what a
philosopher would recognize as rational thought. Despite the insistence of some Orthodox commentators (notably Lossky) on the methodological and even theological importance of antinomy in Orthodox thought, Gregory's reliance on it is relatively spar-
ing. His hyperbolic assertions regarding participation in the Imparticipable, for example,
are clearly analogous to almost any variety of orthodox trinitarian discourse: as God is
three and God is one, but not in the same way three and one, so God is both participable
and imparticipable, though not in the same way. Furthermore, the very hyperbolic, almost defiant, quality of those utterances suggests that Gregory's training in Aristotelian
logic has come into play: he knows the conventions and flouts them deliberately, in the
name of a transcendent, hypostatic Truth, a Logos with whom Aristotle's logic was never
concerned.

Thomas shows no evidence of such calculated defiance of traditional Aristotelianism,
but leave its confines he nevertheless does. We may consider his departure from Aristotle
under two forms: substance and method. The departures in substance are well known,
chief among them Thomas' denial of the eternity of the world. Despite their status as
commonplaces and their frequent attestation in secondary literature, however, Orthodox commentators continue to treat Aquinas as if he were willing to side with Aristotle
against the Christian tradition if need be, when in fact precisely the reverse is true. Thomas' methodological independence is of even greater significance. Had he wished to
follow an Aristotelian pattern, he might have constructed his argument on the ostens-
sible basis of observation, along lines such as these: we see the human person constituted by intellect and will; seeking the origin of these faculties, we suppose a First Cause,
a pattern of intellect and will in some eternal and omnipotent Being; from these faculties posited in God, we develop not only the essential features of the *De Deo uno* but also
of *De Trinitate*. But this is precisely not the Thomistic pattern. Aquinas declares his independence of philosophy in the first question of the *Summa*, where he states that the only
sure ground for theology is revelation. His argument's methodological premise is the
God of scripture, as is the beginning of the *Summa*'s theology proper: it begins with the
doctrine of God and proceeds to anthropology, not the reverse. His assertion of divine
intellect and will is based, not on the major premise of the observed existence of these
qualities in rational creatures and the minor premise of an analogy of being, but on the
assumption of will and intellect in God on the basis of the classical doctrine of God,
expounded in prior tradition and ultimately derived from the biblical depiction of God.

If the methodological difference between Thomas and Gregory does not lie in logi-
cality versus alogicality or illogicality, or in complete acceptance versus total rejection

of philosophy, where does it lie?—for we are clearly dealing with different theological tempers. The very means to which we resorted in analyzing each thinker provide a clue to the nature of their distinctiveness. In Thomas we followed two structuring principles, intellect and will (or knowledge and love), observing how he used them, first in the doctrine of God, then in the doctrine of the Trinity, next in the anthropology, Christology and sacramental theology, and finally, how the movement through the various sections constituted a doctrine of sanctification. Structure and a consistent, sustained meditation on two principles proved to be the wellspring of virtually the whole *Summa*, certainly of its doctrine of deification. Gregory's work required quite a different approach: the examination of a fairly large circle of images, no one of which provides an adequate insight into his doctrine of God, his theological anthropology or his doctrine of sanctification. Instead, he provides a number of lenses through which we may look at God and humanity, pointing out the limitations of many of them. Without providing an explicit synthesis, though, Gregory's images nevertheless yield a coherent theology, whose variegated color is indeed rich: not uniform but perhaps deeper for its very lack of uniformity.

This difference between Thomas and Gregory is striking, but is it evidence for a fundamental difference in method between East and West? To sustain that claim, we would need to show other theologians lining up neatly alongside our figures, and that proves difficult to do. Damascene and Staniloae write more in the manner of Thomas than Gregory; Augustine and Balthasar are methodologically more similar to Gregory than Thomas. The difference we are describing is essentially one of prose structure, which is certainly indicative of a theological temper and a writer's proclivities, audience and purposes, but says nothing about grave, let alone irreconcilable, theological divergence. The most immediately obvious feature of Thomas' prose—the unyielding form of the article, with its objections, corpus and replies—reflects the medieval West's willingness to acknowledge apparent conflicts among the Fathers, and Gregory, no more than Eastern theologians generally, not only does not adopt such a form but is remote from its spirit. Yet this difference, too, is more superficial than material, for Thomas is almost invariably concerned to find common ground with his patristic predecessors. However seemingly disputatious his form, his intentions are usually irenic, certainly more so than Gregory's vis-à-vis Barlaam.

There remains a final question of method, the answer to which proves much more elusive than the others we have considered. Granted that differing modes of exposition are justifiable, granted that degrees of dependence on a clearly articulated philosophical framework may vary, may experience be used as a theological warrant, and if so, under what circumstances? At times, Orthodox critique of the rationalism of Western theology borders on suggesting that spiritual experience may indeed ground theological assertions and seems to suggest this without qualifications. The West hastens to respond with the spectre of subjectivity and private revelation run amok.

The debate is a legitimate one, the questions important, but they are not questions raised by the work of Palamas. Nowhere does Palamas attempt to ground new doctrine by the appeal to private revelation. Nowhere does he announce: "To X has it been revealed that Y," much less "Therefore Y is to be believed by all the faithful." Gregory's use of experience is much more diffuse. Essentially, the *Triads* represents an answer to the question: in what ways and to what degree is the theology of the Christian tradition consonant with hesychast spiritual experience? He does not use experience to ground theology but theology to verify experience. Whether or not the essence-energies distinction constitutes a codification or a novelty, it is not urged by any specifically hesychast practice, but by the assertion of theosis in general.

What of the East's charge, that the West has banished spirituality from theological reflection? This charge merits investigation, but scarcely with respect to Thomas. In its most common form, criticism of Thomas acquires distinctly ad hominem overtones, as though the paucity or alleged absence of explicit reference to prayer, visions or other spiritual experiences in Thomas' theological work proves its detachment from a fully Christian life. The specific answer to this kind of attack can be found in any of the several biographies of Thomas, all of which testify to the depth and fervor of his spiritual life. The ultimate answer to the charge of a narrowly intellectual treatment of Christianity in Thomas' work, however, is the kind of analysis we have just provided, which attempts to show how concern for union with God is the author of Thomas' theology, not its silent partner.

We do encounter genuine difference between Thomas and Gregory in their attitudes to secular knowledge. Here again, though, we are speaking of distinction rather than polarity. Thomas does not uncritically embrace all the latest intellectual fashions, but he is generally more open to the possibility that secular knowledge might prove helpful. Gregory has a healthy respect for intellectual training, as evidenced by his pride in his own grasp of Aristotle, but is on the whole more suspicious of the value of such knowledge for theology. As the comparison of cognates indicated, Thomas readily understands the intellect as an organ of deification in part because for him, intellect is a prime attribute of God. Gregory will speak of knowledge as deification's medium, but because his portrait of God differs in emphasis from that of Thomas, it is more important for him to distinguish between knowledge that is a divine gift and knowledge that comes by means of human effort, of which he is deeply skeptical. What we have here, then, is another difference of emphasis rather than any methodological opposition.

The prime methodological difference between Aquinas and Palamas lies at the literary level, in the structuring principles that shape their works. Theologians have not generally considered literary analysis to fall within their province, perhaps because they believe it more concerned with surface than with substance. I would suggest, however, that failure to attend to literary differences lies at the root of much anti-Thomist and anti-Palamite polemic. Failure to appreciate such formal qualities certainly obscures the logical linkages in Gregory's thought. Failure to grasp the larger structures of Thomas' theology results in an obscured doctrine of deification and of the mystical orientation of the Summa generally—failure to see it, in other words, as a work seminally concerned with the union of God and humanity. Less certainly but still plausibly nonetheless, we may conjecture that Thomas has so often been labelled rationalistic, a manipulator of pagan philosophy and a fabricant of syllogisms, because readers have peered too myopically at individual questions in the Summa, seeing only the relentless forward press of the argument within each one, and concluding on that basis that Thomas was solely concerned with careful reasoning. To grasp the doctrine of deification at all, and certainly to appreciate their authors' positive contribution to the Christian tradition, one must attend to the literary structures of the Summa Theologiae, the Triads and the Capita. Nevertheless, understanding the differences between Thomistic and Palamite structuring principles, far from alienating the two authors from each other, ultimately highlights the compatibility of their doctrines of deification.

This difference between Thomas and Gregory with respect to prose structure is also significant. Thomas' structuring principle, and the tradent of his doctrine of deification, could be described as linear and teleological. The intertwining of his two principles culminates logically in beatific vision and participation in divine life. Gregory's circles of imagery convey a tension: the multiplicity of images and the paucity of definitions express his conviction of the reality of deification and the necessity of speaking of it, yet his demurrals simultaneously proclaim the impossibility of doing so adequately. Thomas stresses the vision of God, Gregory the darkness of divine mystery. Thomas strives, as far as possible, for clarity; Gregory more characteristically reminds us of the poverty of all human language in the face of the Inexpressible.

These differences nevertheless remain those of emphasis, and it would be an exaggeration to describe them simply as the opposition of a kataphatic and an apophatic theology. Both Thomas and Gregory are trying to give a theological account of deification, after all, and both succeed in doing so; both acknowledge the inadequacy of human language to this, or any other, theological task. Nevertheless, they do not have the same level of tolerance for unclarity—Thomas does all he can to avoid it, whereas Gregory uses it as a theological tool to articulate his doctrine of God.

3. Theological Loci

Aside from the large procedural questions pertaining to development of doctrine and theological method, the historical survey also identified as problematic specific theological assertions, notably created grace and beatific vision in the work of Aquinas and the essence-energies distinction in that of Palamas. We have already responded to these questions, either explicitly or implicitly, in the analytical chapters, so we will here merely summarize briefly.

The complaints against Thomas' use of the category created grace are weak on two counts. The first is that Thomas barely uses the term at all, and the Summa's treatise on grace itself, the very place where we would most expect to find it, does so only in an objection. Second, when he does use the term in the Summa, he does so in a context that indicates he seeks not to distinguish between two forms of grace but between two sorts of subjects, divine and human. If Thomas' end is, as we have argued, not to deny a genuine inhabitation by the Holy Trinity, and therefore, real contact with God, but to affirm the unbreachable ontological divide between created and Uncreated, then his end must be deemed fully consonant with that of an Orthodox doctrine of deification. Similarly, if we acknowledge Thomas to be claiming that the beatific vision is a participation in God's self-knowledge and that even this participated vision or knowing remains less than God's own, Orthodox objections to Thomistic beatific vision could only be couched in the form of a dogmatic insistence on the necessity of distinguishing between divine essence and energies.

This last issue proves the most problematic of the three. As we have seen, despite the protestations of some Orthodox writers, the evidence for the distinction's dogmatic status in Orthodoxy is ambiguous: doctrines not authenticated by the first seven councils may have the status of conciliar dogma if they become widely regarded as having such status. Aside from a handful of twentieth-century Orthodox writers, however, there is little evidence the distinction has acquired such force. Furthermore, among those theologians most adamant about its dogmatic status, at least one (Ware) concedes that the doctrine cannot be considered binding upon Westerners. This state of affairs results in two consequences.

First, if the distinction is not dogma, or at least cannot be used as a test of Western orthodoxy, then Aquinas cannot be faulted for failing to distinguish the essence from the energies, a determination that would in any case be anachronistic, given he wrote long before the distinction had any claim to dogmatic status. His caveats regarding vision of the divine essence—that it is both participated knowledge and less than God's own—can thus be taken as an informal equivalent of the distinction, an alternate means to the same end. The second consequence is that Palamas need not be read as espousing a real distinction in divine being, which is the basis of the West's objections with respect to novelty and offense against simplicity. This last point is more open to dispute than the others. There is indeed a textual basis for claiming Palamas regards the distinction as ontological rather than nominal; however there is also textual warrant for believing Palamas himself regarded it as purely nominal. At the very least, we must acknowledge a lack of complete clarity on this point, and this analysis concludes the burden of textual evidence falls on the side of a nominal distinction, at least as far as the *Triads* and the *Capita* are concerned. If such is the case, the West's objections are to an in-principle distinction that preserves both divine transcendence and the authenticity of self-communication, theological desiderata with which Western theology has no quarrel whatsoever. Both theologians, in sum, possess a means of guarding divine transcendence, and it is precisely the differences between these means that pose the greatest problems for ecumenical dialogue. We need not magnify these problems, however, by forgetting that we are talking about differing means to an end that is common.

4. Differences between Aquinas and Palamas

Of the specific theological loci identified as problematic by the historical survey, then, none proves nearly as problematic as has generally been claimed, either because the actual content of the locus in question has been misrepresented or because it does not possess the dogmatic status that has sometimes been claimed for it. These loci do reveal differences between Aquinas and Palamas, but not categorical opposition. The assertion must therefore be one of a substantial consonance between Aquinas and Palamas, although this does not preclude the acknowledgement of differences. These nevertheless do not correspond to the traditional complaints of East and West against one another.

The first is incomparability. We do not here have two theologians saying the same thing, in the first instance simply because Aquinas and Palamas do not always address the same issues. At many points, they cannot be compared, or can be compared only with difficulty or conjecturally. Gregory does not treat intellect and will as such, nor does glory figure prominently in Aquinas' exposition of deification in the sense that Gregory uses it. To an extent, this incomparability reflects, once again, differing emphases. The difficulty of comparing their views of love, for example, results not from its complete absence from Palamas' work but its relative unimportance in his doctrine of deification versus the huge role it plays in the *Summa*. The incomparability cannot be attributed solely to emphasis, however. The Transfiguration figures rarely in Aquinas' work, and when it does, it is not systemically significant. In the Palamite corpus, on the other hand, it functions not just as a favorable rhetorical figure but as one of the most important keys to the doctrine of deification. We do find a parallel to the Transfiguration in Aquinas' work in the beatific vision. Nevertheless, this very parallelism underscores a difference: both Aquinas and Palamas resort to a cherished optical image to designate the heights of human communion with God, but that of Aquinas points to paradisiacal consummation, while that of Palamas points to the possibility of rapturous actualization during earthly life. Although this amounts to a difference of emphasis rather than any outright opposition, it does illustrate a broader trend in the work of each author. Aquinas tends to focus on growth in deiformity towards a culmination of theosis in the next life, while Palamas more readily alludes to divinization in this one.

Second, although Aquinas and Palamas share with the Fathers a common vocabulary of deification, individual terms within that vocabulary may not correspond exactly. Light, for Thomas, more frequently denotes an intellectual illumination; for Gregory, it sometimes designates a visual phenomenon. More significantly, Thomas and Gregory are not always using the term *participation* in the same sense. For Thomas, anything's existence is a participation in divine nature of a sort; even the light of natural reason is a participation in divine light. Such usages differ from Gregory's, for in his lexicon *participation* seems equated solely with deification proper. The significance of this disparity in usage extends no further than a difference we have already encountered, however. Gregory wants to leave open the possibility of divinization in this life but exhibits discomfort with some of his more prosaic cognates, such as virtue and knowledge. Thomas, less inclined to allow for the experience of glory *in via*, binds nature, grace and glory together so tightly that they become inseparable, and consequently a term like *participation* expresses humanity's relation to God at all three of these stages. Each author wants to preserve the uniqueness of deification while showing its continuity with lesser forms of sanctification, yet each possesses a different means of doing so.

Third, the analysis and comparison also uncovered what appears to be an inherent difficulty in articulating a doctrine of deification: it must simultaneously assert two near-contradictories or fall prey to one variety or another of theological error. It must claim God is both available to and engaged with humanity and that God remains transcendent, not entangled in the web of his own creation. Any Christian theology must assert both points, of course, in its Christology, its model of revelation and in any doctrine of sanctification. However, because deification affirms a particularly strong claim of divine self-communication—indeed, maintaining a form of human entrance into divine life that a doctrine of revelation, for instance, need not—it must also make a particularly strong claim of divine transcendence if it is to avoid pantheism. These notes, it seems, resist being sounded as a chord; in articulating them successively, the theologian, inevitably it seems, plays one more loudly than the other. In the case of Aquinas and Palamas, this necessary leaning to one side or the other produces a systemic distinction. Neither theologian, we must stress emphatically, yields up either of the poles; to do so would entail abandonment of the doctrine of deification altogether.

At different points, however, each theologian leans to one side or the other, and they do not always lean in the same direction at the same time. In the context of the vision of God, for example, Aquinas inclines towards the assertion of direct apprehension of God, while Palamas is willing, via the affirmation of the divine essence's absolute inviolability, to restrict human access to God if it seems a compromised transcendence would result. In the context of grace, we see precisely the opposite. When pressed, Aquinas will call grace created when it has been incorporated into the creature, both to preserve creaturely agency and to avoid claiming the creature ceases to be created; Palamas will skirt pantheism by saying the creature becomes by grace uncreated. Acknowledging this parting of ways does not imply that either thinker does not correct his bias elsewhere in his theology. Balancing the immediacy of beatific vision is Aquinas' insistence on the unique identity of essence and existence in God; the counterweight to the inaccessible essence in Palamas' work is the assertion of the genuinely divine yet communicable energies. The inclination towards one pole or another should not, therefore, be viewed as an absolute characteristic of an author's theology, but merely a distinguishing trait that appears in certain, usually highly charged, contexts.

II. Conclusion

We are left, then, with the question of whether a fundamental disparity exists between Eastern and Western models of sanctification, as has been often contended. The terms in which this disparity are usually proposed in a sense place it beneath the scope of this study, inasmuch as the quarrel supposedly concerns an Eastern model of sanctification as deification, versus a Western model characterized in a variety of ways, none of which is deification. Obviously, the detailed description of the Thomistic model of deification presented here, as well as the assertion of its general consonance with the Palamite, intends to answer the charge that deification becomes a purely Eastern doctrine after the patristic period. Yet this claim raises the equally obvious question of why, if Thomas possesses such a carefully elaborated doctrine of deification, the original allegation would have been made at all. The answer is that the traditional motifs and assertions of a doctrine of deification by no means exhaust his notion of sanctification. This study has, for example, given relatively glancing attention to the *Summa*'s subtle and profound treatment of habits and virtues, and much less to the treatise on grace. The language specifically of deification thus coexists in the *Summa* alongside other elements of sanctification. Since, however, there has never been any contention that one must speak of sanctification only in terms of deification, Thomas' synthesis should scarcely trouble the East. The West has no grounds for rejecting deification, not only because it can be found in Aquinas but also because it figures extensively in the patristic corpus and derives ultimately from scripture. While its scriptural grounding may seem inadequate for Reformation tastes, it was evidently not on that basis eschewed by all the Reformers, for recent studies have claimed to find deification prominent in the works of both Luther and Lancelot Andrewes.[2] East and West may thus be said to make different uses of the idea of theosis, but this study indicates that at least until the Middle Ages, one cannot characterize the differences between East and West as deriving from two wholly divergent conceptions of either divinization or sanctification, broadly speaking, and there is increasing reason to believe such a divide cannot even be asserted before the Enlightenment.

The answers we have given here to the most prominent issues aired in the historical survey will undoubtedly not satisfy all students of East-West relations. Some Thomists, for example, will continue to insist that Thomas espouses a notion of created grace, thereby reassuring the Orthodox of its incompatibility with that of Palamas. Similarly, many Orthodox will refuse to accept that Aquinas' notion of beatific vision does not correspond to their idea of direct apprehension of divine essence. Many on both sides will continue to regard Palamas' distinction between essence and energies to be ontological, and many Westerners who do so will find it introduces innovation into the doctrine of God. Nevertheless, the arguments advanced here should serve to indicate these ancient determinations are highly questionable. The ground that Aquinas and Palamas share is vast compared to the points at which they diverge, and considered in context, even their divergences do not reveal diametrical opposition. One does not, therefore, need to choose between them, for in thinking with either one, one does not reject the shape the doctrine takes in the other. Indeed, in most respects, to know and affirm the doctrine of deification in one is implicitly to accept the doctrine of the other. If Aquinas and Palamas are in fact representative of their respective traditions, the grounds on which they assert the union of God and humanity should also provide the basis for asserting substantial common ground between the Eastern and Western forms of Christianity.

NOTES

CHAPTER 1

1. Cited in Nicol, *Church and Society in the Last Centuries of Byzantium*, p. 38.

2. Every, *Misunderstandings between East and West*, p. 9; Geanakoplos, *Byzantine East and Latin West*, p. 1; Meyendorff, *Byzantine Theology*, p. 91; Runciman, *The Eastern Schism*, p. vi; Runciman notes that the first book challenging the 1054 date was Gay's *L'Italie méridionale et l'empire byzantine*, published in Paris in 1904. Dissenting is Southern, *Western Church and Society in the Middle Ages*, p. 67.

3. Every (*Misunderstandings between East and West*, p. 9) opts for the late fifteenth century or perhaps not until 1650. Geanakoplos favors 1204, the Sack of Constantinople by Western crusaders (*Byzantine East and Latin West*, pp. 1–2). Meyendorff notes systematic attempts of Byzantine emperors to reestablish ecclesiastical communion from the thirteenth to the fifteenth centuries (*Byzantine Theology*, p. 91). Runciman, while declining to give any date, notes that Innocent IV speaking in 1245 implied that the breach had only occurred in his lifetime and guesses that Innocent would have placed it at 1206, when the Greeks refused to accept a Latin patriarch and appointed one of their own (*The Eastern Schism*, p. 160). He also notes that Anna Comnena, writing after 1140, assumes throughout the Alexiad that Greeks and Latins are in full communion (ibid., p. 110). Geanakoplos points to the letter of Michael Palaeologus, written circa 1266/67 to Pope Clement, acknowledging that Greeks continued to honor the pope as their spiritual father and chief of all priests (*Emperor Michael Paleologus and the West 1258–82*, p. 201).

4. Notably Norden, whose work *Papsttum und Byzanz* is dedicated to this thesis, p. xv and passim; cf. also Runciman, *The Eastern Schism*, p. v and passim.

5. Meyendorff, "Humanisme nominaliste et mystique chrétienne à Byzance au XIVe siècle" in *Byzantine Hesychasm*, p. (VI) 914 (my translation; all English versions of untranslated secondary literature that follow are my own). Cf. also Pelikan, *Development of Christian Doctrine*, p. 55.

6. Ware, "Scholasticism and Orthodoxy," p. 24.

7. Meyendorff, "The Holy Trinity in Palamite Theology," Fahey and Meyendorff, in *Trinitarian Theology East and West*, p. 26. The view of Fahey, Meyendorff's colecturer in these Patriarch Athenagoras Lectures, differs, asking whether both Aquinas and Palamas have not been over-

177

valued in their respective traditions, "Trinitarian Theology in Thomas Aquinas," in Fahey and Meyendorff, *Trinitarian Theology East and West*, p. 23. He voices the same concern seven years later in "Rome and Byzantium," in Barringer, *Rome and Constantinople*, p. 33.

8. Dejaifve, "East and West," in Armstrong and Fry, *Rediscovering Eastern Christendom*, p. 54.

9. LaCugna, *God for Us*, p. 196. Less polemically, LaCugna views Thomas and Gregory as aptly compared simply because they represent the central ethos of Latin and Greek theology, respectively (ibid., pp. 143–44).

10. "The History of the Question" in *Justification by Faith*, pp. 17–18.

11. Jugie, *Le Schisme byzantin*, p. 383.

12. Schultze, "Latin Theology and Oriental Theology" in *The Unity of the Churches of God*, pp. 200–201. Note however Kuhlmann, who points to disputes over interpretation and status within the tradition with respect to both Palamas and Aquinas: "Palamism was then and is still today a strongly contested teaching, and what is harder to find than an interpretation of Thomas that is acknowledged by all Thomsists?" (*Die Taten des einfachen Gottes*, p. 4).

13. Ware, "Scholasticism and Orthodoxy," p. 17.

14. See, however, chapter 5 for a discussion of the questions surrounding the distinction's status as dogma.

15. Runciman, *The Great Church in Captivity*, pp. 100–101; cf. also pp. 128–29 on broader differences between Eastern and Western forms of mysticism. On the Orthodox side, Barrois echoes this view: "The two versions of soteriology, the version of western scholasticism and the version of Palamism, are incompatible. . . . We have to make a choice" ("Palamism Revisited," p. 229). In Barrois's view, the opposition lies in particular in the difference between an approach via created grace and deification. Note, however, that the ever-conciliatory Philips claims Palamas does not deny the notion of created grace ("La Grâce chez les Orientaux," p. 45). Meyendorff agrees that Palamas distinguishes between deifying grace and the grace of nature, with the stipulation that he does not understand the latter in the "Thomist" sense of created grace (*Introduction à l'étude de Grégoire Palamas*, p. 230).

16. Evdokimov, *L'Orthodoxie*, p. 93, n. 214.

17. Fahey, "Trinitarian Theology in Thomas Aquinas," in Fahey and Meyendorff, *Trinitarian Theology East and West*, pp. 18–19.

18. Hussey and Hart, "Byzantine Theological Speculation and Spirituality," in Hussey, *The Byzantine Empire*, p. 200. Cf. also Every, *Misunderstandings between East and West*, p. 48.

19. LaCugna, *God for Us*, p. 188.

20. Halleux, "Palamisme et scolastique," p. 409.

21. Congar, "Ecclesiological Awareness in the East and in the West from the Sixth to the Eleventh Century" in *The Unity of the Churches of God*, pp. 129–30.

22. Ibid., p. 132; cf. also p. 135.

23. Ibid., p. 146.

24. Harkianakis, *Orthodoxe Kirche und Katholizismus*, p. 73. He is speaking specifically with reference to monasticism, but the point is more widely applicable.

25. Modern Roman Catholic doctrines of grace have often been expressed in ways that make them more immediately congenial to Orthodox sensibilities; see, for example, Avery Dulles' account in "Justification in Contemporary Roman Catholic Theology" in *Justification by Faith*. While these thinkers stress grace as uncreated and the indwelling of the Trinity, however, they do not propound a doctrine of deification proper and thus do not directly address the problem examined in this study.

26. Russo, "Rahner and Palamas," p. 157.

27. Schultze, "Latin Theology and Oriental Theology" in *The Unity of the Churches of God*, p. 200. The classification of the essence-energies distinction as an Oriental (rather than Byzantine) problem is Schultze's.

28. Lossky, "The Procession of the Holy Spirit in the Orthodox Triadology," p. 52.

29. Meyendorff, Byzantine Theology, p. 103.

30. Journet, for one, sees the points of agreement between the two as "innombrables," in "Palamisme et thomisme," p. 430. Mascall claims that, whatever the difference of verbal idiom and philosophical setting, there is fundamental dogmatic and religious agreement between Palamas and Aquinas ("Grace and Nature in East and West," p. 185). Kuhlmann concludes in his study of issues pertaining to the Council of Florence that Palamism does not contradict Catholic dogma and that there is between Latins and Greeks no separation in belief (Die Taten des einfachen Gottes, p. 135).

31. Ware claims that, on the eve of the Council of Florence, educated Greeks had a better understanding of Thomism than Latins had of Palamism—which is, however, a claim of small proportions ("Scholasticism and Orthodoxy," p. 25). Southern notes that the West never discovered the Byzantine church as the Greeks discovered the Latin church in the fourteenth century. Those Greek theologians known in the West, such as Denys and Damascene, seemed remote and stimulated no interest in the Byzantine church (Western Church and Society in the Middle Ages, p. 82).

32. Runciman sees the problem in reverse: the absence of Byzantine interest in the West ("The Place of Byzantium in the Medieval World," in Hussey and Hart, The Byzantine Empire, p. 362). His view fails to account for the relative ease with which one can measure Thomas' limited impact on the East versus an almost total absence of information regarding contemporary Western reception of Palamas.

33. Every, Misunderstandings between East and West, p. 35.

34. Meyendorff notes that it was Prochoros who first wrote refutations of Palamism using Thomist arguments (Byzantine Theology, pp. 106–7).

35. Hussey and Hart, The Byzantine Empire, pp. 196–97.

36. Meyendorff, Byzantine Theology, pp. 105–6. Nicol maintains, though, that Kydones' translations were never noticed beyond a small circle of intellectuals in Constantinople ("The Byzantine Church and Hellenic Learning in the Fourteenth Century," in Byzantium, pp. (XII) 54–55).

37. Ware, "Scholasticism and Orthodoxy," p. 26, and "The Debate about Palamism," p. 57.

38. Barlaam's intellectual optimism is the only respect in which he approaches the Thomist position, Meyendorff notes. Barlaam is especially acerbic regarding Latins in general and Thomas in particular because of the latter's alleged affirmation of the legitimacy of apodictic reasoning about the divine (Byzantine Hesychasm, p. (VI) 910). Cf. also p. (V) 54, where Barlaam is said to attack Aquinas "constantly." Cf. also Runciman, The Great Church in Captivity, p. 139; and Papadopulos, "Thomas in Byzanz," p. 287. Gill claims the association of anti-Palamitism and a pro-Latin stance came about because of Barlaam's Calabrian origins; although graecophone, his Italian origins may have linked him to the Latin church (Byzantium and the Papacy 1198–1400, p. 204). Given that Barlaam was not doctrinally pro-Latin, however, this view may exaggerate knee-jerk reactions on the part of the Byzantines, whose intellectual subtlety surely enabled them to distinguish between regional origin and theological opinion. Tatakis places Barlaam and Kydones together in their opposition to Palamas and links both to Thomas (La Philosophie byzantine, p. 230 and cf. p. 265). Evdokimov also allies Gregoras, Barlaam, Calecas and the Kydones brothers in their anti-Palamitism, Barlaam and the Kydones brothers following Thomas and denying the distinction between divine essence and energies (L'Orthodoxie, p. 26). These analyses, however, proceed not from textual evidence of Barlaam's support for Thomas but from the supposition that opposition to the essence-energies distinction is somehow a hallmark of Thomism.

39. Runciman, The Great Church in Captivity, p. 145.

40. Halleux, "Palamisme et scolastique," pp. 413–14.

41. Runciman, The Last Byzantine Renaissance, p. 48. It is unclear whether this was because the issue itself was perceived as problematical or because its proponents were simply identified with a broadly anti-Thomist stance. Runciman also claims that the doctrine of the energies was de-

nounced by Rome but does not specify when or in what form this denunciation took place or substantiate it.

42. Cf. the dispute between Kuhlmann and Schultze, cited by Stiernon in "Bulletin sur le Palamisme," pp. 296–98. Kuhlmann holds that Florence condemned neither directly nor indirectly the essence-energies distinction, while Schultze believes an indirect condemnation may well be implied. Grumel's view concurs with Kuhlmann's ("Grégoire Palamas, Duns Scot, et Georges Scholarios devant le problème de la simplicité divine," p. 96), while Lossky claims that after Florence and Lyons it became impossible for Roman Catholic theologians not to regard the assertion of the energies as contrary to divine simplicity ("The Procession of the Holy Spirit in the Orthodox Triadology," p. 52).

43. Runciman quotes: "We believe and confess one God, the Father, the Son and the Holy Ghost, to be eternal, and nothing else to be eternal, whether they are called relations or properties or singularities or unities; nor can other things of this sort be part of God since they were taken out of the eternal and are not God" (The Great Church in Captivity, p. 153). Yet Reims does not seem to envisage energies along Palamite lines, which compromise neither divine simplicity, nor the limitation of the divine hypostases to three, nor are "taken out of the eternal" and thus are not God.

44. Gill, Byzantium and the Papacy, 1198–1400, p. 222.

45. Papadopulos, "Thomas in Byzanz," p. 292. Anti-Thomism, he remarks, was a mark of the greater part of the Orthodox hierarchy, p. 277. Cf. also Geanakoplos, Interaction of the "Sibling" Byzantine and Western Cultures in the Middle Ages and Italian Renaissance (330–1600), p. 107.

46. Ibid. Tyn maintains a similar position ("Prochoros und Demetrios Kydones," in Eckert, Thomas von Aquino: Interpretation und Rezeption, p. 842).

47. Gill, Byzantium and the Papacy 1198–1400, p. 252. Gill nevertheless acknowledges that the attempts to stifle "Barlaamism" in the East acquired an anti-Latin overtone: "Palamism had become another obstacle to union, and loyalty to it implied repudiation of union." Countering this view, Ware cautions that no easy classification of Byzantine attitudes toward the West is possible ("Scholasticism and Orthodoxy," p. 26).

48. Papadopulos, "Thomas in Byzanz," p. 277. Papadopulos attributes the relatively muted interest in Thomas to the domination of the hesychast controversy (p. 276). Despite this paucity of evidence, commentators such as Clément are content to claim similarities between the Byzantine humanists and what they imagine to be Thomist positions, such as essentialist conceptions of God, created glory and double knowledge of God (Byzance et le christianisme, p. 34).

49. Ibid., p. 285.

50. Ibid., p. 297.

51. Meyendorff, Byzantine Theology, p. 112.

52. Tyn, "Prochoros und Demetrios Kydones," in Eckert, Thomas von Aquino: Interpretation und Rezeption, p. 907.

53. Cf. also Runciman, who, convinced of a fundamental opposition between Aquinas and Palamas, claimed Scholarios blurred the distinction between essence and energies in order to reconcile it with Thomism. His description leaves doubt whether his interpretation of the energies is also that of Palamas himself (The Last Byzantine Renaissance, p. 82).

54. Papadopulos, "Thomas in Byzanz," p. 277.

55. Southern, Western Church and Society in the Middle Ages, p. 80, bis.

56. Geanakoplos, Interaction of the "Sibling" Byzantine and Western Cultures in the Middle Ages and Italian Renaissance (330–1600), p. 107.

57. Runciman, The Last Byzantine Renaissance, pp. 96–97.

58. Tyn, "Prochoros und Demetrios Kydones," p. 846.

59. Papadopulos, "Thomas in Byzanz," p. 304.

60. Runciman, The Great Church in Captivity, pp. 101 and 105.

61. Geanakoplox, The Interaction of the "Sibling" Byzantine and Western Cultures in the Middle Ages and Italian Renaissance (330–1600), p. 291.

62. Dondaine, "'Contra Graecos: premiers écrits polémiques des Dominicains d'Orient," p. 387.

63. Ibid., p. 390.

64. There are, however, some exceptions to this general silence. Trent's definition of habitus, although directed against Reformation views, may be taken as presupposing a doctrine of imputation foreign to Greek conceptuality (Halleux, "Palamisme et scolastique," p. 417; cf. also Evdokimov, L'Orthodoxie, p. 101, n. 248). Pétau speaks of Palamas' theology as "ridiculous doctrines" (Lossky, The Vision of God, p. 22 and cf. p. 166). Jugie also claims that nineteenth-century Russian theological manuals overtly contradict Palamas, echoing Aquinas (Le Schisme byzantin, p. 382.). Harnack deemed Orthodoxy to be a "perversion of the Christian religion, its reduction to the level of pagan antiquity" (cited in Schmemann, The Historical Road of Eastern Orthodoxy, p. v; Schmemann does not give a reference for this remark, and I have been unable to locate it in Harnack's work). Ware cites J. M. Neale's work of 1850, A History of the Holy Eastern Church, which refers to Palamism as an "absurd and erroneous doctrine" ("The Debate about Palamism," p. 45), and gives further references to seventeenth-century Western thinkers critical of Palamas. These references tend to be fleeting and lacking in documentation, hence the characterization here of the period from 1500 to 1900 as one of silence.

65. Fortescue, The Orthodox Eastern Church, p. vi.

66. Ibid., p. 438. Fortescue acknowledges the horrors, for example, of the Sack of Constantinople as a result of the Fourth Crusade (pp. 225–28) but evidently feels on the balance justified in attributing hostility and intractability solely to the East.

67. Jugie, Le Schisme byzantin, p. 333.

68. Ibid., p. 380.

69. Ibid., p. 380.

70. Ibid., p. 381.

71. Jugie, "Palamas" in Dictionnaire de théologie catholique, 11/2, Col. 1762.

72. Jugie, Le Schisme byzantin, p. 451.

73. Podskalsky, Theologie und Philosophie in Byzanz, pp. 9–10.

74. Tyn, "Prochoros und Demetrios Kydones." If Tyn had worked with primary texts of Palamas to any significant degree, this is not evident from his references or his bibliography.

75. Ibid., pp. 886–87.

76. Ibid., p. 911.

77. Lossky, The Mystical Theology of the Eastern Church, p. 81.

78. Bernhard Schultze, "Hauptthemen der neueren russischen Theologie," in Nyssen, Schulz, and Wiertz, Handbuch der Ostkirchenkunde, Bd. 1, p. 347.

79. Halleux, "Palamisme et scolastique," p. 419. Halleux also documents but one example of Palamas' speaking of the distinction as real, in the Capita 34; cf. chapter 5.

80. Ibid., p. 440.

81. Palamas, Défense des saints hésychastes, p. vii.

82. LaCugna, God for Us, pp. 197–98.

83. Evdokimov: "According to St Thomas, created grace assimilates us to divine nature itself" (L'Orthodoxie, p. 101, n. 247).

84. Lossky, "The Procession of the Holy Spirit in Orthodox Triadology," p. 36.

85. Lossky, The Vision of God, pp. 14–15.

86. Fortescue claims this issue was settled by the conquest of Constantinople: "As for the Azymes, the Turkish armies at their very gates had at last made them see reason" (The Orthodox Eastern Church, p. 214).

87. Meyendorff, Byzantine Theology, p. 2. Cf. also Bria, The Sense of Ecumenical Tradition, p. 74; and

Congar, "Ecclesiological Awareness in the East and in the West from the Sixth to the Eleventh Century," pp. 131–32, in The Unity of the Churches of God; and Geanakoplos, Interaction of the "Sibling" Byzantine and Western Cultures in the Middle Ages and Italian Renaissance (330–1600), p. 60.

88. Evdokimov, L'Orthodoxie, p. 80.

89. Meyendorff, Byzantine Hesychasm, p. (III) 14.

90. Hussey and Hart, "Byzantine Theological Speculation and Spirituality," in Hussey, The Byzantine Empire, p. 201. Kuhlmann agrees that the crux of the difference between Thomas and Gregory lies in the question of whether the experience of God is given in this life or is promised in the next (Die Taten des einfachen Gottes, p. 7).

91. Halleux, "Palamisme et scolastique," p. 424.

92. Tyn, "Prochoros und Demetrios Kydones," p. 883. The quoted passage derives from Lakebrink, Klassische Metaphysik. Eine Auseinandersetzung mit der existentialen Anthropozentrik, Freiburg im Breisgau, 1967, p. 250. This view is not echoed in other scholarship, even by scholars not sympathetic to Palamas, and is difficult to reconcile with the primary texts. As usual, Tyn provides no references to support his view, and the quoted passage appears to refer not to Palamas, but to modern existentialist thought.

93. Bernhard Schultze, "Hauptthemen der neueren russischen Theologie," in Nyssen, Schulz, and Wiertz, Handbuch der Ostkirchenkunde, Bd. 1, p. 347. Cf. also the reference to Schultze in n. 78, this chapter.

94. Lossky, "The Procession of the Holy Spirit in the Orthodox Triadology," p. 48; Halleux, "Palamisme et scolastique," p. 419.

95. Lossky, The Vision of God, p. 13.

96. Ibid., p. 11.

97. Fahey, "Trinitarian Theology in Thomas Aquinas," in Fahey and Meyendorff, Trinitarian Theology East and West, p. 15.

98. Halleux, "Palamisme et scolastique," p. 437.

99. Meyendorff, "Society and Culture in the Fourteenth Century," in Actes du XIVe Congrès International des Études Byzantines, p. 119.

100. Meyendorff, Byzantine Hesychasm, p. (I) 87.

101. Ware, "Scholasticism and Orthodoxy," p. 18.

102. Ibid., p. 18; cf. also Every, Misunderstandings between East and West, p. 38.

103. Kalomiros, Against False Union, p. 38. Ware expresses the same view in more temperate form (The Orthodox Church, p. 1).

104. Kalomiros, Against False Union, p. 38.

105. Ibid., p. iii.

106. Yannaras, "Orthodoxy and the West," p. 287.

107. Note further that Prochoros Kydones, convinced Thomist and translator of the De ente et essentia, was also a monk of Athos (Hussey and Hart, "Byzantine Theological Speculation and Spirituality," in Hussey, The Byzantine Empire, p. 197).

108. Meyendorff, "Society and Culture in the Fourteenth Century," in Actes du XIVe Congrès International des Études Byzantines, p. 115.

109. Meyendorff, "Spiritual Trends in Byzantium in the Late Thirteenth and Early Fourteenth Centuries," in Underwood, Studies in the Art of the Kariye Djami and Its Intellectual Background, p. 101.

110. Yangazoglou, "Philosophy and Theology" esp. pp. 6–9 and 13–16.

111. Norden, Das Papsttum und Byzanz, p. 744.

112. Meyendorff, "Society and Culture in the Fourteenth Century," in Actes du XIVe Congrès International des Études Byzantines, p. 114. Cf. also Nicol, "The Byzantine Church and Hellenic Learning in the Fourteenth Century," in Byzantium, p. (XII) 51.

113. Geanakoplos, Interaction of the "Sibling" Byzantine and Western Cultures in the Middle Ages and Italian

Renaissance (330–1600), p. 49. Cf. also Meyendorff, "Society and Culture in the Fourteenth Century," in *Actes du XIVe Congrès International des Études Byzantines*, p. 120.

114. Gill, *Byzantium and the Papacy 1198–1400*, p. 145.

115. Hussey and Hart, "Byzantine Theological Speculation and Spirituality," in Hussey, *The Byzantine Empire*, p. 186. Cf. also Geanakoplos, *Interaction of the "Sibling" Byzantine and Western Cultures in the Middle Ages and Italian Renaissance (330–1600)*, p. 62. In *Byzantine East and Latin West* (p. 22), Geanakoplos compares *Fount of Knowledge* with the *Summa Theologiae*, pointing out that Damascene's work not only constitutes the basic work of Orthodox theology but was known and used by Aquinas in the composition of the ST.

116. Meyendorff, *Byzantine Theology*, p. 25.

117. Every, *Misunderstandings between East and West*, p. 35. Cf. Meyendorff, *Introduction à l'étude de Grégoire Palamas*, pp. 46–48, 190–91.

118. Meyendorff, *Introduction à l'étude de Saint Grégoire Palamas*, p. 47; cf. also Meyendorff, "Society and Culture in the Fourteenth Century," in *Actes du XIVe Congrès International des Études Byzantines*, p. 116.

119. Nicol, *Church and Society in the Last Centuries of Byzantium*, p. 51.

120. Nicol, "The Byzantine Church and Hellenic Learning in the Fourteenth Century," in *Byzantium*, p. (XII) 49.

121. Ibid., p. 49.

122. Ibid., p. 50; Runciman settles for a similar description, *The Last Byzantine Renaissance*, p. 35; and Sinkewicz in his edition of Palamas, *Capita*, p. 5.

123. Schultze, *Das Gottesproblem in der Osttheologie*, p. 23.

124. Podskalsky, *Theologie und Philosophie in Byzanz*, p. 243.

125. Sherrard, *The Greek East and the Latin West*, p. 120.

126. Ivánka, *Plato Christianus*, pp. 406–7.

127. Halleux, "Palamisme et scolastique," p. 409.

128. Tatakis, *La Philosophie byzantine*, p. 271. Schmemann further notes that Uspensky regards the hesychast controversy as but one episode in the longer drama of the struggle between Aristotelianism and Platonism, a conflict which he claims defines the history of Byzantine thought (*The Historical Road of Eastern Orthodoxy*, p. 236). This view Schmemann firmly rejects as fallacious.

129. The fullest study on this point, Kuhlmann's *Die Taten des einfachen Gottes*, views Thomas and Gregory as having appropriated Denys in markedly different ways, but does not on this basis conclude a fundamental division of East and West.

130. Runciman, *The Great Church in Captivity*, p. 153. Schultze, however, finds common ground between Aquinas and Palamas on precisely the question of analogous knowledge of God (*Das Gottesproblem in der Osttheologie*, p. 32).

131. "The Theology of Light in the Thought of St. Gregory Palamas," in Lossky, *In the Image and Likeness of God*, p. 53.

132. Kilmartin, *Toward Reunion*, p. 55. Again, it is unclear whether this last remark is based on the author's systematic assumptions—that distinctions in God lead logically and necessarily to predication of a superior and inferior deity (why?)—or is conditioned by historical considerations, such as Kilmartin's belief (contestable, as we have seen) that Palamas asserted both distinctions in God and a superior and inferior deity.

133. Every, *Misunderstandings between East and West*, pp. 64–65.

134. Cited by Nicol, *Church and Society in the Last Centuries of Byzantium*, p. 85.

135. Nicol, "The Byzantine Church and Hellenic Learning in the Fourteenth Century" in *Byzantium*, p. (XII) 47.

136. Papadopulos, "Thomas in Byzanz," p. 295.

137. Kalomiris, *Against False Union*, p. 38.

138. Nicol, *Church and Society in the Last Centuries of Byzantium*, p. 84.

139. ST I. 1, 7 ad 1. Cited in Pelikan, *The Growth of Medieval Theology (600–1300)*, p. 285.

140. Runciman, *The Great Church in Captivity*, p. 85.

141. Ibid., p. 128.

142. Tatakis, *La Philosophie byzantine*, p. 263.

143. Ibid., p. 272. Tatakis also regards Palamas' attitude to the mind as determined by the location of the intelligence in the body as opposed to the supposed Aristotelian location of it outside the body.

144. Ibid., p. 263.

145. Every, *Misunderstandings between East and West*, p. 64.

146. Meyendorff, *Byzantine Theology*, pp. 8–9.

147. Hussey and Hart, "Byzantine Theological Speculation and Spirituality," in Hussey, *The Byzantine Empire*, p. 197.

148. Meyendorff, *Byzantine Theology*, p. 140.

149. Sherrard, *The Greek East and the Latin West*, p. 147.

150. Ibid., p. 150.

151. Ibid., pp. 150–51.

152. Tyn, "Prochoros und Demetrios Kydones," in Eckert, *Thomas von Aquino*, p. 883.

153. Ibid., p. 901.

154. Ibid.

155. Ibid., pp. 839, 883, 886–877.

156. Schultze uses a Hegelian analysis of thesis-antithesis-synthesis to describe the essence-energies distinction, but it seems he does not intend to impute a proto-Hegelianism to Gregory himself (*Das Gottesproblem in der Osttheologie*, pp. 26–28; cf. also p. 32).

157. Lialine, "The Theological Teaching of Gregory Palamas on Divine Simplicity," p. 268. Kuhlmann merely points to the difficulty of finding a firm standpoint on which to compare Thomas and Gregory, given that they belong to different intellectual milieux (*Die Taten des einfachen Gottes*, p. 4).

158. Philips, "La Grâce chez les Orientaux," p. 47.

159. Lison, *L'Esprit répandu*; on returning to the texts see esp. pp. 17–18.

160. Blum, "Oikonomia und Theologia," p. 294.

161. Ibid.

162. Philips, "La Grâce chez les Orientaux," p. 50.

163. Lison, *L'Esprit répandu*, p. 131.

164. Ibid., p. 279.

165. Halleux, "Palamisme et scolastique," p. 442.

166. Ware, "Scholasticism and Orthodoxy," p. 16.

167. Meyendorff, *Introduction à l'étude de Grégoire Palamas*, p. 14.

168. Pesch and Peters, *Einführung in die Lehre von Gnade und Rechfertigung*, p. 13.

169. Rusch, "How the Eastern Fathers Understood What the Western Church Meant by Justification" in *Justification by Faith*, pp. 134–35; cf. also Quasten, *Patrology*, vol. 1, pp. 170–71.

170. These references come from Rusch, "How the Eastern Fathers Understood What the Western Church Meant by Justification," in *Justification by Faith*, pp. 134–35.

171. Quasten, *Patrology*.

172. Dalmais, "Divinisation," in *Dictionnaire de spiritualité*, col. 1376.

173. Lot-Borodine "La Doctrine de la 'déification' dans l'Église grecque jusqu'au XIe siècle" (in vol. 105), pp. 6–7.

174. Gross, *La Divinisation du chrétien d'après les pères grecs*, p. 117.

175. Ibid., pp. 134 and 142.

176. Ibid., p. 143.

177. Ibid., pp. 123–24.

178. Dalmais, "Divinisation," col. 1379.

179. Gross, *La Divinisation du chrétien d'après les pères grecs*, p. 185.

180. Ibid., p. 152.

181. Gross attributes to Irenaeus an inchoate distinction between created and uncreated grace (ibid., p. 156), as he does to Clement (p. 294). This may, however, constitute precisely a case of seeing "scholastic" tendencies in works of a quite different nature.

182. Cf. Pesch and Peters, *Einführung in die Lehre von Gnade und Rechtfertigung*, pp. 13–14.

183. Dalmais, "Divinisation," col. 1377.

184. Ibid., col. 1380.

185. Gross, *La Divinisation du chrétien d'après les pères grecs*, p. 163.

186. Ibid., p. 161; Dalmais, "Divinisation," col. 1378.

187. Gross, *La Divinisation du chrétien d'après les pères grecs*, p. 173.

188. Ibid., p. 296.

189. Rusch finds evidence in Nazianzen's *Theological Orations* 37 (13–15) and 38 (8–10) of discussion of theosis, but the treatment there seems so nebulous as scarcely to qualify.

190. Gross, *La Divinisation du chrétien d'après les pères grecs*, pp. 221–22.

191. Lot-Borodine, "La Doctrine de la 'déification' dans l'Église grecque jusqu'au XIe siècle," p. 15.

192. Dalmais, "Divinisation," col. 1385.

193. Gross, *La Divinisation du chrétien d'après les pères grecs*, pp. 239–43.

194. Further examples of deification in the Western patristic tradition may be found in Tertullian, *Against Praxeas* 13 and *On the Resurrection of the Flesh* 49.

195. Gross, *La Divinisation du chrétien d'après les pères grecs*, pp. 257–58; Dalmais, "Divinisation," col. 1383.

196. Gross, *La Divinisation du chrétien d'après les pères grecs*, p. 261.

197. Ibid., pp. 283–84.

198. Ibid., pp. 285–86.

199. Ibid., pp. 295–96.

200. Dalmais, "Divinisation," col. 1385.

201. Gross sees in the Dionysian corpus the twin tendencies of neoplatonic mysticism and pantheism (*La Divinisation du chrétien d'après les pères grecs*, p. 318).

202. Gross asserts none of the Greek Fathers gives a definition (ibid., p. 349), although as we shall see later, Maximus certainly comes close.

203. Cf. Gross: "For all the Greek Doctors, the deification obtained by Christian initiation was normally the point of departure for a continuing ascent towards an ever more perfect divinisation" (ibid., p. 348; cf. also p. 337).

CHAPTER 2

Bibliographic Note. Little of the secondary literature on Thomas sheds any significant light on the issues treated in this chapter. For a very brief treatment of deification in the *Summa*, see Torrell, *Saint Thomas d'Aquin, maître spirituel*, pp. 166–68 and 498–99. For references to or intimations of a Thomistic sensibility (if not actual doctrine) of divinization, see De Letter, "Divine Quasi-Formal Causality," pp. 221–22, "Sanctifying Grace and Divine Indwelling," pp. 65 and 68–69; and "Grace, Incorporation, Inhabitation," pp. 6 and 11; Bourassa, "Adoptive Sonship," *passim*; and "Rôle personnel des Personnes et relations distinctes aux Personnes," p. 167; Pesch and Peters, *Einführung in die Lehre von Gnade und Rechtfertigung*, pp. 45 and 57; Wadell, *The Primacy of Love*, pp. 59–61; M. Donnelly, "Sanctifying Grace," p. 200; and La Taille, "Actuation créée par acte incréé," p. 267. The general premise and outline of this study also bears clear resemblances to Chenu's claim that the structure of the ST is one of *exitus* and *reditus*, emanation and return (*Toward Understanding St. Thomas,* pp. 304–5), although Chenu is not thinking specifically in terms of deification. See also Burnaby, *Amor Dei*, pp. 263–272; and O'Meara, *Thomas Aquinas Theologian*, pp. 57, 59, 95–96 and 123.

For treatments of the *Prima Pars*, the reader should consult, in addition to the preceding, Burrell, *Aquinas*; Cunningham, *The Indwelling of the Trinity*; Davies, *The Thought of Thomas Aquinas*; Flew, *The Idea of Perfection in Christian Theology*; Gilson, *The Philosophy of St. Thomas Aquinas*; O'Mahony, *The Desire of God in the Philosophy of St. Thomas Aquinas*; Persson, *Sacra Doctrine*; and Preller, *Divine Science and the Science of God*. For the differing senses of participation in Thomas' work, see Fabro, *Participation*; Klauder, *A Philosophy Rooted in Love*; McInerny, *St. Thomas Aquinas*; and Te Velde, *Participation and Substantiality*. Thomas' indebtedness to Denys has been most fully examined by O'Rourke, *Pseudo-Dionysius and the Metaphysics of Aquinas*.

1. Quotations from the ST follow the Dominican Province edition.

2. Additional direct references may be found at: I-II.3,1 ad 2; I-II.50,6 resp.; II-II.188,2 ob. 1 (quoting Denys); III.1,2 resp. (quoting Augustine); III.2,1 ad 3; III.16,7 ad 3. The last of these we will consider at the end of the next chapter. The others provide little help in elucidating Thomas' doctrine of deification. Some, as noted, are quotations from other authors (cf. also Suppl. 36,1 resp.); some concern matters peripheral to our study, like the angels (cf. I-II.50,6).

3. Aquinas does not explicitly make this connection between these parts of his argument in Questions 12 and 13, but the presentation here is faithful to the prevailing pattern of logic governing the development of his argument.

4. "Dicendum quod in omnibus nominibus quae de pluribus analogice dicuntur, necesse est quod omnia dicantur per respectum ad unum; et ideo illud unum opportet quod ponatur in definitione omnium."

5. "Natura divina non est communicabilis, nisi secundum similitudinis participationem."

6. That he may assume this position may largely be attributed to a cornerstone of theological anthropology inherited as much from the Fathers as from Aristotle—namely, the definition of the human creature as a rational being. As Persson explains: "As a creature endowed with reason man's primary object is the acquisition of knowledge; whenever, therefore, his understanding is deepened, his nature is brought correspondingly nearer to its perfection. It follows that where knowledge of God has been fully attained, the perfectio hominis is complete. Thus in Thomas salus hominis (salvation of man) and perfectio hominis become quite simply synonymous and interchangeable terms" (*Sacra Doctrina*, p. 36).

7. The idea made its first appearance in Question 12 in Objection 4 to Article 1: "There must be some proportion between the knower and the known, since the known is the perfection of the knower." Nevertheless, since the principle is articulated in an objection, we cannot take it as evidence of Thomas' own views, although it is consistent with what he maintains elsewhere.

8. The consequent of this reasoning: "If the principle of the visual power and the thing seen were one and the same thing, it would necessarily follow that the seer would receive both the visual power and the form whereby it sees, from that one same thing" (I.12,2 resp.).

9. We must also note, though, that because of his strong doctrine of participation, Thomas considers all reasoning to be in virtue of the divine gift of illumination, in one sense: "All things are said to be seen in God and all things are judged in Him, because by the participation of His light we know and judge all things; for the light of natural reason itself is a participation of the divine light [nam et ipsum lumen naturale rationis participatio quaedam est divini luminis]" (I.12,11 ad 3).

10. Thomas does make the point regarding the participation of knower in the known specifically in relation to our knowledge of God in I.12,7 ad 1: "The blessed possess these three things in God; because they see Him, and in seeing Him, possess Him as present, having the power to see Him always; and possessing Him, they enjoy Him as the ultimate fulfilment of desire," and in I.12,9 ad 1: "The created intellect of one who sees God is assimilated to what is

seen in God, inasmuch as it is united to the divine essence, in which the similitudes of all things pre-exist [intellectus creatus videntis Deum assimilatur rebus quae videntur in Deo, inquantum unitur essentiae divinae, in qua rerum omnium similitudines praeexistunt]."

11. "This increase of the intellectual powers is called the illumination of the intellect, as we also call the intelligible object itself by the name of the light of illumination" (I.12,5 resp.).

12. "Lumen istud non requiritur ad videndum Dei essentiam quasi similitudo in qua Deus videatur, sed quasi perfectio quaedam intellectus, confortans ipsum ad videndum Deum."

13. The insistence on the need for grace, the use of images of light and glory and the specific claim of resultant deiformity are all repeated in the next article, I.12,6 resp.

14. Thomas does allow that in beatific vision we see *that* God exists infinitely and is infinitely knowable (I.12,7 ad 3).

15. "Et hoc modo illa quae sunt a Deo, assimilantur ei inquantum sunt entia."

16. Aquinas does use the term *univocal*, which features prominently in Question 12.

17. A second version of recourse to the act-potency distinction can be found in I.14,2 resp. Here, Aquinas' argument depends intermediately on the claim of God's intelligibility established in I.12,1 but primarily on the identification of the intellect's act and its object:

> Since therefore God has nothing in Him of potentiality, but is pure act, His intellect and its object are altogether the same; so that He neither is without the intelligible species, as is the case with our intellect when it understands potentially; nor does the intelligible species differ from the substance of the divine intellect . . . but the intelligible species itself is the divine intellect itself, and thus God understands Himself through Himself [sic seipsum per seipsum intelligit]. (I.14,2 resp.)

Note the similarity between the explanation of divine and human modes of knowing God: although we do not know God to the extent that God knows himself, we know him in the way he knows himself—that is, through himself. Thus to know God at all is to participate in his being, not only because the known must be present in the knower but also because to know God is to participate in his own way of knowing.

18. The view taken here thus differs sharply from that of Edmund Hill, who claims that Thomas reverses Augustine's procedure, beginning from God as first cause, a procedure which Hill, along with Eastern commentators, regards as profoundly misguided. "God as first cause is the one God, so Thomas indeed exemplifies what is said to be the whole Latin tradition of beginning with the divine unity of substance and only then proceeding to the trinity of persons" (*The Mystery of the Trinity*, p. 150). Our position here is that what is significant about the relationship between the *De Deo uno*, the *De Trinitate* and the theological anthropology is that each is governed by the same structures, so that they parallel one another. God as first cause is not somehow prior to God as tripersonal; rather, God, as first cause, is ontologically distinct from nondivine persons. Lonergan also views Aquinas as having started not from God the Father but from God, reserving the question of persons until after the issues of processions and relations. In this respect, he views Thomas as unique but apparently not culpable (*Verbum*, p. 206). Lonergan's view of Thomistic trinitarian doctrine concurs with that presented here inasmuch as he regards the Augustinian psychological analogy as giving a deeper insight into what God is, penetrating to the very core, or essence, of God (ibid., p. 208).

19. That Thomas is here quite deliberately building upon the conception of God he laid out in the previous section becomes clearest in the reply to the second objection: "The more a thing is understood, the more closely is the intellectual conception joined and united to the intelligent agent; since the intellect by the very act of understanding is made one with the object understood. Thus, as the divine intelligence is the very supreme perfection of God, the divine Word is of necessity perfectly one with the source whence He proceeds, without any kind of diversity."

20. "Though will and intellect are not diverse in God, nevertheless the nature of will and

intellect requires the processions belonging to each of them to exist in a certain order. For the procession of love occurs in due order as regards the procession of the Word; since nothing can be loved by the will unless it is conceived in the intellect" (I.27,3 ad 3).

21. "It follows that no other procession is possible in God but the procession of the Word, and of Love" (I.27,5 resp.).

22. In addition to the priority of unity over hypostases (cf. n. 18), Hill sees two differences between the Thomistic and Augustinian models of the Trinity, differences he regards as weaknesses on Thomas' part: first, Thomas does not recognize Augustine's purpose in construing the trinitarian image in the human mind, as an indirect means of understanding the mystery of the eternal processions, and second, that he fails to observe Augustine's point that the temporal missions reveal the eternal processions. In his zealous quest for a pure Augustinianism, Hill may have missed the distinctive characteristics, and merits, of Thomas' doctrine of the Trinity.

23. "Nihil autem quod est in Deo, potest habere habitudinem ad id in quo est, vel de quo dicitur, nisi habitudinem identitatis."

24. "Because subsistence in a rational nature is of high dignity, therefore every individual of the rational nature is called a *person*. Now the dignity of the divine nature excels every other dignity; and thus the name *person* pre-eminently belongs to God" (I.29,3 ad 2).

25. Grace builds only on this innate likeness of those created in *imago Dei*; further degrees of likeness are not claimed for the irrational creature, of whom God is Father only by a trace (cf. I.33,3 resp.).

26. Hill and Persson differ sharply on the relation between trinitarian theology and theological anthropology in Thomas. In Hill's view, Thomas has made the doctrine of the Trinity largely irrelevant to salvation (*The Mystery of the Trinity*, pp. 149—51 and passim). Persson, in contrast, claims that Thomas' doctrine of the Trinity cannot be separated from the relationship between God and the world, because in everything created there is a *representatio Trinitatis* (*Sacra Doctrina*, p. 149). Principe adopts a view similar to Persson's, in which knowledge and love unite so as to be constantly present and continually active in all created reality (*Thomas Aquinas' Spirituality*, pp. 16—17).

27. Since Aquinas himself does not specify what he means by *expressive*, this reading admittedly leans rather strongly in the direction of conjecture; however, it seems entirely compatible with the overall thrust of these passages. The sense of a heightened engagement with creation that seems implied in *expressive* emerges also from the final paragraph of the response: "As the knowledge of God is only cognitive as regards God, whereas regards creatures, it is both cognitive and operative, so the Word of God is only expressive of what is in God the Father, but is both expressive and operative of creatures; and therefore it is said: *He spake and they were made*; because in the Word is implied the operative idea of what God makes" (I.34,3 resp.). While the biblical citation shifts the focus of this passage towards creation, the meaning of *operative* need not be taken so narrowly and may be interpreted to include such redemptive and sanctifying activities as the Word engages in after creation.

28. This quotation applies when the term *love* is taken in a notional sense; Thomas distinguishes this notional sense from the essential sense of *to love*, and in the latter, the Father and the Son love one another by their essence, rather than by the Spirit.

29. Cf. also: "The name Gift involves the idea of belonging to the Giver through its origin; and thus it imports the property of the origin of the Holy Ghost—that is, His procession" (I.38,2 ad 2).

30. "Unum est habitudo missi ad eum a quo mittitur, aliud est habitudo missi ad terminum ad quem mittitur."

31. Cf. also I.43,6 resp.

32. Aquinas reiterates both the Father's true bestowal and his not being sent in the response to Article 5: "Since both to the Son and to the Holy Ghost it belongs to dwell in the soul by grace, and to be from another, it therefore belongs to both of them to be invisibly sent. As to the Fa-

ther, though He dwells in us by grace, still it does not belong to Him to be from another, and consequently He is not sent."

33. "Non igitur secundum quamlibet perfectionem intellectus mittitur Filius, sed secundum talem institutionem vel instructionem intellectus, qua prorumpat in affectum amoris."

34. Thomas alludes briefly to this unity also in the penultimate article: "For as the Father, Son, and Holy Ghost are signified by the diverse names, so also can They each one be signified by different things; although neither separation nor diversity exists among Them" (I.43,7 ad 3) and in Article 5: "The two missions [of Son and Spirit] are united in the root which is grace, but are distinguished in the effects of grace, which consist in the illumination of the intellect and the kindling of the affection. Thus it is manifest that one mission cannot be without the other, because neither takes place without sanctifying grace, nor is one person separated from the other" (I.43,5 ad 3).

35. Aquinas acknowledges the complexity of the question and the justifiability of several different responses to it. However, the view quoted represents the answer he seems to regard as the single most appropriate and accords with the pronouncement of the *sed contra*: "A divine person is sent by one from Whom He does not proceed."

CHAPTER 3

Bibliographic Note. Works that deal in a general fashion with the issues of this chapter include Chenu, *Toward Understanding Saint Thomas*; Congar, *Thomas d'Aquin: sa vision de théologie et de l'Église*; Cunningham, *The Indwelling of the Trinity*; Davies, *The Thought of Thomas Aquinas*; De Letter, "Sanctifying Grace and Divine Indwelling"; Flew, *The Idea of Perfection in Christian Theology*; Gilson, *Saint Thomas moraliste* and *The Philosophy of St. Thomas Aquinas*; Jordan, "Theology and Philosophy"; Merriell, *To the Image of the Trinity*; Morency, *L'Union de grâce selon saint Thomas*; O'Connor, *The Eternal Quest*; O'Mahony, *The Desire of God in the Philosophy of St. Thomas Aquinas*; O'Meara, *Thomas Aquinas Theologian*, pp. 59, 89, 95–96, 123; Persson, *Sacra Doctrina*; Principe, *Thomas Aquinas' Spirituality*; and Rahner, "Concerning the Relationship between Nature and Grace" and "Some Implications of the Scholastic Concept of Uncreated Grace." See also the references to participation in the bibliographic note to chapter 2.

1. This seamless link is sharply denied by LaCugna: "Thomas posits an intradivine self-communication that is really distinct, if not really separate from, whatever self-communication may take place in creation" (*God for Us*, p. 166). Chapters 2 and 3 in their entirety may be taken as an argument against this position.

2. "Sed relatio in Deo ad creaturam non est realis, sed secundum rationem tantum. Relatio vero creaturae ad Deum est relatio realis."

3. "To create is, properly speaking, to cause or produce the being of things. And as every agent produces its like, the principle of action can be considered from the effect of the action; for it must be fire that generates fire. And therefore to create belongs to God according to His being, that is, His essence, which is common to the three Persons. Hence to create is not proper to any one Person, but is common to the whole Trinity."

4. The editor of the Dominican Province edition of the *Summa* takes Aquinas' self-reference here to allude to Question 32; a good case can be made, nonetheless, for Question 12.

5. *Pace* McInerny, who claims that human beings are in the image of God for Thomas because we have free wills (*St. Thomas Aquinas*, p. 52).

6. Merriell implies a similar view when he claims that Thomas locates the principle of analogical likeness between God and humanity in our participation in God's knowledge and love (*To the Image of the Trinity*, p. 221). Merriell thus suggests that the foundation of the *imago Dei* is the *De Deo uno*. Merriell's reading of the *Summa* nevertheless differs from that presented here. While he acknowledges some texts speak of the Spirit's indwelling by grace or charity outside the ques-

tion on divine missions, he regards these as "insignificant" (p. 233) and indeed attributes the infrequency of such usage to Thomas' desire not to overburden the reader by making explicit connections between the various parts of the Summa (p. 233). The reading presented here advocates the opposite view—namely, that it is precisely in the tight connections between the parts that the doctrine of deification (which necessarily entails the union of Uncreated and created) is chiefly to be found. Principe takes the moderate position that Thomas' anthropology views humanity in the Spirit as in the image of the Trinity (Thomas Aquinas' Spirituality, p. 23).

7. "Similitudo quaedam unitas est; unum enim in qualitate similitudinem causat."

8. Or in the interpretative translation of Timothy McDermott, "Dispositions enable us to act as and when we want" (Summa Theologiae: A Concise Translation, p. 225).

9. Aquinas gives a second reason for divine infusion, but it is not relevant to our purposes.

10. "Amatum continetur in amante, inquantum est impressum in affectu eius per quandam complacentiam. E converso vero amans continetur in amato, inquantum amans sequitur aliquo modo illud quod est intimum amati."

11. "It is possible for an act, without charity, to be generically good, but not perfectly good, because it lacks its due order to the last end" (II-II.23, 7 ad 1).

12. "Et quia mater est quae in se concipit ex alio, ex hac ratione dicitur mater aliarum virtutum, quia ex appetitu finis ultimi concipit actus aliarum virtutum, imperando ipsos."

13. The precise terms in which one may conceive the relation between charity and union with God may differ. The assumption here has been that charity attains to God because God is charity. Wadell sees matters somewhat differently: "We can speak of charity as a lifelong conversion to the goodness of God. Through the love given and received in friendship with God, we slowly take on the goodness of God. Doing so brings us likeness to God, a likeness sufficient to enable us to see God as 'another self,' which is the third mark of friendship" (The Primacy of Love, p. 145).

14. Aquinas' subsequent discernment of three degrees of charity, in Article 9, by no means detracts from charity's essential unity and continuity, since these degrees are distinguished "according to the different pursuits to which man is brought by the increase of charity" (II-II.24, 9 resp.) and therefore have nothing to do with charity in and of itself.

15. "When the Holy Ghost moves the human mind the movement of charity does not proceed from this motion in such a way that the human mind be merely moved, without being the principle of this movement, as when a body is moved by some extrinsic motive power. For this is contrary to the nature of a voluntary act, whose principle needs to be itself [cuius oportet principium in ips esse] . . . so that it would follow that love is not a voluntary act, which involves a contradiction, since love, of its very nature, implies an act of the will" (II-II.23,2 resp.).

16. "[Charity] produces an infinite effect, since, by justifying the soul, it unites it to God, this proves the infinity of the Divine power, which is the author of charity" (II-II.23,2 ad 3).

17. "Caritas est dignior anima, inquantum est participatio quaedam Spiritus Sancti." Cunningham insists that the divine persons do not dwell in the soul by charity, on the grounds that Thomas' Aristotelian psychology teaches that love is indifferent to the presence or absence of an object, whereas the Persons are contacted in the indwelling as objects really present (The Indwelling of the Trinity, p. 352).

18. "Charity can be in us neither naturally, nor through acquisition by the natural powers, but by the infusion of the Holy Ghost, Who is the love of the Father and the Son, and the participation of Whom in us is created charity [unde caritas non potest neque naturaliter nobis inesse, neque per vires naturales est acquisita, sed per infusionem Spiritus Sancti, qui est amor Patris et Filii, cuius participatio in nobis est ipsa caritas causata]" (II-II.24,2 resp.).

19. "Since charity surpasses the proportion of human nature . . . it depends, not on any natural virtue, but on the sole grace [ex sola gratia] of the Holy Ghost" (II-II. 24,3 resp.).

20. "Et hoc est quod facit Deus caritatem augendo, scilicet quod magis insit, et quod perfecitius similitudo Spiritus Sancti participetur in anima."

21. Aquinas wants, nonetheless, to preserve free will (I-II.113, 3–5), but for our purposes the emphasis on free will is less important than the all-inclusivity of grace's work.

22. "For the knowledge of any truth whatsoever man needs Divine help, that the intellect may be moved by God to its act. But he does not need a new light added to his natural light, in order to know the truth in all things, but only in some that surpass his natural knowledge" (ibid.).

23. "Patet igitur quod quamlibet Dei dilectionem sequitur aliquod bonum in creatura causatum, quandoque tamen dilectioni aeternae coaeternum."

24. "Alia autem dilectio est specialis, secundum quam trahit creaturam rationalem supra conditionem naturae, ad participationem divini boni."

25. "Secundum hanc dilectionem vult Deus simpliciter creaturae bonum aeternum, quod est ipse."

26. As he establishes beyond doubt at the end of the response: "Accordingly, when a man is said to have the grace of God, there is signified something bestowed on man by God. Nevertheless, the grace of God sometimes signifies God's eternal love [sic igitur per hoc quod dicitur homo gratiam Dei habere, significatur quiddam supernaturale in homine a Deo proveniens. Quandoque tamen gratia Dei dicitur ipsa aeterna Dei dilectio]" (ibid.).

27. "Virtutes autem infusae disponunt hominem altiori modo, et ad altiorem finem; unde etiam oportet quod in ordine ad aliquam altiorem naturam. Hoc est in ordine ad naturam divinam participatam quod dicitur lumen gratiae." The Dominican Province edition mysteriously omits "quod dicitur lumen gratiae" from its translation.

28. "Donum autem gratiae excedit omnem facultatem naturae creatae; cum nihil aliud sit quam quaedam participatio divinae naturae, quae excedit omnem aliam naturam. Et ideo impossibile est quod aliqua creatura gratiam causet. Sic enim necesse est quod solus Deus deificit, communicando consortium divinae naturae per quandam similitudinis participationem, sicut impossibile est quod aliquid igniat nisi solus ignis."

29. The argument here builds on and extends the discussion begun in the early decades of this century, notably in the work of La Taille, although he and his followers regarded themselves as returning to the biblical and patristic tradition, correcting Thomist error in doing so (cf. De Letter "Divine Quasi-Formal Causality," p. 22). La Taille's concern lay chiefly in establishing the unity between what he called created actuation and uncreated act: "Thus this hypothesis emerges: God becomes the Act of a created power. There is, therefore, in this instance a created actuation by an uncreated Act. There is, therefore, a created adaptation of the intelligence to the uncreated Act. This infused adaptation or disposition of the spirit is what is called the light of glory" ("Actuation Créée par Acte Incréé," p. 255). This way of understanding the essential unity of grace while simultaneously acknowledging the created-Uncreated distinction was taken up with particular enthusiasm by De Letter, who insisted on created grace as a disposition and effect of uncreated grace, the disposition to and effect of divine indwelling ("Divine Quasi-Formal Causality," esp. p. 223; "Reciprocal Causality," p. 407; and "Created Actuation by the Uncreated Act"). Similar positions were adopted by Morency, L'Union de grâce, p. 264; Bourassa, "Les Missions divines," p. 49; Bouillard, Conversion et grâce chez S. Thomas d'Aquin, p. 158; Moeller and Philips, Grâce et oecuménisme, p. 36; Pesch, Theologie der Rechtfertigung, p. 632; and Pesch and Peters, Einführung in die Lehre von Gnade und Rechtfertigung, p. 85. Rahner and M. Donnelly insist somewhat more strongly on the value of created grace as a category, but their positions nevertheless largely concur with the preceding authors. See Donnelly, "Sanctifying Grace and Our Union with the Holy Trinity"; Rahner, "Some Implications of the Scholastic Concept of Uncreated Grace." Mascall points out that the very term created grace must be considered suspect because it has acquired "secondary and unfortunate" meanings ("Grace and Nature in East and West," p. 191).

30. Note Davies' insistence that these categories are different ways of thinking about grace; there is, however, only one grace (*The Thought of Thomas Aquinas*, p. 269). Lonergan adopts a similar position, albeit specifically in relation to the commentary on the *Sentences*: "The differences implicit in these distinctions are not the differences of many graces but of the many effects of the one grace" (*Grace and Freedom*, p. 24).

31. "God is the life of the soul after the manner of an efficient cause; but the soul is the life of the body after the manner of a formal cause. Now there is no medium between form and matter, since the form of itself, *informs* the matter or subject; whereas the agent *informs* the subject, not by its substance, but by the form which it causes in the matter." This is the entire text of I.II.110,1 ad 2.

32. Davies notes in connection with Thomas' contention that the soul of Christ does not comprehend the divine essence (III.10,1) that he there invokes a principle derived from Damascene that Uncreated and created be kept strictly separate (*The Thought of Thomas Aquinas*, pp. 315–16). The reference to Damascene suggests that maintaining this classic patristic distinction lies at the forefront of Thomas' concerns in these questions. On the consonance of the Thomistic and patristic doctrines of grace, see Morency (*L'Union de grâce selon S. Thomas*, p. 271).

33. "The gift which is given the human nature, to be united to the Divine Person . . . also is an infinite gift" (III.7,11 ad 1).

34. "The grace of Christ has an infinite effect, both because the aforesaid infinity of grace, and because of the unity of the Divine Person, to whom Christ's soul is united" (III.7,11 ad 2).

35. Cf. *Lexicon of St. Thomas Aquinas*, p. 469.

36. "Ad plenam participationem divinitatis, quae vera est hominis beatitudo et finis humanae vitae. Et hoc collatum est nobis per Christi humanitatem."

37. Cf. also III.2,1 ad 3, where Thomas cites Damascene on the deification of the flesh in virtue of the Incarnation.

38. "Sic ergo dicendum est quod haec unio de qua loquimur, non est in Deo realiter, sed secundum rationem tantum; in humana autem natura, quae creatura est, realiter est."

39. "It belongs to Him, as man, to unite men to God, by communicating to men both precepts and gifts, and by offering satisfaction and prayer to God for men" (III.26,2 resp.).

40. Pesch states the matter in the strongest terms: for Thomas the Incarnation is not only the way to humanity's gracing, it is grace itself (*Theologie der Rechtfertigung*, p. 577).

41. "Anima Christi non est per suam essentiam divina. Unde oportet quod fiat divina per participationem, quae est secundum gratiam."

42. "Cuius sacerdotio configuratur fideles secundum sacramentales characteres."

43. "Quia semper inchoatio alicuius ordinatur ad consummationem ipsius."

44. "Naught can lull man's will, save the universal good. This is to be found, not in any creature, but in God alone; because every creature has goodness by participation. Wherefore God alone can satisfy the will of man" (I-II.2,8 resp.).

45. P. Donnelly documents what he considers to be the erroneous interpretation of many of Aquinas' commentators on this point. Lessius and "many modern theologians," he claims, regard the last end of creatures as a finite good, while Aquinas and Suarez see it as no less than divine intrinsic goodness ("Saint Thomas and the Ultimate Purpose of Creation," p. 83). As far as Donnelly is concerned, the positing of created good as the last end "logically would lead to the denial of God's transcendence, His infinite perfection, His very Divinity" (p. 71).

46. "Man's happiness consists in the knowledge of God, which is an act of the intellect" (I-II.3,4 s.c.).

47. "Man's highest operation is that of his highest power in respect of its highest object: and his highest power is the intellect, whose highest object is the Divine Good, which is the object, not of the practical, but of the speculative intellect. Consequently happiness consists principally in such an operation, viz., in the contemplation of Divine things" (I-II.3,5 resp.). Even here,

Thomas does not entirely exclude the will, for he adds: "Such an operation is most proper to man and most delightful to him."

48. "Visio divinae essentiae convenit omnibus beatis secundum participationem luminis."

49. "Although in this unhappy abode we participate, after a fashion, in the Divine good, by knowledge and love, yet the unhappiness of this life is an obstacle to a perfect participation in the Divine good: hence this very sorrow, whereby a a man grieves for the delay of glory, is connected with the hindrance to a participation of the Divine good" (II-II.28,2 ad 3).

50. "Rectitude of will is necessary for Happiness both antecedently and concomitantly. Antecedently because rectitude of the will consists in being duly ordered to the last end" (I-II.4,4 resp.).

51. "God intends by this precept ['Love God with all your heart'] that man should be entirely united to Him, and this will be realized in heaven, when God will be *all in all*. . . . Hence this precept will be observed fully and perfectly in heaven; yet it is fulfilled, though imperfectly, on the way" (II-II.44,6 resp.).

52. "Et ideo secundum caritatem specialiter attenditur perfectio christianae vitae."

53. "Dicendum quod ea quae sunt divinae naturae, dicuntur de humana natura, non secundum quod essentialiter competunt divinae naturae, sed secundum quod participative derivantur ad humanam naturam. Unde ea quae participari non possunt a natura humana, sicut esse increatum aut omnipotentem, nullo modo de humana natura dicuntur."

CHAPTER 4

1. Ware, for example, complains of selective and narrow reading in R. Williams' article "The Philosophical Structures of Palamism" in his response to the latter, "The Debate about Palamism," p. 57. LaCugna, to give another instance, is content to reach very negative assessments of Palamas' theology on the basis of information coming largely from secondary material; see *God for Us*, chap. 6.

2. Lison, one of the few commentators to undertake a close reading of the entire Palamite corpus, remarks upon this complexity and the consequent difficulty of apprehending Gregory's thought as a whole (*L'Esprit répandu*, p. 18).

3. James L. Kinneavy treats this question intermittently in *A Theory of Discourse* (New York: Norton, 1971), see esp. pp. 127—29.

4. Textual references to the *Triads* are by Roman numeral followed by two Arabic (e.g., III.1.27). References to the *Capita* specify the text, followed by a chapter numer in Arabic (e.g., *Capita* 48). Translations of the *Capita* follow the Sinkewicz edition; translations of the *Triads* are my own, though heavily indebted to Meyendorff's French and Gendle's English.

5. These are the primary direct references to deification and the loci where Palamas allies theosis with a number of cognates at once. These texts are corroborated by a number of direct references that link individual cognates with deification, for example: light, I.3.5, I.3.23, III.1.7, III.1.29, III.1.35; union, I.3.17, II.3.35, II.3.32; knowledge, II.3.17; and grace, III.1.27, *Capita* 69. Numerous texts equate deification with supernatural gift: II.3.68; III.1.7; III.1.8; III.1.26; III.1.31; III.1.34; III.1.35; III.3.13.

6. In his edition of the *Triads*, Meyendorff was unable to locate it (vol. 2, p. 610); Gendle, in the Classics of Western Spirituality (hereafter CWS) edition notes, identifies it as from *Ad Thalas.* 61, PG 90, 636C, and from the *Scholia* 6, ibid. 644C.

7. This section is not a study of Gregory's use of the term ἀρετή but rather brings together a range of concepts whose common denominator is striving in virtue, such as obedience, heeding scripture and the commandments, and turning towards God.

8. "The human spirit . . . surpasses itself and by the victory over the passions acquires an angelic aspect."

9. "The glory which the Father gave [Christ] he himself has given to those obedient to him" (I.3.5).

10. "Now the kingdom of heaven has drawn near to us . . . let us not remove ourselves far from it by living an unrepentant life" (*Capita* 57).

11. "We will only succeed in assimilating and uniting ourselves to God . . . by love and the holy practice of the divine commandments" (II.3.74).

12. "'It is there [in the heart] one must look to see if grace has inscribed the laws of the Spirit'" (he is quoting Macarius).

13. Thus, at any rate, if we assume Gregory to be following the conventional Platonic-Aristotelian scheme.

14. Gregory is highly consistent in using γνωσις, or forms allied to it, for the concept of knowledge, and σοφία for wisdom. Meyendorff notes in the Greek index to his edition of the *Triads* that γνῶσις often functions as the synonym for σοφία. Occasionally, Gregory uses forms related to νοῦς, and so in this section the Greek will be supplied from time to time to alert the reader to the play between intellect, knowledge and wisdom, even though the three are being taken here as variations of a single idea.

15. Mantzarides takes an even stronger view—namely, that Palamas sees that in humanity which is in the image as inhering primarily in the intellect, which he claims Palamas regards as the highest aspect of human nature (*The Deification of Man*, p. 17). Mantzarides' generally high view of the role of knowledge in Palamite theology is also reflected in the correspondence he sees between participation and knowledge (p. 113). However, Sinkewicz differs quite sharply from this view, claiming that for Palamas the human soul is more truly in God's image than the purely intellectual nature of the angels because of its corporeality ("Introduction" to the *Capita*, p. 19). Meyendorff's view approximates that of the Sinkewicz: though Palamas knew of the Dionysian distinction between wisdom ἔξωθεν and ἔνδοθεν, he associated the latter not with νοῦς but with the whole person (*Introduction à l'étude de Saint Grégoire Palamas*, p. 217). Krivosheine takes the middle road, maintaining that Palamas regards possession of a body as necessary to the manifestation of life-giving spirit but not viewing the image as subsisting in corporeality per se ("The Ascetic and Theological Teaching of Gregory Palamas," p. 4).

16. "Salvific perfection in the domain of knowledge and doctrine consists in being in accord with the prophets, the apostles, and quite simply all the Fathers" (II.1.42).

17. Sinkewicz sees matters slightly differently, at least insofar as the *Capita* are concerned. He maintains that knowledge must serve humanity in our true nature and according to our eternal destiny, in Gregory's view ("Introduction" to his edition of the *Capita*, pp. 14—15). Sinkewicz grants that for Gregory saving knowledge consists in knowledge of God and our place before him, and this must be counted superior to all secular learning (ibid.).

18. "This light is not knowledge, and one acquires it neither by affirmations nor negations" (III.2.17).

19. "Union is above all knowledge, although one calls it so metaphorically" (II.3.33).

20. Journet's analysis differs slightly but remains compatible. He distinguishes between three kinds of knowledge of God in Palamas' thought: the natural knowledge of reason, the revealed knowledge of faith and the apophatic knowledge of the gifts. The second two are clearly God's gift, whereas the first is equally clearly a form of knowledge about which Palamas exhibits considerable reservation ("Palamisme et thomisme," p. 430).

21. "They see the vesture of their deification, their intelligence being glorified and filled by the grace of the Word" (I.3.5).

22. "Ἔτι ἡ πρὸς τὰς ἐλλάμψεις ἔνωσις τί γε ἄλλο ἢ ὅρασίζ ἐστιν;"

23. "Although vision lies above negation, the word that expresses it is inferior to the negative way: it progresses by using examples or analogies" (I.3.4). More obscurely, he writes: "The

Archetype is invisible because of the fact of its transcendence, not because one does not see it, but because one sees it" (II.3.26).

24. "[Paul] did not know if it was his intellect or his body which saw. He did not actually see by sensation, but his vision was as clear, even clearer, than that which enables the sensation of perceptible things. He was in ecstasy, ravished by the mysterious sweetness of a vision surpassing all things, all objective thought, and even himself [Ὁρᾷ δ'ἑαυτὸν ὑπὸ τῆς τοῦ ὁρωμένου γλυκυθυμίας ἀπορρήτου ἐκστάντα τε καὶ ἁρπαγέτα οὐ μόνον ταυτὸς πράγματός τε καὶ νοήματος πραγμάτων, ἀλλὰ καὶ ἑαυτοῦ]."

25. Closely related to the question of whether the vision of which Gregory writes entails sense perception is the question of whether the vision of God is reserved for the next life or whether it can be begun here and now (cf. Lossky, The Vision of God, p. 11). This issue is central to the fundamental concept of deification, as we saw in the Introduction. In the texts on vision, however, Gregory's language is somewhat ambivalent. At times, he is clearly speaking of extraordinary visionary experiences, such as that of Paul; at other times, he is clearly speaking of the future (e.g., in the passage below from II.3.24). In yet other loci, he seems to allow the possibility of the vision of God to persons of great holiness, whose "location" is unspecified (e.g., the passage above from I.3.18). From this ambiguity we may only conclude that the in patria–in via question is less important to Palamas than to Lossky. The larger question of the nature of deification in relation to this life and the next will be considered in the conclusion.

26. "When the saints contemplate this divine light within themselves, [they see] it by the divinising communion of the Spirit . . . . as the Gospel says, 'He willed that they should be with him and contemplate his glory'" (I.3.5).

27. Generally, light here translates φῶς, and illumination ἔλλαμψις.

28. Since the texts that link light to other cognates reveal little more than the texts pertaining exclusively to those cognates, we will not examine them here. For texts linking light and knowledge, see II.3.18 and II.3.16; light and glory II.3.20, III.1.7, III.1.18, III.1.22 and Capita 147; light and grace I.3.20, I.3.38, II.3.15, III.1.13; light and union I.3.17 and II.3.25.

29. "'Ἀρχίφωτν ἀκτῖνα καί θεοργικὶν' καλέσας φῶς, ἐνταῦθα δὲ 'θεοποιὸν δῶρον καὶ ἀρχὴν θεότητος.'"

30. "This spiritual light is thus not only the object of vision, but is also the power by which we see" (III.2.14). Cf. III.3.5: "It is not possible to see the light without seeing in the light" (an allusion to Psalm 36:9).

31. The light becomes accessible, nevertheless, "but to eyes that saw in a fashion superior to that of the eyes and had acquired the spiritual power of the spiritual light" (III.1.22).

32. Canévet, "Sens spirituel" in Dictionnaire de spiritualité, p. 599.

33. "Paul was therefore light and spirit, to which he was united, by which he received the capacity for union, having gone out from all beings and become light by grace, and nonbeing by transcendence, that is by exceeding created things" (II.3.37).

34. I am grateful to Rowan Greer for this insight. Lison, however, holds that there is a connection between God, light and love (both ἔρως and ἀγάπη) that Palamas does not fully explain but which suggests that the divine light is the fire of love (L'Esprit répandu, p. 240).

35. He proceeds to extend the identification in III.1.16: "[The saints] commune not only with the glory of Trinity, and it is not the Trinity alone which they contemplate, but also the light of Jesus."

36. He expresses a similar sentiment in III.1.17: "This light is neither an independent reality, nor one foreign to the Divinity."

37. Similarly in II.3.66 he writes: "Even in the created realm, glory and light are not essence," and in the Capita he emphatically denies the light is divine substance (149).

38. Note that Krivosheine admits that Gregory nowhere gives an exact explanation of what he understands by light ("The Ascetic and Theological Teaching of Gregory Palamas," p. 36).

39. Ibid.: "[Christ] also wishes that they see this glory. It is therefore this glory by which we are possessed at the interior of our selves and by which we see God, properly speaking."

40. *Composite* here simply denotes human nature, which as created and mortal, is necessarily composed of component parts, in contrast to divine nature. Cf. CWS edition of the *Triads*, p. 133 n. 26.

41. He expresses much the same sentiment in II.3.66 when he writes: "[Christ] has endowed our nature with a glory and splendour that are divine."

42. "Through this life [the soul] receives also immortality for the body joined to it, for at the proper time the body attains to the promised resurrection and participates in eternal glory" (*Capita* 39; cf. also II.3.66).

43. "They became living icons of Christ and the same as he is, more by grace than by assimilation" (76).

44. "Even the angels could not attain this state [union with the light], at least not without transcending themselves by unifying grace" (II.3.37).

45. "Ὅλος ἄνρθωπος μένων κατὰ ψυχὴν καὶ σῶμα διὰ τὴν φὺσιν καὶ ὅλος γινόμενος Θεὸς κατὰ ψυχὴν καὶ σῶμα διὰ τὴν χάριν καὶ τὴν εμπρέπουσαν αὐτῷ διόλου θείαν τῆς μακαρίας δόξης λαμπρότητα."

46. Although the issue is scarcely important for Palamas' notion of grace per se, for the sake of the later comparison with Aquinas, it is worth noting that several commentators find in Palamas a willingness to speak, at least in some circumstances, of created grace. Cf. Lison, *L'Esprit répandu*, p. 121; and Philips, "La Grâce chez les Orientaux," p. 45. Neither, however, cites texts from the *Triads* or the *Capita*.

47. "Ἐκείνη μὲν γὰρ σξέσις, ει καὶ μή φυική, καὶ α"σχετος, οὐχ ὡς ὑπερφυὴς μόνον, ἀλλὰ καὶ ὡς σχέσις."

48. "Ἀκάματόν τία ἐνέργειαν ὑπὸ τῆς χάριτος ἐλλινομένην συνοῦαν καὶ ἐνερριζωμένην τῇ ψυχῇ."

49. We find the same notion in the *Triads*: "It is through grace that 'the entire Divinity comes to dwell in fullness in those deemed worthy,' and all the saints in their entire being dwell in God, receiving God in his wholeness, and gaining no other reward for their ascent to him than God himself. 'He is conjoined to them as a soul is to its body, to its own limbs,' judging it right to dwell in believers by the authentic adoption, according to the gift and grace of the Holy Spirit" (III.1.27).

50. "Τὴν μὲν ἐκ πίστεως εις ἐνέργειαν προβᾶσαν υιοθεσίαν."

51. What is in these translations rendered by a substantive tends in Gregory's Greek to be a form of the verb μετέχω, though at times he does use the noun μέθεξις.

52. "Ἀμέθεκτος ἄρα καὶ μεθεκτος ὑπάρχει ὁ αὐτὸς Θεος."

53. The closeness of the connection between this cognate and deification is attested by Meyendorff, who not only takes the union in John 17:22–23 as the equivalent of theosis but finds a similar equation in the thought of Gregory of Nyssa (*St. Gregory Palamas and Orthodox Spirituality*, p. 40). Schmemann sees union not only as the core of the need to assert the divine energies but the very heart of Orthodox theology: "[Palamas' doctrine] completes and renews in a creative way the most authentic and basic tendency in the doctrine of Palamas on divine energies (*The Historical Road of Eastern Orthodoxy*, pp. 234–35).

54. The commonality between God and humanity that union asserts grants it a unique status among the cognates, but Palamas does use union in conjunction with other cognates, with apparent contentment. He allies union variously with light (I.3.17; II.3.32 and III.2.14), vision (II.3.25; II.3.52 and III.2.14), knowledge (I.3.19 and II.3.74) and virtue (II.3.74 and, obliquely, I.3.23).

55. "[Our spirit] possesses union that transcends the nature of the spirit and allows it to at-

tach itself to what surpasses it" (I.3.45), and: "Our spirit leaves itself and unites itself to God, but does this by surpassing itself" (I.3.47).

56. The fact that an important category such as love does not rank among the cognates is instructive and serves as a reminder that no single textual approach will succeed in wholly encompassing the text it purports to illuminate. Note also that love has impressed other commentators as an important category in Palamite thought, quite aside from its significance for a comparison with Aquinas. Lison calls for a systematic study of love in Palamas' work (L'Esprit répandu, p. 240), and Le Guillou has executed such a study, albeit on a very limited scale ("Lumière et charité dans de la doctrine palamite de la divinisation").

57. Meyendorff insists upon the connection between this freedom and love: "The person (or hypostasis), in virtue of its freedom (which is the image of God, according to St. Gregory of Nyssa), possesses an *openness*, a capacity *to love* the other and therefore, particularly, to love God, and to know Him in love" ("Introduction" to CWS edition of the Triads, p. 14).

CHAPTER 5

1. Meyendorff, Byzantine Theology, p. 164. Cf. also Mantzarides: the accomplishment of God's intention for humanity depends on human free will, even after the accomplishment of Christ's mission of regeneration (The Deification of Man, p. 20).

2. Cf. Meyendorff: "The Presence itself is not the simple result of 'natural' efforts, whether intellectual, or ascetical, but is the gift of personal divine communion, or deification . . . that transcends all creatures" ("Introduction" to CWS edition of the Triads, p. 17).

3. Sic. See Meyendorff's edition of the Triads, vol. 2, p. 424, note 1.

4. Jugie, "Palamas," col. 1758.

5. Ibid., col. 1762.

6. Ibid., col. 1762.

7. Bouyer takes a position between that of Jugie on the one hand and Gregory's Orthodox proponents on the other. He sees the distinction as "prepared" by the Cappadocians, notably Nazianzen, and furthermore regards it as a direct development of Jewish conceptions of divine transcendence and immanence (Histoire de la spiritualité chrétienne, vol. 2, p. 694).

8. Jugie, Palamas, col. 1761.

9. Ibid., col. 1764.

10. Ibid., col. 1755.

11. Ibid., col. 1760.

12. The term συμβεβεκος πως is not necessarily a blatant blurring of Aristotelian categories in any case. As De Vogel explains (Greek Philosophy, vol. 2, Leiden: Brill, 1960) there is an ambiguity in Aristotle regarding the status of συμβεβεκος as a logical or ontological category (pp. 73—75). Furthermore, between Aristotle and Gregory lies the tradition of Middle Platonism, which both acknowledges the ambiguity in Aristotle just mentioned and often denies the applicability of these categories to nonsensible realities or rejects them altogether. Cf. for example, the discussion of Philo, pp. 178–79, and of later critics of Aristotle up to Plotinus, p. 246, in Dillon's The Middle Platonists (London: Duckworth, 1977). In using an originally Aristotelian term in a modified way, Gregory is thus in the company of major philosophers from Philo to Plotinus, who cannot simply be dismissed as erroneous because their views differed from Aristotle's. (I am grateful to Rowan Greer for this insight.) For a more recent criticism of Palamas for lack of Aristotlian purity, see R. Williams' "The Philosophical Structures of Palamism."

13. Lossky, The Mystical Theology of the Eastern Church, p. 81. Note, however, that the careful and sympathetic Lison also seems to regard the language of greater and lesser divinities as authentic (L'Esprit répandu, p. 98).

14. Halleux, "Palamisme et scolastique," p. 419.

15. In addition to the numerous Western theologians questioning simplicity, the Orthodox writer Barrois has also raised this question specifically with reference to Palamas; see "Palamism Revisited," p. 224.

16. Wendebourg, *Geist oder Energie*, p. 8; and "From the Cappadocian Fathers to Gregory Palamas," p. 196.

17. Ivánka, *Plato Christianus*, p. 428.

18. Journet, "Palamisme et thomisme," p. 443.

19. Jugie, "Palamas," col 1750.

20. Schultze, "Grundfragen des theologischen Palamismus," p. 107.

21. Halleux, "Palamisme et scolastique," p. 421.

22. Grumel, "Grégoire Palamas, Duns Scot et Georges Scholarios devant le problème de la simplicité divine," p. 95.

23. Reid, *Energies of the Spirit*, p. 3. Cf. also p. 128, where he seems more insistent on the reality of the distinction.

24. Lossky, *The Mystical Theology of the Eastern Church*, p. 76.

25. Philips, "La Grâce chez les Orientaux," p. 47. Cf. also Boularand, cited in Stiernon, "Bulletin sur le Palamisme," p. 235.

26. Meyendorff, *Byzantine Theology*, p. 187.

27. Ibid., p. 225.

28. Lossky, *The Mystical Theology of the Eastern Church*, p. 86.

29. Ibid., p. 88.

30. Ibid., p. 73.

31. Cf. also Boularand, cited in Stiernon, "Bulletin sur le Palamisme," p. 235.

32. Trethowan, "Irrationality in Theology and the Palamite Distinction," p. 21.

33. Wendebourg, *Geist oder Energie*, p. 10.

34. *Sic.*; it seems, however, that a "not" is intended before "God."

35. Wendebourg, "From the Cappadocian Fathers to Gregory Palamas," pp. 196–97.

36. Ibid., e.g., pp. 8–9, 11.

37. Ibid., p. 16.

38. Ibid., p. 196.

39. "The created being attains immutability through God. Therefore God's action cannot be an alteration, but must be a gift and revelation of the eternal. Therefore the entry of God into time has its limits. Revelation must be expressed precisely at the point where it happens. God must still be transcendent, at once exalted above his temporal bond (even Christology is no exception)" (Wendebourg, *Geist oder Energie*, p. 43). Wendebourg also decries Palamas' theology for its "Defunctionalisation of the Holy Spirit by the divinising energies" (p. 169).

40. LaCugna, *God for Us*, p. 186.

41. Neither Wendebourg nor LaCugna seems prepared to acknowledge that the identification *oikonomia-theologia* or immanent-economic Trinity might be less than imperative. The stated assumption of both is that failutre to observe these identities results in severely deficient theology. For Wendebourg, the identification is "axiomatic" (*Geist oder Energie*, p. 7), apparently on the basis of a consensus among Hegel, Barth, Rahner, and three minor twentieth-century theologians. LaCugna claims the identity of *oikonomia* and *theologia* originated in the earliest emergence of the doctrine of the Trinity, although she locates the origins of the breach as early as Nicaea (*God for Us*, p. 8). In the end, one gets the impression that LaCugna's insistence on the identity issue derives more from her allegiance to Rahner than to early Christian theology. Note that Lison accepts the identity of the immanent and economic Trinities, but once again in contrast to LaCugna and Wendebourg, finds evidence for precisely this identity in Palamas' thought, and cites Congar to the same effect (*L'Esprit répandu*, p. 58).

42. Wendebourg, *Geist oder Energie*, p. 43. Cf. LaCugna: "By locating the divine persons in the

inaccessible, imparticipable divine essence, Gregory in effect has removed the Trinity from our salvation" (*God for Us*, p. 197). In either case, the pattern is that a particular doctrine of God creates problems for the formulation of desirable doctrines of revelation and the Trinity—the distinction pertains to the doctrine of God.

43. Philips, "La Grâce chez les Orientaux," p. 45.

44. Lison, *L'Esprit répandu*, p. 99.

45. Ibid., p. 273

46. Richter, "Ansätze and Motive für die Lehre des Gregorios Palamas," p. 294.

47. "The problem of Palamism lies in that, philosophically, it also wants to furnish an ontological formula which will supposedly make understandable the nature of grace as the power that imparts participation in God" (Ivánka, *Plato Christianus*, p. 412).

48. Ibid., p. 444.

49. Lossky, *The Mystical Theology of the Eastern Church*, p. 87.

50. Ibid., p. 86.

51. Meyendorff, *St. Gregory Palamas and Orthodox Spirituality*, p. 126. Russo takes a similar view and on that basis finds an important similarity between Rahner and Palamas ("Rahner and Palamas," p. 176).

52. Ware, "The Debate about Palamism," p. 58.

53. The logical connection between superessentialism and impassibility and the rest is mine and not explicitly Gregory's. Nevertheless, this statement of the reasoning is fully consonant with Gregory's own logic.

54. "Πᾶσα φύσις ὡς πορρωτάτω ἐστὶ καὶ παντάπασι ξένη τῆς θείας φύσεως."

55. "Ἐπεὶ μὴ μόνον θεός ἐστιν ὑπὲρ τὰ ὄντα ὤ, ἀλλὰ καὶ ὑπέρθεος."

56. "Τὸν ὑπερανιδρυμένον καὶ ἀπολελυμένον."

57. Note that he continues here, "even though it is called a quasi-accident by some theologians who are indicating solely that it is in God but is not the substance," an attribution of *quasi accident* to others, suggesting that Palamas himself does not favor use of the term. This attestation of his ambivalence regarding the term *quasi accident* indicates Jugie's criticism requires considerable tempering, for it fails adequately to take account of Gregory's own qualification.

58. "The deifying gift of the Spirit is an energy of God" (III.1.31; cf. also III.1.33); "[The deifying gift of the Spirit] is the deifying energy of this divine essence" (III.1.34; cf. also III.1.35); "the divine and divinizing illumination and grace is . . . the energy of God . . . . It is bestowed proportionately upon those who participate and . . . it instills the divinizing radiance to a greater or lesser degree" (*Capita* 69 and cf. 147); "this very radiance and divinizing energy of God, by which the beings that participate are divinized, is a certain divine grace" (*Capita* 93).

59. "Not only is the divine essence unoriginate, but each of its powers is also" (III.2.5; cf. also III.2.19).

60. "[The beings united to the divinity] have received an energy identical to that of the deifying essence, and possessing it in absolute entirety, reveal it through themselves."

61. Gendle finds it possible to interpret this sentence in two quite distinct ways. The meaning assumed here corresponds to what he considers the more likely of the two readings and is the one I myself find most plausible (cf. CWS Triads, pp. 136–37).

62. "This grace is in fact a relationship, albeit not a natural one. . . . But as to the essence of God, that is unrelated, not because it is itself a relation, but because it transcends the supernatural relationships themselves [ἐκείνη μὲν γὰρ σχέσις, εἰ καὶ μὴ φυσική. . . . ἡδὲ οὐσία τοῦ θεοῦ οὐχ ὡς σχεβσις ἄσχετος, ἀλλ᾿ ὡς καὶ αὐτῶν τῶν ὑπερφυῶν σχέσεων ἐπέκεινα]."

63. "Τριῶν ὄντων τοῦ θεοῦ, οὐσίας, ἐνεργείας, τριάδος ὑποστάσεων θείων."

64. Other commentators here also held that Palamas himself attached relatively little importance to the distinction, notably Bouyer and and Florovsky, cited by Stiernon in "Bulletin sur le Palamisme," p. 325.

65. Lossky, *In the Image and Likeness of God*, pp. 53–54.

66. Ware, "God Hidden and Revealed," p. 136.

67. Ibid.

68. Ibid. He repeats this claim in a later article, "The Debate about Palamism," p. 54.

69. Ware, *The Orthodox Church*, p. 202.

70. Bulgakov, *The Orthodox Church*, p. 100.

71. Schmemann, *The Historical Road of Eastern Orthodoxy*, p. 234.

72. Aghiorgoussis, "Christian Existentialism of the Greek Fathers," p. 23.

73. Florovsky, "Saint Gregory Palamas and the Tradition of the Fathers," p. 125.

74. Ibid., p. 129.

75. Jugie, "Palamite (controverse)," col. 1811.

76. Ibid., cols. 1812 and 1814.

77. Ibid., col. 1810. He gives a list of modern Greek thelogians whose theology "contradicts" that of Palamas in col. 1811.

78. Ware, "God Hidden and Revealed," p. 129.

79. Stiernon, "Bulletin sur le Palamisme," p. 292. Note, however, that Yannaras criticizes Trembelas (this is the standard transliteration in English texts) and others for being Westernized, precisely because "they do not know the distinction between the Essence and Energies of God, the qualitative difference that distinguishes Orthodox theology from every other theology and spirituality" ("Orthodoxy and the West," p. 294). This argument, however, is clearly circular: the dogmatic status of the doctrine in question is proved by the fact that all theologians who do not subscribe to it are now deemed Westernized because they do not subscribe to it.

80. Karmiris' text, *A Synopsis of the Dogmatic Theology of the Orthodox Catholic Church*, while disinclined to limit dogma to scripture and promulgations of the first seven councils, and allowing as dogmatic those truths upheld by church conscience, nevertheless places the proceedings of the two hesychast councils on a long list of works described as "minor symbolic books, written later than the 9th century, which are not actually 'symbols' in the strict sense of the word . . . . none of them can be considered a canonical symbol of the Orthodox Church. . . . it is not permitted to employ them as the main and primary sources of Orthodox dogmatic teaching, but simply as relative, auxiliary and completely secondary sources" (pp. 8–9).

81. Staniloae tends to speak of God's being and his works (*being* and *operations* in the English translation of his dogmatics, *The Experience of God*; and *Wesen* and *Werke* in the German translation, *Orthodoxe Dogmatik*), rarely using *energies*. He holds firm to the notion that we have access only to the divine as it is manifested in the created realm but seems to regard the distinction as notional, articulating a position that sounds rather Thomistic: "It is from God himself that the operations originate which are productive of new and various qualities in the world. But we only know them through the prism of the effect they produce in world. God himself changes for our sake in his operations, remaining simple as the source of these operations and being wholly present in each one of them" (*The Experience of God*, p. 126). Note also that Staniloae strongly insists on divine simplicity throughout this chapter, which treats God's operations. Indeed, he comes close to identifying God's simple being and his operations: "The words which have reference to divine operations can also serve as names for God's being" (p. 128).

82. Ibid., p. 125: "Palamas did nothing more than hold fast to this distinction between the being of God and the uncreated operations flowing from it. Nevertheless, while speaking of the variety of divine works, we can sometimes forget to observe that, through each of these operations, it is the God, who is one in being, who is at work."

83. Wendebourg, *Geist oder Energie*, p. 9; she is citing Lossky.

84. LaCugna, *God for Us*, p. 186.

85. Ibid., p. 192.

86. Reid, *Energies of the Spirit*, p. 5. Reid compares Eastern and Western positions to an irenic end, it should be noted. Nevertheless, his claim that the doctrine counts as Orthodox dogma seems at odds with the acknowledgement that there *are* Eastern writers who do not accept the doctrine of the energies. These are the exceptions, he notes (p. 121)—but the fact that there are exceptions rather suggests a status for the distinction as a widely accepted theologoumenon, than as an official dogma.

87. Esser, "Östliche und westliche Theologie," p. 282.

88. Halleux, "Palamisme et scolastique," p. 442.

89. Schultze, "Grundfragen des theologischen Palamismus," p. 108.

90. Ibid., p. 134.

91. Ware, "The Debate about Palamism," p. 55.

92. Ibid., p. 58.

93. Lossky, *The Mystical Theology of the Eastern Church*, p. 76.

94. Meyendorff, *St. Gregory Palamas and Orthodox Spirituality*, p.126. Cf. also his introduction to the CWS edition of the *Triads*: "The distinction in God between 'essence' and 'energy' . . . is nothing but a way of saying that the transcendent God remains transcendent, as He also communicates Himself to humanity" (p. 20).

95. Meyendorff, *Byzantine Theology*, p. 187.

96. Lossky, *The Mystical Theology of the Eastern Church*, p. 88.

CHAPTER 6

1. For a fuller account of the ST specifically in relation to possible definitions of mystical theology, see A. N. Williams, "Mystical Theology Redux, The Pattern of Aquinas' *Summa Theologiae*," *Modern Theology* 12 (1997): 53–74.

2. See, for example, Lossky, *Lancelot Andrewes the Preacher (1555–1626): The Origins of Mystical Theology in the Church of England* (Oxford: Clarendon Press, 1991); Tuomo Mannermaa, "Theosis as a Subject of Finnish Luther Research," in *Pro Ecclesia* 4 (1995): 37–48; and David Yeago, "The Bread of Life: Patristic Christology and Evangelical Soteriology in Martin Luther's Sermons on John 6," *St. Vladimir's Theological Quarterly* 3 (1995): 257–79.

BIBLIOGRAPHY

Aertsen, Jan. *Nature and Creature: Thomas Aquinas's Way of Thought.* Leiden: E. J. Brill, 1988.

Aghiorgoussis, Maximos. "Christian Existentialism of the Greek Fathers: Persons, Essence, and Energies in God." *Greek Orthodox Theological Review* 23 (1978): 15–41.

Allchin, A. M. *The Kingdom of Love and Knowledge: The Encounter between Orthodoxy and the West.* London: Darton, Longman & Todd, 1979.

Aquinas, Thomas. *Summa contra Gentiles.* Translated and edited by Anton C. Pegis, James F. Anderson, Vernon J. Bourke, and Charles J. O'Neil. 5 vols. Garden City, N.Y.: Hanover House. Reprint, Notre Dame, Ind.: University of Notre Dame Press, 1975.

———. *Summa Theologiae: A Concise Translation.* Edited by Timothy McDermott. Westminster, Md.: Christian Classics, 1989.

———. *Summa Theologica.* Translated by Fathers of the English Dominican Province. 5 vols. 1911, rev. 1920. Reprint, Westminster, Md.: Christian Classics, 1981.

Armstrong, A. H., and E. J. B. Fry, eds. *Re-discovering Eastern Christendom: Essays in Commemoration of Dom Bede Winslow.* London: Darton, Longman & Todd, 1963.

Balthasar, Hans Urs von. *Seeing the Form.* Vol. 1 of *The Glory of the Lord: A Theological Aesthetics,* translated by Erasmo Leiva-Merikakis and edited by Joseph Fessio and John Riches. San Francisco: Ignatius, 1982.

Barringer, Robert. "Catholic-Orthodox Dialogue: The Present Position." In Robert Barringer, ed., *Rome and Constantinople,* pp. 55–72.

———, ed. *Rome and Constantinople: Essays in the Dialogue of Love.* Saints Peter and Andrew Lectures. Brookline, Mass.: Holy Cross Orthodox Press, 1984.

Barrois, Georges. "Palamism Revisited." *St. Vladimir's Seminary Quarterly* 19 (1975): 211–31.

Blum, Georg Günter. "Oikonomia und Theologia: der Hintergrund einer konfessionellen Differenz zwischen östlichem und westlichem Christentum." *Ostkirchliche Studien* 38 (1984): 281–301.

Bois, J. "Les Débuts de la controverse hésychaste." *Échos d'Orient* 5 (1901–1902): 353–62.

Bouillard, Henri. *Conversion et grâce chez S. Thomas d'Aquin. Étude historique.* Théologie 1. Paris: Éditions Montaigne, 1944.

Bourassa, François. "Adoptive Sonship: Our Union with the Divine Persons." *Theological Studies* 13 (1952): 309–35.

———. "Les Missions divines et le surnaturel chez Saint Thomas d'Aquin." *Sciences ecclesiastiques* 1 (1948): 41–94.

———. "Présence de Dieu et union aux divines personnes." *Sciences ecclesiastiques* 6 (1954): 5–23.

———. "Rôle personnel des Personnes et relations distinctes aux Personnes." *Sciences ecclesiastiques* 7 (1955): 151–72.

Bouyer, Louis. *La Spiritualité du moyen âge.* Vol. 2 of *Histoire de la spiritualité chrétienne.* Paris: Editions Montaigne, 1961.

Breck, John. "Divine Initiative: Salvation in Orthodox Theology." In John Meyendorff and Robert Tobias, eds., *Salvation in Christ: A Lutheran-Orthodox Dialogue.* Minneapolis: Augsburg, 1992.

Bria, Ion. *The Sense of Ecumenical Tradition: The Ecumenical Witness of the Orthodox.* Geneva: WCC Publications, 1991.

Brisbois, Ed. "Désir naturel et vision de Dieu." *Nouvelle Revue Théologique* 54 (1927): 81–97.

———. "Le Désir de voir Dieu et la métaphysique du vouloir selon Saint Thomas." *Nouvelle Revue Théologique* 63 (1936): 978–89, 1089–1113.

Broglie, Guy de. "Sur la place du surnaturel dans la philosophie de Saint Thomas." *Recherches de sciences religieuses* 15 (1925): 5–53.

Bulgakov, Sergius. *The Orthodox Church.* Translation revised by Lydia Kesich. Crestwood, N.Y.: St. Vladimir's Seminary Press, 1988.

Burnaby, John. *Amor Dei: A Study of the Religion of St Augustine.* London: Hodder and Stoughton, 1938.

Burrell, David B. *Aquinas: God and Action.* Notre Dame, Ind.: University of Notre Dame Press, 1979.

Calian, Carnegie Samuel. *Theology without Boundaries: Encounters of Eastern Orthodoxy and Western Tradition.* Louisville, Ky.: Westminster/John Knox Press, 1992.

Cessario, Romanus. *The Godly Image: Christ and Salvation in Catholic Thought from St Anselm to Aquinas.* Petersham, Mass.: St. Bede's Publications, 1990.

Chenu, M.-D. *Toward Understanding Saint Thomas.* Translated by A. M. Landry and D. Hughes. Library of Living Catholic Thought. Chicago: Regnery, 1964.

Clément, Olivier. *Byzance et le christianisme.* Mythes et religions. Paris: Presses Universitaires de France, 1964.

Congar, M.-J. "La Déification dans la tradition spirituelle de l'Orient d'après une étude récente." *Vie Spirituelle* 1935: 91–107.

Congar, Yves. *After Nine Hundred Years: The Background of the Schism between the Eastern and Western Churches.* New York: Fordham University Press, 1959.

———. "Le sens de l' 'économie' salutaire dans la 'théologie' de S. Thomas d'Aquin (Somme Théologique)." In *Thomas d'Aquin: sa vision de théologie et de l'Église.* London: Variorum, 1984. Originally published in *Festgabe Joseph Lortz.* Edited by E. Iserloh and P. Mann. Bd. 2: *Glaube und Geschichte.* Baden-Baden: Bruno Grimm, 1957.

Contos, Leonidas C. "The Essence-Energies Structure of Saint Gregory Palamas with a Brief Examination of its Patristic Foundation." *Greek Orthodox Theological Review* 12 (1967): 283–94.

Copleston, F. C. *Aquinas.* London: Penguin, 1955.

Corbin, Michel. *Le Chemin de la théologie chez Thomas d'Aquin.* Paris: Beauchesne, 1974.

Cunningham, Francis L. B. *The Indwelling of the Trinity: A Historico-Doctrinal Study of the Theory of St. Thomas Aquinas.* Dubuque, Iowa: Priory Press, 1955.

Dalmais, Irénée-H. "Divinisation. II: Patristrique grèque." In *Dictionnaire de spiritualité, ascétique et mystique, doctrine et histoire,* vol. 3. Paris: Beauchesne, 1937– .

Daniélou, Jean. *Platonisme et théologie mystique: essai sur la doctrine spirituelle de Saint Grégoire de Nysse.* Paris: Éditions Montaigne, 1944.

Davies, Brian. *The Thought of Thomas Aquinas.* Oxford: Clarendon, 1992.

Dejaifve, Georges. "East and West: Two Theologies, One Faith." In A. H. Armstrong and E. J. B. Fry, eds., *Re-discovering Eastern Christendom,* pp. 51–62.

De Letter, P. "Created Actuation by the Uncreated Act: Difficulties and Answers." *Theological Studies* 18 (1957): 60–92.

———. "Divine Quasi-Formal Causality." *Irish Theological Quarterly* 27 (1960): 221–28.

———. "Grace, Incorporation, Inhabitation." *Theological Studies* 19 (1958): 1–31.

———. "Reciprocal Causality: Some Applications in Theology." *The Thomist* 25 (1962): 382–418.

———. "Sanctifying Grace and Divine Indwelling." *Theological Studies* 14 (1953): 242–72.

———. "Sanctifying Grace and Divine Indwelling: Fr. de la Taille and St Thomas." *Gregorianum* 41 (1960): 63–69.

Doig, James C. *Aquinas on Metaphysics: A Historico-Doctrinal Study of the Commentary on the Metaphysics.* The Hague: Nijhoff, 1972.

Dondaine, Antoine. "Contra Graecos: premier écrits polémiques des Dominicains d'orient." *Archivum Fratrum Praedicatorum* 21 (1951): 320–446.

Donnelly, Malachi J. "Sanctifying Grace and Our Union with the Holy Trinity: A Reply." *Theological Studies* 13 (1952): 190–204.

Donnelly, Philip J. "Saint Thomas and the Ultimate Purpose of Creation." *Theological Studies* 2 (1941): 53–83.

Esser, Ambrosius. "Östliche und westliche Theologie." *Freiburger Zeitschrift für Philosophie und Theologie* 9 (1962): 279–84.

Evdokimov, Paul. *L'Orthodoxie.* Bibliothèque théologique. Neuchâtel: Delachaux et Niestlé, 1959.

Every, George. *Misunderstandings between East and West.* Ecumenical Studies in History, 4. Richmond, Va.: John Knox, 1966.

———. "Theosis in Later Byzantine Theology." *Eastern Churches Review* 2 (1968–1969): 243–52.

Fabro, Cornelio. *Participation et causalité selon S. Thomas d'Aquin.* Louvain: Publications Universitaires de Louvain, 1961.

Fahey, Michael A. "Orthodox Ecumenism and Theology: 1978–83." *Theological Studies* 44 (1983): 625–92.

———. "Rome and Byzantium: Sister Churches Prepare for the Third Millenium." In Robert Barringer, ed., *Rome and Constantinople,* pp. 9–34.

Fahey, Michael A., and John Meyendorff. *Trinitarian Theology East and West: St. Thomas Aquinas—St. Gregory Palamas.* Patriarch Athenagoras Memorial Lectures. Brookline, Mass.: Holy Cross Orthodox Press, 1977.

Falenga, Anthony J. *Charity the Form of the Virtues according to Saint Thomas.* Catholic University in America Studies in Sacred Theology, 2nd ser., 18. Washington, D.C.: Catholic University of America Press, 1948.

Flew, R. Newton. *The Idea of Perfection in Christian Theology: An Historical Study of the Christian Ideal for the Present Life.* [Oxford]: Oxford University Press, 1934.

Florovsky, Georges. "Saint Gregory Palamas and the Tradition of the Fathers." *Greek Orthodox Theological Review* 5 (1959–1960): 119–31. Also published as "Grégoire Palamas et la patristique." *Istina* 8 (1961–1962): 115–25.

Fortescue, Adrian. "Hesychasm." In *The Catholic Encyclopedia,* vol. 7, pp. 301–303.

———. *The Orthodox Eastern Church.* London: Catholic Truth Society, 1929.

Gavin, Frank. *Some Aspects of Contemporary Greek Orthodox Thought.* The Hale Lectures, 1922. Milwaukee: Morehouse, 1923.

Geanakoplos, Deno John. *Byzantine East and Latin West: Two Worlds of Christendom in Middle Ages and Renaissance.* Studies in Ecclesiastical and Cultural History. New York: Barnes and Noble, 1966.

———. *Emperor Michael Palaeologus and the West 1258–1282: A Study in Byzantine-Latin Relations.* Cambridge: Harvard University Press, 1959.

————. *Greek Scholars in Venice: Studies in the Dissemination of Greek Learning from Byzantium to Western Europe.* Cambridge: Harvard University Press, 1962.

————. *Interaction of the "Sibling" Byzantine and Western Cultures in the Middle Ages and Italian Renaissance (330–1600).* New Haven: Yale University Press, 1976.

Gill, Joseph. *Byzantium and the Papacy 1198–1400.* New Brunswick, N.J.: Rutgers University Press, 1979.

Gill, Joseph, and Edmund Flood. *The Orthodox: Their Relations with Rome.* Glen Rock, N.J.: Paulist, 1964.

Gilson, Étienne. *The Philosophy of St. Thomas Aquinas,* 3rd ed. translated by Edward Bullough and edited by G. A. Elrington. New York: Dorset, n.d.

————. *Saint Thomas moraliste.* Biblliotheque d'histoire de la philosophie. 2nd ed. aug. Paris: Vrin, 1974.

Greer, Rowan A. *Broken Lights and Mended Lives: Theology and Common Life in the Early Church.* University Park: Pennsylvania State University Press, 1986.

"Grégoire Palamas" [by the editors of Istina]. *Istina* 19 (1974): 257–59.

Gross, Jules. *La Divinisation du chrétien d'après les pères grecs: contribution historique à la doctrine de la grâce.* Paris: J. Gabalda, 1938.

Grumel, V. "Grégoire Palamas, Duns Scot et Georges Scholarios devant le problème de la simplicité divine." *Echos d'Orient* 34 (1935): 84–96.

Halleux, André de. "Palamisme et scolastique: exclusivisme dogmatique ou pluriformité théologique?" *Revue théologique de Louvain* 4 (1973): 409–42.

————. "Palamisme et Tradition." *Irénikon* 48 (1975): 479–93.

Harkianakis, Stylianos. *Orthodoxe Kirche und Katholizismus: ähnliches und verschiedenes.* Munich: Kösel, 1975.

Héris, V. "L'Amour naturel de Dieu d'aprés Saint Thomas." In *Mélanges thomistes.* Bibliothèque thomiste 3. Paris: Vrin, 1934.

Hill, Edmund. *The Mystery of the Trinity.* Introducing Catholic Theology 4. London: Chapman, 1985.

Holmes, Urban T., III. *A History of Christian Spirituality: An Analytical Introduction.* San Francisco: Harper & Row, 1980.

Houdret, Jean-Philippe. "Palamas et les Cappadociens." *Istina* 19 (1974): 260–71.

Hunter, H. D. "Gregory Palamas." In *New Catholic Encyclopedia,* vol. 10, pp. 872–74.

Hussey, J. M., ed. *The Byzantine Empire.* Vol. 4 of *The Cambridge Medieval History.* Part 2, Government, Church and Civilisation. Cambridge: At the University Press, 1967.

Hussey, J. M., and T. A. Hart. "Byzantine Theological Speculation and Spirituality." In J. M. Hussey, ed., *The Byzantine Empire,* vol. 4, pt. 2 of *The Cambridge Medieval History,* pp. 185–205.

Hussey, M. Edmund. "The Palamite Trinitarian Models." *St. Vladimir's Seminary Quarterly* 16 (1972): 83–89.

————. "The Persons-Energy Structure in the Theology of St. Gregory Palamas." *St. Vladimir's Seminary Quarterly* 18 (1974): 22–43.

Ivánka, Endre von. "Das Dogma der orthodoxen Kirche im Spiegel der wichtigsten Glaubensurkunden." In Wilhelm Nyssen, Hans-Joachim Schulz, and Paul Wiertz, eds., *Handbuch der Ostkirchenkunde.* Bd. 1, pp. 289–320.

————. *Plato Christianus: Übernahme und Umgestaltung des Platonismus durch die Väter.* Einsiedeln: Johannes Verlag, 1964.

Jordan, Mark D. "Theology and Philosophy." In Norman Kretzmann and Eleonore Stump, eds., *The Cambridge Companion to Aquinas.* Cambridge: Cambridge University Press, 1993.

Journet, Charles. "Palamisme et thomisme: à propos d'un livre récent." *Revue thomiste* 60 (1960): 429–52.

Jugie, M[artin]. "Grégoire Palamas" in *Dictionnaire de théologie catholique,* vol. 11, pt. 2, pp. 1735–76.

————. "Palamite (controverse)" in *Dictionnaire de théologie catholique,* vol. 11, pt. 2, pp.1777–1818.

————. *Le Schisme byzantin: aperçu historique et doctrinal.* Paris: P. Lethielleux, 1941.

Justification by Faith. Edited by H. George Anderson, Austin Murphy, and Joseph A. Burgess. Lutherans and Catholics in Dialogue 7. Minneapolis: Augsburg, 1985.

Kalomiros, Alexander. *Against False Union. Humble Thoughts of an Orthodox Christian concerning the Attempts for Union of the One, Holy, Catholic and Apostolic Church with the So-Called Churches of the West*. Translated by George Gabriel. Boston: Holy Transfiguration Monastery, 1967.

Karmiris, John. *A Synopsis of the Dogmatic Theology of the Orthodox Catholic Church*. Translated by George Dimopoulos. N.p.: Christian Orthodox Edition, 1973.

Kenny, Anthony. *Aquinas*. Past Masters. New York: Hill and Wang, 1980.

Kern, Cyprien. "Les Élements de la théologie de Grégoire Palamas." *Irénikon* 20 (1947): 6–33, 164–93.

Kilmartin, Edward J. *Toward Reunion: The Roman Catholic and the Orthodox Churches*. New York: Paulist, 1979.

Klauder, Francis J. *A Philosophy Rooted in Love: The Dominant Themes in the Perennial Philosophy of St. Thomas Aquinas*. Lanham, Md.: University Press of America, 1994.

Krivosheine, Basil. *The Ascetic and Theological Teaching of Gregory Palamas*. Eastern Churches Quarterly. 3 (1938) Nos. 1–4). Reprint, London: Geo. E. J. Coldwell, [1954].

Kuhlmann, Jürgen. *Die Taten des einfachen Gottes: eine römisch-katholische Stellungnahme zum Palamismus*. Das östliche Christentum, n. F., H. 21. Würzburg: Augustinus-Verlag, 1968.

LaCugna, Catherine Mowry. *God for Us: The Trinity and Christian Life*. San Francisco: HarperSanFrancisco, 1991.

La Taille, Maurice de. "Actuation créée par acte incréé: lumière de gloire, grâce sanctifiante, union hypostatique." *Recherches de science religieuse* 18 (1928): 253–68.

Leeming, Bernard. "Orthodox-Catholic Relations." In A. H. Armstrong and E. J. B. Fry, eds., *Rediscovering Eastern Christendom*, pp. 15–50.

Le Guillou, M.-J. "Lumière et charité dans la doctrine palamite de la divinisation." *Istina* 19 (1974): 329–38.

A Lexicon of St. Thomas Aquinas based on the Summa Theologica and Selected Passages of His Other Works. Compiled by Roy J. Deferrari, M. Inviolata Barry, and Ignatius McGuiness. N.p.: Catholic University Press of America, 1948.

Lialine, Clement. "The Theological Teaching of Gregory Palamas on Divine Simplicity: Its Experimental Origin and Practical Issue." *Eastern Churches Quarterly* 6 (1945–1946): 266–87.

Lison, Jacques. *L'Esprit répandu: la pneumatologie de Grégoire Palamas*. Patrimoines, orthodoxie. Paris: Cerf, 1994.

The Living God: A Catechism for the Christian Faith. Translated by Olga Dunlop. 2 vols. Crestwood, N.Y.: St Vladimir's Seminary Press, 1989.

Lonergan, Bernard J. F. *Grace and Freedom: Operative Grace in the Thought of St. Thomas Aquinas*. Edited by J. Patout Burns. London: Darton, Longman & Todd, 1971.

————. *Verbum: Word and Idea in Aquinas*. Edited by David B. Burrell. Notre Dame, Ind.: University of Notre Dame Press, 1967.

Lossky, Vladimir. *In the Image and Likeness of God*. Edited by John H. Erickson and Thomas E. Bird. Crestwood, N.Y.: St Vladimir's Seminary Press, 1985.

————. *The Mystical Theology of the Eastern Church*. [Translated by members of the Fellowship of St. Alban and St. Sergius.] Crestwood, N.Y.: St. Vladimir's Seminary Press, 1976.

————. "The Procession of the Holy Spirit in the Orthodox Triadology." Translated by Edward Every. *Eastern Churches Quarterly* 7 (1947–1948): 31–53.

————. *The Vision of God*. Translated by Asheleigh Moorhouse. Crestwood, N.Y.: St. Vladimir's Seminary Press, 1983.

Lot-Borodine, M. "La Doctrine de la 'déification' dans l'Église grecque jusqu'au XIe siècle." *Revue de l'Histoire des Religions* 105 (1932): 5–43; 106 (1932): 525–74; 107 (1933): 8–55.

McInerny, Ralph. *St. Thomas Aquinas*. Boston: Twayne, 1977. Reprint, Notre Dame, Ind.: University of Notre Dame Press, 1982.

Mantzarides, Georgios I. *The Deification of Man: St Gregory Palamas and the Orthodox Tradition*. Translated by Liadain Sherrard. Contemporary Greek Theologians 2. Crestwood, N.Y.: St. Vladimir's Seminary Press, 1984.

————. "Tradition and Renewal in the Theology of Saint Gregory Palamas." *Eastern Churches Review* 9 (1977): 1–18.

Marshall, Bruce D. "Action and Person: Do Palamas and Aquinas Agree about the Spirit?" In *Der Heilige Geist: Ökumenische und reformatorische Untersuchungen*. Veröffentlichungen der Luther-Akademie Ratzeburg. Erlangen: Martin-Luther-Verlag, 1996.

Mascall, E. L. "Grace and Nature in East and West." *Church Quarterly Review* 164 (1963): 181–98, 332–47.

Merriell, D. Juvenal. *To the Image of the Trinity: A Study in the Development of Aquinas' Teaching*. Studies and Texts 96. Toronto: Pontifical Institute of Medieval Studies, 1990.

Meyendorff, John. *Byzantine Hesychasm: Historical, Theological and Social Problems*. Collected Studies. Reprint, London: Variorum, 1974.

————. *Byzantine Theology: Historical Trends and Doctrinal Themes*. 2nd ed. rev. New York: Fordham University Press, 1979.

————. *Introduction à l'étude de Grégoire Palamas*. Patristica Sorbonensia 3. Paris: Editions du Seuil, 1959.

————. "New Life in Christ: Salvation in Orthodox Theology." *Theological Studies* 50 (1989): 481–99.

————. *St. Gregory Palamas and Orthodox Spirituality*. Translated by Adele Fiske. [Crestwood, N.Y.]: St. Vladimir's Seminary Press, 1974.

————. "Society and Culture in the Fourteenth Century. Religious Problems." In *Actes du XIVe Congrès International des Études Byzantines*. Bucharest, 6–12 Septembre, 1971. Bucharest: Editura Academici Republicii Socialiste România, 1974.

————. "Spiritual Trends in Byzantium in the Late Thirteenth and Early Fourteenth Centuries." In Paul A. Underwood, ed., *Studies in the Art of the Kariye Djami and Its Intellectual Background*. Vol. 4 of *The Kariye Djami*. Bollingen Series 70. Princeton, N.J.: Princeton University Press, 1975.

Minet, Paula. *Vocabulaire théologique orthodoxe*. Catachèse orthodoxe. Paris: Cerf, 1985.

Moeller, C., and G. Philips. *Grâce et oecuménisme*. Chevetogne: [Éditions de Chevetogne, 1957].

Morency, Robert. *L'Union de grâce selon saint Thomas*. Studia Collegii Maximi 8. Montreal: Éditions de l'Immaculée-Conception, 1950.

————. "L'Union du juste à Dieu par voie de connaissance et d'amour." *Sciences ecclesiastiques* 2 (1949): 27–79.

Mulard, R. "Désir naturel de connaître et vision béatifique." *Revue de sciences philosophiques et théologiques* 14 (1925): 5–19.

Nellas, Panayiotis. *Deification in Christ: Orthodox Perspectives on the Nature of the Human Person*. Translated by Norman Russell. Contemporary Greek Theologians, 5. Crestwood, N.Y.: St. Vladimir's, 1987.

Nichols, Aidan. *Rome and the Eastern Churches: A Study in Schism*. Collegeville, Minn.: Liturgical Press, 1992.

Nicol, Donald M. *Byzantium: Its Ecclesiastical History and Relations with the Western World*. Collected Studies. Reprint, London: Variorum, 1972.

————. *Church and Society in the Last Centuries of Byzantium*. The Birkbeck Lectures, 1977. Cambridge: Cambridge University Press, 1979.

Norden, Walter. *Das Papsttum und Byzanz. Die Trennung der beiden Mächte und das Problem ihrer Wiedervereinigung bis zum Untergange des byzantinischen Reichs (1453)*. Berlin: N.p., 1903. Reprint, New York: Burt Franklin, n.d.

Nyssen, Wilhelm, Hans-Joachim Schulz, and Paul Wiertz, eds. *Handbuch der Ostkirchenkunde*. 2 vols. Neu erarb. Ausg. Düsseldorf: Patmos, 1984.

O'Connor, Williams R. *The Eternal Quest: The Teaching of St. Thomas Aquinas on the Natural Desire for God.* New York: Longmans, Green, 1947.

O'Mahony, James E. *The Desire of God in the Philosophy of St. Thomas Aquinas.* Dublin: Cork University Press, 1929.

O'Meara, Thomas Franklin. *Thomas Aquinas Theologian.* Notre Dame, Ind.: University of Notre Dame Press, 1997.

Origen. *Origen: An Exhortation to Martrdom, Prayer, First Principles Book IV, Prologue to the Commentary on the Song of Songs, Homily XXVII on Numbers.* Translated by Rowan Greer. New York: Paulist, 1979.

O'Rourke, Fran. *Pseudo-Dionysius and the Metaphysics of Aquinas.* Studien und Texte zur Geschichte des Mittelalters, Bd. 32. Leiden: E. J. Brill, 1992.

Palamas, Gregory. *Defense des saints hésychastes: introduction, texte critique, traduction et notes.* Edited and translated by John Meyendorff. Etudes et documents, fasc. 30–31. Louvain: Spicilegium Sacrum Lovaniense, 1959.

———. *The One Hundred and Fifty Chapters: A Critical Edition, Translation and Study.* Edited and translated by Robert E. Sinkewicz. Studies and Texts 83. Toronto: Pontifical Institute of Medieval Studies, 1988.

———. *The Triads.* Edited by John Meyendorff and translated by Nicholas Gendle. The Classics of Western Spirituality. New York: Paulist, 1983.

Papadopulos, Stylianos G. "Thomas in Byzanz. Thomas-Rezeption und Thomas-Kritik in Byzanz zwischen 1354 und 1435." *Theologie und Philosophie* 49 (1974): 274–304.

Patterson, Robert Lect. *The Conception of God in the Philosophy of Thomas Aquinas.* London: George Allen & Unwin, 1933.

Pegis, Anton C. "Creation and Beatitude in the *Summa contra Gentiles* of St. Thomas Aquinas." *Proceedings of the American Catholic Philosophical Association* 29 (1955): 52–62.

———. "Nature and Spirit: Some Reflections on the Problem of the End of Man." *Proceedings of the American Catholic Philosophical Association* 23 (1949): 62–79.

———. *Saint Thomas and the Greeks.* The Aquinas Lecture 1939. Milwaukee: Marquette University Press, 1939.

Pelikan, Jaroslav. *Development of Christian Doctrine: Some Historical Prolegomena.* New Haven: Yale University Press, 1969.

———. *The Growth of Medieval Theology (600–1300).* Vol. 3 of *The Christian Tradition: A History of the Development of Doctrine.* Chicago: University of Chicago Press, 1978.

———. *The Spirit of Eastern Christendom (600–1700).* Vol. 2 of *The Christian Tradition: A History of the Development of Doctrine.* Chicago: University of Chicago Press, 1974.

Persson, Per Erik. *Sacra Doctrina: Reason and Revelation in Aquinas.* Translated by Ross Mackenzie. Philadelphia: Fortress Press, 1970.

Pesch, Otto Hermann. *Theologie der Rechtfertigung bei Martin Luther und Thomas von Aquin: Versuch eines systematisch-theologischen Dialogs.* Walberger Studien, Theologische Reihe, Bd. 4. Mainz: Matthias-Grünewald, 1967.

Pesch, Otto Hermann, and Albrecht Peters. *Einführung in die Lehre von Gnade und Rechtfertigung.* Die Theologie. Darmstadt: Wissenschaftliche Buchgesellschaft, 1981.

Philips, G. "La Grâce chez les Orientaux." *Ephemerides Theologicae Lovanienses* 48 (1972): 37–50.

Podskalsky, Gerhard. *Theologie und Philosophie in Byzanz: Der Streit um die theologische Methodik in der spätbyzantinischen Geistesgeschichte (14./15. Jh.), seine systematischen Grundlagen und seine historische Entwicklung.* Byzantinisches Archiv, H. 15. Munich: C. H. Beck, 1977.

Pomazansky, Michael. *Orthodox Dogmatic Theology: A Concise Exposition.* Translated by Seraphim Rose. Platina, Calif.: Saint Herman of Alaska Brotherhood, 1984.

Preller, Victor. *Divine Science and the Science of God: A Reformulation of Thomas Aquinas.* Princeton, N.J.: Princeton University Press, 1967.

Principe, Walter H. *Thomas Aquinas' Spirituality.* Etienne Gilson Series 7. Toronto: Pontifical Institute of Medieval Studies, 1984.

Pseudo-Dionysius the Areopagite. *Pseudo-Dionysius: The Complete Works*. Translated by Colm Luibheid. Classics of Western Spirituality. New York: Paulist, 1987.

Quasten, Johannes. *Patrology*. 4 vols. 1950. Reprint, Westminster, Md.: Christian Classics, 1983.

Rackl, Michael. "Die griechische Übersetzung der Summa Theologiae des hl. Thomas von Aquin." *Byzantinische Zeitschrift 24* (1923–1924): 48–60.

Rahner, Karl. "Concerning the Relationship between Nature and Grace" and "Some Implications of the Scholastic Concept of Uncreated Grace" in *God, Christ, Mary and Grace*. Vol. 1 of *Theological Investigations*. Translated by Cornelius Ernst. Baltimore: Helicon, 1961.

Reid, Duncan. *Energies of the Spirit: Trinitarian Models in Eastern Orthodox and Western Theology*. American Academy of Religion Academy series 96. Atlanta: Scholars Press, 1997.

Richter, Gerhard. "Ansätze und Motive für die Lehre des Gregorios Palamas von den göttlichen Energien." *Ostkirchliche Studien* 31 (1982): 281–96.

Roberts, Alexander, and James Donaldson, eds. *Ante-Nicene Fathers*. 1885–1886. Reprint, Peabody, Mass.: Hendrickson, 1994.

Romanides, John S. "Notes on the Palamite Controversy and Related Topics." *Greek Orthodox Theological Review* 6 (1960): 186–205 and 9 (1963–1964): 225–70.

Runciman, Steven. *Byzantine Civilisation*. London: Edward Arnold, 1933.

———. *The Eastern Schism: A Study of the Papacy and the Eastern Churches during the XIth and XIIth Centuries*. Oxford: Clarendon, 1955.

———. *The Great Church in Captivity: A Study in the Patriarchate of Constantinople from the Eve of the Turkish Conquest to the Greek War of Independence*. Cambridge: At the University Press, 1968.

———. *The Last Byzantine Renaissance*. Wiles Lectures 1968. Cambridge: At the University Press, 1970.

———. "The Place of Byzantium in the Medieval World." In J. M. Hussey and T. A. Hart, eds, *The Byzantine Empire*, vol. 4, pt. 2 of *The Cambridge Medieval History*, pp. 354–75.

Russo, Gerry. "Rahner and Palamas: A Unity of Grace." *Saint Vladimir's Theological Quarterly* 32 (1988):157–80.

St. Thomas Aquinas 1274–1974: Commemorative Studies. Toronto: Pontifical Institute of Medieval Studies, 1974.

Schaff, Philip, ed. *Nicene and Post-Nicene Fathers*. First Series. 1886–1889. Reprint, Peabody, Mass.: Hendrickson, 1994.

Schaff, Philip, and Henry Wace, eds. *Nicene and Post-Nicene Fathers*. Second Series. 1890–1900. Reprint, Peabody, Mass.: Hendrickson, 1994.

Schmemann, Alexander. *The Historical Road of Eastern Orthodoxy*. Translated by Lydia W. Kesich. New York: Holt, Rinehart and Winston, 1963.

Schultze, Bernhard. *Das Gottesproblem in der Osttheologie*. Aevum Christianum, Salzburger Beiträge zur Religions- und Geistesgeschichte des Abendlandes 7. Münster: Aschendorff, 1967.

———. "Grundfragen des theologischen Palamismus." *Ostkirchliche Studien* 24 (1975): 105–35.

———. "Hauptthemen der neueren russischen Theologie." In Wilhelm Nyssen, Hans-Joachim Schulz and Paul Wiertz eds., *Handbuch der Ostkirchenkunde*, Bd. 1, pp. 321–89.

Sherrard, Philip. *The Greek East and the Latin West: A Study in the Christian Tradition*. London: Oxford University Press, 1959.

Southern, R. W. *Western Church and Society in the Middle Ages*. (Penguin History of the Church). London: Penguin, 1970.

Staniloae, Dumitru. *The Experience of God*. Translated and edited by Ioan Ioanită and Robert Barringer. Brookline, Mass.: Holy Cross Orthodox Press, 1994.

———. *Orthodoxe Dogmatik*. Translated by Hermann Pitters. 2 vols. Ökumenische Theologie, Bd. 12. Zürich: Benziger, 1985.

———. *Theology and the Church*. Translated by Robert Barringer. Crestwood, N.Y.: St. Vladimir's Seminary Press, 1980.

Stiernon, D. "Bulletin sur le Palamisme." *Revue des études byzantines* 30 (1972): 233–337.

Szepticky, Andrew. "Eastern and Western Mentality." *Eastern Churches Quarterly* 9 (1951–1952): 392–401.

Tatakis, Basile. "La Philosophie byzantine." In *Histoire de la Philosophie*, fasc. suppl. 2, edited by Émile Bréhier. Paris: Presses Universitaires de France, 1949.

Te Velde, Rudi A. *Participation and Substantiality in Thomas Aquinas*. Studien und Texte zur Geistesgeschiche des Mittelalters; Bd. XLVI. Leiden: E. J. Brill, 1995.

Torrell, Jean-Pierre. *Initiation à saint Thomas d'Aquin: sa personne et oeuvre*. Vestigia 13; Pensée antique et médievale. Fribourg: Éditions Universitaires Fribourg Suisse, 1993.

———. *Saint Thomas d'Aquin, maître spirituel*. Initiation 2. Vestigia 19; Pensée antique et médievale. Fribourg: Éditions Universitaires Fribourg Suisse, 1996.

Trethowan, Illtyd. "Irrationality in Theology and the Palamite Distinction." *Eastern Churches Review* 9 (1977): 19–26.

Tsirpanlis, Constantine N. *Introduction to Eastern Patristic Thought and Orthodox Theology*. Theology and Life 30. Collegeville, Minn.: Liturgical Press, 1991.

Tugwell, Simon, ed. and trans. *Albert & Thomas: Selected Writings*. Classics of Western Spirituality. New York: Paulist, 1988.

Tyn, Thomas. "Prochoros und Demetrios Kydones. Der byzantinische Thomismus des 14. Jahrhunderts." In Willehad Paul Eckert, ed., *Thomas von Aquino: Interpretation und Rezeption. Studien und Texte*. Walberger Studien, Philosophische Reihe, Bd. 5. Mainz: Matthias-Grünewald, 1974.

The Unity of the Churches of God. Translated by Polycarp Sherwood. Baltimore: Helicon, 1963.

Vailhé, S. "Greek Church." In *The Catholic Encyclopedia*, vol. 6, pp. 752–72.

Wadell, Paul J. *The Primacy of Love: An Introduction to the Ethics of Thomas Aquinas*. New York: Paulist, 1992.

Ware, Kallistos. "The Debate about Palamism." *Eastern Churches Review* 9 (1977): 45–63.

———. "God Hidden and Revealed: The Apophatic Way and the Essence-Energies Distinction." *Eastern Churches Review* 7(1975): 125–36.

———. *The Orthodox Church*, new ed. London: Penguin, 1993.

———. *The Orthodox Way*. Crestwood, N.Y.: St. Vladimir's Orthodox Theological Seminary, 1979.

———. "Scholasticism and Orthodoxy: Theological Method as a Factor in the Schism." *Eastern Churches Review* 5 (1973): 16–27.

———. "Tradition and Personal Experience in Later Byzantine Theology." *Eastern Churches Review* 3 (1971): 131–41.

Wendebourg, Dorothea. "From the Cappadocian Fathers to Gregory Palamas: The Defeat of Trinitarian Theology." *Studia Patristica* 14, Pt. 1 (1982): 194–98.

———. *Geist oder Energie: Zur Frage der innergöttlichen Verankerung des christlichen Lebens in der byzantinischen Theologie*. Münchener Universitäts-Schriften, Bd. 4. Münchener Monographien zur historischen und systematischen Theologie. Munich: Chr. Kaiser Verlag, 1980.

Whiting, Philip, ed. *Byzantium: An Introduction*. New York: New York University Press, 1971.

Williams, Rowan D. "The Philosophical Structures of Palamism." *Eastern Churches Review* 9 (1977): 27–44.

Wippel, John F. *Metaphysical Themes in Thomas Aquinas*. Studies in Philosophy and the History of Philosophy 10. Washington, D.C.: The Catholic University Press of America, 1984.

Yangazogalou, Stavros. "Philosophy and Theology: The Demonstrative Method in the Theology of Saint Gregory Palamas." *Greek Orthodox Theological Review* 41 (1996): 1–18.

Yannaras, Christos. "The Distinction between Essence and Energies and Its Importance for Theology." *St. Vladimir's Seminary Quarterly* 19 (1975): 232–45.

———. "Orthodoxy and the West." *Eastern Churches Review* 3 (1971): 286–300.

INDEX

9 780195 124361